SERIES

(ex•ploring)

1. To investigate in a systematic way: examine. 2. To search
into or range over for the purpose of discovery.

Microsoft® Office

SharePoint Designer
2007

BRIEF

PEARSON

Prentice
Hall

**Upper Saddle River
New Jersey 07458**

Robert T. Grauer

Daniela Marghitu

Library of Congress Cataloging-in-Publication Data

Grauer, Robert T.,
Microsoft Office SharePoint designer 2007 / Robert T. Grauer, Daniela Marghitu.
    p. cm.
ISBN-13: 978-0-13-235051-8
ISBN-10: 0-13-235051-3
 1. Microsoft SharePoint (Electronic resource) 2. Intranets (Computer networks) 3. Web servers. I. Marghitu,
Daniela. II. Title.
    TK5105.875.I6G7 2007
    006.7'8—dc22
                          2007051099

VP/Publisher: Natalie E. Anderson
Senior Acquisitions Editor: Melissa Sabella
Director, Product Development: Pamela Hersperger
Product Development Manager: Eileen Bien Calabro
Editorial Project Manager: Meghan Bisi
Development Editor: Pat Gillivan, Triple SSS Press
Editorial Assistant: Melissa Arlio
AVP/Executive Editor, Media: Richard Keaveny
Editorial Media Project Manager: Ashley Lulling
Production Media Project Manager: Lorena Cerisano
Marketing Manager: Maggie Moylan
Marketing Assistant: Angela Frey
Senior Managing Editor: Cynthia Zonneveld
Associate Managing Editor: Camille Trentacoste
Production Project Manager: Ruth Ferrera-Kargov
Senior Operations Director: Nick Sklitsis
Senior Art Director: Jonathan Boylan
Art Director: Anthony Gemmellaro
Cover Design: Anthony Gemmellaro
Cover Illustration/Photo: Courtesy of Getty Images/Laurent Hamels
Composition: GGS Book Services
Full-Service Project Management: GGS Book Services
Printer/Binder: Banta/Menasha
Typeface: 10/12 Palatino

Microsoft, Windows, Vista, Word, PowerPoint, Outlook, FrontPage, Visual Basic, MSN, The Microsoft Network,
and/or other Microsoft products referenced herein are either registered trademarks or registered trademarks of the
Microsoft Corporation in the U.S.A. and other countries. Screen shots and icons reprinted with permission from
the Microsoft Corporation. This book is not sponsored or endorsed by or affiliated with the Microsoft Corporation.

Pearson Education Ltd., London   Pearson Education Australia PTY, Limited
Pearson Education Singapore, Pte. Ltd   Pearson Education North Asia Ltd
Pearson Education, Canada, Ltd   Pearson Educación de Mexico, S.A. de C.V.
Pearson Education–Japan   Pearson Education Malaysia, Pte. Ltd.

10 9 8 7 6 5 4 3
ISBN-13: 978-0-13-235051-8
ISBN-10: 0-13-235051-3

Dedications

To Marion—my wife, my lover, and my best friend.

Robert Grauer

To Stefania—I live for you, my little angel!

To Dan—I love you, my high school sweetheart, loving husband, and best friend!

To my parents—Thank you for dedicating your lives to me and Stefania. All that I accomplished in life would have not been possible without your unconditional love and support!

Daniela Marghitu

# About the Authors

Dr. Robert T. Grauer

Dr. Robert T. Grauer is an Associate Professor in the Department of Computer Information Systems at the University of Miami, where he has been honored with the Outstanding Teacher Award in the School of Business. He is the vision behind the Exploring Series, which is about to sell its 3 millionth copy.

Dr. Grauer has written more than 50 books on programming and information systems. His work has been translated into three foreign languages and is used in all aspects of higher education at both national and international levels.

Dr. Grauer also has been a consultant to several major corporations including IBM and American Express. He received his Ph.D. in operations research in 1972 from the Polytechnic Institute of Brooklyn.

Dr. Daniela Marghitu

Dr. Daniela Marghitu is a professor in the Computer Science and Software Engineering Department at Auburn University where she teaches Web Design and Web Application Development courses and has coordinated the traditional and independent learning computer literacy courses since 1996. She is the founder and director of the Auburn University Computer Literacy Academy for children (dealing with disabilities) and other innovative K12 outreach computer literacy courses.

She has published two books for the Prentice Hall Exploring Series, over 30 peer reviewed articles and international conference papers, has been a consultant to several major companies including Prentice Hall, McGraw-Hill, and Course Technology, and has given numerous presentations at national and international professional events. She serves on several not-for-profit organizations boards and committees including the IEEE Virtual Instructor Pilot Research Group (VIPRG) and UPA World Usability Day.

She currently resides in Alabama with her husband and daughter. When she is not teaching, writing, or doing research, she dedicates all her free time to her daughter, husband, and parents.

Contents

CHAPTER ONE | Introduction to Microsoft Office SharePoint Designer 2007: What Is a Web Site? 1

CHAPTER TWO | Web Sites and Web Pages: Designing and Building Standard Web Sites and Web Pages 111

CHAPTER THREE | Microsoft Office 2007 Documents and Web Forms: Integrating Microsoft Office 2007 Documents and Adding Interactive Web Forms to Microsoft Office SharePoint Designer 2007 Web Sites 257

APPENDIX A | HTML, XHTML, XML, and CSS: Microsoft Office SharePoint Designer 2007 User-Friendly Tools for Working with HTML, XHTML, XML, and CSS   345

Acknowledgments

The success of the Exploring series is attributed to contributions from numerous individuals. First and foremost, our heartfelt appreciation to Melissa Sabella, senior acquisitions editor, for providing new leadership and direction to capitalize on the strength and tradition of the Exploring series while implementing innovative ideas into the Exploring Office 2007 edition. Scott Davidson, senior marketing manager, was an invaluable addition to the team who believes in the mission of this series passionately and did an amazing job communicating its message.

During the first few months of the project, Eileen Clark, senior editorial project manager, kept the team focused on the vision, pedagogy, and voice that has been the driving force behind the success of the Exploring series. Claire Hunter, market development editor, facilitated communication between the editorial team and the reviewers to ensure that this edition meets the changing needs of computer professors and students at the collegiate level.

Laura Town, developmental editor, provided an objective perspective in reviewing the content and organization of selected chapters. Jenelle Woodrup, editorial project manager, provided valuable assistance in communication among team members and keeping the files moving into production. Eileen Calabro, product development manager, facilitated communication among the editorial team, authors, and production during a transitional stage. Doug Bell and the whole team at GGS worked through software delays, style changes and anything else we threw at them to bring the whole thing together. Art director Blair Brown's conversations with students and professors across the country yielded a design that addressed the realities of today's students with function and style.

The new members of the Exploring author team would like to especially thank Bob Grauer for his vision in developing Exploring and his leadership in creating this highly successful series.

Maryann Barber would like to thank Bob Grauer for a wonderful collaboration and providing the opportunities through which so much of her life has changed.

Daniela Marghitu, author of SharePoint Designer, would like to convey her very special appreciation to Melissa Sabella and Natalie Anderson for their constant support; to the renowned author, Robert Grauer, for always believing in her and being her mentor. She would also like to convey her deepest gratitude and respect to Pat Gillivan, development editor for SharePoint Designer. Last, but certainly not least, she would like to acknowledge all the Auburn University undergraduate and graduate students that have worked with her for the past 12 years, especially those that were involved with the developing of the Auburn University Web sites that she has used as examples in this book.

The Exploring team would like to especially thank the following instructors who drew on their experience in the classroom and their software expertise to give us daily advice on how to improve this book. Their impact can be seen on every page:

Bob McCloud, Sacred Heart University

Cassie Georgetti, Florida Technical College

Dana Johnson, North Dakota State University

Dick Albright, Goldey-Beacom College

Jackie Lamoureux, Central New Mexico Community College

Jim Pepe, Bentley College

Judy Brown, The University of Memphis

Julie Boyles, Portland Community College

Lancie Anthony Affonso, College of Charleston

Michele Reader

Mimi Duncan, University of Missouri – St. Louis

Minnie Proctor, Indian River Community College

Richard Albright, Goldey-Beacom College

We also want to acknowledge all the reviewers of the Exploring 2007 series. Their valuable comments and constructive criticism greatly improved this edition:

Aaron Schorr
Fashion Institute of Technology

Alicia Stonesifer
La Salle University

Allen Alexander, Delaware
Tech & Community College

Amy Williams, Abraham
Baldwin Agriculture College

Anne Edwards
Central New Mexico Community College

Annie Brown
Hawaii Community College

Barbara Cierny
Harper College

Barbara Hearn
Community College of Philadelphia

Barbara Meguro
University of Hawaii at Hilo

Barbara Stover
Marion Technical College

Bette Pitts
South Plains College

Beverly Fite
Amarillo College

Bill Wagner
Villanova

Brandi N. Guidry
University of Louisiana at Lafayette

Brian Powell
West Virginia University – Morgantown
Campus

Carl Farrell
Hawaii Pacific University

Carl Penzuil
Ithaca College

Carole Bagley;
University of St. Thomas

Catherine Hain
Central New Mexico CC

Charles Edwards
University of Texas of the Permian Basin

Christine L. Moore
College of Charleston

David Barnes
Penn State Altoona

David Childress;
Ashland Community College

David Law, Alfred
State College

Dennis Chalupa
Houston Baptist

Diane Stark
Phoenix College

Dianna Patterson
Texarkana College

Dianne Ross
University of Louisiana at Lafayette

Dr. Behrooz Saghafi
Chicago State University

Dr. Gladys Swindler
Fort Hays State University

Dr. Joe Teng
Barry University

Dr. Karen Nantz
Eastern Illinois University.

Duane D. Lintner
Amarillo College

Elizabeth Edmiston
North Carolina Central University

Erhan Uskup
Houston Community College

Fred Hills, McClellan
Community College

Gary R. Armstrong
Shippensburg University of Pennsylvania

Glenna Vanderhoof
Missouri State

Gregg Asher
Minnesota State University, Mankato

Hong K. Sung
University of Central Oklahoma

Hyekyung Clark
Central New Mexico CC

J Patrick Fenton
West Valley College

Jana Carver
Amarillo College

Jane Cheng
Bloomfield College

Janos T. Fustos
Metropolitan State College of Denver

Jeffrey A Hassett
University of Utah

Jennifer Pickle
Amarillo College

Jerry Kolata
New England Institute of Technology

Jesse Day
South Plains College

John Arehart
Longwood University

John Lee Reardon
University of Hawaii, Manoa

Joshua Mindel
San Francisco State University

Karen Wisniewski
County College of Morris

Karl Smart
Central Michigan University

Kathryn L. Hatch
University of Arizona

Krista Terry
Radford University

Laura McManamon
University of Dayton

Laura Reid
University of Western Ontario

Linda Johnsonius
Murray State University

Lori Kelley
Madison Area Technical College

Lucy Parker,
California State University, Northridge

Lynda Henrie
LDS Business College

Malia Young
Utah State University

Margie Martyn
Baldwin Wallace

Marianne Trudgeon
Fanshawe College

Marilyn Hibbert
Salt Lake Community College

Marjean Lake
LDS Business College

Mark Olaveson
Brigham Young University

Mary Logan
Delgado Community College

Nancy Sardone
Seton Hall University

Patricia Joseph
Slippery Rock University.

Patrick Hogan
Cape Fear Community College

Paula F. Bell
Lock Haven University of
Pennsylvania

Paulette Comet
Community College of Baltimore County,
Catonsville

Pratap Kotala
North Dakota State University

Richard Blamer
John Carroll University

Richard Herschel
St. Joseph's University

Richard Hewer
Ferris State University

Robert Gordon
Hofstra University

Robert Marmelstein
East Stroudsburg University

Robert Stumbur
Northern Alberta Institute of
Technology

Roberta I. Hollen
University of Central Oklahoma

Roland Moreira
South Plains College

Ron Murch
University of Calgary

Rory J. de Simone
University of Florida

Ruth Neal
Navarro College

Sandra M. Brown
Finger Lakes Community College

Sharon Mulroney
Mount Royal College

Stephanie Jones
South Plains College

Stephen E. Lunce
Midwestern State University

Steve Schwarz
Raritan Valley Community College

Steven Choy
University of Calgary

Susan Byrne
St. Clair College

Thomas Setaro
Brookdale Community College

Todd McLeod
Fresno City College

Vickie Pickett
Midland College

Vipul Gupta
St Joseph's University

Vivek Shah
Texas State University - San Marcos

Wei-Lun Chuang
Utah State University

William Dorin
Indiana University Northwest

Finally, we wish to acknowledge reviewers of previous editions of the Exploring series—we wouldn't have made it to the 7th edition without you:

Alan Moltz
Naugatuck Valley Technical Community College

Alok Charturvedi
Purdue University

Antonio Vargas
El Paso Community College

Barbara Sherman
Buffalo State College

Bill Daley
University of Oregon

Bill Morse
DeVry Institute of Technology

Bonnie Homan
San Francisco State University

Carl M. Briggs
Indiana University School of Business

Carlotta Eaton
Radford University

Carolyn DiLeo
Westchester Community College

Cody Copeland
Johnson County Community College

Connie Wells
Georgia State University

Daniela Marghitu
Auburn University

David B. Meinert
Southwest Missouri State University

David Douglas
University of Arkansas

David Langley
University of Oregon

David Rinehard
Lansing Community College

David Weiner
University of San Francisco

Dean Combellick
Scottsdale Community College

Delores Pusins
Hillsborough Community College

Don Belle
Central Piedmont Community
College

Douglas Cross
Clackamas Community College

Ernie Ivey
Polk Community College

Gale E. Rand
College Misericordia

Helen Stoloff
Hudson Valley Community
College

Herach Safarian
College of the Canyons

Jack Zeller
Kirkwood Community College

James Franck
College of St. Scholastica

James Gips
Boston College

Jane King
Everett Community College

Janis Cox
Tri-County Technical College

Jerry Chin
Southwest Missouri State
University

Jill Chapnick
Florida International University

Jim Pruitt
Central Washington University

John Lesson
University of Central Florida

John Shepherd
Duquesne University

Judith M. Fitspatrick
Gulf Coast Community College

Judith Rice
Santa Fe Community College

Judy Dolan
Palomar College

Karen Tracey
Central Connecticut State University

Kevin Pauli
University of Nebraska

Kim Montney
Kellogg Community College

Kimberly Chambers
Scottsdale Community College

Larry S. Corman
Fort Lewis College

Lynn Band
Middlesex Community College

Margaret Thomas
Ohio University

Marguerite Nedreberg
Youngstown State University

Marilyn Salas
Scottsdale Community College

Martin Crossland
Southwest Missouri State University

Mary McKenry Percival
University of Miami

Michael Hassett
Fort Hayes State University

Michael Stewardson
San Jacinto College – North

Midge Gerber
Southwestern Oklahoma State
University

Mike Hearn
Community College of Philadelphia

Mike Kelly
Community College of Rhode Island

Mike Thomas
Indiana University School of Business

Paul E. Daurelle
Western Piedmont Community
College

Ranette Halverson
Midwestern State University

Raymond Frost
Central Connecticut State University

Robert Spear, Prince
George's Community College

Rose M. Laird
Northern Virginia Community College

Sally Visci
Lorain County Community College

Shawna DePlonty
Sault College of Applied Arts and
Technology

Stuart P. Brian
Holy Family College

Susan Fry
Boise State Universtiy

Suzanne Tomlinson
Iowa State University

Vernon Griffin
Austin Community College

Wallace John Whistance-Smith
Ryerson Polytechnic University

Walter Johnson
Community College of Philadelphia

Wanda D. Heller
Seminole Community College

We very much appreciate the following individuals for painstakingly checking every step and every explanation for technical accuracy, while dealing with an entirely new software application:

Barbara Stover

Barbara Waxer

Bill Daley

Beverly Fite

Dawn Wood

Denise Askew

Elizabeth Lockley

James Reidel

Janet Pickard

Janice Snyder

Jeremy Harris

John Griffin

Joyce Nielsen

LeeAnn Bates

Mara Zebest

Mary Pascarella

Michael Meyers

Sue McCrory

Preface

The Exploring Series

Exploring has been Prentice Hall's most successful Office Application series of the past 15 years. For Office 2007 Exploring has undergone the most extensive changes in its history, so that it can truly move today's student "beyond the point and click."

The goal of Exploring has always been to teach more than just the steps to accomplish a task – the series provides the theoretical foundation necessary for a student to understand when and why to apply a skill. This way, students achieve a broader understanding of Office.

Today's students are changing and Exploring has evolved with them. Prentice Hall traveled to college campuses across the country and spoke directly to students to determine how they study and prepare for class. We also spoke with hundreds of professors about the best ways to administer materials to such a diverse body of students.

Here is what we learned

Students go to college now with a different set of skills than they did 5 years ago. The new edition of Exploring moves students beyond the basics of the software at a faster pace, without sacrificing coverage of the fundamental skills that everybody needs to know. This ensures that students will be engaged from Chapter 1 to the end of the book.

Students have diverse career goals. With this in mind, we broadened the examples in the text (and the accompanying Instructor Resources) to include the health sciences, hospitality, urban planning, business and more. Exploring will be relevant to every student in the course.

Students read, prepare and study differently than they used to. Rather than reading a book cover to cover students want to easily identify what they need to know, and then learn it efficiently. We have added key features that will bring students into the content and make the text easy to use such as objective mapping, pull quotes, and key terms in the margins.

Moving students beyond the point and click

All of these additions mean students will be more engaged, achieve a higher level of understanding, and successfully complete this course. In addition to the experience and expertise of the series creator and author Robert T. Grauer we have assembled a tremendously talented team of supporting authors to assist with this critical revision. Each of them is equally dedicated to the Exploring mission of **moving students beyond the point and click.**

Key Features of the Office 2007 revision include

- **New** **Office Fundamentals Chapter** efficiently covers skills common among all applications like save, print, and bold to avoid repetition in each Office application's first chapter, along with coverage of problem solving skills to prepare students to apply what they learn in any situation.

- **New** **Moving Beyond the Basics** introduces advanced skills earlier because students are learning basic skills faster.

- **White Pages/Yellow Pages clearly** distinguish the theory (white pages) from the skills covered in the Hands-On exercises (yellow pages) so students always know what they are supposed to be doing.

- **New** **Objective Mapping** enables students to skip the skills and concepts they know, and quickly find those they don't, by scanning the chapter opener page for the page numbers of the material they need.

- **New** **Pull Quotes** entice students into the theory by highlighting the most interesting points.

- **New** **Conceptual Animations** connect the theory with the skills, by illustrating tough to understand concepts with interactive multimedia.

- **New** **More End of Chapter Exercises** offer instructors more options for assessment. Each chapter has approximately 12–15 exercises ranging from Multiple Choice questions to open-ended projects.

- **New** **More Levels of End of Chapter Exercises,** including new Mid-Level Exercises tell students what to do, but not how to do it, and Capstone Exercises cover all of the skills within each chapter.

- **New** **Mini Cases with Rubrics** are open ended exercises that guide both instructors and students to a solution with a specific rubric for each mini case.

Instructor and Student Resources

Instructor Chapter Reference Cards

A four page color card for every chapter that includes a:
- *Concept Summary* that outlines the KEY objectives to cover in class with tips on where students get stuck as well as how to get them un-stuck. It helps bridge the gap between the instructor and student when discussing more difficult topics.

- *Case Study Lecture Demonstration Document* which provides instructors with a lecture sample based on the chapter opening case that will guide students to critically use the skills covered in the chapter, with examples of other ways the skills can be applied.

The Enhanced Instructor's Resource Center on CD-ROM includes:

- **Additional Capstone Production Tests** allow instructors to assess all the skills in a chapter with a single project.

- **Mini Case Rubrics** in Microsoft® Word format enable instructors to customize the assignment for their class.

- **PowerPoint® Presentations** for each chapter with notes included for online students.

- **Lesson Plans** that provide a detailed blueprint for an instructor to achieve chapter learning objectives and outcomes.

- **Student Data Files**

- **Annotated Solution Files**

- **Complete Test Bank**

- **Test Gen Software with QuizMaster**

TestGen is a test generator program that lets you view and easily edit testbank questions, transfer them to tests, and print in a variety of formats suitable to your teaching situation. The program also offers many options for organizing and displaying testbanks and tests. A random number test generator enables you to create multiple versions of an exam.

QuizMaster, also included in this package, allows students to take tests created with TestGen on a local area network. The QuizMaster Utility built into TestGen lets instructors view student records and print a variety of reports. Building tests is easy with Test-Gen, and exams can be easily uploaded into WebCT, BlackBoard, and CourseCompass.

Prentice Hall's Companion Web Site

www.prenhall.com/exploring offers expanded IT resources and downloadable supplements. This site also includes an online study guide for student self-study.

Online Course Cartridges

Flexible, robust and customizable content is available for all major online course platforms that include everything instructors need in one place.
www.prenhall.com/webct
www.prenhall.com/blackboard
www.coursecompass.com

Visual Walk-Through

chapter 3 | **Access**

Customize, Analyze, and Summarize Query Data

Creating and Using Queries to Make Decisions

bjectives

After you read this chapter you will be able to:

1. Understand the order of precedence (**page 679**).
2. Create a calculated field in a query (**page 679**).
3. Create expressions with the Expression Builder (**page 679**).
4. Create and edit Access functions (**page 690**).
5. Perform date arithmetic (**page 694**).
6. Create and work with data aggregates (**page 704**).

Hands-On Exercises

Exercises	Skills Covered
1. CALCULATED QUERY FIELDS (PAGE 683) **Open:** chap3_ho1-3_realestate.accdb **Save:** chap3_ho1-3_realestate_solution.accdb **Back up as:** chap3_ho1_realestate_solution.accdb	• Copy a Database and Start the Query • Select the Fields, Save, and Open the Query • Create a Calculated Field and Run the Query • Verify the Calculated Results • Recover from a Common Error
2. EXPRESSION BUILDER, FUNCTIONS, AND DATE ARITHMETIC (page 695) **Open:** chap3_ho1-3_realestate.accdb (from Exercise 1) **Save:** chap3_ho1-3_realestate_solution.accdb (additional modifications) **Back up as:** chap3_ho2_realestate_solution.accdb	• Create a Select Query • Use the Expression Builder • Create Calculations Using Input Stored in a Different Query or Table • Edit Expressions Using the Expression Builder • Use Functions • Work with Date Arithmetic
3. DATA AGGREGATES (page 707) **Open:** chap3_ho1-3_realestate.accdb (from Exercise 2) **Save:** chap3_ho1-3_realestate_solution.accdb (additional modifications)	• Add a Total Row • Create a Totals Query Based on a Select Query • Add Fields to the Design Grid • Add Grouping Options and Specify Summary Statistics

Access 2007   677

Objective Mapping

allows students to skip the skills and concepts they know and quickly find those they don't by scanning the chapter opening page for the page numbers of the material they need.

Case Study

begins each chapter to provide an effective overview of what students can accomplish by completing the chapter.

CASE STUDY

West Transylvania College Athletic Department

The athletic department of West Transylvania College has reached a fork in the road. A significant alumni contingent insists that the college upgrade its athletic program from NCAA Division II to Division I. This process will involve adding sports, funding athletic scholarships, expanding staff, and coordinating a variety of fundraising activities.

Tom Hunt, the athletic director, wants to determine if the funding support is available both inside and outside the college to accomplish this goal. You are helping Tom prepare the five-year projected budget based on current budget figures. The plan is to increase revenues at a rate of 10% per year for five years while handling an estimated 8% increase in expenses over the same five-year period. Tom feels that a 10% increase in revenue versus an 8% increase in expenses should make the upgrade viable. Tom wants to examine how increased alumni giving, increases in college fees, and grant monies will increase the revenue flow. The Transylvania College's Athletic Committee and its Alumni Association Board of Directors want Tom to present an analysis of funding and expenses to determine if the move to NCAA Division I is feasible. As Tom's student assistant this year, it is your responsibility to help him with special projects. Tom prepared the basic projected budget spreadsheet and has asked you to finish it for him.

Case Study

Your Assignment

- Read the chapter carefully and pay close attention to mathematical operations, formulas, and functions.

- Open *chap2_case_athletics*, which contains the partially completed, projected budget spreadsheet.

- Study the structure of the worksheet to determine what type of formulas you need to complete the financial calculations. Identify how you would perform calculations if you were using a calculator and make a list of formulas using regular language to determine if the financial goals will be met. As you read the chapter, identify formulas and functions that will help you complete the financial analysis. You will insert formulas in the revenue and expenditures sections for column C. Use appropriate cell references in formulas. Do not enter constant values within a formula; instead enter the 10% and 8% increases in an input area. Use appropriate functions for column totals in both the revenue and expenditures sections. Insert formulas for the Net Operating Margin and Net Margin rows. Copy the formulas.

- Review the spreadsheet and identify weaknesses in the formatting. Use your knowledge of good formatting design to improve the appearance of the spreadsheet so that it will be attractive to the Athletic Committee and the alumni board. You will format cells as currency with 0 decimals and widen columns as needed. Merge and center the title and use an attractive fill color. Emphasize the totals and margin rows with borders. Enter your name and current date. Create a custom footer that includes a page number and your instructor's name. Print the worksheet as displayed and again with cell formulas displayed. Save the workbook as **chap2_case_athletics_solution**.

Key Terms

are called out in the margins of the chapter so students can more effectively study definitions.

Pull Quotes

entice students into the theory by highlighting the most interesting points.

Tables

A **table** is a series of rows and columns that organize data.

A **cell** is the intersection of a row and column in a table.

> The table feature is one of the most powerful in Word and is the basis for an almost limitless variety of documents. It is very easy to create once you understand how a table works.

A **table** is a series of rows and columns that organize data effectively. The rows and columns in a table intersect to form **cells**. The table feature is one of the most powerful in Word and is an easy way to organize a series of data in a columnar list format such as employee names, inventory lists, and e-mail addresses. The Vacation Planner in Figure 3.1, for example, is actually a 4x9 table (4 columns and 9 rows). The completed table looks impressive, but it is very easy to create once you understand how a table works. In addition to the organizational benefits, tables make an excellent alignment tool. For example, you can create tables to organize data such as employee lists with phone numbers and e-mail addresses. The Exploring series uses tables to provide descriptions for various software commands. Although you can align text with tabs, you have more format control when you create a table. (See the Practice Exercises at the end of the chapter for other examples.)

Vacation Planner			
Item	Number of Days	Amount per Day (est)	Total Amount
Airline Ticket			449.00
Amusement Park Tickets	4	50.00	200.00
Hotel	5	120.00	600.00
Meals	6	50.00	300.00
Rental Car	5	30.00	150.00
Souvenirs	5	20.00	100.00
TOTAL EXPECTED EXPENSES			$1799.00

Figure 3.1 The Vacation Planner

In this section, you insert a table in a document. After inserting the table, you can insert or delete columns and rows if you need to change the structure. Furthermore, you learn how to merge and split cells within the table. Finally, you change the row height and column width to accommodate data in the table.

Inserting a Table

You can create a table from the Insert tab. Click Table in the Tables group on the Insert tab to see a gallery of cells from which you select the number of columns and rows you require in the table, or you can choose the Insert Table command below the gallery to display the Insert Table dialog box and enter the table composition you prefer. When you select the table dimension from the gallery or from the Insert Table dialog box, Word creates a table structure with the number of columns and rows you specify. After you define a table, you can enter text, numbers, or graphics in individual cells. Text

Tables | Word 2007   197

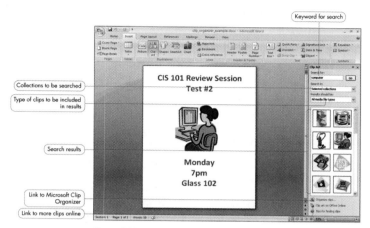

Keyword for search

Collections to be searched

Type of clips to be included in results

Search results

Link to Microsoft Clip Organizer

Link to more clips online

Figure 3.18 The Clip Art Task Pane

White Pages/ Yellow Pages

clearly distinguishes the theory (white pages) from the skills covered in the Hands-On exercises (yellow pages) so students always know what they are supposed to be doing.

You can access the Microsoft Clip Organizer (to view the various collections) by clicking Organize clips at the bottom of the Clip Art task pane. You also can access the Clip Organizer when you are not using Word; click the Start button on the taskbar, click All Programs, Micros... Clip Organizer. Once in the Organi... ous collections, reorganize the exi... add new clips (with their associate... the bottom of the task pane in Figu... and tips for finding more relevant c...

Insert a Picture

In addition to the collection of clip... you also can insert your own pictur... ital camera attached to your compu... Word. After you save the picture to... on the Insert tab to locate and inser... opens so that you can navigate to t... insert the picture, there are many c... mands are discussed in the next sec...

Formatting a Grap...

(Remember that graphical elements should enhance a document, not overpower it.)

When you inse... fined size. For... very large and... resized. Most t... within the d...

Refer to Figure 3.24 as you complete Step 2.

a. Click once on the clip art object to select it. Click **Text Wrapping** in the Arrange group on the Picture Tools Format tab to display the text wrapping options, and then select **Square**, as shown in Figure 3.24.

You must change the layout in order to move and size the object.

b. Click **Position** in the Arrange group, and then click **More Layout Options.** Click the **Picture Position tab** in the Advanced Layout dialog box, if necessary, then click **Alignment** in the *Horizontal* section. Click the **Alignment drop-down arrow** and select **Right**. Deselect the **Allow overlap check box** in the *Options* section. Click **OK**.

c. Click **Crop** in the Size group, then hold your mouse over the sizing handles and notice how the pointer changes to angular shapes. Click the **bottom center handle** and drag it up. Drag the side handles inward to remove excess space surrounding the graphical object.

d. Click the Shape **Height box** in the Size group and type **2.77**.

Notice the width is changed automatically to retain the proportion.

e. Save the document.

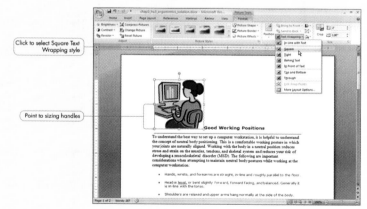

Click to select Square Text Wrapping style

Point to sizing handles

Figure 3.24 Formatting Clip Art

Refer to Figure 3.25 as you complete Step 3.

a. Press **Ctrl+End** to move to the end of the document. Click the **Insert tab**, and then click **WordArt** in the Text group to display the WordArt gallery.

b. Click **WordArt Style 28** on the bottom row of the gallery.

The Edit WordArt Text dialog box displays, as shown in Figure 3.25.

Summary

1. **Create a presentation using a template.** Using a template saves you a great deal of time and enables you to create a more professional presentation. Templates incorporate a theme, a layout, and content that can be modified. You can use templates that are installed when Microsoft Office is installed, or you can download templates from Microsoft Office Online. Microsoft is constantly adding templates to the online site for your use.

2. **Modify a template.** In addition to changing the content of a template, you can modify the structure and design. The structure is modified by changing the layout of a slide. To change the layout, drag placeholders to new locations or resize placeholders. You can even add placeholders so that elements such as logos can be included.

3. **Create a presentation in Outline view.** When you use a storyboard to determine your content, you create a basic outline. Then you can enter your presentation in Outline view, which enables you to concentrate on the content of the presentation. Using Outline view keeps you from getting buried in design issues at the cost of your content. It also saves you time because you can enter the information without having to move from placeholder to placeholder.

4. **Modify an outline structure.** Because the Outline view gives you a global view of the presentation, it helps you see the underlying structure of the presentation. You are able to see where content needs to be strengthened, or where the flow of information needs to be revised. If you find a slide with content that would be presented better in another location in the slide show, you can use the Collapse and Expand features to easily move it. By collapsing the slide content, you can drag it to a new location and then expand it. To move individual bullet points, cut and paste the bullet point or drag-and-drop it.

5. **Print an outline.** When you present, using the outline version of your slide show as a reference is a boon. No matter how well you know your information, it is easy to forget to present some information when facing an audience. While you would print speaker's notes if you have many details, you can print the outline as a quick reference. The outline can be printed in either the collapsed or the expanded form, giving you far fewer pages to shuffle in front of an audience than printing speaker's notes would.

6. **Import an outline.** You do not need to re-enter information from an outline created in Microsoft Word or another word processor. You can use the Open feature to import any outline that has been saved in a format that PowerPoint can read. In addition to a Word outline, you can use the common generic formats Rich Text Format and Plain Text Format.

7. **Add existing content to a presentation.** After you spend time creating the slides in a slide show, you may find that slides in the slide show would be appropriate in another show at a later date. Any slide you create can be reused in another presentation, thereby saving you considerable time and effort. You simply open the Reuse Slides pane, locate the slide show with the slide you need, and then click on the thumbnail of the slide to insert a copy of it in the new slide show.

8. **Examine slide show design principles.** With a basic understanding of slide show design principles you can create presentations that reflect your personality in a professional way. The goal of applying these principles is to create a slide show that focuses the audience on the message of the slide without being distracted by clutter or unreadable text.

9. **Apply and modify a design theme.** PowerPoint provides you with themes to help you create a clean, professional look for your presentation. Once a theme is applied you can modify the theme by changing the color scheme, the font scheme, the effects scheme, or the background style.

10. **Insert a header or footer.** Identifying information can be included in a header or footer. You may, for example, wish to include the group to whom you are presenting, or the location of the presentation, or a copyright notation for original work. You can apply footers to slides, handouts, and Notes pages. Headers may be applied to handouts and Notes pages.

Summary

links directly back to the objectives so students can more effectively study and locate the concepts that they need to focus on.

More End-of-Chapter Exercises with New Levels of Assessment

offer instructors more options for assessment. Each chapter has approximately 12-15 projects per chapter ranging from multiple choice to open-ended projects.

Practice Exercises

reinforce skills learned in the chapter with specific directions on what to do and how to do it.

New Mid-Level Exercises

assess the skills learned in the chapter by directing the students on what to do but not how to do it.

New Capstone Exercises

cover all of the skills with in each chapter without telling students how to perform the skills.

Mini Cases with Rubrics

are open ended exercises that guide both instructors and students to a solution with a specific rubric for each Mini Case.

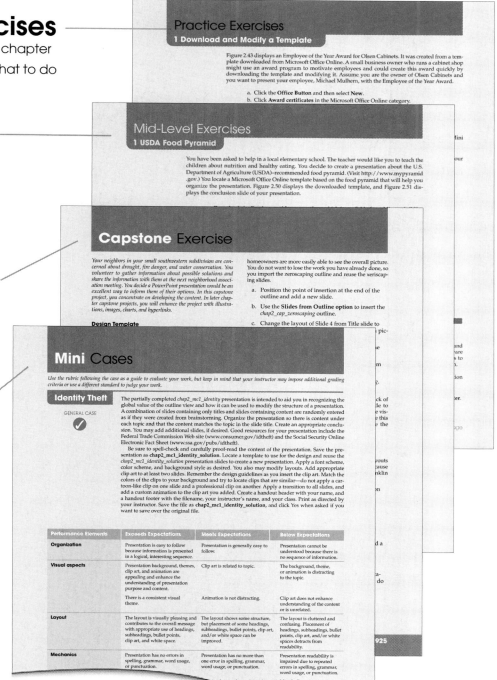

Introduction to Microsoft Office SharePoint Designer 2007

What Is a Web Site?

Objectives

After you read this chapter, you will be able to:

1. Get started with the Internet and the World Wide Web **(page 3)**.
2. Understand Web browsers and markup languages: Hypertext Markup Language (HTML), Extensible Hypertext Markup Language (XHTML), and eXtensible Markup Language (XML) **(page 7)**.
3. Use Cascading Style Sheets (CSS) **(page 15)**.
4. Define Web sites **(page 18)**.
5. Get started with SharePoint Designer 2007 **(page 25)**.
6. Identify SharePoint Designer 2007 tools for creating Web sites **(page 49)**.
7. Open and close a Web site **(page 54)**.
8. Describe Web site views **(page 54)**.
9. Open and close a Web page **(page 60)**.
10. Describe Web page views **(page 60)**.
11. Describe basic Web page elements **(page 62)**.
12. Identify SharePoint Designer 2007 tools for creating Web pages **(page 64)**.
13. Understand the principles of good Web page design **(page 71)**.
14. Save work and exit SharePoint Designer **(page 90)**.

Hands-On Exercises

Exercises	Skills Covered
1. IDENTIFYING SHAREPOINT DESIGNER INTERFACE COMPONENTS AND USING HELP (page 45) Case Study–Related	• Start SharePoint Designer, Identify Interface Components, Use the ScreenTips, and Use the Status Bar • Close the Toolbox Pane, Close the Apply Styles Pane, Reset Workspace Layout, Use the View Menu to Display the Picture Toolbar, and Close the Picture Toolbar • Use SharePoint Designer Help and Print a Help Topic
2. INTRODUCTION TO SHAREPOINT DESIGNER TOOLS FOR CREATING WEB SITES (page 57) Case Study–Related Open: chap1_ho2_emptysite and chap1_ho2_webpackage.fwp Save as: chap1_ho2_website_solution and chap1_ho2_webpackage_solution	• Start SharePoint Designer, Open a Web Site, Use the Remote Web Site View to Back Up a Web Site, and Import a Web Package • Explore the SharePoint Designer Web Site Views • Create a Web Package and Close a Web Site
3. EXPLORING BASIC WEB PAGE ELEMENTS AND SHAREPOINT DESIGNER TOOLS FOR CREATING WEB PAGES (page 91) Case Study–Related Open: chap1_ho3_website_org Save as: chap1_ho3_compatibility_report	• Open a Web Site and Open a Web Page • Get Acquainted with Web Page Elements • Get Acquainted with HTML Tags Corresponding to Web Page Elements • Check Compatibility, Close the Web Page, and Exit SharePoint Designer

CASE STUDY

Can Someone Help Me Create My Personal Web Site, Please?

The ever-growing power of personal computers, extensive interconnection of computers and users, and the development of user-friendly Web-authoring applications have empowered more people to design and create personal or family Web sites and Web sites for small, medium, or large businesses and organizations. You might be wondering how you can build a Web site too!

Michael is an outstanding Ph.D. student in the Computer Science and Software Engineering department. He chooses SharePoint Designer to develop his personal Web site because of the software's friendly graphic user interface (GUI) and its rich set of professional tools for designing, building, and customizing Web sites or Web pages and for publishing, managing, and promoting Web sites. SharePoint Designer also makes it easy to integrate external data and Microsoft Office suite files into your Web site and to create custom Data Views and online forms. And these are only a few of the SharePoint Designer features that help users of every skill level, from the newest beginners to professional Web designers.

Natalie wants to build her own personal Web site. Michael, as the lab instructor in Natalie's Introduction to Personal Computer Applications class, has offered to help her develop her personal Web site using SharePoint Designer. For a start, he has provided Natalie with a generic personal Web site that she can explore to get acquainted with the SharePoint Designer window, SharePoint Designer Web site views, SharePoint Designer Web page views, basic elements of a Web page, and SharePoint Designer tools for creating Web sites and Web pages.

Your Assignment

- Read the chapter, paying special attention to Hands-On Exercises 1, 2, and 3, which help you get acquainted with the SharePoint Designer interface and SharePoint Designer tools for creating Web sites and Web pages.
- Put yourself in Natalie's place; open the Web site *chap1_case_personal*, which contains a generic personal Web site, and create a backup Web site, **chap1_case_personal_solution**.
- Explore all the reports available within the Reports Web site view.
- Open the *default.htm* home page.
- Explore the Web page views of the home page.
- Open the Web site Dynamic Web template, *master.dwt*, using the Format menu.
- Display the Split view of *master.dwt*.
- Position the mouse pointer before the Photo Gallery hyperlink in the horizontal navigation bar and type **Family** in the Design view.
- Position the mouse pointer over the Photo Gallery hyperlink (in the horizontal navigation bar placed within the footer layer) and double-click; position the insertion point in Code view before *Photo Gallery* and type **Family**.
- Position the mouse pointer, in Code view, between the <h1></h1> pair tags within the masterhead layout, select the text included between the <h1></h1> pair tags, and type **Natalie's Web Site**.
- Center align the <h1> heading, setting the value of the align attribute using the Tag Properties task pane.
- Save *master.dwt* using the File menu and allow all the files attached to *master.dwt* to be updated.
- Save *default.htm*.
- Run the Compatibility Checker, review, save the Compatibility report as **compatibility_report.htm**, and fix the compatibility error reported.
- Run the Accessibility Checker, review, and, if there are errors reported, save the Accessibility report as **accessibility_report.htm**.
- Export the *chap1_case_personal_solution* Personal Web site as a Personal Web Package in the SharePoint Designer template folder as **natalie_personal_webpackage.fwp**.
- Close the *chap1_case_personal_solution* Personal Web site and exit SharePoint Designer.

Introduction to the Internet, World Wide Web, Web Sites, and SharePoint Designer 2007

The unprecedented evolution of personal computers was powered by Bill Gates's launch of Microsoft® in the mid-1970s and the Defense Advanced Research Projects Agency's (DARPA) launch of the Internet in 1968, and was ignited by Tim Berners-Lee's invention of the World Wide Web in 1989. Personal computers are now an essential part of everyday life for learning, teaching, communication, business transactions, and accessing entertainment. In the workplace, at home, and in the classroom, the Internet has empowered more people to develop and manage their own personal or business Web sites. Many people choose Microsoft Office SharePoint Designer to help them achieve this goal. Microsoft Office SharePoint Designer 2007 is a new product based on Microsoft Office FrontPage® 2003, ASP.NET, and SharePoint technologies that guides you through the process of designing, creating, and editing Web pages and Web sites. It enables you to publish Web pages and Web sites and assists you in testing, validating, maintaining, and managing a Web site.

(*Four decades after the inception of the Internet and almost two decades since the inception of the World Wide Web, while the global digital divide is still a reality, slowly but surely the Internet and World Wide Web are becoming part of our daily life.*)

In this section, you will learn about the core concepts behind the Internet, World Wide Web, and Web sites. After you have mastered these basics, you will start learning about the SharePoint Designer 2007 interface and how you can customize it. In addition, you will learn how you can use Help to get assistance in using SharePoint Designer.

Getting Started with the Internet and the World Wide Web

At home, at work, or at school, children, teenagers, adults, and senior citizens spend more and more time in front of computers, which are no longer a luxury but rather a commodity in the developed countries. There are also international efforts made toward eliminating the so-called global digital divide, which is a term used to describe the great discrepancies in opportunity to access the Internet between developed and developing countries or even between different regions of developed countries. Four decades since the inception of the Internet and almost two decades since the inception of the World Wide Web, while the global digital divide is still a reality, slowly but surely the Internet and World Wide Web are becoming part of our daily life.

Understand the Internet

Communications is the process of moving data within or between computers.

Communications devices provide the hardware and software support for connecting computers to a network.

A **network** consists of a group of computers connected to share resources such as output devices, servers, and information.

The **Internet** is a huge collection of computers and networks located all over the world.

Communications is the process of moving data within or between computers. In order to move data between computers, communications devices are necessary. *Communications devices* provide the hardware and software support for connecting computers to a network. A *network* consists of a group of computers connected to share resources such as output devices (for example, printers), servers, and information. The *Internet* is a huge collection of computers and networks located all over the world. It has dramatically changed the way people use computers. People use the Internet in a great variety of ways, such as to gather information, share resources, read and send e-mail, shop online, trade stocks, participate in discussions and chat groups, and download software.

Figure 1.1 shows the three ways your computer can connect to the Internet: dial-up, direct, and broadband. Dial-up connections use a modem to call in to a server that is connected to the Internet. Direct (or dedicated) connections access the Internet through a local area network (LAN). Broadband connections are based on new and advanced communications technologies and devices, such as Digital Subscriber Lines (DSL), cable modems, satellites, and wireless technology. Bandwidth is the amount of data passing, within a time interval, through a phone line, cable line, or DSL line connection to transfer information from and to a Web site via your computer. It is usually measured in bits-per-second (bps) or Megabits-per-second (Mbps), or (for Web sites) in GigaBytes (GB)/month.

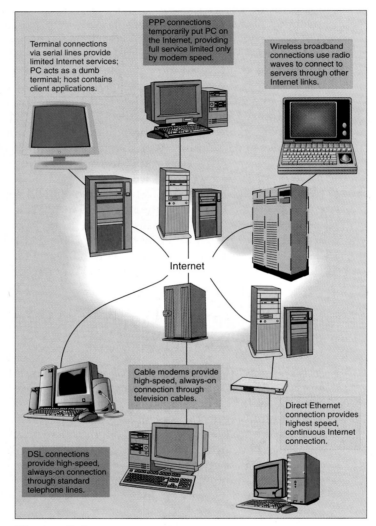

Figure 1.1 Ways to Connect to the Internet

An ***Internet Service Provider (ISP)*** is a company that provides the hardware system, the software applications, and a Point of Presence (PoP), or a connection, necessary for your computer to access the Internet.

A ***protocol*** represents a set of rules used to transmit data on the Internet.

You connect to the Internet using an ***Internet Service Provider (ISP)***. An ISP is a company that provides the hardware system, the software applications, and a Point of Presence (PoP), or a connection, necessary for your computer to access the Internet. Although the Internet is technically only an infrastructure of computers, a network of networks, most people think of the Internet as the network and the data it contains. After you connect to the Internet, you can easily retrieve and send information with just a click of the mouse. A ***protocol*** represents a set of rules used to transmit data on the Internet. The most well-known and commonly used part of the Internet is the World Wide Web (WWW).

File Transfer Protocol (FTP) is the second most popular protocol on the Internet and is used to transfer files between computers.

Telnet is a popular Internet resource that allows users to log in to and use a remote computer.

Transmission Control Protocol (TCP)/Internet Protocol (IP) represents the main set of protocols used for transmitting data on the Internet.

Understand the World Wide Web

The *World Wide Web (Web, WWW)* is the graphical, user-friendly side of the Internet, which enables users to view and share graphics and multimedia documents electronically and remotely over the Internet.

The *World Wide Web* (also called the *Web* or *WWW*) is the graphical, user-friendly side of the Internet, which enables users to view and share graphics and multimedia documents electronically and remotely over the Internet. The WWW has no centralized control or any type of central administration. Theoretically, anybody can retrieve information from the WWW and publish information on it. The WWW is basically a huge collection of Web sites created by individuals and governmental, professional, and academic organizations.

TIP Does Anyone Own or Manage the Internet or the WWW?

Although the U.S. government funded the research for the technologies that constitute the foundation of the Internet, no individual or organization actually owns and manages the Internet or the WWW. However, as a global service, the Internet is collaboratively managed by a group of organizations such as the National Science Foundation (NSF), the Internet Society (ISOC), the Internet Engineering Task Force (IETF), the Internet Corporation for Assigned Names and Numbers (ICANN), the Internet Architecture Board (IAB), and the **World Wide Web Consortium (W3C)**, an open forum of companies and organizations with the mission to lead the Web to its full potential.

The **World Wide Web Consortium (W3C)** is an open forum of companies and organizations with the mission to lead the Web to its full potential.

Today, the WWW is the driving force of the Internet. Its history started in 1989, when Timothy Berners-Lee and other researchers working at CERN, a European particle physics laboratory, brought to life this module of the Internet. Their aim was to create an information system that would make it easier for researchers around the world to locate and share data. They initially developed a system of *hypertext documents*, electronic files that can be easily accessed by a mouse click.

Hypertext documents are electronic files that can be easily accessed by a mouse click.

TIP Sir Timothy Berners-Lee

According to the official W3C Web site (go to http://www.w3.org, click on People under the W3C Team section, then click on Berners-Lee), Sir Timothy Berners-Lee is a graduate of Oxford University, England. Sir Timothy Berners-Lee, also known as the Father of the Web, now holds the 3Com Founders chair at the Computer Science and Artificial Intelligence Laboratory (CSAIL) at the Massachusetts Institute of Technology (MIT) and directs W3C. In December 2003, Queen Elizabeth II made him a Knight Commander of the Order of the British Empire, and in June 2007 Tim Berners-Lee was appointed Member of the Order of Merit by Queen Elizabeth II.

A **Web page** is a document on the WWW that has been coded to provide static or dynamic content for users to view and access.

Web pages are interconnected through a series of **hypertext links** (or **links**), which can be text or objects.

A *Web page* is a document on the WWW that has been coded to provide static or dynamic content for users to view and access. Web page developers today use the Berners-Lee hypertext approach to link documents. The documents are interconnected through a series of *hypertext links* (or *links*), which can be text or objects. Hypertext links on a Web site can link to their own documents or to other locations on the Web.

Understanding Web Browsers and Markup Languages: Hypertext Markup Language (HTML), Extensible Hypertext Markup Language (XHTML), and eXtensible Markup Language (XML)

In 1991, CERN released the first text-oriented browser. However, the explosive growth of the revolutionary hypertext approach started in 1992, when the first graphically oriented browser, Mosaic, was conceived by the National Center for Supercomputing Applications at the University of Illinois at Urbana–Champaign. This approach later evolved into the fundamental method of sharing and retrieving information on the Internet. The relationship among HTML, XML, and XHTML, as today's core markup languages, is still an area of considerable confusion on the Web; thus, this section aims to clear this confusion.

> The relationship among HTML, XML, and XHTML, today's core markup languages, is still an area of considerable confusion on the Web; thus, this section aims to clear this confusion.

Get Started with Web Browsers

Web browsers are software applications, installed on your computer, designed to assist you with navigating the Web, retrieving a Web page from its host server, interpreting its content, and displaying it on your computer.

Web browsers are software applications, installed on your computer, designed to assist you with navigating the Web, retrieving a Web page from its host server, interpreting its content, and displaying it on your computer. Although there are many Web browsers available, the three most popular Web browsers are Microsoft Internet Explorer®, Firefox®, and Safari™ (the default browser of the Apple computers). Figure 1.2 shows the toolbars of the Internet Explorer browser that provides user-friendly Web navigation and Web site and Web page management tools (all other popular browsers provide similar features). Approximately 95% of all computers use Internet Explorer or Firefox (http://www.mozilla.com/en-US/firefox) to browse the Internet. Of the other Web browsers on the market, the following five are most popular:

- **Mozilla:** http://www.mozilla.org mission.html (freeware).
- **Opera:** http://www.opera.com (freeware browser developed as a research project in Norway's telecommunications company, Telenor, in 1994, which branched out into an independent development company named Opera Software ASA in 1995).
- **Lynx:** http://lynx.browser.org (freeware text browser).
- **Netscape® Navigator™:** http://browser.netscape.com (freeware).
- **Amaya™:** http://www.w3.org/Amaya (freeware developed by the World Wide Web Consortium).

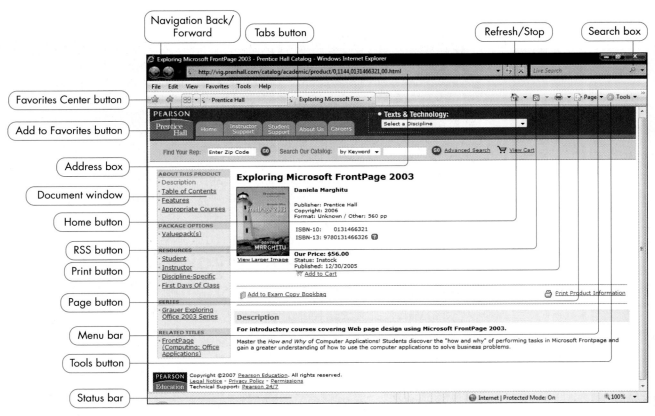

Navigation Back/Forward · Tabs button · Refresh/Stop · Search box

Favorites Center button
Add to Favorites button
Address box
Document window
Home button
RSS button
Print button
Page button
Menu bar
Tools button
Status bar

Figure 1.2 Internet Explorer Browser Window

TIP Internet Privacy and Security

The Internet user-friendly functionalities are now part of billions of people's lives. Regrettably, this has also transformed the Internet into a "promised land" for individuals interested in advertising their services or products, in tracking your Web browsing activities, and in even less ethical actions such as stealing people's copyrighted work and personal information. It is becoming more and more challenging to avoid all the unwanted side effects of the Internet's amazing success. To learn more about this topic visit the Liberty Alliance Project (http://www.projectliberty.org), the Internet Security Squad (http://www.internetsecuritysquad.com), and the Microsoft Trustworthy Computing (http://www.microsoft.com/mscorp/twc/default.mspx) Web sites.

A *markup language* is a language that describes the format of Web page content through the use of tags.

Tags are specific codes that indicate how the text should be displayed when the document is opened in a Web browser.

Hypertext Markup Language (HTML) is the markup language most commonly used to create Web pages and was developed from the more complicated Standard Generalized Markup Language (SGML).

Get Started with Hypertext Markup Language (HTML)

Web pages are created using markup languages. A *markup language* is a language that describes the format of Web page content through the use of tags. *Tags* are specific codes that indicate how the text should be displayed when the document is opened in a Web browser. It is the job of the Web browsers to interpret these tags and render the text accordingly. *Hypertext Markup Language (HTML)* is the markup language most commonly used to create Web pages and was developed from the more complicated Standard Generalized Markup Language (SGML).

TIP Standard Generalized Markup Language (SGML)

SGML was invented by Dr. Charles F. Goldfarb in 1974 and further developed into International Standard 8879 (ISO 8879), which was published October 15, 1986. SGML is a platform-independent computer language and is the parent technology for HTML, XHTML, and XML.

HTML was created to simplify the SGML language so that anyone could learn to use it. HTML documents contain a combination of American Standard Code for Information Interchange (ASCII) text and tags. Computers can understand only numbers. *ASCII*, which was created by the American National Standards Institute (http://www.ansi.org), is the common numeric code used by computers. The standard ASCII character set consists of 128 decimal numbers ranging from zero through 127 assigned to letters, numbers, punctuation marks, and the most common special characters. The extended ASCII character set consists of 128 decimal numbers and ranges from 128 through 255, representing additional special, mathematical, graphic, and foreign characters.

ASCII is the common numeric code used by computers.

Although HTML is often called the "language of the Web," it is not a programming language. HTML defines the page layout, fonts, graphic elements, and hypertext links to other documents on the Web. So it could be better defined as a descriptive language. HTML has critical features for distributing information remotely:

- HTML enables Web developers to give users access to other HTML documents and other types of documents and files distributed across the WWW via elements called hyperlinks, which you will learn more about in Chapter 2.

- HTML enables developers to create Web page documents that can be displayed to all visitors, regardless of the computer platform, operating system, and Web browser they use.

Because it is created using unformatted text, you can write an HTML document in a simple text program (such as Windows Notepad or WordPad), in a word processing program (such as Microsoft Word), or in a Web authoring program (such as SharePoint Designer 2007). HTML documents normally have the file extension .htm or .html. Opening an HTML document in a text editor could reveal the following text and tags:

```
<html>

<body>

<p style="text-align: center">
Welcome to Patrick Taylor's Home Page <br/>
1912 Magnolia Street <br/>
Auburn, AL 36849 <br/>
334.111.2222
</p>

</body>

</html>
```

Figure 1.3 HTML Document Viewed in a Text Editor

Tags are mostly used in pairs to indicate the beginning and end of a Web page element or format. As shown in Figure 1.3, tags usually begin with the less than sign (<), end with the greater than sign (>), and are not case sensitive. The end tag always contains a forward slash (/). For example, the <p> tag in the preceding code tells the browser to begin applying the paragraph format, which inserts a blank line at the end of the paragraph. The tag </p> indicates the end of the paragraph.

HTML tags follow a specific syntax, which is a set of rules or standards developed by the W3C. The generic syntax of an HTML tag used in pairs (or two-sided) is <tag attributes> text </tag>. However, some HTML tags, also called empty tags, are not used in pairs. For example, the <br/> tag forces a break in the current line of text. In the previous example, the <br/> tag is one of the HTML tags that is not used in a pair; it does not have an end tag. Whereas HTML W3C standards allow you to omit some end tags, XHTML W3C standards require them for every element, even the empty ones. To maximize the compatibility with browser, you should add a space and a forward slash to empty elements, as shown in Figure 1.3, and include independent end tags for the non-empty tags. In addition to the tags that are used to define Web page elements, HTML also has attributes that further define the way Web page elements display in Web browsers. These attributes can help define the style, color, size, width, height, and source of the element. Web developers can assign a specific value to each attribute. They then include the attribute with the start tag in the HTML code document. In Figure 1.3, the style attribute is added to the <p> tag. The code center aligns the text. Figure 1.4 shows how an HTML document appears when viewed in Internet Explorer and in Notepad.

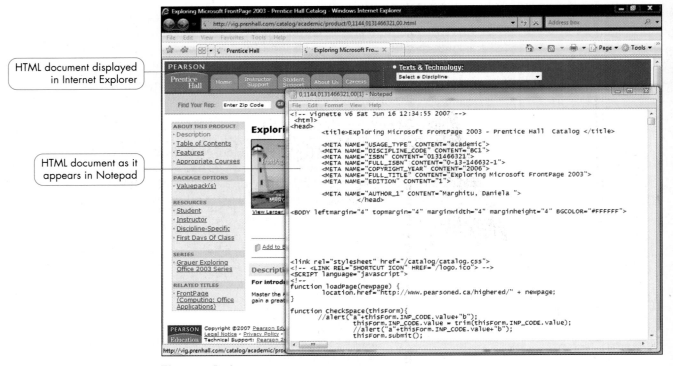

Figure 1.4 HTML Document as It Appears in Internet Explorer and Notepad

TIP   Cross-Browser and Cross-Platform Issues

Unfortunately, although HTML defines the way Web page elements should be displayed, the way a Web page is displayed in different browsers might vary. Fonts, colors, tables, and hyperlinks are only a few of the many Web page elements that could appear differently in Firefox than they do in Microsoft Internet Explorer. The same Web page might also be displayed differently on computers using different operating systems. For example, fonts and colors might look different on an Apple® computer than they would on a Sun® workstation. These two issues are called cross-browser and cross-platform issues, and they are still causing problems for Web developers. The W3C is working on ways to eliminate these problems. One of the SharePoint Designer features enables you to preview a Web page in different browsers and different versions of browsers. You will learn more about how to avoid many cross-browser and cross-platform problems in Chapters 2 and 3.

In the beginning, HTML's development was not overseen by any organization. Web developers were able to make any type of improvements they felt were needed. To win as much of the market share as possible, two major browser companies, Microsoft and Netscape, enriched HTML with new features called extensions. You learn more about HTML in Appendix A.

TIP   Internet Explorer and Netscape Navigator HTML Extensions

Extensions are basically HTML tags and tag attributes that were not initially included in the W3C official HTML standard. Although some extensions have been added to the W3C official standard, extensions that are not part of the W3C standard usually are unevenly supported by today's most popular browsers, Microsoft Internet Explorer and Firefox.

Deprecated HTML tags and tag attributes are tags that might or might not be supported by all browsers, and thus they are not recommended for use.

By creating these unique extensions, developers, in a sense, generated two different HTML standards. Many of these features were not supported by all browsers, creating some major cross-browser compatibility issues. To deal with these problems, the W3C created a comprehensive set of recommended HTML standards and specifications. The W3C standards indicate the format that should be applied to standard tags. The standards also declare many of the HTML tags and tag attributes as *deprecated*, which means that they might or might not be supported by all browsers, and thus they are not recommended for use. To eliminate the cross-browser issues, the W3C standard is supposed to be followed by all browser manufacturers. Unfortunately, this is not yet the case.

TIP   W3C HTML Standards

If you want to read more about the W3C HTML standards and specifications, you can check them out at the W3C Web site (go to http://www.w3.org, click HTML under W3C A to Z, and then click HTML 4.01). SharePoint Designer assists you in developing standard Web pages in line with W3C standards and specifications. You will learn more about how to develop standard Web sites and Web pages in Chapter 2 as well as Appendix B in the Chapters and Appendices of this textbook.

Over the years, millions of Web pages have been and continue to be created with HTML, which remains the most popular markup language. However, despite its popularity, HTML has some drawbacks. All Web developers should be aware of the following limitations and flaws when using HTML:

- HTML does not enable users to structure, define, and process data. For example, you can use HTML to build forms, but you cannot validate, send, and retrieve the form's information to and from a database. To accomplish these types of tasks, a Web developer needs to employ code written in scripting languages such as JavaScript®, Microsoft Active Server Pages (ASP), or Sun Java Server Pages (JSP™).

- HTML is not extensible. In other words, it includes a finite set of tags and does not enable users to create new custom tags; thus it cannot be changed to meet specific developers' needs for describing data content. The extensibility issue is discussed in greater detail later in this chapter.

- Although HTML includes a wide range of syntax rules, it does not enforce these rules. If you forget an HTML rule, the only way that you will know it is by manually validating the way the HTML code is displayed in one or more browsers.

- HTML features are not consistently supported by all browsers; thus an HTML document might be displayed differently on one browser than on another. For example, some browsers require the </p> end tag and some do not.

TIP **What is a Scripting Language?**

A scripting language is less powerful than traditional programming languages, such as Java® and C++, in which programs are sets of commands interpreted and then executed one by one. Each scripting language employs a scripting engine and does not require the compilation. Depending on where a script code is interpreted (that also means where the scripting engine is located), scripting languages are divided into two main categories: client-side and server-side. A script code written in a server-side scripting language is interpreted on the Web server before the requested Web page is sent back to the client. When an HTML document containing code written in a client-side scripting language is loaded in a browser, a scripting engine built into the Web browser interprets the code. A scripting engine (or interpreter) is a program that translates code one line at a time into an executable format each time the program runs. Consequently, scripting languages commonly run more slowly than traditional programming languages.

Microsoft Active Server Pages (ASP) and Sun Java Server Pages (JSP) are two of the most popular server-side scripting languages used to develop interactive Web sites that interface with databases or other data sources (such as an XML document). JavaScript is one of the most popular client-side scripting languages, and its scripting engine is supported by all major browsers, such as Internet Explorer and Firefox. JavaScript (initially named LiveScript) was developed by Netscape, starting 1995, as a solution to the need to make Netscape Navigator's newly added support for Java applets more accessible to non-Java programmers and Web designers. Netscape and Sun jointly announced the new JavaScript scripting language on December 4, 1995, calling it a "complement" to both HTML and Java. It is able to meet the needs of most Web developers who want to create dynamic Web pages. JavaScript is used by Web developers for such things as automatically changing a formatted date on a Web page, causing a linked page to appear in a pop-up window, causing text or a graphic image to change during a mouse rollover, obtaining information about the current Web browser, navigating to Web pages that have been opened during a Web browser session, or validating data submitted via an HTML form.

Get Started with Extensible Hypertext Markup Language (XHTML)

Extensible Hypertext Markup Language (XHTML) is a newer markup language that was designed to overcome some of the problems generated by HTML.

Extensible Hypertext Markup Language (XHTML) is a newer markup language that was designed to overcome some of the problems generated by HTML. XHTML is considered a transitional solution between HTML and XML because it is not extensible. XHTML gives you the opportunity to write well-formed and valid documents that work in all browsers and that can be read by all XML-enabled applications. Thus, until all browsers are upgraded to fully support XML, XHTML will continue to be a worthy solution.

Although there are many similarities between HTML and XHTML, there are also some important differences:

- XHTML code has to be well-formed and valid.

- XHTML tags are case sensitive.

- In XHTML, the empty tags that were inherited from HTML, such as <img>, <br> and <hr>, have the following syntax: <img/>, <br/>, and <hr/>.

TIP   W3C XHTML Standards

If you want to read more about the W3C XHTML standards and specifications, you can check them out at the W3C Web site (go to http://www.w3.org, click XHTML under W3C A to Z, and then click specs (XHTML, HTML4,...).

Get Started with Extensible Markup Language (XML)

eXtensible Markup Language (XML) enables data to be shared and processed via the Internet and across software applications, operating systems, and hardware computer platforms.

eXtensible Markup Language (XML), based on the SGML standard, enables data to be shared and processed via the Internet and across software applications, operating systems, and hardware computer platforms.

Because, unlike HTML, XML is an extensible language, developers can create specific custom tags, describing the data content for each document. Developers also like XML because they can prevent many code errors by employing an XML parser and because XML has the ability to define data content. The following two code examples show how the same data content can be coded in HTML (Figure 1.5) and XML (Figure 1.6).

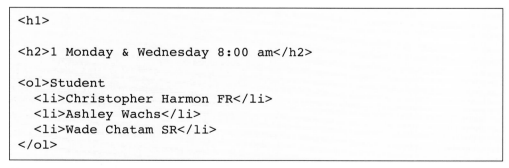

```
<h1>

<h2>1 Monday & Wednesday 8:00 am</h2>

<ol>Student
  <li>Christopher Harmon FR</li>
  <li>Ashley Wachs</li>
  <li>Wade Chatam SR</li>
</ol>
```

Figure 1.5 HTML Code

```
<course>COMP1000 Personal Computer Application </course>

<section>1 Monday & Wednesday 8:00 am
  <student>Christopher Harmon FR</student>
  <student>Ashley Wachs</student>
  <student>Wade Chatam SR</student>
</section>
```

Figure 1.6 XML Code

XML (and SGML) can also be used to create other markup languages called XML applications. Two of the most popular XML applications are MathML (http://www.w3.org/Math) and VoiceXML (http://www.voicexml.org).

After an XML document is created, it has to be evaluated by an application called **XML parser**. An XML parser interprets the document code to make sure that the document meets the following criteria:

XML parser is an application that evaluates XML documents.

A **well-formed** XML document contains no syntax errors and obeys all W3C specifications for XML code.

- **Well-formed.** The document contains no syntax errors and obeys all W3C specifications for XML code (http://www.w3.org/XML). Some common syntax errors can be caused by ignoring the case sensitivity of XML tags or by omitting one or more tags. As previously discussed, HTML never gives you any type of feedback regarding syntax errors.

- **Valid.** The document is well formed and satisfies the rules included in the attached document type definition or schema.

A **valid** XML document is a well-formed document that also satisfies the rules included in the attached document type definition or schema.

A **document type definition (DTD)** can force an XML document to follow a uniform data structure, thus eliminating many code errors that can occur.

A **schema** is an XML document that includes the definition of one or more XML document's content and structure.

XML supports an optional document type definition and XML schema. These documents define all the components that an XML document is allowed to contain as well as the structural relationship among these components. A *document type definition (DTD)* can force an XML document to follow a uniform data structure, thus eliminating many code errors that can occur. The DTD can be internal, included in the XML document itself; external, stored in an external .dtd file; or a combination of internal and external components. The power of a DTD is increased when using external components because the same external DTD can be applied to more than one XML file. A *schema* is an XML document that includes the definition of one or more XML document's content and structure. Two of the most popular schemas are the XML schema (http://www.w3.org/XML/Schema.html), developed by W3C in 2001, and the Microsoft schema, XDR. In an effort to support developers that have to use both schemas, Microsoft has developed an application, the XDR-XSD Converter, which converts XDR schemas to XML schemas (http://www.microsoft.com/downloads/details.aspx?FamilyID=5f6505a1-359e-47bf-8963-f4affaf87566&DisplayLang=en).

TIP Doctype Declarations and W3C-Recommended DTDs

When developing HTML, XHTML, or XML documents, it is important to add a Doctype declaration and W3C-recommended DTDs. To read more about Doctype declarations and W3C-recommended DTDs, see the W3C Recommended DTDs to use in your Web document Web page (go to http://www.w3.org/QA/2002/04/valid-dtd-list.html).

The Microsoft XML parser is called MSXML and is built into Internet Explorer versions 5.0 and above. However, it needs to be separately downloaded and installed. Netscape developed its own parser, called Mozilla, which is built into Navigator version 6.0 and higher. Although these are the most popular, many other

XML editors and parsers are available, such as Altova® XMLSpy® (http://www.altova.com/products/xmlspy/xml_editor.html), an award-winning XML editor for modeling, editing, transforming, and debugging XML technologies.

TIP   What Is a Programming Language?

If HTML, XHTML, and XML are markup languages and JavaScript, ASP, and JSP are scripting languages, then what is a programming language? A programming language consists of a set of instructions that tell computers what actions to perform. Programming languages are often categorized in three groups that also reflect the historical development of computer languages: machine language, assembly language, and high-level language. Today, most programmers use a high-level language. A high-level language is expressed in English-like phrases, and thus is easier for programmers to read and write. A single high-level language programming statement can accomplish the equivalent of many, perhaps hundreds, of machine language instructions. However, high-level language code must be translated into machine language to be executed by the computer because computers can only understand binary numbers. A compiler (or interpreter) is a software application that translates each statement in the program into a sequence of machine language instructions. Working with high-level languages enables the programmer to ignore the underlying details required for the machine language. There are two main categories of high-level programming languages: procedural, such as Fortran, and object oriented, such as Java.

HTML can define the way data are formatted and displayed only on a Web page, whereas XML code describes the type of information contained in the document. The XML code does not indicate how data are to be formatted or displayed. Consequently, it must use Cascading Style Sheet (CSS) or Extensible Style Sheet (XSL) languages to build style sheets that can be embedded into the XML document or linked to it. The CSS contains formatting instructions for each element. For example, the CSS external style sheet code shown in Figure 1.9 contains styles for the six HTML headings that will be formatted accordingly across all Web pages that will be linked to the style sheet. Using a CSS to format XML documents provides Web developers with the same formatting features found in HTML, but with greater flexibility:

Style sheets describe how documents are presented on screens or in print, or even how they are pronounced.

Style sheet languages are computer languages for expressing style sheets.

The **Cascading Style Sheet (CSS)** has become the standard style sheet language used on the Web.

- By attaching different style sheets to an XML document, you can change the way it appears in a browser.

- By changing a style sheet attached to multiple XML documents, you can change the way all these XML documents are displayed in a browser.

The good news is that learning to work with HTML and XHTML makes it easier to learn XML.

Using Cascading Style Sheets (CSS)

Although several style sheet languages have been developed, the **Cascading Style Sheet (CSS)** has become the standard style sheet used on the Web.

Conforming to the W3C, *style sheets* describe how documents are presented on screens or in print, or even how they are pronounced. *Style sheet languages* are computer languages for expressing style sheets. W3C and Web designers have advocated style sheets, starting with HTML, as tools for separating a document's presentation from its content. Although several style sheet languages have been developed, the *Cascading Style Sheet (CSS)* has become the standard style sheet language used on the Web.

TIP Extensible Style Sheet Language (XSL)

XSL was developed by the W3C as an improved method for formatting XML documents, allowing developers to transform XML data files into a wide variety of popular file formats, such as HTML and portable document format (PDF). XSL is still supported by fewer browsers than CSS.

Although the CSS was initially developed for HTML, it is currently used in HTML, XML, and XHTML. CSS is a robust formatting language that successfully separates a Web page's content from its appearance. One of the biggest advantages to using CSS is that when the style sheet is changed, all the Web pages created with that CSS are automatically updated. Although the CSS is useful and has experienced rapid growth on the WWW, it is new enough that it can still generate some problems. For example, some browsers still do not fully support it. To learn more about W3C CSS standards and which browsers support CSS, visit this dedicated Web page of the W3C: http://www.w3.org/Style/CSS.

You can use three different types of CSS style codes to format the HTML code of your Web pages:

Inline style codes are included in the start tag by using the tag's style attributes.

- **_Inline styles_**: Inline style codes are included in the start tag by using the tag's style attributes. Inline style codes override the styles defined in internal and external styles. In Figure 1.7 the <body> tag is using the inline styles.

Internal style codes are usually included in the <head> section of an HTML document and have the following syntax: <style>style declarations</style>.

- **_Internal styles_**: Internal style codes are usually included in the <head> section of an HTML and have the following syntax: <style>style declarations</style>. Internal style codes override the format defined in a linked external style sheet. In Figure 1.8, two internal styles are defined in the <head> section.

External style codes are included in separate files used to specify the formatting of any HTML document to which they are linked.

- **_External styles_**: External style codes are included in separate files used to specify the formatting of any HTML document to which they are linked. These style codes are kept in a document with a .css file extension and are linked to the HTML document using the <link> HTML tag. In Figure 1.8, an external style kept in the au_template3.css style sheet is linked. Figure 1.9 displays the content of an external style sheet in which the layout.css style sheet is imported.

TIP Linking External Style Sheets

An external style sheet also can be linked using the CSS @import directive added inside the HTML <style> tag. For example, the @import url("layout.css"); CSS code (shown in Figure 1.9) links the layout.css to the HTML document. The CSS @import directive is not supported by old browsers, such as Netscape Navigator 4.0. You can learn more about linking CSS style sheets in Chapter 2 and Appendix A.

```
<body onload="FP_preloadImgs(/*url*/button4E.jpg',/*url*/
'button4F.jpg',
/*url*/'button51.jpg',/*url*/'button52.jpg',/*url*/
'button54.jpg',/*url*/'button55.jpg',
/*url*/'button57.jpg',/*url*/'button60.jpg',/*url*/
'button5D.jpg',/*url*/'button5E.jpg',
/*url*/'button4.jpg',/*url*/'button5.jpg')"bgcolor="#052C5C"
style="background-repeat: noleftmargin="10" rightmargin="10"
bottommargin="10" marginwidth="0" marginheight="0">
```

Figure 1.7   Inline Styles

```html
<head>
<meta http-equiv="Content-Type" content="text/html;
charset=utf-8"/>
<!-- BEGIN EDIT AREA A - Enter Description, Keywords, and
Other Meta Tags -->
<meta name="title" content="Auburn University SUMMER
OUTREACH
COMPUTER LITERACY PROGRAM FOR CHILDREN (dealing with
disabilities)" />
<meta name="description" content="Auburn University SUMMER
OUTREACH COMPUTER LITERACY PROGRAM FOR CHILDREN (dealing
with disabilities)" />
<meta name="keywords" content="Daniela Marghitu Computer
Literacy Children With disabilities Alice Mindstorms Robots
Diversity"/>
<meta http-equiv="content-style-type" content="text/css" />
<meta http-equiv="content-script-type"
content="text/javascript"/>
<!-- END EDIT AREA A -->
<!-- BEGIN EDIT AREA B - Enter Page Title -->
<title>SUMMER COMPUTER LITERACY ACADEMY FOR CHILDREN (COMP
CAMP) (Dealing with Disabilities)</title>
<!-- END EDIT AREA B -->
<!-- Link Style Sheets -->
<link rel="stylesheet" type="text/css"
href="au_template3.css" />
<base target="_self">

<style type="text/css">
.style1 {
    color: #F47723;
}
.style2 {
    font-size: 9.0pt;
    font-family: Verdana;
    color: black;
    margin-left: 0in;
    margin-right: 0in;
}
</style>

</head>
```

Figure 1.8 Internal Styles

```
<head>
@import url("layout.css");
body {
        font-family: Georgia, "Times New Roman", Times, serif;
        font-size: small;
        background-image: url("../images/background_tile.gif");
        background-repeat: repeat;
}
h1 {
        font-size: xx-large;
        color: #000;
}
h2 {
        font-size: x-large;
        font-style: italic;
        color: #000;
}
h3 {
        font-size: large;
        font-style: italic;
        color: #000;
}
h4 {
        font-size: medium;
```

Figure 1.9 Content of an External Style Sheet

Meta tags represent one of the tools that you can use to ensure that the content of your Web site has the proper topic identification and ranking by search engines.

A **Web site** is a collection of Web pages, files, and folders gathered together and published on the Internet.

Publishing a Web site consists of transferring all the Web site's files and folders to a Web server.

A **server** is a computer that provides clients with access to files and printers as shared resources on a computer network.

A **client** is a user machine that connects to the server and receives information from it.

A **Web server** is a special kind of server that is connected to the Internet and that runs specialized software applications, enabling it to handle requests from clients to access information from Web sites.

TIP   Using Meta Tags

Meta tags, shown in Figure 1.8 represent one of the tools that you can use to ensure that the content of your Web site has the proper topic identification and ranking by search engines. SharePoint Designer Web pages automatically include default meta tags that indicate the language used and how the Web page should be displayed. A Web designer can add user-defined meta tags to a Web page. These tags identify the kinds of topics included in the pages of the Web page. You learn more about adding user-defined meta tags to a Web page using SharePoint Designer in Chapter 2 and Appendix A.

An inline style takes precedence over an internal style, which takes precedence over an external style sheet. If you have two styles with the same weight in a document, the style declared last has precedence. You can learn more about formatting with CSS in Appendix A.

Defining Web Sites

A **Web site** is a collection of Web pages, files, and folders gathered together and published on the Internet. **Publishing** a Web site consists of transferring all the Web site's files and folders to a Web server. A **server** is a computer that provides clients with access to files and printers as shared resources on a computer network; a **client** is a user machine that connects to the server and receives information from it. A **Web server**, on the other hand, is a special kind of server that is connected to the Internet and that runs specialized software applications, enabling it to handle requests from clients to access information from Web sites.

Before publishing your Web site to a Web server and making it available to Internet visitors, you can develop it on any disk drive of a computer or a local network. From that drive, you can test all Web pages and files in your Web site. However, specific testing can be accomplished only after the Web site is published on a Web server.

Static Web page content displays the same information every time it is viewed unless the Web developer makes and saves specific changes in the HTML code. **Dynamic Web page** content changes as users interact with it. (For example, using JavaScript, you can change the color of a text line, or a button can change when a user moves the mouse pointer over it.) Dynamic Web pages, using a server-side scripting language such as ASP.NET or JSP, enable users to access and retrieve information from databases so that they can display different information to users depending on their data requests and the formatting choices. Dynamic Web pages always make use of a scripting language. All Web pages included in a Web site can be accessed via the Web site home page. The home page is the main page and the "opening gate" to any Web site. It is usually also defined as the index or table of contents for a Web site because it provides access to and information about all the Web pages and files included in the Web site.

Define Internet Resources: URLs, URIs, and URNs

A **Uniform Resource Identifier (URI)** is a compact string of characters used to identify or name a resource. The main purpose of this identification is to enable interaction with representations of the resource over a network, typically the WWW, using specific protocols. A **Uniform Resource Locator** (**URL**) is a specific kind of URI that assigns each Web page a unique WWW address. For example, "http://www.auburn.edu" is a URI that identifies a resource (Auburn University homepage) and implies that a representation of that resource (such as the home page's current HTML code, as encoded characters) is obtainable via HTTP from a network host named www.auburn.edu.

> **TIP** Uniform Resource Name (URN)
>
> Another specific type of URI is the Uniform Resource Name (URN). Although URNs are formatted similar to URLs, they do not necessarily specify a downloadable resource. The purpose of a URN is simply to provide a globally unique name for something, not necessarily to provide a name that points to a Web-based resource. A URN can be used to talk about a resource without implying its location or how to reference it. For example, the URN "urn:isbn: 0-958-11041-1" is a URI that, like an International Standard Book Number (ISBN), allows one to talk about a book, but does not suggest where and how to obtain an actual copy of it.

The URL can be found in the Location or Address box of your browser's document window, as shown in Figure 1.2. All URLs follow the format shown in Figure 1.10. The first portion of the URL identifies the communication protocol that was used to control the file transfer process. **HTTP**, short for **Hypertext Transfer Protocol**, is the most popular communication protocol used to transfer Web pages. FTP is another communication protocol used for transferring information via the Internet (mainly for uploading files to a server or downloading files from a server). Typically, the communication protocol is followed by a separator, such as a colon and two slashes (://). The **domain name** comprises the first part that identifies the Web page's host, which can be a Web server or computer on the Internet, and a second part called the top-level domain. The **top-level domain** can be either a generic three-letter suffix indicating the type of organization to which the Web page host belongs (such as .edu and .org) or a two-letter suffix designated for each country (such as .us for United States and .au for Australia). The Internet Assigned Numbers Authority

---

Static Web page content displays the same information every time it is viewed unless the Web developer makes and saves specific changes in the HTML code.

Dynamic Web page content changes as users interact with it.

A **Uniform Resource Identifier (URI)** is a compact string of characters used to identify or name a resource.

A **Uniform Resource Locator (URL)** is a specific kind of URI that assigns each Web page a unique WWW address.

Hypertext Transfer Protocol (HTTP) is the most popular communication protocol used to transfer Web pages.

The **domain name** comprises the first part of the URL that identifies the Web page's host, which can be a Web server or computer on the Internet, and a second part of the URL called the top-level domain.

The **top-level domain** can be either a generic three-letter suffix indicating the type of organization to which the Web page host belongs or a two-letter suffix designated for each country.

The **path name** and file name of the URL specify the location of the Web page on the host computer.

Web site (http://www.iana.org/domain-names.htm) provides a full list of all top-level domain names currently approved. The **path name** and file name specify the location of the Web page on the host computer.

Figure 1.10   URL Structure

The Core Types of Web Sites:
Intranets, Extranets, and Portals

> The WWW includes millions of public Web sites that provide information to anyone who can connect to them using a browser; however there are some special-purpose Web sites with particular characteristics.

An *intranet* consists of Web pages and other resources that are only available inside a company.

The Web includes millions of public Web sites that provide information to anyone who can connect to the WWW using a browser; however, there are some special-purpose Web sites with particular characteristics. Three important types of Web sites are intranets, extranets, and portals.

As well as having a public presence on the Internet, many companies maintain a private Intranet behind a security firewall. An *intranet* consists of Web pages and other resources that are only available inside the company. Intranets have a low cost of ownership because they use the standard technologies of the Internet. They increase internal communication while using less paper—for phone books, manuals, forms, and so forth. They pull information out of corporate databases in a form everyone can use. Intranets have proved valuable for all kinds of organizations: For example, credit card companies work with many banks, and an Intranet can be used as a central repository for information about all the banks that the company works with. Software companies use intranets as a way of locating reusable software components, whereas law firms have used intranets to draw information from worldwide sources on topics such as trials and laws and regulations from many countries. These are just a few of the many contexts in which intranets have been successfully used.

An *extranet* is a Web site that allows access only to selected users, such as customers, suppliers, or other trading partners.

An *extranet* falls somewhere between the Internet and an organization's intranet. Only selected users, such as customers, suppliers, or other trading partners, are allowed access. Extranets can range from highly secure Business-to-Business (B2B) systems to self-registration systems like those frequently used for downloading evaluation software. Extranets can be used, for example, to allow Web shopper customers to log in to check the status of their orders over a secure connection, or by users of courier companies to check where their deliveries are at any point in time.

> **TIP** — Business-to-Business (B2B) and Business-to-Consumers (B2C)
>
> On the Internet, B2B, also known as e-biz, is the exchange of products, services, or information between businesses rather than between businesses and consumers. Although initially interest centered on the growth of retailing on the Internet (also called e-tailing), forecasts are that B2B revenue will far exceed business-to-consumers (B2C) revenue in the near feature.

A *portal* is a special kind of Web application that acts as a gateway into a number of other applications.

A *portal* is a special kind of Web application. Its role is to act as a gateway into a number of other applications. Portal architecture is typically used to present a number of portlets, which are window-based links into other applications. Portals also commonly provide features for personalization, so that users can customize the portlets that are represented and also change the layout, look, and feel of the portal. Portals are frequently used by public sites, such as Google™, that encourage user registration. They are also often used by companies as a route into the various applications provided on the company intranet. In the mobile context, portals are a popular way for mobile service providers to enable easy access to the mobile Internet. Mobile portals provide links to various applications within the "walled garden" of services provided by the mobile network carrier, as well as more general access to the mobile Internet.

Describe Web Applications

A **Web application** (or **webapp**) is a software application that is accessed with a Web browser over a network such as the Internet, an intranet, or an extranet.

Complex Web sites are also called Web applications. A **Web application** (or **webapp**) is a software application that is accessed with a Web browser over a network such as the Internet, an intranet, or an extranet. The main reason for the increased popularity of Web applications is that Web applications can be updated and maintained without distributing and installing software on potentially thousands of client computers.

A Web application resides on a central server and provides a large variety of services to a wide range of clients. The following are the core components of a Web application:

- **Web server:** The Web application runs on the Web server.

- **Active and static documents:** If a client requests a static document, the Web server locates the file and sends it back to the client; the client browser interprets the static documents. If a client requests an active document, the Web server processes the document before sending it back to the client.

- **Processing engine:** Specialized software, such as ASP.NET, installed on the Web server that processes the active documents.

Understand How Search Engines Work

The WWW is a rich source of information on nearly every topic imaginable. However, searching for information within the more than two billion pages of the WWW often can be a challenge. Good Web authors start planning strategies for promoting their Web sites as soon as they begin designing them. The "build it and they will come" philosophy does not apply to building and publishing a Web site. Web designers need to implement some standard design requirements to make their Web sites easy for search engines to find. In order to understand these design requirements, you need to be familiar with search engines and the way they work.

Organizations called search providers develop and maintain Web sites that help you locate the precise information you want. Search providers maintain large databases of information pulled from the WWW and Internet. These databases include URL addresses, content descriptions or classifications, and the keywords that appear on the Web pages. Specially designed programs called spiders, or Web crawlers, are constantly browsing the WWW and updating these databases.

Search engines are powered by the huge amount of information managed by search providers. To learn more about the dynamic connection between search providers and search engines, you might consider reading the article "Who Powers Whom? Search Providers Chart" at http://searchenginewatch.com/reports/article.php/2156401. To stay up to date with the latest trends and statistics on search engines, go to the ClickZ Web site (http://www.clickz.com) and do a search for "search engines."

Search engines usually refer to Web search engines, which are specialized software applications that help you to find information on the WWW and Internet. Search engines offer two different types of searches:

- Keyword search: Keyword searches require you to enter a key word or phrase that relates to the information you want to find. The search engine will then compare your keyword to the information in its database and return a hit list, which is a list of Web sites that contain the key word or phrase you want to find. Each hit contains a hyperlink to the referenced Web page. The search engine orders the list based on the probability of finding the requested information in those sites. Some of the most popular keyword search engines are Google (http://www.google.com), Alta Vista™ (http://www.altavista.com), and AlltheWeb (http://www.alltheweb.com).

- Directory (index) search: A directory search provides a directory, or index, of core topics, such as health, arts, science, society, or real estate. After you select the topic you want to search, the search engine displays a list of related subtopics. Select a subtopic to see more subtopic options to browse through or a form to complete to narrow your search. For example, if you select real estate, you are presented with a form for identifying the kind of housing you want to find. After you narrow your search, you are presented with a hit list that is essentially the same as the kind of hit list you see in a keyword search. One of the most popular directory search browsers is the Open Directory Project (http://dmoz.org), which also has keyword search capabilities.

Search engines usually refer to Web search engines, which are specialized software applications that help you to find information on the WWW and Internet.

The Internet also offers a number of specialized search engines. These search engines focus their searches on topic-specific Web sites, a process which cuts down on the amount of time required to refine your search results to the specific area you want to research. Among the most popular specialized search engines are Medsite® (http://www.medsite.com), which provides medical-related information for experts in the field as well as for casual browsers, and HistoryNet (http://www.historynet.com), which provides resources related to the history of the United States.

Recent research studies, such as the "Invisible or Deep Web: What It Is, Why It Exists, How to Find It, and Its Inherent Ambiguity" study located at http://www.lib.berkeley.edu/TeachingLib/Guides/Internet/InvisibleWeb.html, have shown that none of the current search engines can provide a complete list of the resources available for any one search topic. Consequently, you should consider using several search engines, especially when you need to search for important information.

Understand the Internet Copyright Laws

Internet law is the application of many different types of traditional law to the virtual world of the Internet.

Internet law is the application of many different types of traditional law to the virtual world of the Internet. Internet law comprises a number of distinct subcategories including the Internet Copyright. ISOC provides a comprehensive "Guide to Internet Law" at http://www.isoc.org/internet/law.

Enforcing copyrights over the Internet is a rather new and complicated area even for the most experienced Internet content developers and owners, whether you are a copyright owner attempting to enforce your rights or an individual or business accused of infringing on the copyright rights of others. Internet copyright infringement runs the scope of copyrightable Internet assets, from Web site graphics, to eBooks, to photos, to MP3 and video files, to Web text content. President Clinton signed into law, on October 28, 1998, the Digital Millennium Copyright Act (DMCA), 17 USC § 512 (http://www.copyright.gov/legislation/dmca.pdf). DMCA legislation implements two 1996 World Intellectual Property Organization (WIPO) treaties—the WIPO Copyright Treaty and the WIPO Performances and Phonograms Treaty (http://www.wipo.int/copyright/en/activities/wct_wppt/wct_wppt.htm)—and also addresses a number of other significant copyright-related issues.

Getting Started with SharePoint Designer 2007

Microsoft Office SharePoint Designer 2007 is a new product based on Microsoft Office FrontPage 2003, ASP.NET, and SharePoint technologies that guides you through the process of designing, creating, and editing Web pages and Web sites. It enables you to publish Web pages and Web sites and assists you in testing, validating, maintaining, and managing a Web site. SharePoint Designer assists Web developers in creating and managing Web sites with its easy-to-use graphical user interface and its many built-in features, such as templates, wizards, Web packages, Web components, and Web parts.

> Microsoft Office SharePoint Designer 2007 is a new product based on Microsoft Office FrontPage 2003, ASP.NET, and SharePoint technologies that guides you through the process of designing, creating, and editing Web pages and Web sites. It enables you to publish Web pages and Web sites and assists you in testing, validating, maintaining, and managing a Web site.

SharePoint Designer is easy to learn and use because it uses a what-you-see-is-what-you-get (WYSIWYG) interface. This simply means that instead of looking at the HTML code while you are editing your Web page, you can view your Web page the way it will look in a Web browser. Thus, without any previous knowledge of HTML coding, you can use SharePoint Designer to assist you in designing, developing, viewing, testing, validating, publishing, and managing high-quality personal and professional Web sites.

SharePoint Designer offers many easy-to-use integration features that enable you to work with any kind of Microsoft Office 2007 suite of application files. SharePoint Designer also offers integration features for in-demand file types, including most multimedia and graphic standards, such as Apple QuickTime®, Macromedia® Flash®, Java applets, and XML files.

The **Accessibility Checker** assists you in creating universally accessible Web sites that are in compliance with the W3C Web Content Accessibility Guidelines (WCAG) (http://w3c.org/TR/WCAG20) and Section 508 of the Rehabilitation Act: Electronic and Information Technology Accessibility Standards (http://www.access-board.gov/508.htm).

The **Compatibility Checker** assists you in creating Web pages based on Web standards such as HTML, XHTML, and CSS.

SharePoint Designer provides a built-in **Accessibility Checker** that assists you in creating universally accessible Web sites that are in compliance with the W3C Web Content Accessibility Guidelines (WCAG) (http://w3c.org/TR/WCAG20) and Section 508 of the Rehabilitation Act: Electronic and Information Technology Accessibility Standards (http://www.access-board.gov/508.htm). It also comes with another great tool called the **Compatibility Checker**, which assists you in creating Web pages based on Web standards such as HTML, XHTML, and CSS. Therefore,

SharePoint Designer Web sites are compatible with any browser that supports these Web standards. You will learn more about SharePoint Designer accessibility and compatibility tools later in this chapter, in Chapters 2 and 3, and Appendix B.

TIP Microsoft Office 2007 Online

To learn more about the new SharePoint Designer features, you can visit the SharePoint Designer home page of Microsoft Office Online at http://office. microsoft.com/en-us/sharepointdesigner/FX100487631033.aspx. This Web site provides comprehensive online training and technical assistance for all SharePoint Designer features. You can also get great ideas and tips from other SharePoint Designer users.

Identify SharePoint Designer 2007 Interface Components

Before installing SharePoint Designer on a computer you should carefully review the following SharePoint Designer software and hardware system requirements:

- Personal computer with a 700MHz processor or higher.
- 128MB RAM or higher.
- 1.5GB of available hard-disk space.
- A CD-ROM or DVD drive.
- A 1024x768 or higher resolution monitor.
- The Microsoft Windows XP with Service Pack 2 (SP2) or Microsoft Windows Vista™ operating systems.
- Internet Explorer 6.0 or later, 32-bit browser only.
- Mozilla Firefox 2.0.0.4 or later.
- Internet access for Internet functionality.

TIP SharePoint Designer 2007
Advanced Features

SharePoint Designer provides professional tools that can be used equally for designing and developing standard Web sites or for building and customizing advanced Microsoft SharePoint Web sites and workflow-enabled applications based on SharePoint technologies. Some features of SharePoint Designer also require the Microsoft .NET Framework version 2.0. The purpose of this textbook is to introduce you to the Web design and development of standard Web sites using SharePoint Designer not requiring the SharePoint Technologies. To learn more about Microsoft SharePoint, visit the Microsoft SharePoint Products and Technologies dedicated Web site (http://www.microsoft.com/sharepoint/default.mspx) and the SharePoint Products and Technologies Community (http://sharepoint.microsoft.com/sharepoint/default. aspx).

When you launch SharePoint Designer, by default, a blank page named Untitled_1.htm is displayed in Page view, shown in Figure 1.11. Notice that the file name appears as a tab located in the upper-left corner of the work area. A similar tab appears for each Web page that you open. You can easily switch between opened Web pages by clicking these tabs.

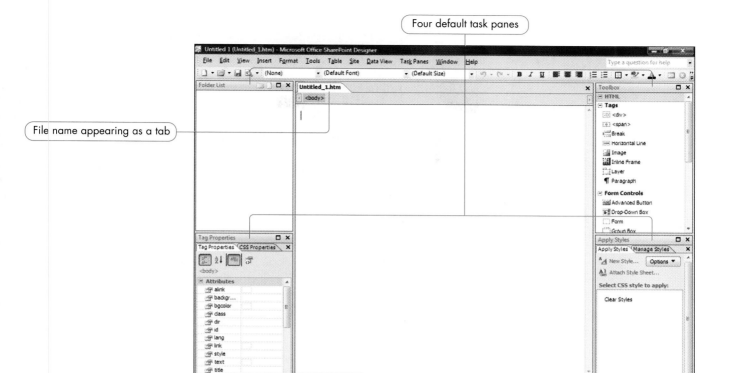

Figure 1.11 SharePoint Designer Interface Containing a New Blank Page

---

TIP Opening SharePoint Designer

Check your desktop. Depending on the installation method used, you might have a SharePoint Designer icon on your Windows desktop. If so, you can save time by double-clicking this icon to start SharePoint Designer. If SharePoint Designer was recently used on your computer, you can start SharePoint Designer by pointing to Microsoft Office SharePoint Designer 2007 from the Start menu.

As shown in Figure 1.11, the SharePoint Designer default interface is an upgraded version of the FrontPage 2003 default interface, and it does not match the standard Office 2007 design concepts and layout. In this section, you learn about components of the SharePoint Designer default interface, which includes a title bar, menu bar, toolbars, status bar, task panes, and document window; these components are further described in Table 1.1.

> The SharePoint Designer default interface is an upgraded version of the FrontPage 2003 default interface, and it does not match the standard Office 2007 design concepts and layout.

TIP Microsoft Expression Web

If you had the chance to see the new Microsoft Expression Web application you might wonder about the differences between this application and Microsoft Office SharePoint Designer. The fundamental difference between these two applications is that Microsoft Expression Web does not provide any tools for building and customizing advanced Microsoft SharePoint Web sites based on SharePoint technologies. Instead, Microsoft Expression Web provides a set of Web site templates for developing an organization, personal, or small business Web site. However, this set of Web site templates also can be used in Microsoft Office SharePoint Designer. You will learn more about this topic later in this chapter.

Table 1.1 SharePoint Designer Default Interface

Components	Description
Title bar	Provides information about the file that you have open and always shows the name of the application as well as the location and name of the Web site that you are creating or editing.
Menu bar	Is located directly beneath the title bar and displays the names of each of the SharePoint Designer menus. When you click a menu name, the menu appears.
Toolbars	Are combinations of related buttons that you can choose to perform tasks without using the menus. Each button displays a graphic icon suggesting its functionality. A common toolbar is the default SharePoint Designer toolbar a, which includes the most frequently used functionalities from the Standard toolbar shown in Figure 1.12 and the Formatting toolbar shown in Figure 1.13.
Views bar	Enables you to change the view of an open file or of all Web pages included in the Web site. When a Web page is open you can select Design View, Code View, or Split View, as shown in Figure 1.11. When a Web site is open and no Web pages are open, the Views bar shows the six Web site views. You learn about Web page and Web site views later in this chapter.
Status bar	Is formed by five sections providing information about the open files and enables you to customize the SharePoint Designer interface and some of its functionalities. Table 1.2 includes a concise description of the information and tools provided by its five sections.
Task panes	Contain the most common options for the particular view that you are using. This feature can improve your productivity by eliminating the need to hunt through menus to find the options you need (for example, the Toolbox task pane assists you in inserting HTML tags). Table 1.3 includes a concise description of the four default task panes for SharePoint Designer, also shown in Figure 1.11, as well as some of the most popular task panes.
Document window	Displays the content of the latest open Web page. If no Web page is open, it displays a view of all Web site files.

Shortcut menus are short menus that display a list of commands related to the item you right-clicked within the SharePoint Designer window.

TIP SharePoint Designer Shortcut Menus

SharePoint Designer uses also *shortcut menus*, which are short menus that display a list of commands related to the item you right-clicked within the SharePoint Designer window.

File Menu | Reference

File Menu Command	Functionality
New	Displays the New submenu that enables you to create a new Page or Web site; a new HTML, ASPX, or CSS document; and Folder. You can also create a new Web page from a Dynamic Web Template or from a Master Page.
Open	Displays the Open File dialog box that enables you to open a document or file.
Open Site	Displays the Open Site dialog box that enables you to open a Web site.
Close	Closes a document.
Close Site	Closes a Web site.
Save	Saves a document or a file.
Save As	Displays the Save As dialog box that enables you to save a document or file at a required location and with a new name.
Save All	Enables you to save all the documents and files that were previously open and modified.
Reset to Site Definition	Resets a customized Web page (built upon a template) to the Web site definition. It applies only to Web pages published on a server running Microsoft Office SharePoint Server 2007.
Detach from Page Layout	Detaches a Web page from a publishing page layout. It applies only to Web pages published on a server running Microsoft Office SharePoint Server 2007.
Publish Site	Displays the Remote Web Site Properties dialog box that enables you to create or navigate to a remote Web Site, to optimize the HTML code using the options on the Optimize HTML tab, and to publish a Web site using the options on the Publishing tab.
Import	Displays the Import submenu that enables you to import a File, import a Web site using the Import Site wizard, or to import a Personal Web Package.
Export	Displays the Export submenu that enables you to export a File, a Personal Web Package, or a SharePoint Site template, and to Save a Web part to a Site Gallery or file. The SharePoint Site Template and Save a Web part To commands apply only to Web sites and Web pages published on a server running Microsoft Office SharePoint Server 2007.
Preview in Browser	Enables you to see what a Web page will look like in a Web browser without having to first save or publish your page.
Print	Displays the Print submenu that enables you to Print or Print Preview the active page or to display the Print Page Setup using the Page Setup command.
Properties	Displays the Page Properties dialog box that enables you to add or modify properties related to an active page.
Recent Files	Enables you to open a file from a list of files you have recently opened.
Recent Sites	Enables you to open a Web site from a list of Web sites you have recently opened.
Exit	Exits the SharePoint Designer application.

Microsoft IntelliSense technologies (IntelliSense) help you minimize errors when working directly in the Code view with the markup language and tags that comprise the site, including HTML, XHTML, ASP.NET, and CSS.

Microsoft IntelliSense technologies (IntelliSense), as a result of the built-in syntax and tag-structuring support, help you minimize errors when working directly in the Code view with the markup language and tags that comprise the site, including HTML, XHTML, ASP.NET, and CSS. The Split view feature provides a contextual view of the portion of the code that you are working on—providing both a WYSIWYG view and a code view in the same pane. The Tag Inspector can validate the markup code as well as point out anomalies. When editing a Web page in the Office SharePoint Designer 2007 Code view, IntelliSense can also suggest commands based on the work you are doing, enabling you to develop pages quicker and more efficiently. You learn more about Microsoft IntelliSense technologies (IntelliSense) in Chapter 2 and Appendices A and B.

The Standard toolbar, shown in Figure 1.12, includes buttons linked to menu commands, such as Cut, Copy, Paste, Open, and Save. It also contains a Help button that you can click to access the SharePoint Designer Help system. The Formatting toolbar, shown in Figure 1.13, includes buttons linked to formatting commands, such as creating and formatting lists, setting text styles, and aligning text.

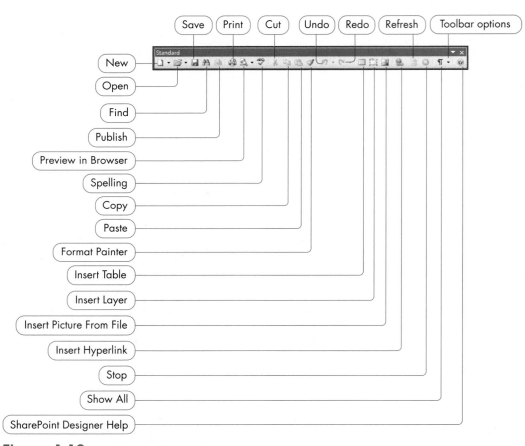

Figure 1.12 Standard Toolbar

Figure 1.13 Formatting Toolbar

SharePoint Designer also includes an entire set of specialized toolbars that can help you work with SharePoint Designer features in a more productive way. Some of the most frequently used specialty toolbars are the Picture toolbars and Table toolbar. You can make any toolbar visible in the SharePoint Designer window with one of the following methods:

- Choose Toolbar on the View menu to see a list of available toolbars. To display one, just click its name.

- Right-click an empty area of any visible toolbar to display a shortcut menu. To display a toolbar, click its name.

TIP   Showing the Pictures Toolbar

You can also display the Pictures toolbar by right-clicking any image included on a Web Page and selecting Show Pictures Toolbar from the shortcut menu that appears.

The SharePoint Designer status bar is a fully upgraded version of the FrontPage 2003 status bar, providing new and powerful tools. Its default location is at the bottom of the SharePoint Designer window and is formed by two areas: the message area is located on the left side and the indicators are located on the right side. If you move the mouse pointer over each of the six indicators described in Table 1.2, a ScreenTip is displayed showing the information provided by that indicator. For example, if you move the mouse pointer over the Download Statistics indicator of the status bar, a ScreenTip providing information about the HTML page size, linked data size, total download size, and linked data file count will be displayed as shown in Figure 1.14. You can customize the status bar by double-clicking or right-clicking the indicators, changing settings, and enabling or disabling features.

Figure 1.14 Status Bar Download Statistics Feature

> **TIP ScreenTips**
>
> ScreenTips are small windows that display descriptive text and appear when you point to a command or control. SharePoint Designer does not support the Enhanced ScreenTips that are available in Access™, Excel®, PowerPoint®, and Word 2007.

Table 1.2 SharePoint Designer Status Bar

SharePoint Designer Status Bar Areas	Options
Message Area	Located on the left side of the status bar, the message area shows information about hyperlinks, file names, locations, and more.
Visual Aids	This indicator enables you to show or hide on a Web page in Design view all invisible and empty elements and properties. When visual aids indicators are OFF, the Web page layout in Design view looks almost identical to the Web page layout in the browser.
Style Application	This indicator enables you to view and customize the SharePoint Designer CSS settings using the Style Application toolbar (double-click indicator to display the Style Application toolbar) and the CSS tab of the Page Editor Options dialog box (right-click indicator and click CSS Options to display the Page Editor Options dialog box); see Figure 1.15.
Download Statistics	This indicator informs you of the size of the HTML page, the size of the data linked to the HTML page, the size of the total download, and the number of files linked to the HTML page; see Figure 1.14.
HTML/XHTML Schema	This indicator enables you to view the Default Document Type and to choose a doctype and a secondary schema of the authoring document using the Authoring tab of the Page Editor Options dialog box (double-click indicator to display the Authoring tab of the Page Editor Options dialog box); see Figure 1.16.
CSS Schema	This indicator enables you to see and set the CSS schema available in CSS IntelliSense; see Figure 1.16.

SharePoint Designer default configuration enables CSS styles to be automatically generated in certain operations related to creating and formatting Web pages. However, very often you might want to save all CSS styles into an external style sheet so that you can use the external style sheet for more than one Web page. To prevent SharePoint Designer from generating CSS styles automatically, use the Style Application toolbar or right-click the Style Application indicator, point to Mode, and then point to Manual.

Manual and Auto options on the CSS tab of the Page Editor Options dialog box

Manual and Auto options on the Style Application toolbar

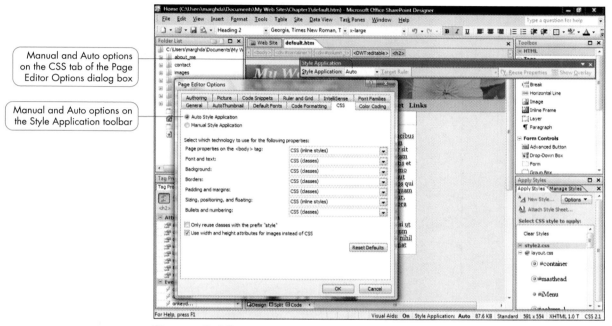

Figure 1.15 Using the Style Application Indicator

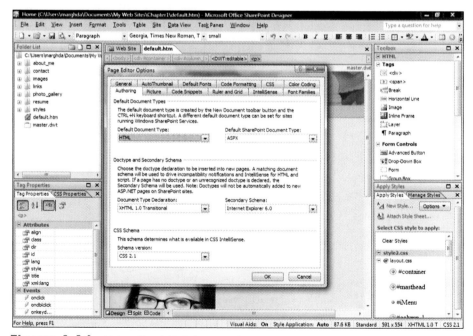

Figure 1.16 Using the HTML/XHTML Schema and CSS Schema Indicators

SharePoint Designer introduces a new Task Panes menu that displays task panes organized in six groups, as shown in Figure 1.17. These six groups are also part of the SharePoint Designer default workspace. When you open each group for the first time, task panes are displayed by default as merged task panes that cover the same space and are laid one behind the other. Each merged task pane is available by clicking its corresponding tab.

Table 1.3 SharePoint Designer Core Task Panes

SharePoint Designer Task Pane	Options
Folder List	View the Web site as a hierarchical list of documents and folders.
Tag Properties/CSS Properties	Apply HTML properties (attributes) and CSS properties (styles) to HTML tags using just the WYSIWYG interface.
Toolbox	Add HTML tags and form controls.
Apply Styles/Manage Styles	Apply CSS styles. Manage CSS styles. Insert new tables and cells.
Layout Tables	Set up table properties. Select a table layout.
Clipboard	View a thumbnail of any item, such as text and graphics, that can be copied or pasted. Collect up to 24 copied items. Paste all copied items at once or one at a time. Delete all copied items.
Behaviors	Add built-in SharePoint Designer behaviors (scripting code that can assist you when adding interactivity to your Web pages).
Layout Tables and Cells	Insert new tables and cells. Set up table properties. Select a table layout.
Layers	Add, delete, and modify layers.

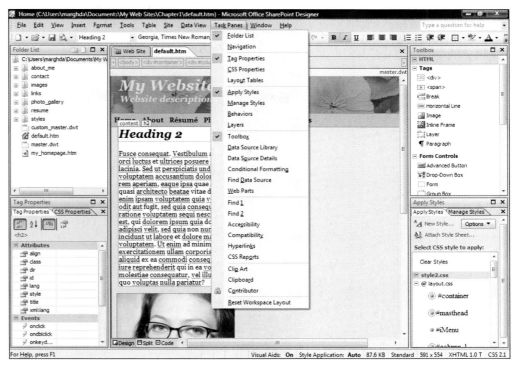

Figure 1.17 SharePoint Designer Task Panes Menu

TIP   Floating and Merging Individual Task Panes

SharePoint Designer allows you to change the default group of task panes by floating and merging individual task panes. You can also restore the default task pane layout at any time using the Reset Workspace Layout command on the Task Panes menu.

Customize the SharePoint Designer 2007 Interface

Figure 1.11 shows how the SharePoint Designer window looks the first time it is opened. You might want to make changes, such as closing one or more of the task panes in the SharePoint Designer window to give yourself a larger workspace. You can move, hide, customize, and reset toolbars. You can also enable speech and handwriting recognition or create a personal toolbar containing all the special features that you like best. The user-friendly interface enables you to customize features to suit your needs.

You can customize the SharePoint Designer toolbars and menu bars using the Customize dialog box. Click the View menu, point to Toolbars to open the Toolbars submenu, and click Customize to open the Customize dialog box.

Customize Toolbars Using the Customize Dialog Box Tabs | Reference

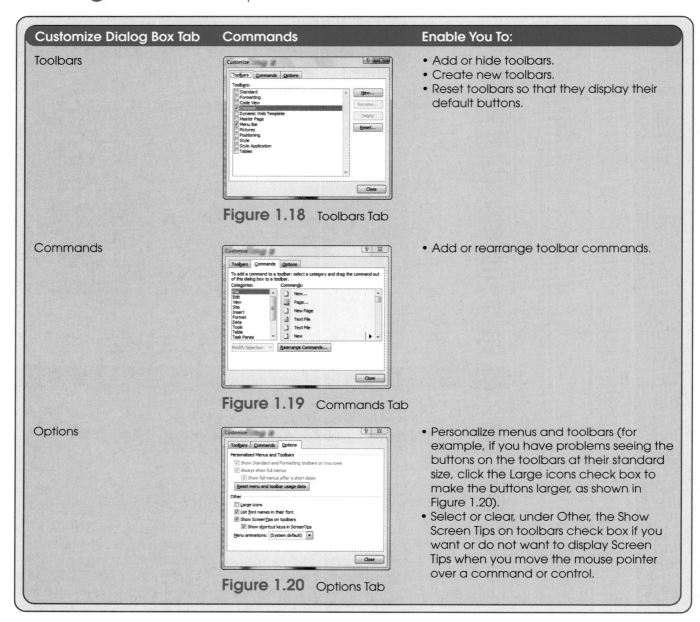

Customize Dialog Box Tab	Commands	Enable You To:
Toolbars	**Figure 1.18** Toolbars Tab	• Add or hide toolbars. • Create new toolbars. • Reset toolbars so that they display their default buttons.
Commands	**Figure 1.19** Commands Tab	• Add or rearrange toolbar commands.
Options	**Figure 1.20** Options Tab	• Personalize menus and toolbars (for example, if you have problems seeing the buttons on the toolbars at their standard size, click the Large icons check box to make the buttons larger, as shown in Figure 1.20). • Select or clear, under Other, the Show Screen Tips on toolbars check box if you want or do not want to display Screen Tips when you move the mouse pointer over a command or control.

TIP Creating New Toolbars

SharePoint Designer enables you to create a new toolbar that contains your favorite features. To create a new toolbar, click the Toolbar tab in the Customize dialog box, click the New button, type the desired name of the toolbar in the New Toolbar box, and click OK. Then, using the Commands tab and Options tab described previously, add commands and options to your toolbar.

The **Language bar** is a toolbar that automatically appears on your desktop, in the Windows Vista operating system, when you add text services such as input languages, speech recognition, handwriting recognition, or Input Method Editors (IME).

When working in the Windows Vista operating system, the **Language bar** automatically appears on your desktop when you add text services such as input languages, speech recognition, handwriting recognition, or Input Method Editors (IME), a program that enables users to enter East Asian text by converting regular keystrokes into East Asian characters.

TIP Speech Recognition Features

To use speech recognition features, such as speaking the names of menu commands, toolbar buttons, dialog box commands, and so on, you will first need to set up Windows Vista using the Ease of Access Center. As this manuscript is being written, the Windows Vista speech recognition tool does not work for SharePoint Designer, although it works with all Microsoft applications that come with Windows Vista as well as with Microsoft Office Word and PowerPoint. Ease of Access was called Accessibility Options in Windows XP. Ease of Access Center and Accessibility Options can be found in the Accessories folder of the Start/All Programs menu. To learn more about the accessibility features of the Microsoft Office 2007 system, see the Microsoft Accessibility in the 2007 Microsoft Office System Web site (http://www.microsoft.com/enable/products/office2007/default.aspx).

If the Language bar is not showing in Windows Vista, you will need to check Show the Language bar on the desktop in the Language Bar Settings dialog box that you can find within the Regional and Language Options. If you work with Windows XP and cannot see the Language toolbar, right-click the Task bar, point to Toolbars, and click Language bar. When you are finished using the Language bar features, you can close it by right-clicking the Language bar to open the shortcut menu, clicking Close, and then clicking OK in the Language Bar dialog box, as shown in Figure 1.21.

Figure 1.21 Language Bar

TIP Changing Your Screen Resolution

You can change the resolution of your computer screen if your specific needs and preferences require it. Your needs could be based on accessibility (such as vision) problems or editing and authoring requirements. If you work on a computer with Windows Vista, choose Start, Control Panel, Appearance and Personalization, Personalization, and then click Display Settings to modify your screen resolution and other display settings. If you work on a computer with Windows XP, choose Start, Control Panel, and then click Display to modify your screen resolution and other display settings.

In SharePoint Designer, you can have multiple task panes open simultaneously. To create your custom layout, you can open and close a task pane or you can close a group of task panes. SharePoint Designer also enables you to merge, dock, float, stack, and resize task panes, as described in Table 1.4. Once you have arranged the task panes in a layout that meets your preferences, SharePoint Designer automatically uses this layout the next time the application is launched. You can restore the default task pane layout at any time by clicking Reset Workspace Layout on the Task Panes menu.

Table 1.4 Arrange the SharePoint Designer Task Panes

Task Pane Layout Arrangement Option	Description
Open	• To open a task pane, click its name on the Task Panes menu, shown in Figure 1.17. • A task pane always opens in the position in which it was most recently closed. • A check mark attached to a task pane name on the Task Panes menu indicates that the task pane is visible. • If a task pane is open but not visible, it is because it is merged with other task panes. Therefore, to make it visible, you will need to click that task pane on the Task panes menu.
Close	• To close an individual task pane, click Close (see Figure 1.22). • To close a group of task panes, click Close on the task pane name title bar (see Figure 1.22).
Merge	• To merge a task pane or a group of task panes, point to the task pane name title bar and, when the pointer becomes a four-headed arrow, drag the title bar to another task pane. • To see an individual task pane in a group of merged task panes, click the task pane name tab (see Figure 1.23).
Dock	• To dock a task pane horizontally or vertically to an edge of the program window, point to the task pane name title bar, and when the pointer becomes a four-headed arrow, drag the title bar to an edge of the program window (see Figure 1.24). • The Page view will automatically adjust its size to include the docked task pane.
Float	• You can float a task pane, drag it, and place it anywhere, even outside the program window (see Figure 1.25). If you drag the task pane to the edge of the program window, it might become docked. To avoid this, hold down CTRL while you drag.
Stack	• You can stack individual or groups of task panes so they cover the same vertical or horizontal space along the edge of the SharePoint Designer window.
Resize	• You can resize a docked pane when the pointer becomes a split line; see Figure 1.26. • You can resize a floating pane when the pointer becomes a double-headed arrow.

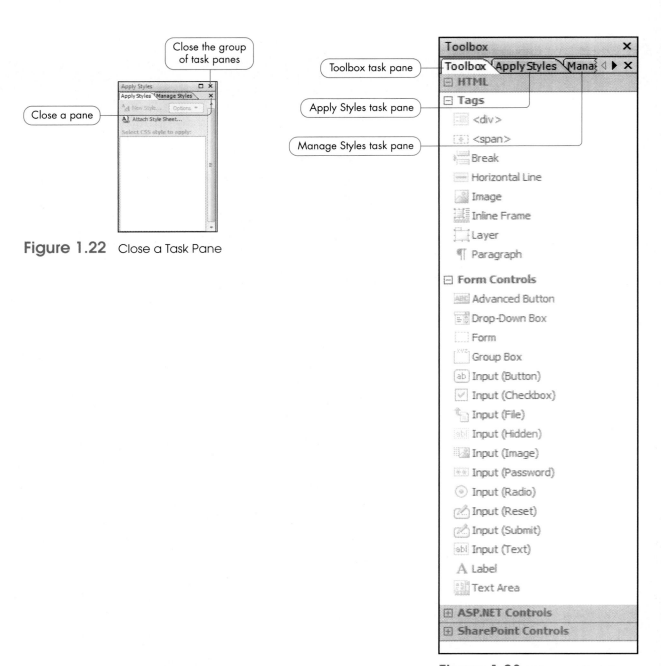

Figure 1.22 Close a Task Pane

Figure 1.23 Merged Task Panes

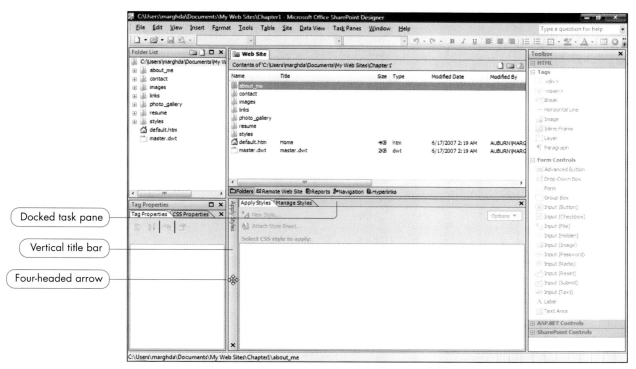

Figure 1.24 Docked Task Pane

Docked task pane

Vertical title bar

Four-headed arrow

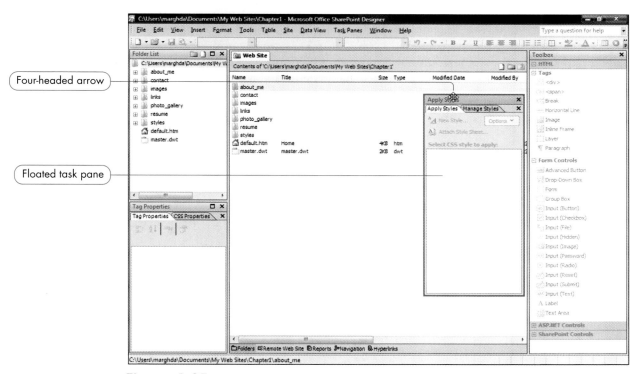

Figure 1.25 Floated Task Pane

Four-headed arrow

Floated task pane

Split line

Figure 1.26 Resizing a Docked Task Pane

Use SharePoint Designer 2007 Help

We all need help in almost any daily activity, from assembling an outdoor grill to getting acquainted with a new iPod®. SharePoint Designer, as with all Microsoft Office 2007 applications, includes a wide range of features that assist you in accomplishing anything from a simple task to a complex project. Help files are automatically saved on your computer when you install SharePoint Designer. Microsoft Office Online also provides, via its dedicated Microsoft Web site, extensive help and access to up-to-date products, files, and graphics.

To access the SharePoint Designer Help window, shown in Figure 1.27, you can use any of the following methods:

- Press F1.
- Click the Help button on the right edge of the Standard toolbar.
- Type a key term in the Search box placed on the right edge of the Common toolbar and hit Enter.

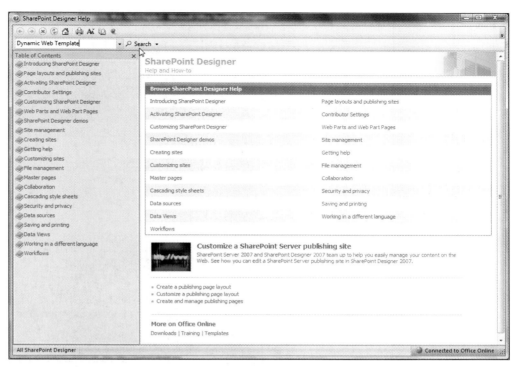

Figure 1.27 SharePoint Designer Help Window

Within the SharePoint Designer Help window you can browse general topics, access more information on Office Online, or, if you know the topic you need help with, you can type a key term in the Search box to display relevant help files. To display a comprehensive table of contents, click the Show Table of Contents button. Once you have located the needed information, you can generate a hard copy by clicking the Print button. Figure 1.27 shows all these methods.

As you work with a dialog box, you might need help with some of the many options contained in it. For example, if you open the Customize dialog box and want help with the Dynamic Web Template toolbar, click the Help button on the title bar of the dialog box to display specific help, as shown in Figure 1.28.

Figure 1.28 Help with Dialog Boxes

Hands-On Exercises

1 | Identifying SharePoint Designer 2007 Interface Components and Using Help

Skills covered: 1. Start SharePoint Designer, Identify Interface Components, Use the ScreenTips, and Use the Status Bar **2.** Close the Toolbox Pane, Close the Apply Styles Pane, Reset Workspace Layout, Use the View Menu to Display the Picture Toolbar, and Close the Picture Toolbar **3.** Use SharePoint Designer Help and Print a Help Topic

---

Step 1
Start SharePoint Designer, Identify Interface Components, Use the ScreenTips, and Use the Status Bar

Refer to Figure 1.29 as you complete Step 1.

a. Click **Start** to display the Start menu. Click **All Programs**, click **Microsoft Office**, and then click **Microsoft Office SharePoint Designer 2007** to open the program.

> **TROUBLESHOOTING:** If a dialog box appears asking you if you want to make SharePoint Designer the default Web editor, clear **Always perform this check when starting SharePoint Designer**, and then click **NO**.

b. Identify the SharePoint Designer interface components described in Table 1.1.

c. Click **Tools**, click **Customize** to display the Customize dialog box, and click the **Options tab**. On the Options tab, check the **Show ScreenTips on Toolbars check box** if it is not already checked, and then click the **Close button**.

d. Move the mouse pointer over the **Download Statistics** indicator of the status bar.

A ScreenTip providing information about the HTML page size, linked data size, total download size, and linked data file count is displayed.

e. Move the mouse pointer over the **HTML/XHTML schema** indicator of the status bar.

A ScreenTip providing information about the HTML/XHTML schema being used on the doctype of the active Web page is displayed.

f. Double-click the **HTML/XHTML schema** indicator to display the Page Editor Options dialog box, carefully review the sections of the Authoring tab, and then click **OK** to close the Page Editor Options dialog box.

> **TROUBLESHOOTING:** If you are not familiar with doctype and schemas, go to the W3C Web site and search for more information.

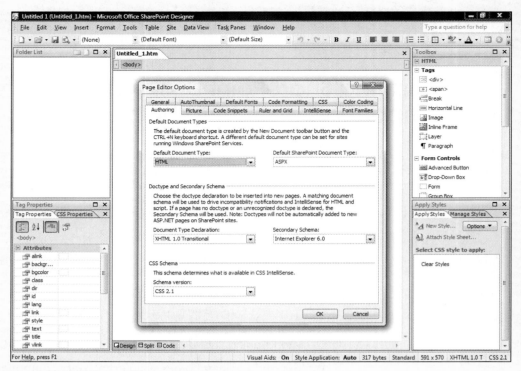

Figure 1.29 SharePoint Designer Interface

Step 2

Close the Toolbox Pane, Close the Apply Styles Pane, Reset Workspace Layout, Use the View Menu to Display the Picture Toolbar, and Close the Picture Toolbar

Refer to Figure 1.30 as you complete Step 2.

a. Click the **Close button** on the Toolbox pane window to remove this task pane from the Workspace Layout.

b. Click the **Close button** on the Apply Styles pane window to remove this task pane from the Workspace Layout.

c. Click **Task Panes** on the Menu bar, and then click **Reset Workspace Layout** to restore the original layout.

d. Click **View** on the Menu bar, point to the toolbars, and then click **Pictures** to display the Pictures toolbar.

e. Click the **Close button** on the Pictures toolbar to close it.

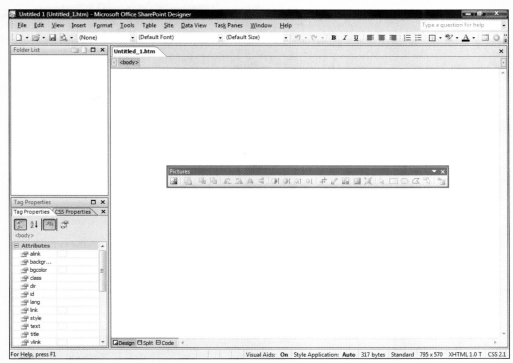

Figure 1.30 Customizing the SharePoint Designer Interface

Refer to Figure 1.31 as you complete Step 3.

a. Click **Help** on the Menu bar, and then click **Microsoft Office SharePoint Designer Help**.

SharePoint Designer Help displays.

b. Click **Saving and printing** in the Table of Contents, and then click the topic **Print a file**.

The help topic displays.

TROUBLESHOOTING: If you do NOT have a printer that is ready to print, skip Step 3c and continue with the exercise.

c. Turn on the attached printer, be sure it has paper, and then click the **SharePoint Designer Help Print button**.

The Help topic prints on the attached printer.

d. Click the **Close button** on SharePoint Designer Help.

SharePoint Designer Help closes.

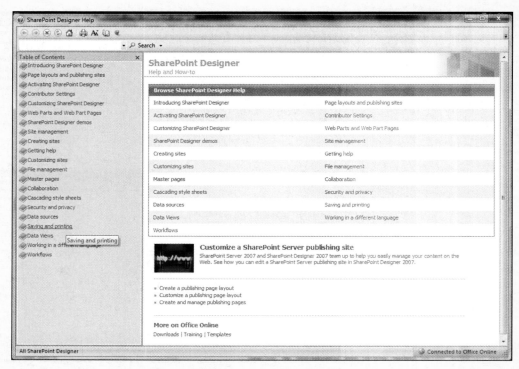

Figure 1.31 Using the SharePoint Designer Help

Introduction to Web Sites

With SharePoint Designer's complete set of Web authoring tools, you can create (and edit) standard Web sites from scratch, from one of the SharePoint Designer Web site templates and wizards (using CSSs to control the format and layout of pages) or from a Personal Web Package.

As previously discussed in this chapter, a Web site is a collection of Web pages, files, and folders put together and published on the Internet by an individual, organization, or business. All high-quality Web sites need to have the following core characteristics:

- A solid, up-to-date, secure, and accessible structure.
- A consistent, easy-to-navigate layout.
- An attractive appearance.

Disk-based Web sites are Web sites located on a floppy disk, zip disk, CD, USB flash drive, or hard disk on your local machine or any other machine on a network that you can access.

WebDAV is an application protocol for creating, editing, and publishing files on a Web server.

With SharePoint Designer's complete set of Web authoring tools, you can create (and edit) standard Web sites from scratch, from one of the SharePoint Designer Web site templates and wizards (using CSSs to control the format and layout of pages), or from a Personal Web Package. Such Web sites include Web sites built on Windows SharePoint Services, *disk-based Web sites* (Web sites located on a floppy disk, zip disk, CD, USB flash drive, or hard disk on your local machine or any other machine on a network that you can access), and Web sites built on FrontPage Server Extensions. SharePoint Designer 2007 can also open and edit Web sites directly with FTP and Web-based Distributed Authoring and Versioning (WebDAV).

As previously discussed in this chapter, FTP is one of the most popular communication protocols, enabling a user to transfer files between remote locations within a network. Using FTP software application commands, such as listing, renaming, or deleting files and folders, Web developers can easily work with the files on a remote location. *WebDAV* is an application protocol for creating, editing, and publishing files on a Web server. It enables multiple authors of a Web site to change files and file properties simultaneously without overwriting each other's work.

> **TIP** WebDAV
>
> More and more students and educators are using the WebCT and Blackboard online management applications that assist students in their classes by creating, managing, organizing, and housing a Web-based learning environment. WebDAV supports local access to both the Manage Files folder and the Course Backup folder of the WebCT and Blackboard applications.

In this section, you explore the SharePoint Designer tools for creating Web sites. You learn how to open and close a Web site. You also explore the SharePoint Designer Web site Views.

Identifying SharePoint Designer 2007 Tools for Creating Web Sites

A *page template* is a template that includes all the appropriate Web page elements, including page settings and formatting.

A *Web site template* is a template formed by a group of page templates and contains navigation elements that connect the pages.

Each Web site is associated with a Web folder. A Web folder is a Windows folder configured to store all files included in a Web site. Although SharePoint Designer offers many different templates, the templates can be divided into two basic categories. A *page template* is a template that includes all the appropriate Web page elements, including page settings and formatting. A *Web site template* is a template formed by a group of page templates and contains navigation elements that connect the pages. SharePoint Designer enables you to customize existing templates or create new ones. You can also download and install many additional templates from the Internet.

SharePoint Designer also offers a wizard, similar to the wizards in other Microsoft applications, such as the Microsoft Excel Text Import Wizard or Microsoft Access Import Text Wizard and Link Text Wizard. The SharePoint Designer *wizard* consists of a series of steps that guide you through the process of designing Web pages and Web sites or importing already created Web sites.

SharePoint Designer provides two default categories of Web site templates, General and SharePoint, available on the Web Site tab of the New dialog box, as shown in Figure 1.32. The templates in both categories produce Web sites that can support ASP.NET functionality, and all of the templates can be used on a server running Windows SharePoint Services 3.0. However, only the templates in the SharePoint Templates category produce Web sites that already include collaborative SharePoint content such as Web Parts and SharePoint lists and document libraries. You can manually add this type of content, in the process of customization, to Web sites that you create using templates in the General category, but this content is not automatically included in such sites.

A *wizard* consists of a series of steps that guide you through the process of designing Web pages and Web sites or importing already created Web sites.

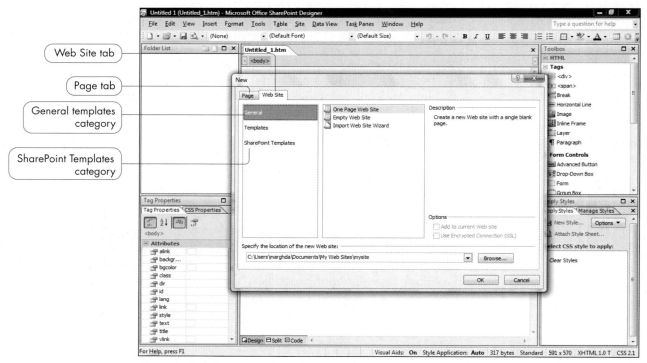

Figure 1.32 SharePoint Designer General Web Site Templates

TIP FrontPage Server Extensions, SharePoint Services, and Visual Studio Extensions

FrontPage Server Extensions and SharePoint Services 2.0 (built-in components of Microsoft Windows Server 2003) are special sets of programs and scripts that support all UNIX and Windows-based Web servers, such as Microsoft Internet Information Server (MIIS), Apache, Linux, and SunOS. When Web developers publish their Web sites to a server on which these programs and scripts have been installed, they have access to many advanced features. FrontPage Server Extensions and SharePoint Services 2.0 provide SharePoint Designer users with features required to create Web pages that can connect to the Internet and search, retrieve data from, or modify databases, or in some way cause the information on the screen to change. No previous knowledge of other programming or scripting languages, such as JavaScript and VBScript, is required when developing these sophisticated and dynamic Web pages. ***SharePoint Services 3.0*** (the latest release of SharePoint Services) provides support for authoring, publishing, organizing, and finding information on the Web and a foundation for Web-based applications. To learn more about SharePoint Services, see the Microsoft Windows SharePoint Services Overview Web site (http://www.microsoft.com/technet/windowsserver/sharepoint/techinfo/overview.mspx).

SharePoint Designer enables you to customize SharePoint Web sites and build reporting tools and Web-based custom applications without writing any code. The Visual Studio® 2005 Extensions for Windows SharePoint Services enable developers to build SharePoint applications such as Web parts, Blank Site Definition, and Team Site Definition and to use the browser and Microsoft Office SharePoint Designer to customize the content of their Web sites.

Office SharePoint Designer 2007 can publish through the HTTP protocol to Web servers running FrontPage Server Extensions or Windows SharePoint Services and publish through FTP, WebDAV, or the file system to any Web server supporting those protocols. Web pages that depend on SharePoint Services or ASP.NET will not work on other servers. For a comprehensive list of FrontPage components that require the FrontPage Server Extensions, visit the Microsoft Office Online Web site (http://support.microsoft.com/?id=281532). Because there is no 2003 version of the Server Extensions, this page also applies to SharePoint Designer and FrontPage 2003.

SharePoint Services 3.0 (the latest release of SharePoint Services) provides support for authoring, publishing, organizing, and finding information on the Web and a foundation for Web-based applications.

Import Web Site Wizard allows you to create a new Web site by importing files either from an existing Web site or from a folder on your computer or a network.

One Page Web site creates a Web site incorporating only one blank page.

Empty Web site creates just the Web site folder with no files included.

The two templates in the General category produce very basic Web sites that are a good place to begin when you want to build a site from scratch, whereas the ***Import Web Site Wizard*** allows you to create a new Web site by importing files either from an existing Web site or from a folder on your computer or a network:

- ***One Page Web site*** creates a Web site incorporating only one blank page.
- ***Empty Web site*** creates just the Web site folder with no files included; see Figure 1.32.

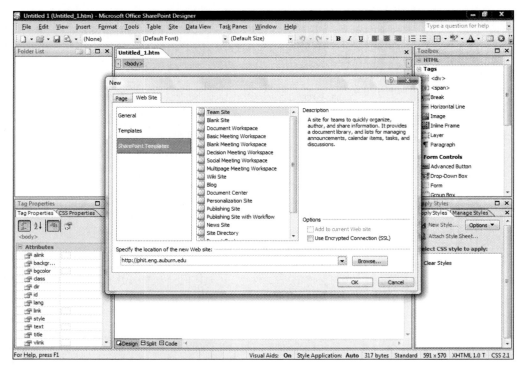

Figure 1.33 SharePoint Designer SharePoint Templates

My Templates is an induced category of templates that appears on the Web site tab of the New dialog box only if you have previously saved a Web package in the user Web template folder on your computer.

My Templates is an induced category of templates that appears on the Web site tab of the New dialog box only if you have previously saved a Web package in the user Web template folder on your computer. Depending on which operating system you are using, the Web template folder is by default located as follows:

- Windows Vista: C:\Users\user name\AppData\Roaming\Microsoft\ SharePoint Designer\Webs.

- Microsoft Windows XP or Microsoft Windows Server 2003: C:\Documents and Settings\user name\Application Data\Microsoft\SharePoint Designer\Webs.

Web Package (.fwp) enables you to share or reuse Web pages or an entire Web site.

Web Package (.fwp) enables you to share or reuse Web pages or an entire Web site. To create a Web Package (in SharePoint Designer or Expression Web), on the File menu, click Open Site. In the Open Site dialog box, browse to and click the Web site that you want to package, and then click Open. On the File menu, point to Export, and then click Personal Web Package. To view the dependencies of files as you select them for inclusion in the Web package, click Show Dependencies at the bottom of the dialog box. Dependencies are additional, associated files (such as linked image, video, PDF, or CSS files) that the selected files require in order to work properly. In the Dependency checking list, do one of the following:

- To show all dependent files, click Check all dependencies.
- To show all dependent files except pages linked by hyperlinks, click Check all dependencies, except hyperlinks. If you choose this option, CSS files are excluded as well. If you want to include CSSs when you export a Web package, click Check all dependencies.

TIP   Web Packages

Web packages represent a great way to duplicate a Web site structure, but they cannot include elements such as subsites or security and permissions settings. However, a Web package can include custom link bars. You will learn about subsites, permission settings, and custom link bars in Chapter 2.

If you wish to remove files from the Web package, click those files in the Files in Package list, and then click Remove (choosing another option in the Dependency checking list does not remove files that have already been added to the Web package). Once you finish adding all the files that you want to the Files in Package list, click OK, and then, in the File name box, enter a name for the Web package. By default, if you clicked Properties and typed a title for the Web package, that title appears here as the file name. In the File Save dialog box, browse to the location where you want to save the Web package, and then click Save. After you finish creating a Web package, you can import, using the Import command from the file menu, and deploy its corresponding .fwp file into as many Web sites as you want. If the Web package was exported in the default Web template folder of the SharePoint Designer, it will be displayed within the My Template category on the Web site tab of the New dialog box, as shown in Figure 1.34.

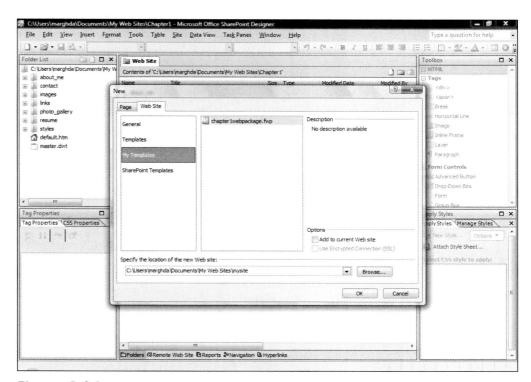

Figure 1.34 SharePoint Designer My Templates

You can also import a Web package within a Web site using the File/Import/ Personal Web Package command, as shown in Figure 1.35, which will display the File Open dialog box. Once you locate and double-click the .fwp file of the Web package, the File Open dialog box is closed and the Import Web Package dialog box is displayed, enabling you to select the Destination and Items from Web package. Click the Import button to start transferring the Web Package files.

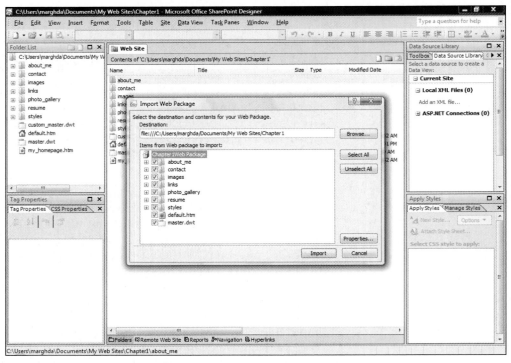

Figure 1.35 Import a Personal Web Package

Opening and Closing a Web Site

As with all Microsoft Office applications, you can create a new Web site or open an already existing one. In SharePoint Designer, you open a Web site with the Open Site command from the File menu or the drop-down list on the Common or Standard toolbar's Open button.

To close a Web site in SharePoint Designer, click File on the Menu bar and click Close Site. If you exit SharePoint Designer, without closing a Web site, the next time you launch SharePoint Designer, the same Web site opens. However, SharePoint Designer closes without warning you that an existing Web site is still open.

Describing Web Site Views

> SharePoint Designer contains a collection of views that provide different ways to look at the content of a Web site in the main SharePoint Designer window and to help you throughout the process of designing, publishing, and managing a Web site.

SharePoint Designer contains a collection of views that provide different ways to look at the content of a Web site in the main SharePoint Designer window and to help you throughout the process of designing, publishing, and managing a Web site. You can use the Site menu to choose one of the Web site views: *Page view*, *Folders view*, *Remote Web site view*, *Reports view*, *Navigation view*, and *Hyperlinks view*. You can also select a view by clicking the corresponding button at the bottom of the document window.

Web Site View | Reference

Web Site Views	Options	Description
Folders view	**Figure 1.36** SharePoint Designer Folders View	• When you create a new Web site, it is displayed in the Folders view by default. • You can use Folders view to open, close, create, delete, copy, rename, and move folders and files; to preview files in the browser; to select files you do not need to publish; and to publish files, as shown on the shortcut menu in Figure 1.36. • Folders view can also provide useful information about files, such as title, size, type, modified date (the date when the last change was made to the file), and whether the Don't Publish option has been selected.
Remote Web site view	**Figure 1.37** SharePoint Designer Remote Web Site View	• You can use Remote Web site view to publish an entire Web site or individual Web pages to a local or remote site and to save a backup copy of your Web site; see Figure 1.37. • You can publish in both directions, moving files easily between the local and remote site. • You can also synchronize files to make sure that all local sites are up to date with recent changes published to the remote site. (This can be helpful if you have local sites on different computers or different people developing the same Web site.) • The Remote Web site view uses icons and descriptive text to provide information on the publish status of files, such as Don't Publish, Changed, Unchanged, Unmatched, New, and Conflict, as shown in Figure 1.37. • You learn more about SharePoint Designer's Remote view in Chapter 2.
Reports view	**Figure 1.38** SharePoint Designer Reports View	• Reports view provides access to a set of site reports, organized in five categories, as shown in Figure 1.38. • Through the Reports view, you can access a comprehensive set of site reports and statistics, such as total number and size of picture files, unlinked files (files that cannot be reached directly from the Web site home page), slow pages (pages that need more than 30 seconds to be downloaded), older files (files that have not been updated within 72 days), and broken links (links that are targeting unavailable files). These reports offer a great way to test and validate a Web site. • You learn more about how to use Reports view in Chapter 2.
Navigation view	**Figure 1.39** SharePoint Designer Navigation View	• Navigation view, as shown Figure 1.39, provides a tree-like diagram of your Web pages and helps you add a new or already existing Web page to a Web site and/or to the Web site navigational structure. • You can also use it to remove a Web page from the Web site or just from its Navigational structure. • You can move a page to a new location in the site's navigational structure with a mouse click. • You can develop the navigational flow of your Web site. This is highly recommended because it properly updates SharePoint Designer Web components, such as banners and link bars. • You learn more about how to use the Navigation view in Chapter 2.

Web Site Views	Options	Description
Hyperlinks view	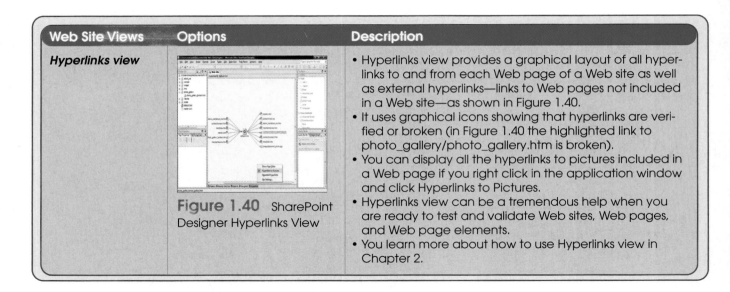 **Figure 1.40** SharePoint Designer Hyperlinks View	• Hyperlinks view provides a graphical layout of all hyperlinks to and from each Web page of a Web site as well as external hyperlinks—links to Web pages not included in a Web site—as shown in Figure 1.40. • It uses graphical icons showing that hyperlinks are verified or broken (in Figure 1.40 the highlighted link to photo_gallery/photo_gallery.htm is broken). • You can display all the hyperlinks to pictures included in a Web page if you right click in the application window and click Hyperlinks to Pictures. • Hyperlinks view can be a tremendous help when you are ready to test and validate Web sites, Web pages, and Web page elements. • You learn more about how to use Hyperlinks view in Chapter 2.

TIP Using Remote Web Site View to Synchronize Files

If you choose to synchronize files using the Remote Web site view, all files from the remote site are downloaded into your local site. Consequently, any file posted on the remote site by you or any other person who has access to the remote site is downloaded to your local site.

2 | Introduction to SharePoint Designer 2007 Tools for Creating Web Sites

Skills covered: 1. Start SharePoint Designer, Open a Web Site, Use the Remote Web Site View to Back Up a Web Site, and Import a Web Package **2.** Explore the SharePoint Designer Web Site Views **3.** Create a Web Package and Close a Web Site

Step 1 **Start SharePoint Designer, Open a Web Site, Use the Remote Web Site View to Back Up a Web site, and Import a Web Package**	Refer to Figure 1.41 as you complete Step 1. **a.** Click **Start** to display the Start menu. Click (or point to) **All Programs**, click **Microsoft Office**, then click **Microsoft Office SharePoint Designer 2007** to open the program. **b.** Click **File** on the Menu bar, click **Open Site** to open the Open Site Dialog box, navigate to the Exploring SharePoint Designer folder, click the **chap1_ho2_emptysite** Web site folder, and then click the **Open button**. You can now see the chap1_ho2_emptysite in Folders view.

c. Select **Remote Web Site** at the bottom of the document window and click the **Remote Web Site Properties button**.

The Remote Web Site Properties Dialog box displays.

d. Click the **Browse button** to open the New Publish Location dialog box, navigate to the location where you want to save your solutions, and click the **Open button** to close the New Publish Location dialog box. In the Remote Web site location box, type **\chap1_ho2_website_solution**, click **File System** in the *Remote Web server type* section, and then click the **OK button**.

TROUBLESHOOTING: If a dialog box appears asking you if you would like to create a Web site at that location, click Yes.

The path of the newly created chap1_ho2_website_solution backup folder is now showing on the right upper corner of the SharePoint Designer document window.

e. Click the **Publish Web site button** to create the backup and click **Open your Remote Web site in SharePoint Designer** in the *Status* section.

The empty chap1_ho2_website_solution is now displayed in Folders view.

f. Click **File** on the Menu bar, select **Import**, and then select **Personal Web Package**.

The File Open dialog box displays so that you can navigate to the Exploring SharePoint Designer folder.

g. Click the **chap1_ho2_webpackage.fwp** Personal Web Package, and then click the **Open button**.

The Import Web Package dialog box is displayed.

h. Click the **Import button** to start importing the files contained in the chap1_ho2_webpackage.fwp Personal Web Package and click **OK** when a dialog box appears indicating that the Web package deployment is complete.

When the transfer is finished, you should see the folders and documents contained in the imported Web Package in the Folder List task pane and in Folders view.

TROUBLESHOOTING: If a Security Warning dialog box appears asking you if you want to run this software, click Run.

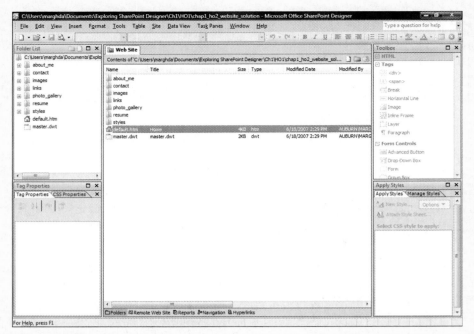

Figure 1.41 Web Site Including All Files of the Imported Web Package

Refer to Figure 1.42 as you complete Step 2.

a. Select **Reports** at the bottom of the document window.

> You should see the Site Summary, including all the SharePoint Designer reports.

b. Click **Recently added files** to see the files in the current Web site that have been created in the last 30 days.

c. Click the **drop-down arrow** at the right of the Recently Added Files tab and select **Site Summary**.

> You should see the Site Summary, including all the SharePoint Designer reports.

d. Click **Unlinked files** to see the files that cannot be reached via your home page.

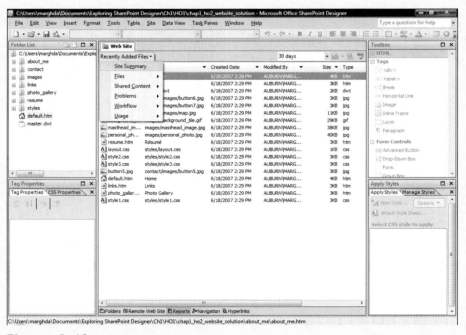

Figure 1.42 Switching Out from the Recently Added Files Report

Refer to Figure 1.43 as you complete Step 3.

a. Click **File** on the Menu bar, point to **Export**, and then select **Personal Web Package**.

The Export Web Package dialog box displays.

b. Click the **Add button** to transfer all files in the new Web Package.

c. Click the **Properties button** and type **chap1_ho2_webpackage_solution** in the Title box of the Export Web Package dialog box.

A file name may contain up to 255 characters. Spaces and commas are not allowed in the file name.

d. Click the **OK button** to create the new Web Package and close the Web Package Properties dialog box.

e. Click the **OK button** to close the Export dialog box.

The File Save dialog box displays.

f. Navigate to the location where you want to store your completed files.

g. Click **Save** or press **Enter**. Click **OK** to close the pop-up box.

h. Click **File** on the Menu bar and click **Close Site**.

TROUBLESHOOTING: If there are other SharePoint Designer tabs on the Windows task bar, you might want to click each of them to maximize the SharePoint Designer application window, click File, and click Close Site.

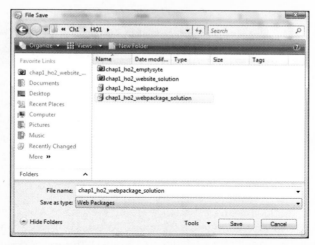

Figure 1.43 Saving a New Web Personal Package

Introduction to Web Pages

To design and develop high-quality Web pages, you focus on more than just the content and appearance of your Web pages. You also need to consider their global usability and accessibility and address the challenging cross-browser and cross-platform issues. SharePoint Designer can assist you in creating a new Web page from scratch or based on a Web page template, in importing a preexisting Web page into a Web site, and in removing, changing, or customizing a Web page. You can easily add, format, or set the properties for a wide range of Web page elements, from simple text elements to rather sophisticated form elements or Web Components. SharePoint Designer also empowers Web developers with advanced tools for maximizing the accessibility and compatibility of Web pages.

> SharePoint Designer can assist you in creating a new Web page from scratch or based on a Web page template, in importing a preexisting Web page into a Web site, and in removing, changing, or customizing a Web page. You can easily add, format, or set the properties for a wide range of Web page elements, from simple text elements to rather sophisticated form elements or Web Components.

In this section, you learn how to open and close a Web page. You explore the SharePoint Designer views and the basic elements of a Web page. You learn about the requirements of good Web page design. You explore the SharePoint Designer tools for creating Web pages, maximizing their compatibility and accessibility.

Opening and Closing a Web Page

While working in the Folders or Navigation Web site views, you can open a SharePoint Designer Web page in three ways: from the File menu, from the Open button on the Common toolbar and Standard toolbar, or by double-clicking the name of the Web page document.

TIP **Opening a SharePoint Designer Web Page Using the Open Button**

The Open button on the Standard toolbar also has two options and icons:

- The Open option enables you to open a Web page.
- The Open Site option enables you to open a Web site.

You should always use the Open Site option if you want SharePoint Designer to make any changes on the Web pages global (meaning the changes apply to all Web pages of the Web site).

To close a SharePoint Designer Web page, click File on the Menu bar and click Close. If any changes were made to the Web page, SharePoint Designer displays a box to verify changes. Click Yes if you want to save changes; click No if you want to ignore all changes. Click Cancel if you want to cancel closing the page.

TIP **Closing a Web Page**

You can also close a Web page if you right-click the Web page's tab and click Close. If you close a Web site, all opened Web pages are also closed.

Describing Web Page Views

Page view displays the Web page that is being edited.

The Web page that is being edited is referred to as the *current page* or the *active page*.

The SharePoint Designer *Page view* displays the Web page that is being edited. The Web page that is being edited is referred to as the *current page* or the *active page*. For each opened Web page, SharePoint Designer displays a tab positioned to the right of the Web Site tab. There are four types of Page subviews: *Design view, Code view, Split view,* and *Preview in Browser view*.

Web Page Views | Reference

Web Page View	Options	Description
Design view	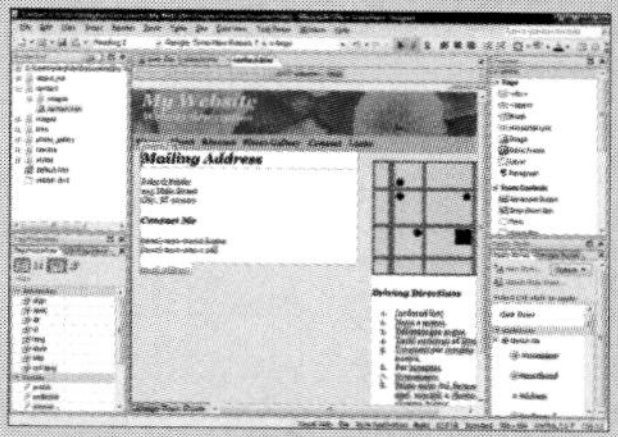 **Figure 1.44** SharePoint Designer Design View	• You design and edit Web pages in Design view with just minimal WYSIWYG authoring experience. • When you open a Web page, this is the default view, as shown in Figure 1.44.
Code view	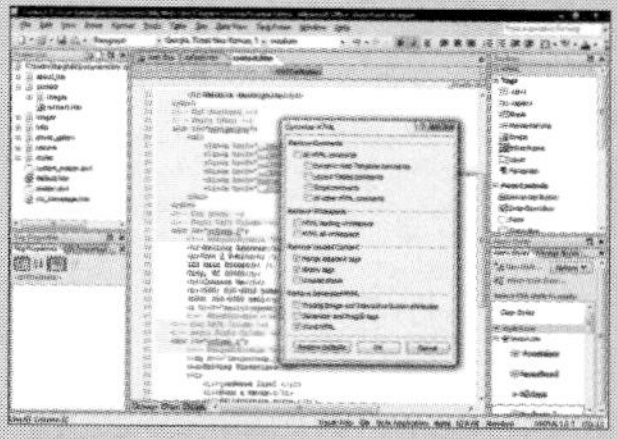 **Figure 1.45** SharePoint Designer Code View	• You view, add, and edit HTML tags in Code view. • The Optimize HTML tool assists you in selectively removing comments, white space, and unused content, as shown in Figure 1.45. (To open the Optimize HTML in any Web page view, click Tools on the menu bar and select Optimize HTML.)
Split view	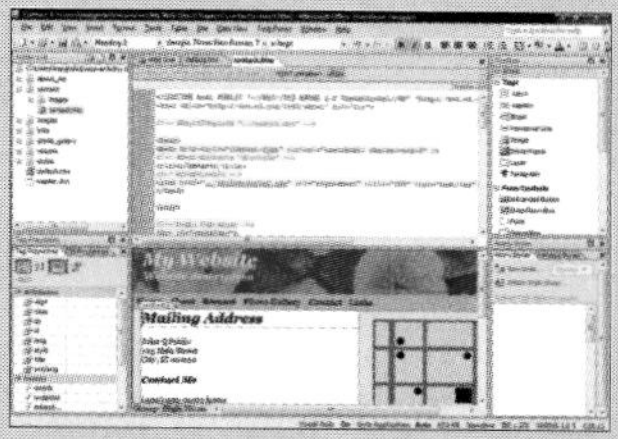 **Figure 1.46** SharePoint Designer Split View	• You can simultaneously display the Code view and Design view of the Web page content in a split screen format. • You use this view to make changes in Code view and immediately see the changes in Design view, or vice versa, as shown in Figure 1.46.
Preview in Browser view	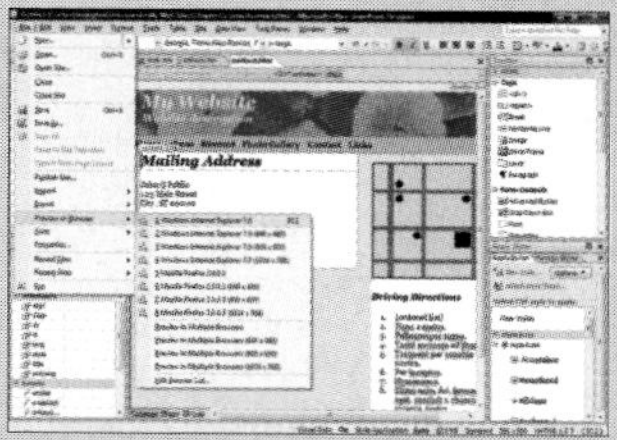 **Figure 1.47** SharePoint Designer Preview in Browser View	• You can see what a Web page will look like in a Web browser without having to first save or publish your page. • You use this view while developing a Web page to check minor changes, as shown in Figure 1.47.

TIP   Preview in Browser

In contrast with FrontPage 2003, in SharePoint designer the Preview in Browser feature is available only via the File menu.

Describing Basic Web Page Elements

Each Web page has its own individual design and functionality. However, all Web pages use a combination of generic Web page elements, such as text, images, hyperlinks, frames, and forms, to name just a few. All these elements have characteristics that you can modify so that they display and function the way you want them to. Each basic Web page element falls into one of the following categories: Web page title, Web page background, Heading, Numbered list, Bulleted list, Hyperlinks, URL, Inline images, Tables, CSS Layouts, and Forms.

Basic Web Page Elements | Reference

Web Page Element	Description
Web page title	The title of a Web page is the text that appears on the title bar of the browser window when a Web page is loaded, as shown in Figure 1.48.
Web page background	The background of a Web page can be a solid color, as shown in Figure 1.48, or a graphic image. A background graphic can be tiled or repeated across the entire body of the Web page.
Heading	The headings on the page are usually used to differentiate between different sections of the Web page, as shown in Figure 1.48.
Numbered list	Numbered lists are a way to display items in sequential order, with each item preceded by a number.
Bulleted list	Bulleted lists are a way to display unordered items, with each item preceded by a graphic character called a bullet, as shown in Figure 1.48.
Hyperlinks	A hyperlink, or link, is specially coded text or a graphic object that a visitor can click to transfer to another location on the same page or to another site, as shown in Figure 1.48.
URL	The URL is the unique address of the page. (Refer to Figure 1.48.)
Inline images	Inline images display graphic images that are stored in a separate file that can be located within the same Web site or outside the Web site, as shown in Figure 1.48. Although a Web page is loaded in a browser, the image is merged with the Web page body. Theoretically, the image can be any format, but most browsers support only Graphics Interchange Format (GIF) and Joint Photographic Experts Group (JPEG) images, whereas the number of browsers that support the Portable Network Graphics (PNG) image format is slowly but surely growing. An inline image can also be used as the background of a Web page. An *image map* is a more elaborate inline image; its area is divided into hyperlinked sections called hotspots. In Chapter 2, you learn about using inline images to enhance Web pages.
Tables	Tables are grid structures of rows and columns and represent an effective way to organize and display information (tabular data). Tables also can be used to control the layout of Web pages, but it is highly recommended that you use CSS to control Web page layout. In Chapter 2, you learn about using tables in developing Web pages.
CSS Layouts	CSS Layouts enable you to accurately position and format the elements of your Web pages by creating and applying CSS styles. You can place CSS Layouts in external style sheets and easily use them for as many Web pages as needed. By using them, you also minimize the code required for developing Web pages. In Chapter 2 and Appendix A, you will learn about using CSS layout styles in designing Web pages.
Graphics	SharePoint Designer can assist you in adding graphics, or pictures, to your Web page. You can use graphics from its rich ClipArt collections, a file, a scanner, or a digital camera. In Chapter 2, you learn more about using graphics to enhance Web pages.
Forms	Your viewers use forms to enter or retrieve data from a file, database, or Web page, or to search the Internet or a Web site. Some core form elements are text areas that allow users to enter text, radio buttons, check boxes, and select boxes that enable users to make and send selections to the server, as shown in Figure 1.48.

Figure 1.48 Web Page Elements

Identifying SharePoint Designer 2007 Tools for Creating Web Pages

SharePoint Designer's comprehensive set of user-friendly tools can be used to create a wide variety of standard Web pages in line with Web standards such as XHTML and CSS. The Web pages can be created from scratch or by employing templates and CSS layouts. SharePoint Designer 2007 provides support for creating and editing ASP.NET pages using a Microsoft ASP.NET Development Server. You can also use SharePoint Designer 2007 to open, modify, and enhance Web pages created in any version of Microsoft FrontPage and Expression Web. If you wish to create a new Web page based on an existing one, you will need to open the file, choose File, select the Save As command, type the desired name of the new Web page, and click Save.

Microsoft ASP.NET Development Server is available in Microsoft Office SharePoint Designer as well as Microsoft Expression Web. If you work on a personal computer using Windows XP, the installation of this server requires the previous installation of Microsoft .NET Framework 2.0 (http://msdn2.microsoft.com/enus/netframework/aa731542.aspx). Windows Vista, by default, includes .NET Framework 3.0. To learn more about how to install the Microsoft ASP.NET Development Server, see the "How to Install the Microsoft ASP.NET Development Server That Is Available in Expression Web" article from the Microsoft Knowledge Base (http://support.microsoft.com/default.aspx/kb/928697).

To create a new Web page, go to the File, New command to display the New dialog box as shown in Figure 1.49 (if you click the New Page icon on the Common toolbar, a new untitled .htm document is added to the file list). The New dialog box displays the options for creating a new Web page. The easiest way to master the New dialog box options for creating a new Web page is to view these options in five groups according to their general functions, as shown in the New dialog box options reference (Table 1.5).

Microsoft ASP.NET Development Server is available in Microsoft Office SharePoint Designer as well as Microsoft Expression Web.

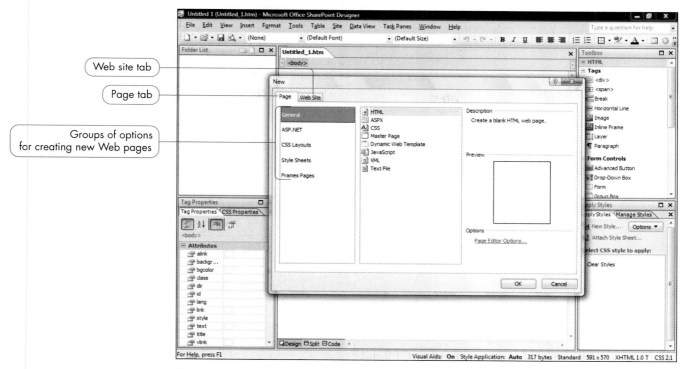

Figure 1.49 New Dialog Box

If, for example, you choose to create a new Web page using one of the nine layouts available within the CSS Layouts group, you will need to click CSS Layouts, click one of the nine predefined layouts, and then click OK to close the New dialog box. A new untitled .htm document will be created as well as a new untitled .css file already attached to the .htm file (shown in Figure 1.50). When you save the newly created .htm document, you will be automatically required to save its attached untitled .css file.

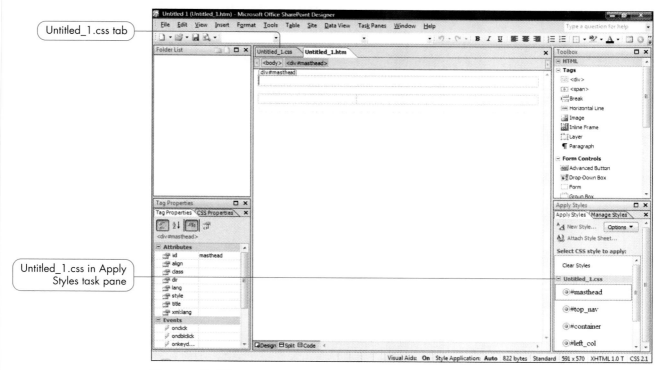

Figure 1.50 Creating a New Web Page Using SharePoint Designer CSS Layouts

The Style Sheets group of options enables you to create a blank style sheet or a custom style sheet using one of the 12 available options. If you choose to create a style sheet using one of these 12 options, a new, untitled .css will be created. Using the Attach Style Sheet command from the Apply Styles Task pane, you can attach this new style sheet to all HTML pages, selected Web pages, or just the Current Page. The Attach Style Sheet dialog box enables you to attach the style sheet using the Link or Import options (see Figure 1.51).

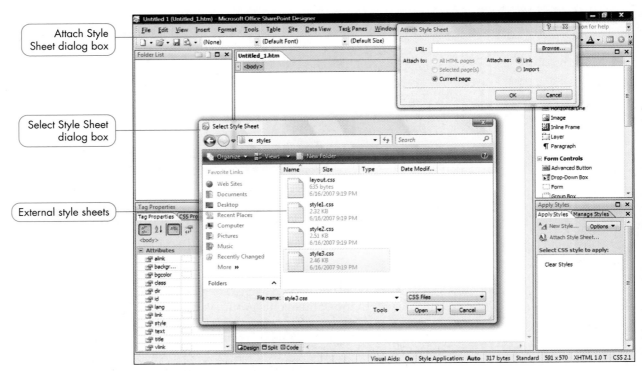

Figure 1.51 Creating a New Web Page Using SharePoint Designer Style Sheets

Table 1.5 New Dialog Box Options

Group	Options	Description
General	HTML	Create a blank HTML Web page.
	ASPX	Create a new ASP.NET Web Form.
	CSS	Create a blank Cascading Style Sheet.
	Master Page	Create a Master Page for Web Applications.
	Dynamic Web Template	Create a Dynamic Web Template.
	Java Script	Create a JavaScript file.
	XML	Create an XML file.
	Text File	Create a blank text file.
	Create from Dynamic Web Template	Create a new Web page based on an existing Dynamic Web Template
	Create from Master Page	Create a new Web page based on an existing Master Page.

Table 1.5 New Dialog Box Options (continued)

Group	Options	Description
ASP.NET	ASPX	Create a new ASP.NET Web Form.
	Master Page	Create a Master Page for Web Applications.
	Web User Control	Create an ASP.NET server control.
	Web Configuration	Create a file used to configure Web Applications.
	Site Map	Create a site map. This file requires ASP.NET 2.0 or above.
	Create from Master Page	Create a new Web page based on an existing Master Page.
CSS Layouts	Nine Web page layouts	Nine Web page layouts.
Style Sheets	Thirteen Web page formatting style sheets	Thirteen Web page formatting style sheets.
Frames Pages	Ten templates for frames pages	Ten templates for frames pages.

TIP Master Page

A master page is an ASP.NET page that has the file name extension ".master" and enables you to create a consistent appearance and layout for the dynamic Web pages of your Web site or Web application located on a server running Windows SharePoint Services 3.0 or Office SharePoint Server 2007. As with Dynamic Web Templates, master pages can be used to create a single page template, and then this template is used to develop multiple pages in Web applications.

A **Dynamic Web template** enables you to automatically update common features of many attached Web pages.

Editable regions are sections of the Web template that can be modified within any Web page built upon the Dynamic Web template.

Static or **noneditable regions** are sections of the Dynamic Web template that can be edited only through the Dynamic Web template.

By using a **Dynamic Web template** instead of a standard template, you can automatically update common features of many Web pages by modifying just one file: the Dynamic Web template. The Dynamic Web template can also contain "protected regions" that can only be modified by modifying the template file. This prevents a member of the design team from accidentally modifying a feature that should be common to all Web pages within the site. The Dynamic Web template feature also helps Web developers provide consistency across the pages of their Web sites, which makes maintenance and future additions to their Web sites easier. You can create a Dynamic Web template from any existing Web page by saving the file as a .dwt file. A Dynamic Web template includes editable and noneditable (or static) regions (see Figure 1.52). **Editable regions** are sections of the Web template that can be modified within any Web page built upon the Dynamic Web template. Static or **noneditable regions** are sections of the Dynamic Web template that can be edited only through the Dynamic Web template.

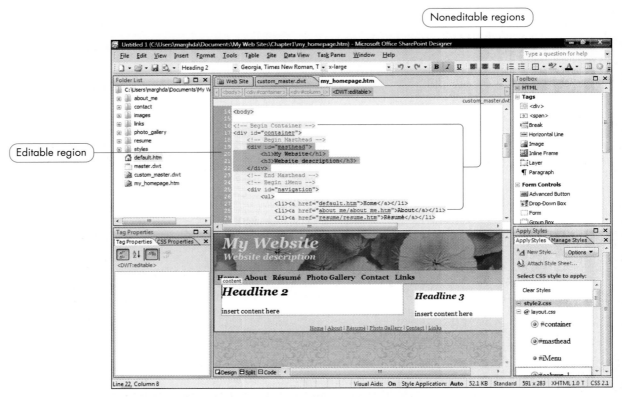

Figure 1.52 Dynamic Web Template Editable and Noneditable Regions

To open the Dynamic Web Template attached to a Web page, select Dynamic Web Template on the Format menu, and then click Open Attached Dynamic Web Template. To format an area of the Dynamic Web Template as an editable region, highlight the area, click Format on Menu bar, point to Dynamic Web Template, and click Manage Editable Regions to open the Editable Regions dialog box. Type a name for the new editable region in the Region name text box and click the Add button, as shown in Figure 1.53. The newly created editable region is outlined in orange and displays a tab identifying the name of the editable region, as shown in Figure 1.54. Click Close to close the dialog box and save the Dynamic Web template.

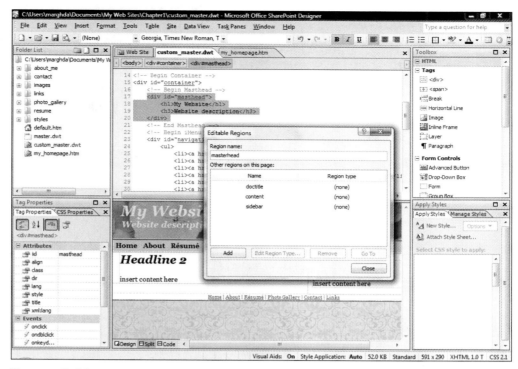

Figure 1.53 Editable Regions Dialog Box

New editable region in Code view

New editable region in Design view

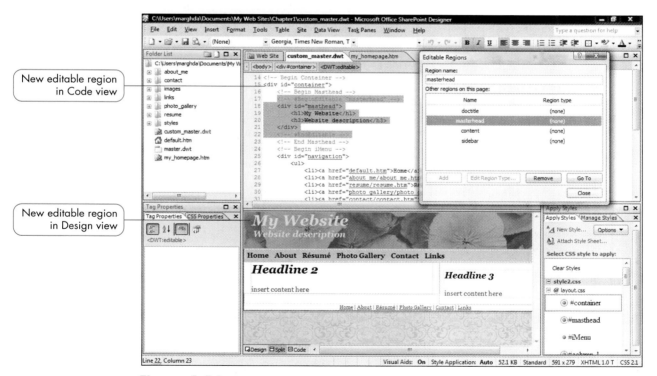

Figure 1.54 New Editable Region

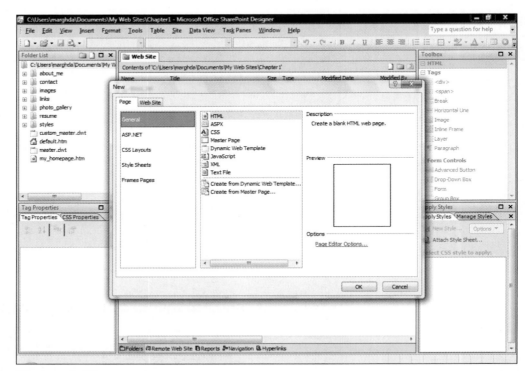

Figure 1.55   Creating a New Web Page from a Dynamic Web Template

The New Dialog box enables you to add a new Web page to a Web site from an existing Dynamic Web template, as shown in Figure 1.55. You can also attach or detach a Dynamic Web Template using the commands of the Format menu Dynamic Web Template submenu (see Figure 1.56).

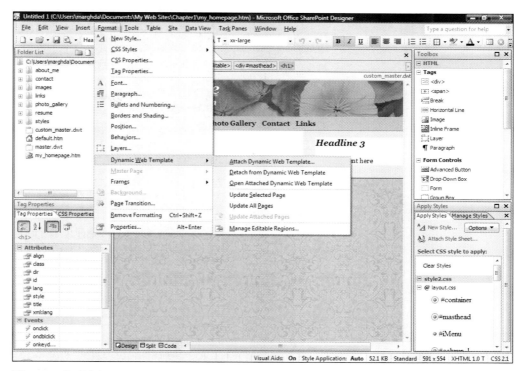

Figure 1.56 Dynamic Web Template Submenu Commands

Understand the Principles of Good Web Page Design

A Web page is a pure representation of the designer's professional and personal background, expertise in solving technical design and development issues, and, last but most definitely not least, personal creativity and artistic skills. However, there are certain key factors that all professional designers and Web developers consider essential to good Web page design (see Table 1.6).

> A Web page is a pure representation of the designer's professional and personal background, expertise in solving technical design and development issues, and, last but most definitely not least, personal creativity and artistic skills. However, there are certain key factors that all professional designers and Web developers consider essential to good Web page design.

Table 1.6 Key Design Factors for Developing Good Web Pages

Design Factor	Description
Usability	A usable Web site is easy to navigate and accessible. You should always keep in mind that you design your Web pages for the people who will be visiting them. The quality of your design will be measured by visitors' satisfaction.
Navigation	Web pages must be easy to navigate. Always consider using Web page templates, link bars, hyperlinks, and bookmarks to create a clear, robust navigational structure for your Web pages.
Compatibility	Web pages need to appear the same (or as close to that as possible) in all browsers, in all versions of the same browser, and on all computer platforms.
Accessibility	Web pages need to be accessible to all people, including those with different types of total and partial disabilities. You should always consult World Wide Web Consortium's (W3C) Web site to stay on top of the latest standards and requirements.
Consistency	Web users do not like surprises. They expect the information on a Web page to be laid out as it was on previous pages of the same Web site. To ensure the consistency of your Web pages from the early stages of development, you should always sketch a draft of your Web pages before starting the actual construction, and you should develop and use Web page templates.
Validity	The validity of a Web page needs to be thoroughly tested before it is published. If a Web site does not display and function properly, it can cause more pain than gain for your visitors, and they will leave your site to find another one. (You learn about testing and validating Web pages in Chapters 2 and 3.)
Attractiveness	A Web page will be attractive only if it is designed as precisely as a NASA space shuttle and as beautifully as the Mona Lisa. Think like an engineer and feel like an artist when you design a Web page; that is an important key to success.

Many companies such as Microsoft, IBM®, and Sun Microsystems and organizations such as the World Wide Web Consortium (W3C) have developed Web-design guidelines that help beginning and experienced Web developers create well-structured, easy-to-navigate, accessible, and attractive Web pages. Each company's Web design guidelines are created to ensure that every page included in its Web site has a consistent look and feel. A well-designed company Web site is a great way of advertising its business, improving its relationship with current customers, and attracting new customers by providing rich, accurate, and updated information. You can find some of the most popular Web design guidelines at the following Web sites:

- **IBM Web design guidelines:** http://www.ibm.com.

- **Research-Based Web Design & Usability Guidelines:** http://www.usability.gov/guidelines.

- **Web Monkey, The Web Developer's Resource:** http://webmonkey.wired.com/webmonkey/index.html.

A good Web designer, especially a beginner, needs to review the core Web design guidelines before starting to draw the rough sketch of the Web page layout on a piece of paper. This process should continue from inception until a Web page is developed and tested. To avoid having to redo or patch work, a good Web designer should keep in mind the following design principles from the earliest stage of the design process:

- Each Web page should have its own personality.

- Each Web page should have its own unique goal. A Web page that covers multiple topics, concepts, goals, or purposes can be confusing.

- Each Web page should provide information about related or secondary topics and concepts by containing links to extra sources of information.

Learn About Working with Colors

Using colors in a creative way can have a tremendous effect on the appearance and content of a Web page. Colors should be used to emphasize key words in a Web page, to differentiate between a Web page's sections, and to provide a background page color that does not affect the page's readability. Thus, you need to use color in a meaningful way, keeping a balance between the clean white space of your Web page and the colored space.

It has, so far, proved to be impossible for computers to replicate all the colors that exist in nature. The quality of the color that a computer is able to create depends on the computer platform, operating system, graphics card, and monitor. However, newer computers using newer operating systems, such as Windows XP, Windows Vista, Mac® OS X v10.4 "Tiger," Mac OS X v10.3 "Panther," and Linux 2.6, offer the best color control.

The first color monitors displayed 16 colors. (See Appendix C, "Colors and Web Design", available on the Companion Web site.) At this time, some Web users have access to only an 8-bit computer system, which can display only 256 colors. When Web pages are created using all the colors available on today's more common and sophisticated 24-bit systems, older Web browsers are not able to display them. Web developers avoid color-related display issues by using a Web-safe palette. Whenever a browser has to render a color not included in its palette, it uses a process called dithering, or combining similar colors included in its palette to match as close as possible the indicated color. A Web-safe palette (WSP) is a palette made up of 216 colors that look the same in all browsers, platforms, monitors, and resolutions. Browsers use this built-in palette when they need to render colors on monitors with only 256 colors (also called 8-bit color monitors).

In any computer environment, a color can be identified by a color name or a value. In Web design, HTML enables you to specify a color using one of the 147 Web color names. To see a list of all these 147 Web color names, visit the W3C Web site at http://www.w3.org/TR/SVG11/types.html#ColorKeywords.

A color value is a numerical expression that accurately represents a color. In Web design, colors can be created as a blend of the three colors used by all computers: red, green, and blue. (These blends are called simply RGB.) The intensity of each of these three colors can vary between a color value of 0, indicating the total absence of this color, and 255, representing the highest level of that color's intensity. For example, the (0, 128, 0) RGB triplet corresponds to a shade of green.

Although the RGB triplet formula is often used in computer applications, HTML accepts only color values entered in hexadecimal format (a string of six characters). Thus, when using color in designing a Web page, the RGB triplet of a color needs to be converted into a hexadecimal format. For example, the hexadecimal color value that corresponds to the (0, 128, 0) RGB shade of green is (00,80,00).

Using color hexadecimal values in Web design increases the color portability (its capability to look the same in all browsers, platforms, monitors, and resolutions). However, even when you use hexadecimal color values in your Web design, different computers and operating systems display the same colors differently. In addition, each Web browser displays colors a little bit differently. Thus, even Web browsers represent an impediment in defining portable colors.

In SharePoint Designer 2007, you can easily use the hexadecimal values of the safe colors via the More Colors dialog box. To access the More Colors dialog box, display the Page Properties dialog box for the active page by pulling down the File menu, clicking the Properties command, and selecting the Formatting tab. Then click a drop-down arrow for one of the controls, such as Text, in the Colors area. Click the More Colors button, as shown in Figure 1.57, to open the More Colors dialog box. Click the desired color sample in the hexagonal array shown in Figure 1.58, click OK to close the dialog box, and click OK to close the Page Properties dialog box and finish setting the text color of the Web page.

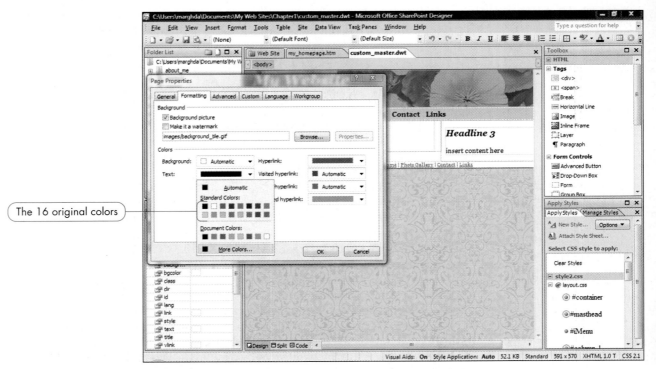

The 16 original colors

Figure 1.57 Working with Colors

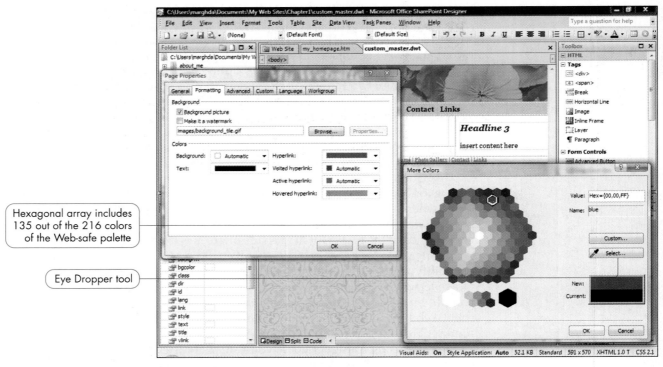

Hexagonal array includes 135 out of the 216 colors of the Web-safe palette

Eye Dropper tool

Figure 1.58 More Colors Dialog Box

CHAPTER 1 | Introduction to Microsoft Office SharePoint Designer 2007

The hexagonal array of the More Colors dialog box displays only the 135 most commonly used of the 216 safe colors (see Figure 1.58). If the color you want to use does not appear in the hexagonal array, you can still use it. First find its corresponding hexadecimal value using Appendix C (available on the Companion Web site) or the W3cSchool Web site (http://www.w3schools.com/html/html_colors.asp). Type the value in the Value field of the More Colors dialog box, and then click OK to close the More Colors dialog box. The Eye Dropper tool, found on the Select button in the More Color dialog box shown in Figure 1.58, captures any color that can be seen on your screen, such as in graphics, menus, and even other applications. So if you are browsing the Web and see the perfect blue on a Web page, you can use this handy tool to duplicate that exact shade of blue on your page. You might need to resize the SharePoint Designer window so that you can capture colors from another program interface.

SharePoint Designer enables you to create custom colors with the Custom button. However, using the Custom button to create a custom color does not guarantee that you are creating a color that is included in the Web-safe palette. The Custom button in the More Colors dialog box takes you to the Color dialog box, which is also the default Windows color selector.

To create a custom color, select an empty box in the Custom Colors section. Then click a color in the Color Spectrum box. Finally, click and drag the left arrow up and down the gradient bar until you reach a desired color. The color you choose appears in the Color/Solid box.

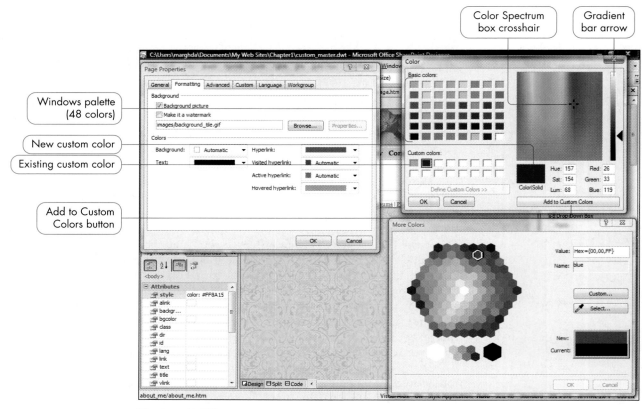

Figure 1.59 Color Dialog Box

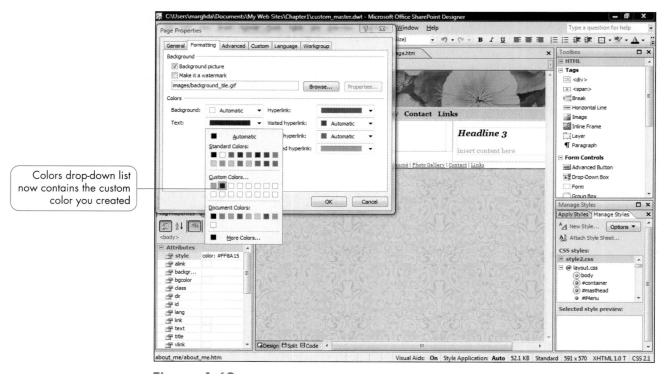

Figure 1.60 Color Drop-Down List Containing the New Custom Color

Microsoft Office SharePoint Designer 2007 Modify Style Dialog Box

In SharePoint Designer, you can also modify the properties of a Dynamic Web Template or Web page using the Tag Properties, CSS Properties, and Manage Styles task panes. For example, to change the colors of a Dynamic Web Template, the style attribute of the <body> tag needs to be updated. If you click the style attribute, and then click the button placed to the right of its current color hexadecimal value (see Figure 1.61), the Modify Style dialog box appears, enabling you to modify inline styles of the <body> tag. Using the Manage Styles task pane, you can modify the CSSs already created, add a new style, or attach a CSS. Using the CSS Properties task pane, you can modify all CSS properties of the <body> tag included in internal and external CSS styles. You will learn more about the SharePoint Designer capabilities to work with CSS in Chapter 2 and Appendix A.

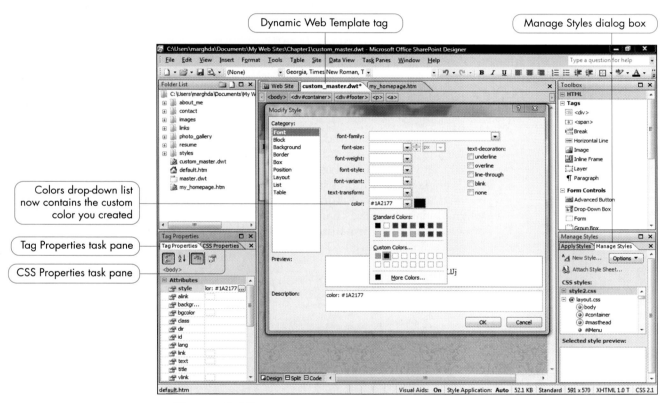

Figure 1.61 Modify Style Dialog Box

You should always remember that your Web pages might have visitors with different types of color vision deficiencies. To accommodate them, follow Section 508 of the Rehabilitation Act Standards (http://www.section508.gov/index.cfm?FuseAction =Content&ID=12), the Electronic and Information Technology Accessibility Standards (http://www.access-board.gov/508.htm), and the W3C accessibility guidelines (http://www.w3.org/TR/WCAG10-CSS-TECHS).

To read more about these standards, launch your Internet browser and type the uniform resource locators (URLs) in the address bar of the browser. Click Edit on the Menu bar, click Find (on This Page), type color in the Find dialog box, and click the Find Next button to locate all the color related issues.

In SharePoint Designer, you can change the text color, size, style, and character spacing of your text, and apply special text effects, such as underline, superscript, or subscript. You should use different fonts to emphasize key words, titles, subtitles, and different sections of text on your Web page. However, to create a clean, professional-looking Web page, do not use more than three fonts in a Web page.

Fonts are specially designed sets of text and symbol characters. Many sets of fonts are installed with most operating systems; however, you can also obtain specialized fonts by searching the Internet, visiting your local computer store, or ordering them from the software company that has designed the operating system you are using. The most common fonts are Arial, Courier, and Helvetica. If a Web page contains a font that is not installed on a visitor's computer, the visitor's browser applies its default font. Although you can use just about any font you want on your Web sites, it is important to use common fonts when designing your Web pages. This enables visitors to see the content the way you intended, instead of with the replacement fonts provided by their browsers.

TIP   CSS Styles

When using the SharePoint Designer Font feature to format the text, by default, you are actually generating or changing internal CSS styles. The HTML <style> tag enables you to specify a list of fonts. You should always specify at least one common font to increase the chances of overriding a browser's default font settings. In Appendix A, you will learn more about the CSS styles.

To use a unique font and ensure that it will appear the same in all browsers, you can use a graphics program—even Window's Paint will do—to create an image of the text that you formatted using a special font. You then add the image of the text to your Web page as a graphic instead of as typed text. However, be aware that adding your text in the form of a graphic increases the size of your Web page. SharePoint Designer enables you to change fonts using the Font dialog box (available from the Format menu), the Formatting or Common toolbar, or the Modify Style dialog box (see Figure 1.61). Figure 1.62 shows the Font dialog box and the Common toolbar.

Figure 1.62 Options for Setting Style Font Attributes

Design for Usability

You design Web pages and Web sites to be used by people. Therefore, the focus of Web designers should be on the visitors of their Web site rather than on the technology used to develop it. In other words, to be successful, your Web pages need to be easy to use. Who are the intended visitors? What are their skills and knowledge? What are the services and/or products you are providing? What type of user/customer support will your visitors need? These are just a few of the questions you should have in mind when designing a Web site for usability.

The ***usability*** of your Web site can be defined as a measure of the quality of your Web site visitors' experience. How can you make your Web site more usable? How can you test and evaluate the usability of your Web site? These are important issues to consider when designing your Web pages and sites.

The ***usability*** of your Web site can be defined as a measure of the quality of your Web site visitors' experience.

In our professional and personal lives, we enjoy having tools that are easy to use. One of the essential elements of usability is navigation. Whether we are driving a car or browsing the Internet, we all like to be able to navigate easily, to know where we are going and how to get there. When designing a Web site, it is your responsibility to make sure that all your Web site visitors can navigate and use your pages without too much frustration. To build a clear, robust navigational structure for a Web site, from the first steps of the designing process you always need to keep track of the following site elements:

- The number of Web pages within the Web site and the relationship between them.
- The number of hyperlinks on each Web page and whether the address of each is correct or updated.
- The type of navigation elements (such as navigation bars, menus, and hyperlinks) you use to make your Web site visitor's experience a pleasant one.

Link bars are one of the most popular and helpful navigational tools. Link bars can contain custom links or links based on the Web site's navigational structure. To insert link bars in your Web page, click Insert on the Menu bar and click Web Component to display the Insert Web Component dialog box, shown in Figure 1.63.

Then, depending on the type of link bar you want to create, continue with one of the following steps:

- **Bar with custom links:** Enables you to assign any links you want to the link bar, within the Web site or externally, in addition to the appropriate text.

- **Bar with back and next links:** Enables you to create a link bar that includes only Back and Next buttons that link to pages within the Web site.

- **Bar based on navigation structure:** Enables you to create a link bar based upon the navigational structure of the Web site.

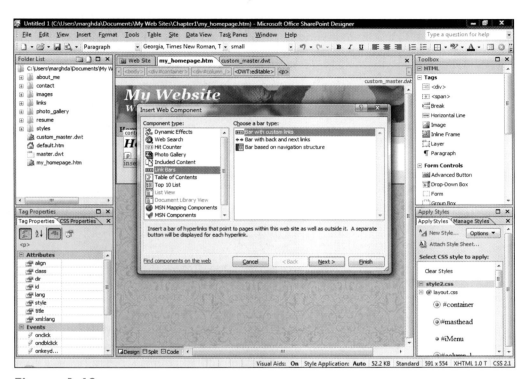

Figure 1.63 Link Bars

TIP Microsoft Office SharePoint Designer 2007 Navigation Tools and Team Development Issues

If you are not the only developer of a Web site and other developers might not choose to use SharePoint Designer, it is not wise to take advantage of the SharePoint Designer Navigation tools. The link bars that these Navigation tools create are tied directly to the SharePoint Designer standards and requirements, which might not be recognized by other applications. You will learn more about Share Point Designer navigation tools in Chapter 2.

Design for Compatibility

A computer platform is defined by the type of hardware and operating system in use on a given computer. Why do Web pages look different when viewed on the same computer platform when using different Internet browsers, or even different versions of the same browsers? What causes these problems and is there a way you can correct them? Let us try to find some answers to these questions that continue to challenge Web designers.

The cross-platform compatibility issue is the result of the way different browsers or browser versions display Web pages on different computer platforms. The cross-browser compatibility issue is the result of the way different browsers display the same Web pages on the same computer platform. Because you cannot predict the computer platform and browser your users will be using when they view your Web site, it is your responsibility, as the designer, to address potential cross-platform and cross-browser compatibility issues in your design.

The W3C is developing specifications, guidelines, software, and tools to lead the Web to its full potential by eliminating the cross-browser and cross-platform compatibility issues. The W3C is joining efforts with companies such as Microsoft, Netscape Communications Corporation, IBM, Sun, and Oracle® and governmental organizations such as the U.S. Department of Health and Human Services (http://www.hhs.gov) to develop a universal standard for Web design focused on eliminating the cross-browser and cross-platform compatibility issues. Despite all these efforts, Web designers often need to develop different versions of the same Web page to make sure their page has the same appearance and functionality in all browsers and on all platforms.

TIP   How PNG Format Helps

Using the most popular GIF or JPG graphic formats in Web design can cause the images to be displayed differently. A new file format—PNG—might eventually replace GIF. PNG stores the screen gamma value (the relationship between the brightness of a pixel as it appears on the screen and the numerical value of that pixel) used by the computer platform in a standard place within the file that most browsers, image viewers, and authoring tools know how to find, read, and display. Thus, the lightness and contrast of the image automatically adjusts to fit the computer system on which it is displayed, without any adjustments from the image designer or image viewer. To read more about PNG, visit the W3C PNG (Portable Network Graphics) Specification Web site (http://www.w3.org/TR/REC-png-multi.html).

SharePoint Designer comes with a competitive set of tools that can help Web designers avoid some of these compatibility issues. The Compatibility Reports enable you to verify that the Web pages in your site are in compliance with the W3C Web standards. The Compatibility Reports command, on the Tools menu, displays the Compatibility Checker dialog box, in which you can identify any areas of your Web site that do not behave as anticipated and address these issues. You first select the page(s) that will be checked for compatibility. Then you need to select the appropriate criteria for compatibility checking:

- **Check HTML/XHTML compatibility with:** This Compatibility Checker dialog box option, shown in Figure 1.64, enables designers to improve the HTML/XHTML compatibility of their Web pages with browsers and browsers' versions of their choice, and with W3C HTML/XHTML standards.

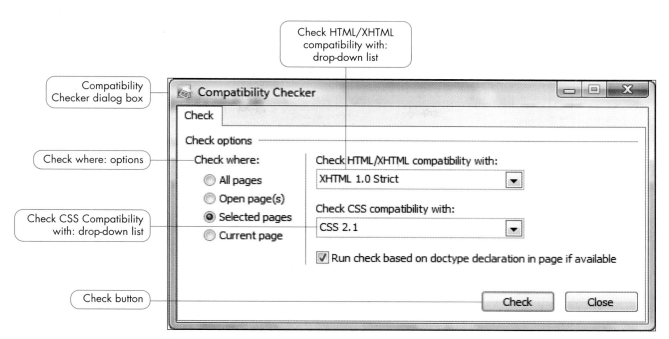

Figure 1.64 Check Compatibility Dialog Box

- **Check CSS compatibility with:** This Compatibility Checker dialog box option, shown in Figure 1.64, enables designers to check the CSS compatibility of their Web pages when using a selected CSS schema (CSS2.1 is the default schema).

When you click the Check button, the checker searches your pages for errors. Click OK when the search is complete, and if you have any errors, they appear in Compatibility task pane. If you see an error listed in the Compatibility task pane, click the Generate HTML Report button. SharePoint Designer generates a Compatibility report, as shown in Figure 1.65. To fix a compatibility error, double-click the listed error in the Compatibility task pane. SharePoint Designer opens the document (if is not already open) and selects the code section where the incompatibility is located. You can also right-click an error in the Compatibility task pane and choose Go to page or you can manually switch to Code view and scroll to the indicated line number.

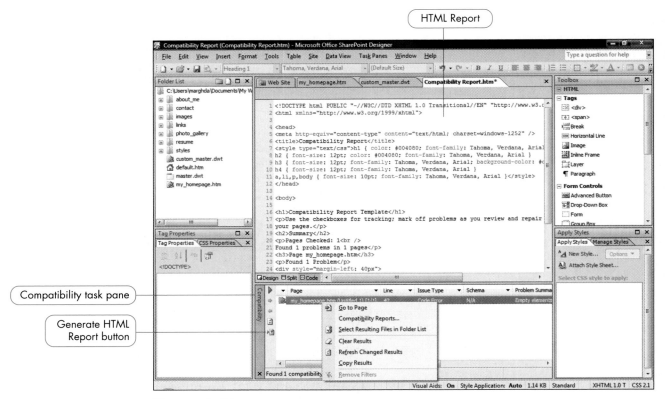

Figure 1.65 Working with the Compatibility Report

TIP **Check Browser Behavior**

Unfortunately, there might be situations where some cross-browser (or incompatibility) issues cannot be solved; therefore you might need to create alternative versions of your Web pages for specific browsers or browser versions. SharePoint Designer provides you with the Check Browser behavior tool, which assists you in making sure your Web pages display correctly in all browsers. You will learn how to use this tool in Appendix B.

Preview in Browser is also a useful compatibility feature that enables you to select the browser, the browser version, and screen resolution you want to use to preview your Web page. You can also preview a Web page in multiple browsers at the same time, as shown in Figure 1.66. Using this tool, you can preview your Web page in a wide combination of browsers, browser versions, and screen resolutions. Browsers need to be installed on your computer. If a browser is installed on your computer, you can add it to the SharePoint Designer browser list using the Edit Browser List command (see Figure 1.66). Pull down the File menu, click Preview in Browser, and select browser, browser version, and screen resolution to preview a Web page.

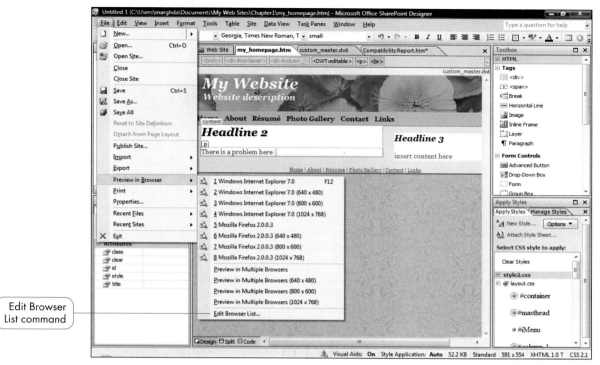

Edit Browser List command

Figure 1.66 Preview in Browser Feature

TIP Testing Your Web Site on Multiple Computer Platforms

Just as it is important to preview your Web page on different browsers and different releases of the same browser, it can also be helpful to preview your page on different computer platforms and on different versions of the same operating system. By doing this you avoid having your Web pages look different or lose some of their functionalities caused by incompatibilities between computer platforms and versions of the same operating system. On a PC, you can normally install only one version of the Windows operating system. Thus, the only way to test older versions of Windows is to install them on a separate computer, set up a dual-boot system, or run a software virtualization solution such as the freeware Microsoft Virtual PC 2007 (http://www.microsoft.com/windows/products/winfamily/virtualpc/default.mspx).

Virtual PC emulates the hardware of a PC, enabling users to run PC operating systems, such as Windows 98, Windows 2000, Windows XP, and Linux, within a virtual machine environment. There is also a Virtual PC 7.0 version for Mac operating systems, which enables Mac users to run Windows applications on their computers. The Mac (Intel®) computers support Windows operating systems. To read more about how Microsoft products are supported by Mac (Intel) computers, see the Microsoft Office Q&A: Intel-Based Macs Web site (http://www.microsoft.com/mac/default.aspx?pid=macIntelQA).

Design for Accessibility

According to the Disability Statistics Center, there are 1.3 million Americans with visual impairments, 1.2 million with hearing impairments, and 1.2 million with impairments that interfere with the mobility of shoulders and upper extremities. These kinds of impairments are likely to affect their ability to browse the Internet and access your Web site. If your Web site does not comply with accessibility guidelines, these people might not be able to access your Web pages.

TIP   Differences Between Accessibility and Usability

Although accessibility and usability have many related requirements and goals, they are not identical. Usability issues affect all Web page users equally, whereas accessibility issues affect only people with special needs and disabilities.

Accessibility means that a page can be accessed—read and used—by any person regardless of special needs or disabilities.

What does accessibility have to do with Web pages? **Accessibility** means that a page can be accessed—read and used—by any person regardless of special needs or disabilities. An accessible Web page has to be compatible with screen reading and screen magnification software—applications that help people with visual challenges— and with natural language speech applications that people with poor arm or finger motion use. It also needs to offer text equivalents for multimedia content for people with hearing impairments.

TIP   Color Vision Deficiencies and Related Issues, Standards, and Solutions in Web Design

aDesigner is a disability simulator developed by IBM (http://www.alphaworks. ibm.com/tech/adesigner) that enables Web designers to test their Web pages for accessibility and usability related to visually impaired persons' needs. There are two modes in aDesigner: blind and low vision. The low-vision mode also simulates how users with color vision deficiencies perceive Web pages.

How can you design and develop a page that is as accessible as possible? Design your Web pages in compliance with the W3C's Web Content Accessibility Guidelines (WCAG) (go to http://www.w3.org/WAI/guid-tech.html) and with Section 508 of the Rehabilitation Act. Section 508 of the Rehabilitation Act is a set of standards and guidelines that require access to electronic and information technology procured by Federal agencies (http://www.section508.gov). The Access Board (http://www.access-board. gov/about.htm) "is an independent Federal agency devoted to accessibility for people with disabilities" and has developed accessibility standards for the various technologies covered by the Section 508 Law (http://www.access-board.gov/508.htm). At the time this manuscript was being developed, the Telecommunications and Electronic and Information Technology Advisory Committee (TEITAC, http://teitac.org), a federal advisory committee providing recommendations for updates of accessibility standards issued under section 508 of the Rehabilitation Act and guidelines under section 255 of the Telecommunications Act, was working on providing the Access Board with a major proposal for updating Section 508. The updated Section 508 document was expected to be released in October 2007.

SharePoint Designer 2003 contains a feature called the Accessibility Reports. This tool can tell you how well your design complies with the existing W3C and government standards. To access the Accessibility Checker dialog box, click Tools and then click the Accessibility Reports command. The Accessibility Checker dialog box displays, as shown in Figure 1.67. To use the Accessibility Checker, you should first select, under Check for, the accessibility guidelines you want to check against. Second, under Check where, decide which pages you want the Accessibility Checker to check. The Accessibility Checker can check specific pages or the whole site. Third, under Show, indicate if you wish to look for errors and warnings.

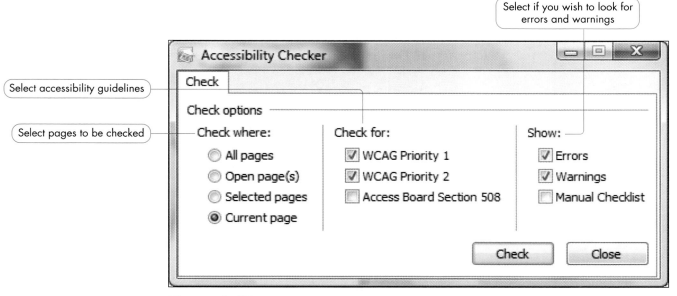

Figure 1.67 Accessibility Checker Dialog Box

When you click the Check button, the checker searches your pages for errors. Click OK when the search is complete, and if you have any errors, they appear in the Accessibility task pane. If you see an error list in the Accessibility task pane, click the Generate HTML Report button. SharePoint Designer generates an accessibility report, as shown in Figure 1.68.

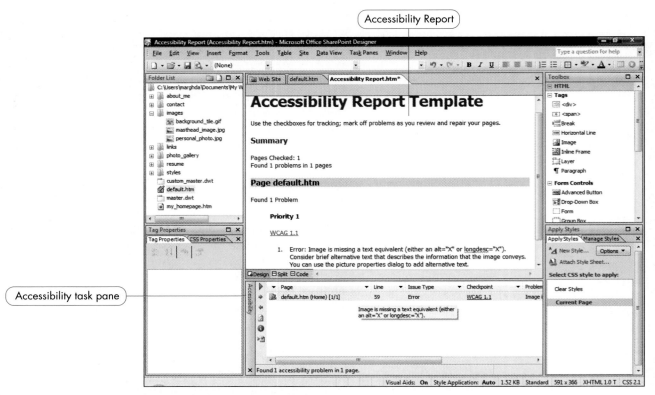

Figure 1.68 Result of the First Accessibility Check

In the example shown, no alternative text is provided for an image. This is one of the key issues related to Web page accessibility. Alternative text is displayed when the graphic is downloading, when it cannot be found, or when a visitor moves the pointer mouse over it. For visually impaired people who rely on a screen-reading application to convert graphics on the screen to spoken words, the presence of the alternative text for any graphic is extremely important.

You can add alternative text to your figures by using the alt attribute in the Tag Properties task pane, as shown in Figure 1.69. (You will learn about how to add pictures to a Web page in Chapter 2.) After you make your corrections, run the Accessibility Checker again to be sure that there are no other errors.

Figure 1.69 Correcting Accessibility Errors

Tag Properties task pane

TIP   Bobby

One of the first and most well-known accessibility checkers is Bobby™ (http://www.watchfire.com/products/webxm/bobby.aspx). It was first released in 1996. Watchfire® Corporation, Bobby's provider, launched Watchfire WebXACT™ in 2003 (http://webxact.watchfire.com), a free online service that allows users to test single Web pages for quality, privacy, and accessibility issues. WebXACT is the first free online service to provide comprehensive Web page testing for all of these critical issues. What makes WebXACT such a valuable tool is that it empowers Web developers to check the accessibility of their Web pages for all three Web Content Accessibility Guidelines (WCAG) priorities (http://www.w3.org/TR/WAI-WEBCONTENT/full-checklist.html), whereas the SharePoint Designer Accessibility Checker checks for the first two WCAG priorities. The third WCAG priority, not covered by SharePoint Designer, refers to the accessibility guidelines for design elements, such as images, audio elements, tables, and forms. However, the first two WCAG priorities are the most important ones in developing accessible Web sites. Bobby and the SharePoint Designer Accessibility Checker check accessibility by applying the Section 508 rules. To read more about the WebXACT free online service, see also the Watchfire WebXACT launching announcement (http://www.watchfire.com/news/releases/5-12-03.aspx). To read more about the evaluation, repair, and transformation tools that you can use for developing more accessible Web content, visit the dedicated W3C Web page at http://www.w3.org/WAI/ER/existingtools.html.

Saving Work and Exiting SharePoint Designer 2007

Before you exit SharePoint Designer, you should save and close any open Web sites or pages. If you try to exit SharePoint Designer without saving your changes, SharePoint Designer prompts you to confirm whether you want to save your work, as shown in Figure 1.70. If you do not close the open Web site before exiting, SharePoint Designer automatically opens that Web site the next time you start it. To exit SharePoint Designer, click File and click Exit.

Figure 1.70 Exiting SharePoint Designer

TIP Stop SharePoint Designer 2007 from Automatically Opening the Last Web Site

To prevent SharePoint Designer from automatically opening the last Web site view when it loads, you can follow these steps:

1. Choose Tools, Application Options.
2. Click the General tab.
3. Choose the *Clear the Open last Web site automatically when SharePoint Designer starts* check box.

Hands-On Exercises

3 | Exploring Basic Web Page Elements and SharePoint Designer 2007 Tools for Creating Web Pages

Skills covered: 1. Open a Web Site and Open a Web Page **2.** Get Acquainted with Web Page Elements **3.** Get Acquainted with HTML Tags Corresponding to Web Page Elements **4.** Check Compatibility, Close the Web Page, and Exit SharePoint Designer

<table>
<tr>
<td>

Step 1

Open a Web Site and Open a Web Page

</td>
<td>

Refer to Figure 1.71 as you complete Step 1.

a. Click **Start** to display the Start menu. Click **All Programs**, click **Microsoft Office**, and then click **Microsoft Office SharePoint Designer 2007** to open the program (if it is not already open).

b. Click **File** on the Menu bar and click **Open Site**. Click the **Look in down-drop arrow** and navigate to the location of your data files to locate the Web folder **chap1_ho3_website_org**. Click the **chap1_ho3_website_org** Web folder, and then click the **Open button** to open it.

c. Double-click the **default.htm** Web page to open it.

d. Click the **Close button** of the Toolbox task pane. Click the **Close button** of the Apply Styles task pane.

</td>
</tr>
</table>

Figure 1.71 Design View of the STARBRIGHT CHILDREN'S FOUNDATION Web Site Home Page

Step 2

Get Acquainted with Web Page Elements

Refer to Figure 1.72 as you complete Step 2.

a. Analyze the Web page; pinpoint and create a list with all the Web page elements included: headings, lists, hyperlinks, URLs, inline images, and graphics. Save your work as a Word document so your instructor can grade it.

b. Click the **Preview in Browser** command and pinpoint all the Web page elements included.

> **TROUBLESHOOTING:** If you do NOT have an Internet connection, skip Step 2c and continue with the exercise.

c. Click the hyperlinks to see the targeted Web sites.

d. Move the mouse pointer over the pictures included to see the text.

The area of the document window is now extended.

Figure 1.72 Preview in Browser View of the STARBRIGHT CHILDREN'S FOUNDATION Web Site Home Page

Refer to Figure 1.73 as you complete Step 3.

a. Click the **Code view button**.

b. Identify the HTML tags that correspond to the Web page elements you found in Design view.

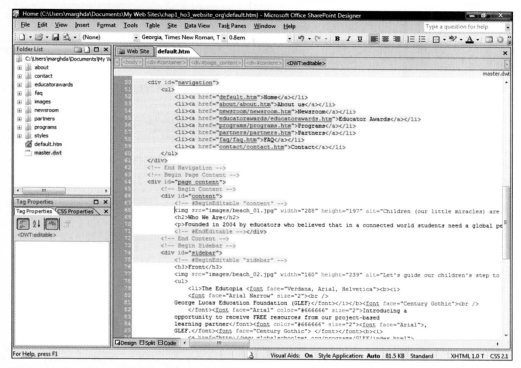

Figure 1.73 Code View of the STARBRIGHT CHILDREN'S FOUNDATION Web Site Home Page

Refer to Figure 1.74 as you complete Step 4.

a. Click **Tools** and click **Compatibility Reports**.

The Compatibility Checker dialog box is now displayed.

b. Check the **Current page option**. Select **HTML 4.01 Strict in the Check HTML/XHTML compatibility with: drop-down list**. Select **CSS2.1** in the **Check CSS compatibility with: drop-down list**, and then click the **Check button**.

The Compatibility task pane is now displayed and includes 12 compatibility problems.

c. Click the **Generate HTML Report button**.

The Compatibility Report.htm Web page is now displayed in Design view.

d. Move the mouse pointer over the first line in the Compatibility task pane and read the additional information displayed in the ScreenTip.

e. Click the **Save button** on the Common toolbar, locate the folder where you want to save your solutions in the Save As dialog box, type **chap1_ho3_ compatibility_report** in the File name box, and then click the **Save button**.

f. Click **File** and click **Close**.

> **TROUBLESHOOTING:** If you saved the Compatibility Report outside the chap1_ho3_website_org Web folder, you can see two SharePoint Designer tabs on the Windows task bar. Click File on the Menu bar and click Exit to close the active SharePoint Designer tab.

g. Click **Task Panes** on the menu bar and click **Reset Workspace Layout**. Pull down the **File menu** and click **Exit**.

> **TROUBLESHOOTING:** If you are asked to save changes to default.htm, click No.

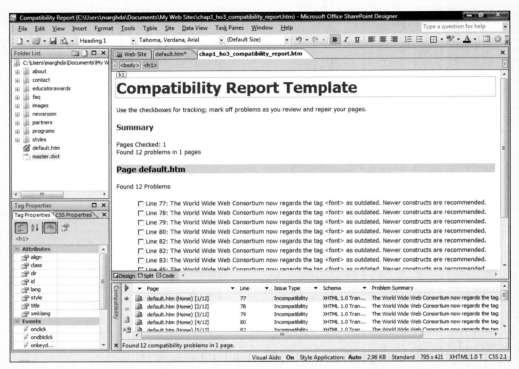

Figure 1.74 Saved Compatibility Report for the STARBRIGHT CHILDREN'S FOUNDATION Web Site Home Page

TIP Saving Changes When Exiting SharePoint Designer

When you make a change to a Web page, SharePoint Designer displays an asterisk in the Web page tag until you save the Web page. As soon as you save the Web page changes, the asterisk disappears. When exiting a Web site, if you made any changes while working on its Web pages, SharePoint Designer prompts you to verify whether you want to save your changes. If you choose not to save changes, your work will be lost.

Summary

1. **Get started with the Internet and the World Wide Web.** You learned about the software and hardware structure and the functionalities of the Internet and World Wide Web.

2. **Understand Web browsers and markup languages: Hypertext Markup Language (HTML), Extensible Hypertext Markup Language (XHTML), and eXtensible Markup Language (XML).** HTML, XHTML, and XML represent the core markup languages used to develop Web pages. Web browsers are software applications designed to assist you in navigating the Web, retrieving a Web page, interpreting its content, and displaying it on your computer.

3. **Use Cascading Style Sheets (CSS).** CSSs have become the standard style sheet used on the Web; they successfully separate the content of a Web page from its appearance. You can use three different types of CSS style codes to format your Web pages: inline styles, internal styles, and external styles.

4. **Define Web sites.** Web sites include sets of Web pages, files, and folders gathered and published on the Internet. Once published, each Web page is given a unique WWW address called a URL. Among the millions of Web sites published on the Internet, there are three important types of Web sites having particular characteristics: intranets, extranets, and portals. Web search engines offer two different types of searches for information retrieval on the WWW: keyword search and directory search. Content developers and owners can use Internet law to enforce their copyrightable Internet assets such as Web site graphics, eBooks, photos, and MP3 or video files.

5. **Get started with SharePoint Designer.** You learned to identify, use, and customize the elements of the SharePoint Designer interface, such as bars, toolbars, task panes, and the document window. When you need help while working with SharePoint Designer, you can use the Help feature from your computer or get help at Microsoft Office Online. You can get context-sensitive help by clicking Help within dialog boxes.

6. **Identify Microsoft Office SharePoint Designer 2007 tools for creating Web sites.** SharePoint Designer provides you with two categories of Web site templates, General and SharePoint. The General category is comprised of two templates, which enable you to create either a Web site incorporating only one blank page or only an empty Web site folder. The Import Web site Wizard allows you to create a new Web site by importing files from another Web site. The My Site Templates induced category of templates can be used to develop new Web sites from Web packages previously saved in the user template folder. You can create a Web package using the Export command, and you can import a Web package using the Import command.

7. **Open and close a Web site.** To retrieve all the files incorporated into a Web site folder you have previously saved, you use the Open Site command. To close a Web site, you use the Close Site command.

8. **Describe Web site views.** SharePoint Designer provides you with seven Web site views to help you in the process of designing, publishing, and managing a Web site: Page, Folders, Remote Web site, Reports, Navigation, Hyperlinks, and Preview in Browser views.

9. **Open and close a Web page.** You can open a Web page file that you have previously saved from the Open command on the File menu, the Open button, or by double-clicking the name of the Web page documents. To close a Web page, you use the Close command.

10. **Describe Web Page Views.** You can use four types of Page subviews, Design view, Code view, Split view, and Preview in Browser view, in the process of designing, developing and modifying a Web page.

11. **Define basic Web page elements.** Although each Web page has its own design and functionality, web page design includes combinations of the same set of elements, such as text, images, hyperlinks, graphics, CSS layouts, and forms.

12. **Identify Microsoft Office SharePoint Designer 2007 tools for creating Web pages.** Using SharePoint Designer, you can develop a Web page either from scratch or by employing the user-friendly set of page templates and CSS layouts; you can open, modify, and enhance a Web page created in any version of Microsoft Office FrontPage or Microsoft Expression Web. A SharePoint Designer Dynamic Web template empowers you to automatically update features of all Web pages to which it is attached.

...continued on Next Page

13. Understand the principle of good Web page design. All Web designers and Web developers take into consideration a set of core factors defining good Web page design, such as usability, navigation, compatibility, accessibility, consistency, validity, and attractiveness.

14. Save work and exit SharePoint Designer. You exit SharePoint Designer using the Exit command. If you did not save all new or modified Web pages, SharePoint Designer will alert you. If you do not close the open Web site before exiting, SharePoint Designer will automatically open the same Web site the next time you start the program.

Key Terms

Multiple Choice

1. Which of the following items is not part of the SharePoint Designer window?

   (a) Title bar

   (b) Status bar

   (c) Personal toolbar

   (d) Common toolbar

2. Which of the following is not one of the SharePoint Designer views?

   (a) Page view

   (b) Folders view

   (c) XML view

   (d) Navigation view

3. Which of the following items is not a Web page element?

   (a) An image

   (b) A table

   (c) A frame

   (d) A task pane

4. Which of the following items is not a markup language?

   (a) XML

   (b) Java

   (c) XHTML

   (d) HTML

5. In SharePoint Designer, you cannot open a Web site using:

   (a) The File menu

   (b) The Standard toolbar

   (c) The Formatting toolbar

   (d) The Status bar

6. Which of the following documents can you create assisted by SharePoint Designer tools?

   (a) HTML

   (b) ASPX

   (c) XML

   (d) All of the above

7. In SharePoint Designer, which of the following can you NOT do using Task panes?

   (a) Create Layout Tables.

   (b) Run the Compatibility Checker.

   (c) View and modify HTML tag attributes.

   (d) Create a new Web page from a Dynamic Web template.

8. When designing a Web page, you should NOT take into consideration the following criteria:

   (a) Web page content needs to be easy to navigate.

   (b) Web page content needs to comply with Section 508 of the U.S. Rehabilitation Act and the W3C's Web Content Accessibility Guidelines (WCAG).

   (c) Web pages might be displayed differently on different computer platforms.

   (d) SharePoint Designer enables you to preview a Web page only in Internet Explorer and Netscape Navigator.

9. Which of the following statements about using colors in designing your Web pages is incorrect?

   (a) Web page colors can be set using color names and color hexadecimal values.

   (b) Custom colors might not be part of the WSP.

   (c) Using color names ensures more color portability.

   (d) HTML accepts only hexadecimal value for colors.

10. When working with a Web page that has a Dynamic Web template attached:

    (a) You cannot detach the Dynamic Web template.

    (b) You cannot edit the noneditable regions of the Web page in any SharePoint Designer view.

    (c) You can modify the noneditable regions of the Dynamic Web template in Design view.

    (d) You can attach the Dynamic Web template to another Web page.

11. When working in SharePoint Designer with task panes:

    (a) You cannot float a task pane.

    (b) You cannot dock a task pane.

    (c) You can merge task panes.

    (d) You cannot stack a task pane.

12. SharePoint Designer does not support:

(a) Authoring a Web site

(b) Publishing a Web site

(c) Managing a Web site

(d) Compiling Java code

13. You can write an HTML document using:

(a) SharePoint Designer

(b) Microsoft Word 2007

(c) Windows Notepad

(d) All of the above

14. Which of the following statements about SharePoint Designer is correct?

(a) SharePoint Designer's interface is very much like any other Office 2007 suite application interface.

(b) Using SharePoint Designer, you cannot manage a Web site created in any FrontPage version.

(c) SharePoint Designer assists you in developing standard Web pages and Web sites.

(d) The SharePoint Designer Common toolbar offers all features provided by the Standard and Formatting toolbars.

15. The Compatibility Reports tool cannot assist you in:

(a) Detecting for what browser a Web page is incompatible

(b) Maximizing the HTML/XHTML compatibility of your Web pages

(c) Maximizing the CSS compatibility of your Web pages

(d) Generating and saving a compatibility report HTML document

16. The Accessibility Reports tool cannot assist you in:

(a) Checking the accessibility of your Web pages for Access Board Section 508 recommendations

(b) Checking the accessibility of your Web pages for WCAG Priority 3

(c) Generating and saving an accessibility report HTML document

(d) Locating the accessibility errors in the Code view of your Web pages

Practice Exercises

1 Identifying and Customizing Interface Components

Three years ago, as an undergraduate student in the Personal Computer Applications course, you learned FrontPage 2003. As a result of your excellent work in this class, you have been hired as an undergraduate teaching assistant in the Personal Computer Applications course, and, as part of your new assignment, you will help students working on their assignments in the Personal Computer Applications course laboratory. Your faculty supervisor is providing you with a notebook computer so that you can start getting acquainted with SharePoint Designer 2007. Proceed as follows:

a. Choose **Start**, **All Programs**, **Microsoft Office**, **Microsoft Office SharePoint designer 2007** to start SharePoint Designer 2007. You should see a blank HTML document.

b. Click the **Close button** in the upper-right corner of the document window to close the blank *untitled_1.htm* document.

c. Click **File** on the Menu bar and click **Open Site**. Navigate to the SharePoint Designer Exploring folder and open the *chap1_ pe1_website* Web site folder.

d. Identify the Folder List task pane. Can you see all the folders and documents included in the Web site? Double-click **index.htm** in the Folder List task pane.

e. Identify the Toolbox task pane. It contains a list with common Web page elements.

f. Identify the Apply Styles task pane. It contains the Apply Styles tab, active by default, and Manage Styles tab. The Apply Styles tab displays a list of CSS styles used in this Web site.

g. Click the **Manage Styles tab**, and in the Manage Styles task pane, click the **Maximize button**. The Manage Styles task pane now covers the whole area of the right column while you can still see, collapsed, the Toolbox task pane.

h. Point to the **Tag Properties task pane title bar**, and when the pointer becomes a four-headed arrow, drag the title bar to the right until it docks below the document window. The title bar is now displayed vertically.

i. Point to the **Tag Properties task pane title bar** and drag upwards to float it. Now you can move the Tag Properties task pane anywhere on your computer screen.

j. Point to the top edge of the **CSS Properties task pane** and, when the pointer becomes a two-headed arrow, drag the top edge up to resize the task pane and display more of its options.

k. On the status bar, point to the **Download Statistics indicator**. A ScreenTip providing information about the HTML page size, linked data size, total download size, and linked data file count is now displayed.

l. Compare the SharePoint Designer workspace displayed on your computer with Figure 1.75.

m. Click the **Close button** in the upper-right corner of the document window to close the *index.htm* document. Click **File** on the Menu bar and click **Close Site** to close the Web site.

n. Click **Task Panes** on the Menu bar, and then click the **Reset Workspace Layout command**. All task panes are now reset to their default locations.

...continued on Next Page

Figure 1.75 Identifying and Customizing Interface Components

2 Exploring SharePoint Designer Web Site Views

Locate and open the *chap1_pe2_website* Web site folder. Proceed as follows:

a. Click the **Hyperlinks button** on the Views bar. In the document window, you should see all the links associated with the home page.

b. Click the **Close button** in the upper-right corner of the Toolbox task pane and Apply Styles task pane to close them.

c. Click and drag to your right the scroll bar at the bottom of the document window so you can properly see all the elements of the Hyperlinks view.

d. If you cannot see any hyperlink to a .jpg file, right-click anywhere within the document window and click **Hyperlinks to Pictures**. The Hyperlinks view will now display all pictures embedded in index.htm.

e. Click the **plus sign** near *master.dwt* to view all the hyperlinks associated with the Dynamic Web template.

f. Compare the Web site Hyperlinks view displayed on your screen with Figure 1.76.

g. Click the **Reports button** on the Views bar to switch to Site Summary list of Reports. Click **Recently added files**. The list of all files in the Web site created in the last 30 days is now displayed.

h. Click the **drop-down arrow** to the right of the **Recently Added Files button**, point to **Files**, and then point to **Recently changed files**. The list of all files in the Web site changed in the last 30 days is now displayed.

i. Click the **drop-down arrow** to the right of the **Recently changed Files button**, point to **Share Content**, and then point to **Dynamic Web Templates**. The list of all files in the Web site attached to the *master.dwt* Dynamic Web template is now displayed.

j. Click **Task Panes** and click **Reset Workspace Layout** to reset the SharePoint Designer workspace to its default layout. Click **File** and click **Close Site** to close the Web site.

...continued on Next Page

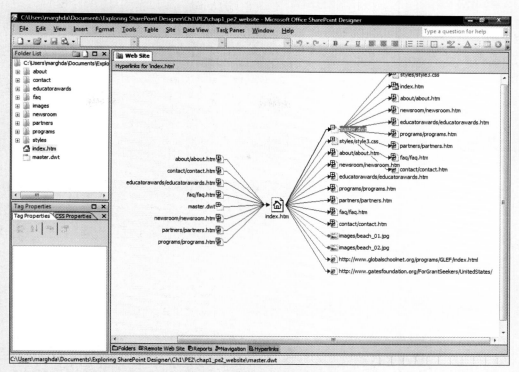

Figure 1.76 Exploring SharePoint Designer Web Site Views

3 Teaching and Research Lab Web Site

Your Education Psychology professor asked you to help her develop a Web site for her teaching and research lab using a generic Web site she was given by a colleague that she already has been working on. You will open the *chap1_ pe3_com_lab* Web site folder, explore and check for accessibility of the home page and Courses Web page, and then present a report of your findings to your professor.

   a. Double-click **index.htm** in the Folder List task pane to open the home page in Design view.

   b. Click the **Split button** on the Views bar. The document window is now split into the Code view and Design view.

   c. Locate and right-click the **<img> tag** in Code view, and then point to **Select Tag**. The corresponding image is highlighted in Design view.

   d. Look at the Quick Tag Selector, at the top of the document window. The <img> tag is selected. Look at the <img> tag properties in the Tag Properties task pane.

   e. Click **Accessibility Reports** on the Tools menu, click **Current page**, and click the **Check button** to launch the Accessibility Checker.

   f. Click the **Generate HTML Report button** in the Accessibility task pane. Right-click the **Accessibility Report.htm* tab** and click **Save**. In the Save As dialog box, locate the folder where you want to save the solutions, type **Accessibility_report_home_ page.htm** in the File name box, and click the **Save button**.

   g. Right-click the **Accessibility_report_home_page.htm tab** and click **Close**. Click the **Close button** on the Accessibility task pane vertical title bar.

   h. Click the **plus sign** to the left of the courses folder in the Folder List task pane and double-click **courses.htm** to open it.

   i. Locate and right-click the **<table> tag** in Code view, and then point to **Select Tag**. The corresponding table is highlighted in Design view.

   j. Look at the Quick Tag Selector, at the top of the document window. The <table> tag is selected. Look at the <table> tag properties in the Tag Properties task pane.

...continued on Next Page

k. Click **Accessibility Reports** on the Tools menu, click **Current page**, and click the **Check button** to launch the Accessibility Checker.

l. Click the **Generate HTML Report button** in the Accessibility task pane. Right-click the **Accessibility Report.htm* tab** and click **Save**. In the Save As dialog box, locate the folder where you want to save the solutions, type **Accessibility_report_ courses_page.htm** in the File name box, and click the **Save button**.

m. Right-click the **Accessibility_report_courses_page.htm tab** and click **Close**. Click the **Close button** on the Accessibility task pane vertical title bar.

n. Click **File** and click **Close Site** to close the Web site. If prompted to save your changes, click **No**.

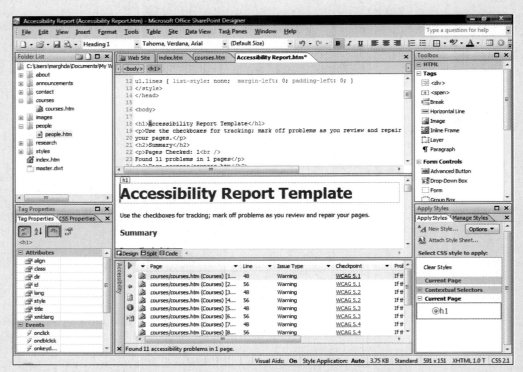

Figure 1.77 Exploring SharePoint Designer Web Page Views and Accessibility Reports

Mid-Level Exercises

Many members of your sorority have family and friends in the states devastated by the mighty Katrina and Rita hurricanes. As part of their "Help Katrina & Rita hurricane victims" initiative, the members of your sorority have asked you to start creating for the sorority a Web site dedicated to help the Hurricane victims. Visitors can use this Web site to stay updated on the aftermath of the two hurricanes, to donate money and needed items, or to volunteer their time and energy for helping the devastated communities. Figure 1.78 shows the completed stage one of the Web site. Use this figure as a guide.

a. Start SharePoint Designer. Create a new **chap1_mid1_katrina_solution** Web site folder site using the Empty Web Site template.

b. Import the *chap1_mid1_katrina* Personal Web Package file into the newly created Web site.

c. Open the *default.htm* home page and use the Split view to see the editable regions of the Dynamic Web template attached to the home page. Close the Toolbox task pane and Apply Styles task pane.

d. Right-click anywhere within an editable region of *default.htm* and click **Page Properties**.

e. Change the word *Home* in the Title bar of the General Tab to **Help Katrina & Rita Hurricane Victims** and close the Page Properties dialog box.

f. Set **On** the Visual Aids indicator if it is showing *Off*.

g. Change the Heading 2 text of the <h2> tag to **Hurricanes Katrina & Rita**.

h. Change the Heading 3 text of the <h3> tag to **New Orleans after Hurricane Katrina**.

i. Press **F9** to cycle through the errors in Code view. Move the mouse pointer over the highlighted HTML code and learn more about the error. Press **Backspace** to remove the highlighted error.

j. Press **F9** again. Move the mouse pointer over the highlighted HTML code and learn more about the error. Press **Backspace** to remove the highlighted error. Move the mouse pointer over the highlighted HTML code and learn more about the error. Press **Backspace** to remove the highlighted error. Press **F9** again to make sure no other error exists.

k. Save *default.htm* using the **Save button**, switch to Design view, and compare your SharePoint Designer workspace to Figure 1.78.

l. Reset the workspace layout, close the Web page, close the Web site, and Exit SharePoint Designer.

...continued on Next Page

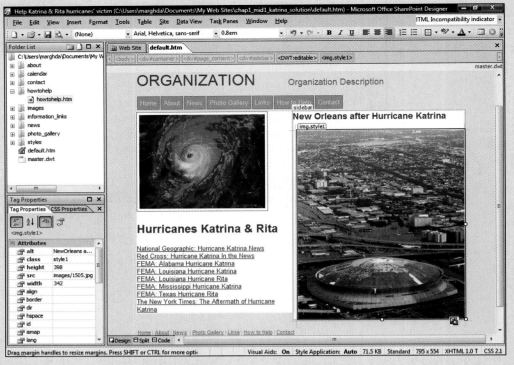

Figure 1.78 Using a Personal Web Package to Create the Web Site for a Small Nonprofit Organization

2 Customizing a Dynamic Web Template for a Small Nonprofit Organization

You have to further customize the Dynamic Web template of the Help Katrina & Rita hurricane victims initiative Web site and add new headlines on the Web site home page.

a. Start SharePoint Designer. Open the *chap1_mid2_katrina* Web site folder site. Open *master.dwt* and save it as **katrina.dwt**.

b. Select **Split view** and position your mouse pointer, in the Design view section, after **Contact** in the horizontal navigation bar.

c. Move your mouse pointer, in the Code view section, to the right after the **</li> tag**, press **Enter** and type **<l** . Intellisense will prompt you to insert the **<li> </li> tags**.

d. Position your mouse pointer, in the Code view section, between the two **<li> </li> tags** (if it is not already there) and enter **<a**. Intellisense will prompt you to insert the **<a> </a> tags**.

e. Move your mouse pointer, in the Code view section, to your left and position it after **<a**. Press the **Space bar** and on the Intellisense list, double-click the **href** attribute. Use Intellisense again to open the Edit Hyperlink dialog box. Type **http://www.weather. com/newscenter/hurricanecentral** in the Address box and close the Edit Hyperlink dialog box.

f. Move your mouse pointer to your right, position it between the **<a>** and **</a> tags**, and type **Weather.com Hurricane Central**.

...continued on Next Page

g. In Design view, double-click the word **ORGANIZATION** and type **Help Katrina & Rita hurricane victims**.

h. In Code view, double-click the **<h3> tag** placed above the horizontal navigation bar and press **Backspace** to remove it. Save **katrina.dwt**.

i. Open *default.htm* in Design view. Attach the *katrina.dwt* Dynamic Web template to *default.htm* using the Attach Dynamic Web Template dialog box. Save **default.htm**.

j. Preview in Browser default.htm and compare it with Figure 1.79.

k. Close all files, reset the SharePoint Designer workspace, close the Web site, and exit SharePoint Designer.

Figure 1.79 Customizing a Dynamic Web Template of a Small Nonprofit Organization

3 Add a New Web Page to the Teaching and Research Lab Web Site Using a Dynamic Web Template and CSSs

You have to add a new Lab Accessibility Web page to the Teaching and Research Lab Web site using a Dynamic Web Template and CSSs.

a. Start SharePoint Designer. Open the *chap1_mid3_comp_lab* Web site folder site. Using the Remote Web Site view, create a **chap1_mid3_comp_lab_solution** Web site backup. Click **Open your Remote Web site in SharePoint Designer** to open the *chap1_mid3_comp_lab_solution* Web site folder.

b. Create a new accessibility folder.

...continued on Next Page

c. Click **Create from Dynamic Web Template** on the New menu and create a new Web page attached to *master.dwt*. Save the new Web page in the *access* folder as **accessibility.htm.**

d. Click **Attach Style Sheet** on the Apply Styles task pane and attach as a link to the current page the *styles/style1.css* CSS style sheet. You can now see style1.css highlighted in the Apply Styles task pane.

e. Click **Open Attached Dynamic Web Template** on the Dynamic Web Template submenu. You can now see style2.css highlighted in the Apply Styles task pane.

f. Click anywhere within the Welcome message text line, click the **Center button** on the Common toolbar, and observe the changes shown in the Tag Properties task pane, as shown in Figure 1.80.

g. Save **accessibility.htm**, close all files, reset the SharePoint Designer workspace, close the Web site, and exit SharePoint Designer.

Figure 1.80 Creating a New Web Page Using a Dynamic Web Template and CSSs

Capstone Exercise

Your family asked you to start developing a family Web site. You decided to make this family Web site part of your personal Web site, which you plan to develop using SharePoint Designer. You learned in your Personal Computer Applications class that, even if there are important upgrades in SharePoint Designer, it can still open, edit, manage, and publish any Web site created in FrontPage 2003. Kevin, your older brother, provides you with an old practice Web site that he developed using the FrontPage 2003 Personal Web site template. You will explore in SharePoint Designer the Personal Web site created by Kevin in FrontPage 2003. You will start developing a new Web site using SharePoint Designer and a generic Web package. You will create a custom default Dynamic Web template for your personal Web site.

Exploring a FrontPage 2003 Customized Personal Web Site

You will open and explore in SharePoint Designer a Personal Web site created in FrontPage 2003.

a. Open the Web site folder *chap1_cap_KevinsPersonalWebSite*. Explore the Hyperlinks Web site view and check if there are any broken links.

b. Open *index.htm*. Using the Split view, identify all the Web page elements included in index.htm. Take notes about the differences between the code of this Web page and Web pages you have seen so far created with SharePoint Designer. Save all your findings as a Word document and hand it to your professor for grading.

c. Move the mouse pointer over the **Quirks indicator** on the right side of the status bar, and then go to the Microsoft Web site (http://www.microsoft.com) and search for Quirks Rendering Mode.

d. Run the **Compatibility Checker**. Generate, review, and save the *Compatibility Report.htm* document as **fp_compatibility_report1_solution.htm**. Close the saved report and close the Compatibility task pane.

e. Run the **Accessibility Checker**. Generate, review, and save the *Accessibility Report.htm* document as **fp_accessibility_report1_solution.htm**. Close the saved report and close the Accessibility task pane.

f. Open the Romania subsite and open *index.html*.

g. Using the Split view, identify all the Web page elements included in index.html. Take notes about the differences between the code of this Web page and Web pages you have seen so far created with SharePoint Designer. Save your notes as a Word document, print it, and hand it to your instructor.

h. Run the **Compatibility Checker**. Generate, review, and save the *Compatibility Report.htm* document as

fp_compatibility_report2_solution.htm. Close the saved report and close the Compatibility task pane.

i. Run the **Accessibility Checker**. Generate, review, and save the *Accessibility Report.htm* document as **fp_accessibility_report2_solution.htm**. Close the saved report and close the Accessibility task pane.

j. Close the Web site.

Create Your Personal Web Site from a Generic Personal Web Package

You will start creating your personal Web site from a given Personal Web package using the SharePoint Designer New dialog box.

a. Place a copy of *chap1_cap_personalwebsitepackage* in the SharePoint Designer default template folder.

b. Start creating your new personal Web site, **chap1_cap_mypersonalwebsite_solution**, using the SharePoint Designer New dialog box and the My Templates category of Web site templates.

c. Explore the Hyperlinks view of the Web site and see the Web pages attached to *master.dwt*, the Dynamic Web Template.

d. Open *default.htm* and change its Web page Title to **Welcome to My Web Site!** Save the home page and preview it in a browser.

e. Explore the editable regions of the document using the Split view.

f. Open the Dynamic Web template attached to *default.htm* and explore the editable regions using the Editable Regions dialog box.

Create a Custom Dynamic Web Template

You will customize the Dynamic Web Template of your personal Web site, update all the attached Web pages, and export the Web site as **chap1_cap_mypersonalwebpackage_solution**.

a. Switch to the Split view of the Dynamic Web Template and place the mouse above the **<!- -Begin Footer - - > line**.

b. Insert the following new line of code using the Toolbox HTML task pane and Intellisense: **<div id="news"> <h3>Headline 3</h3><p>Insert content here</p></div>**.

c. Select the new **<div> element** of the Dynamic Web template added in the previous step and add it to the Editable Regions with the name **new**.

d. Select the **Photo Gallery hyperlink** and change the text to **My Family**. Save the Dynamic Web template and update all pages attached to it.

e. Rename the photo_gallery folder **myfamily**. Rename *photo_gallery.htm* **myfamily.htm**. Update all pages that have hyperlinks to this Web page.

f. Export the Web site as **chap1_cap_ mypersonalwebpackage_solution**.

g. Close the Web site and exit SharePoint Designer.

Mini Cases

Use the rubric following the case as a guide to evaluate your work. However, keep in mind that your instructor may have additional grading criteria or use a different standard to evaluate your work.

Campus Bookstore Web Site

GENERAL CASE

As part of your campus library job, you have to customize the Dynamic Web template of a generic small business Web site to match the specifics of the library business. To successfully do this, carefully study this chapter as well as the two appendices. Open the *chap1_mc1_bookstore* Web site and create a backup Web site, **chap1_mc1_bookstore_solution**. Open *master.dwt* and use Intellisense to add a new Online Shopping hyperlink (with the attribute href="services/OnlineShopping.htm") to the vertical and horizontal navigation bars. Using the Tag Properties task pane, add adequate values to the alt attribute of the <img> tag. Save **master.dwt** and update all Web pages attached to the master.dwt. Open *default.htm* and, using the Tag Properties task pane, add adequate values to the alt attributes of the <img> tag. Save **default.htm**. Run the Compatibility Checker and make sure there are no errors. Run the Accessibility Checker and make sure there are no errors. Preview in Browser the default.htm file. Close all files, close the Web site, and exit SharePoint Designer.

Performance Elements	Exceeds Expectations	Meets Expectations	Below Expectations
Customize the Web site template	All modifications are correctly implemented.	All modifications are implemented.	No modification was implemented.
Modify the home page	All modifications are correctly implemented.	All modifications are implemented.	No modification was implemented.
Compatibility Reports and Accessibility Reports	Both Compatibility and Accessibility Reports run with no errors.	Both Compatibility and Accessibility Reports run with some errors.	Both Compatibility and Accessibility Reports run with all errors.

Microsoft Office Discussion Groups

RESEARCH CASE

There is a large international community of Office 2007 developers that help each other through online discussion groups. One of the most professional and helpful Office 2007 discussion groups is the one organized by Microsoft. Use Microsoft Internet Explorer to open the Microsoft Office Discussion Groups home page (http://www.microsoft.com/office/community/en-us/default .mspx). Select the Office group and click General Questions. Search for your most relevant 10 topics (key terms) covered in this chapter and print or save the most useful information. Provide your instructor with a copy of your printed report. You can also post a new question, but be aware that you will be required to have a .Net Passport, which you can obtain free of charge.

Performance Elements	Exceeds Expectations	Meets Expectations	Below Expectations
Identify 10 relevant topics	Identify 10 relevant topics.	Identify 8 relevant topics.	Identify 6 relevant topics.
Find useful information	Identify and find useful information for each topic.	Information is too brief.	No information.

Mini Cases Continued...

Standard Web Pages

DISASTER RECOVERY

Open the *chap1_mc3_comp_lab* Web site folder from the Exploring SharePoint Designer folder and then open the *index.htm* Web page that contains several incompatibility and code errors. Carefully study Appendices A and B. Use Intellisense and the Compatibility Reports to help you identify the errors in *default.htm* and fix them. Generate and save the compatibility HTML Report with the initial errors as **chap1_mc3_report_errors.htm**. Correct and explain the errors. The Web site with the corrected index.htm document should be backed up as **chap1_mc3_comp_lab_solution**. If you are prompted by the Dynamic Web Template Alert, check the Keep all changes option.

Performance Elements	Exceeds Expectations	Meets Expectations	Below Expectations
Incompatibility	Corrected all 3 errors.	Corrected 2 errors.	Corrected 1 error.
Code error	Corrected all 3 errors.	Corrected 2 errors.	Corrected 1 error.
Explain the error	Complete and correct explanation of each error.	Explanations are too brief to fully explain errors.	No explanations.

Microsoft Office SharePoint Designer 2007

Web Sites and Web Pages

Designing and Building Standard Web Sites and Web Pages

bjectives

After you read this chapter, you will be able to:

1. Design a Web site (page 113).
2. Build a Web site (page 118).
3. Publish SharePoint Designer 2007 Web sites and subsites (page 124).
4. Test and validate a Web site (page 129).
5. Publish changes to a Web site (page 135).
6. Design a Web page (page 147).
7. Build a Web page (page 148).
8. Work with Web page content (page 152).
9. Check the spelling of your text (page 158).
10. Use hyperlinks and lists in organizing a Web page (page 159).
11. Work with tables and layout tables (page 172).
12. Enhance a Web page using graphics, multimedia, and Web components (page 191).
13. Print a Web page (page 227).

Hands-On Exercises

Exercises	Skills Covered
1. BUILD, CUSTOMIZE, PUBLISH, TEST, AND VALIDATE A WEB SITE WITH SUBSITES (page 140) **Case Study–Related** Open: chap2_ho1_data Save as: chap1_ho1_solution and chap1_ho1_solution_remote	• Start SharePoint Designer, Create a One-Page Web Site, and Create Two New Folders • Import .css and .gif Files, Import a Dynamic Web Template, Attach a Dynamic Web Template to a Web Page, and Open a Dynamic Web Template • Create a Subsite and Modify the Navigation Layout of a Web Site • Publish a Web Site with Subsites • Test and Validate a Web Site with Subsites • Publish Changes to a Web Site
2. CREATING AND ENHANCING A WEB PAGE IN SHAREPOINT DESIGNER 2007 (page 229) **Case Study–Related** Open: chap2_ho2_website and chap2_ho2_sketch1_data.pdf, pmf.wav Save as: chap2_ho2_website_solution	• Start SharePoint Designer, Open a Web Site, Create a New Folder, Add a New Web Page in Navigation View, and Format the New Web Page • Add Text Content to a Web Page and Format Text Using CSS Inline Styles and External Style Sheets • Organize a Web Page Using Hyperlinks and Format Hyperlinks Using CSS Styles • Organize a Web Page Using Lists and Format Lists Using CSS Styles • Insert a Standard Table, Format a Standard Table, and Add Content to a Standard Table • Add Graphics to a Web Page and Create an Auto Thumbnail • Add a Plug-In Web Component to a Web page, Add a Page Banner Web Component to a Dynamic Web Template, and Add a Marquee Web Component to a Dynamic Web Template

CASE STUDY

The DestinQuest Company Web Site

Case Study

Stefania, Nadia, Emily, and Codi are four intelligent and enthusiastic best friends who, as soon as they graduated from college three years ago, decided to build their own successful real estate company, named DestinQuest, based in Destin, Florida.

Initially they planned to provide services related to buying, selling, and renting properties situated in the little paradise surrounding the Destin area. They now own their business headquarters building, which is well placed in Destin's business district and furnished with modern and stylish office furniture and equipment. They have also opened two more offices in Vail, Colorado, and Catalina Island, California. One of the important things they learned in school was how much a well-developed e-business Web site can help in promoting, publicizing, and managing their business. In one of their college computer courses, they were introduced to Microsoft FrontPage 2003 and its powerful and friendly tools and features for designing, developing, publishing, and managing professional Web sites. Three years ago, they hired Melissa to help them develop a FrontPage Web site to promote, publicize, and manage their company. Thanks to their efforts and Melissa's skills, they have a functional Web site, and their DestinQuest company is constantly expanding, making a lot of progress in the Destin, Vail, and Catalina Island real estate business. Now, they have hired Melissa to fully upgrade their e-business Web site using SharePoint Designer 2007.

Your Assignment

- Read the chapter, paying special attention to Hands-On Exercises 1 and 2, which help you get acquainted with SharePoint Designer tools for developing standard Web sites and Web pages.
- You will put yourself in Melissa's place and open the *chap2_case_DestinQuest* Web site folder, which contains the partially completed Web site, and create a **chap2_case_DestinQuest_solution** backup Web site folder.
- Study the structure of the Web site, the Dynamic Web Template, and the content of the home page.
- Open the Dynamic Web Template and replace the graphic logo with *DestinQuest_Logo.png* available in the images folder. Insert a Date and Time Web Component as instructed in the home page.
- Using the Dynamic Web Template create a register_destinquest_newsletter.htm Web page in the promotions folder.
- Link the register_destinquest_newsletter.htm Web page to the related h4 headline on the home page.
- On the home page, insert a graphic link, using BD21300_.gif from the images folder, to the right of the *Check DestinQuest Real Estate Listings* h4 headline, and link it to the DestinQuestRealEstateListings.xps document in the data_files folder.
- On the home page, insert a graphic link, using BD21300_.gif from the images folder, to the right of the *Download DestinQuest Poster* h4 headline, and link it to the DestinQuest_Poster.docx document in the data_files folder.
- Highlight the *Check the DestinQuest 2008 rental rates* text line on the home page and insert a link to a DestinQuestCondoRates.htm document in the data_files folder.
- Highlight the *Learn about DestinQuest services for business, professional and family event settings* text line on the home page and insert a link to a DestinQuest.htm document in the data_files folder.
- Locate the three current broken hyperlinks using the Site Summary reports and the Hyperlinks View.
- Insert a Photo Gallery Web Component in the photo_gallery.htm Web page. Use the images available in the images folder.
- Close the DestinQuest Web site and exit SharePoint Designer.

Introduction to Web Site Development

As discussed in Chapter 1, a Web site is a collection of Web pages, files, and folders published on the Internet by an individual, organization, or business. To design and develop a high-quality Web site, you should focus on more than just the content and appearance of your Web pages. You also need to consider their global usability and accessibility and address the challenging cross-browser and cross-platform issues. The main steps required to create a Web site include the following:

- Creating a rough sketch of your Web site's navigational structure.
- Creating a rough sketch of the layout for each Web page included in your site.
- Creating your Web site's navigational structure from scratch or by using the tools provided by SharePoint Designer.
- Creating your own personalized content.
- Testing and validating your Web site, although specific tests can be accomplished only after the Web site is published on a Web server.
- Obtaining a Web site hosting account or Uniform Resource Locator (URL) from a hosting service, such as an Internet Service Provider (ISP).
- Publishing your Web site to the World Wide Web (WWW).

In this section, you learn how to design and build a Web site, how to create subsites and publish Web sites with subsites, how to test and validate a Web site, and how to publish changes applied to a Web site.

Designing a Web Site

Have you ever seen early sketches of paintings or sculptures created by famous artists such as Picasso or Leonardo DaVinci? Have you ever seen the blueprints of some architectural monuments, such as the Brooklyn Bridge or the Eiffel Tour? Did you ever admire the sophisticated, elegant fashion design sketches of a famous couturier such as Coco Channel or Versace? They all represent the artist's or architect's technical and artistic vision of how their work should look when finished. A set of good practices that you can apply to all Web development projects should consist of the following five core phases: defining the project, developing the project Web site structure, designing the visual interface, building and integrating the project, and launching (publishing) and maintaining the project.

TIP — Web Development Project Phases

To read more about the five core phases of a professional Web development project, visit the Web Redesign 2.0: Workflow That Works Web site (http://www.web-redesign.com).

> For a Web developer, the navigational layout of a Web site is the equivalent of an artist's sketch or an architect's blueprint.

For a Web developer, the navigational layout of a Web site is the equivalent of an artist's sketch or an architect's blueprint. It can be designed as a tree-like structure or as an organizational chart showing the hierarchical relationship between the Web pages included in a Web site. Let us consider, as an example, the case of creating the navigational layout of a real estate company's Web site. The Web site's home page should be at the top of the chart. At the second level, beneath the home page, you place pages dedicated to each main division of the company, and one dedicated to its agents: real estate sales, real estate rentals, and real estate agents. The third level should include Web pages focused on the two main categories of the real estate business: residential and commercial. The fourth level includes a list of Web pages that describe individual properties or complexes. Figure 2.1 shows the navigational layout created using a Microsoft Office Word organization chart (you can simply draw it on a piece of paper). Later in this chapter, you will also learn how to develop a Web page from a sketch and the importance of always taking into consideration the core criteria of good Web page design.

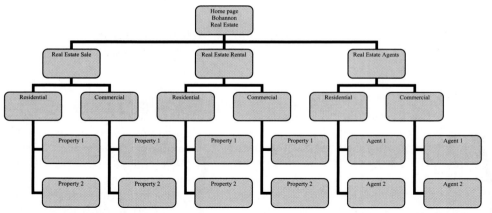

Figure 2.1 Navigational Layout of a Web Site Designed as an Organizational Chart

TIP Hyperlinks

Chapter 1 discussed that a Web page can include links targeting Web pages that are part of the same Web site or other Web sites (see Figure 2.2). When sketching the navigational layout of a Web site, keep in mind that the Web pages within a Web site are connected via hyperlinks. It is best if your site visitors can reach any Web page within your Web site in one step. At times, you might find that one step is not possible; when one step is not possible, try not to use too many.

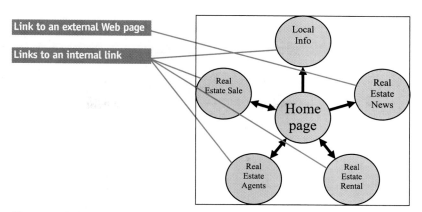

Figure 2.2 Navigational Layout of a Web Page Designed as an Organization Chart

SharePoint Designer Navigation view provides a bar of buttons (see Figure 2.3). You use the buttons to build and modify the Web site's navigational structure, view the navigational structure in Portrait and Landscape mode, zoom the navigational structure, and view sections of the Web site's navigational structure called subtrees. You can also use the Navigation view to build link bars based on the navigational structure.

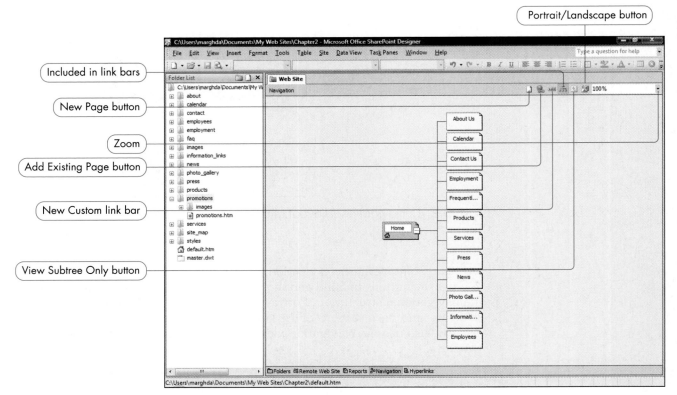

Figure 2.3 Navigation View

TIP Microsoft Expression Web and Web Site Navigation Structure

Microsoft Expression Web does not provide the Navigation Web site view and Navigation task pane; therefore, you will not be able to modify the navigation structure of a Web site created in SharePoint Designer.

To add an existing Web page to the Web site's navigational structure, click the Web page in the Folders List, drag it beneath or to the right (depending on the selected view of the navigational structures) of the higher-level page to which you want it linked, and drop the Web page, as shown in Figures 2.4 and 2.5.

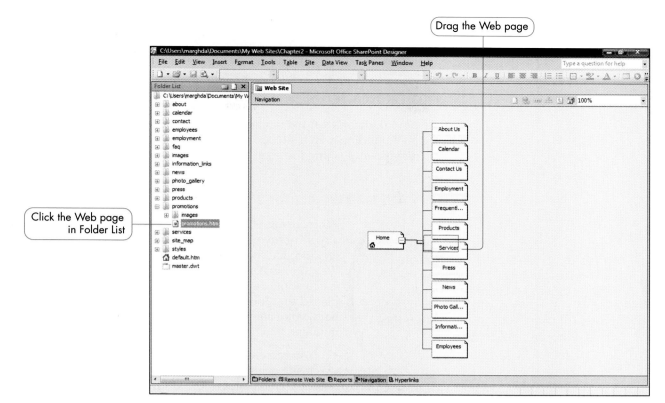

Figure 2.4 Dragging the Existing Page

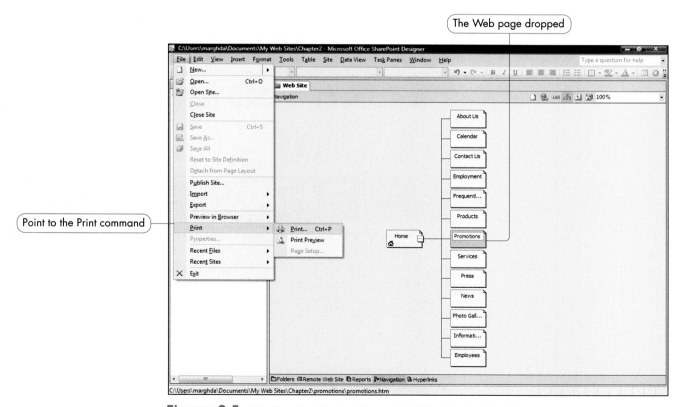

Figure 2.5 Printing the Portrait Layout of the Navigation View

You can print the Web site's navigational structure so that you can review it without having a computer. To print the Navigation view of a Web site, point to the Print command on the File menu and click Print (see Figure 2.5).

Building a Web Site

You are now familiar with the navigational structure of a Web site. Let us see what the stages of building a Web site are and how SharePoint Designer can assist you in successfully accomplishing the goals of these stages.

Use SharePoint Designer 2007 Tools for Building a Web Site

(Most developers find that they are better organized when they store all their Web sites in a single unique folder. If more than one developer is working on the same Web site, the Web site needs to be placed in a location that all developers can access.)

When using SharePoint Designer, you can place a Web site in any location on your hard disk drive. However, most developers find that they are better organized when they store all their Web sites in a single unique folder. If more than one developer is working on the same Web site, the Web site needs to be placed in a location that all developers can access. After you have your navigational layout sketched, there are three ways in which you can develop a SharePoint Designer Web site:

- You can create, using an appropriate General template, an empty Web site or a Web site containing only one Web page to which, one by one, you add, import, or modify Web pages or import the content of a Personal Web Package.

- You can import a preexisting Web site using the Import Web Site Wizard.

- You can create, using an appropriate template, a Personal Web Package or SharePoint Templates.

In Windows Vista, the default location for SharePoint Designer Web sites is the My Web Sites folder, which is nested in the Documents folder. In Windows XP, the default location for SharePoint Designer Web sites is the My Webs folder, which is nested in the My Documents folder. The My Documents folder is automatically created on your hard drive when the operating system is installed. After creating a new Web site using a template, wizard, or Personal Web Package, you can customize it at the Web-site or Web-page level.

> **TIP** **Initial Hardware Support for Developing a Web Site**
>
> Web sites can contain many Web pages and other types of files. Consequently, whereas you can develop a Web site on a CD, zip disk, or flash drive, if at all possible, always create a backup of your Web site on your computer's hard disk or an account on a server for developing a Web site. This way, if you lose the CD, zip disk, or flash drive, you can always continue your work using the backup copy.

> The CSS external style sheets offer you several significant advantages for building and customizing a Web site.

In Chapter 1, you were introduced to Cascading Style Sheets (CSSs) and to the SharePoint Designer tools that can assist you in controlling the positioning and formatting of your Web page elements by creating and applying CSS styles. (Appendix A also covers these topics in more depth.) The CSS external style sheets offer you several significant advantages for building and customizing a Web site:

- You can make changes across multiple pages simply by editing styles only in the external styles sheet.

- You save time and eliminate potential errors or style inconsistencies by making changes only in the external styles sheet.

- You reduce the size of your Web site by using only one file, including the external style sheet; therefore, you minimize the time needed to download your Web site.

To attach a new external style sheet to one or more pages included in a Web site, using SharePoint Designer, click the Apply Styles pane tab, click Attach Style to open the Attach Style Sheet dialog box, enter the path to the style sheet in the URL: box, or click the Browse button to display the Select Style Sheet dialog box and locate it, as shown in Figure 2.6. In the Attach to: section, click Current page or All HTML pages, depending on your design requirements. In the Attach as section, click Link if you wish to link the external style sheet using the <link> HTML tag, as shown in Figure 2.7, or click Import if you wish to link the external style sheet using the CSS @import directive. The @import directive allows developers to import style rules from other external style sheets. If you wish to remove a link to an external style sheet, click the Manage Styles task pane tab, right-click on the external style sheet you want to remove, and click Remove Link (see Figure 2.7).

Figure 2.6 Linking an External Style Sheet

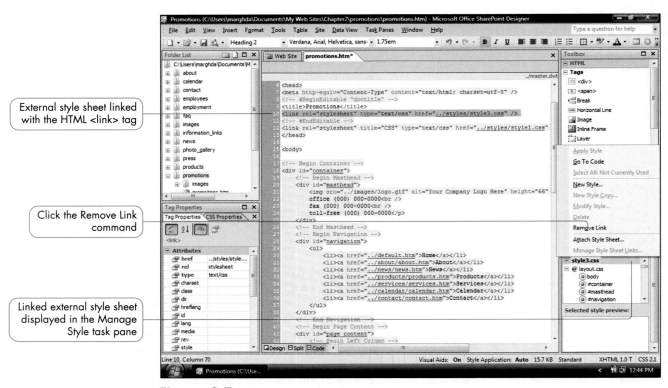

Figure 2.7 Removing a Link to an External Style Sheet

Callouts in figure:
- External style sheet linked with the HTML <link> tag
- Click the Remove Link command
- Linked external style sheet displayed in the Manage Style task pane

> When using a Dynamic Web Template to build and maintain your Web site pages, it is highly recommended that you link an external style sheet to the Dynamic Web Template instead of linking an external style sheet to each Web page.

When using a Dynamic Web Template to build and maintain your Web site pages, it is highly recommended that you link an external style sheet to the Dynamic Web Template instead of linking an external style sheet to each Web page. This way, the style sheet is automatically available to any Web page attached to the Dynamic Web Template. The procedure for attaching and removing an external style sheet to and from a Dynamic Web Template is identical to the procedure presented previously. When you save the Dynamic Web Template, a Microsoft Office SharePoint Designer box will be displayed inquiring if you would like to update all files attached to the Dynamic Web Template, as shown in Figure 2.8.

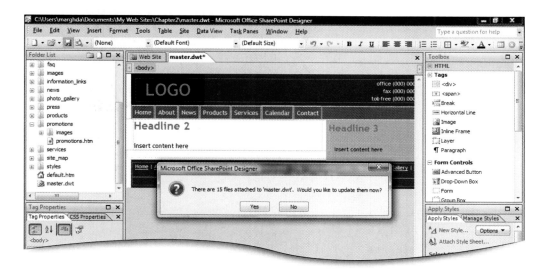

Figure 2.8 Attaching an External Style Sheet to a Dynamic Web Template

┌───┐

TIP   Accessible Web Pages Using CSS Styles

Some users have browsers that do not support style sheets, and some users turn off style sheets or need to apply their own custom style sheet. Therefore, develop Web pages that are comprehensible and usable without style sheets. Read Appendix B to learn more about this topic.

SharePoint Designer enables you to detach a Dynamic Web Template from a Web page or to attach a Dynamic Web Template to only one Web page or group of Web pages without affecting the formatting of the rest of the Web pages in the Web site. However, each additional Dynamic Web Template increases the size of your Web site and negatively affects the consistent appearance of the Web site. You should carefully weigh the advantages of personalizing a Web page against the disadvantages mentioned here.

Import a Web Page

> You might need to personalize an imported Web page because the default Dynamic Web Template and CSS styles of your Web site will not be automatically applied to the imported Web page.

Often, you might want to reuse an entire Web page you already created. You can import an existing Web page into your Web site using the Import dialog box available from the File menu. Click the File menu, point to Import, and click File to open the Import dialog box. Click the Add button to open the Add File to Import List dialog box and click the Web page you want to use. After you select the file you want, click OK twice to close both dialog boxes and return to the Web page. You might need to personalize the imported Web page because the default Dynamic Web Template and CSS styles of your Web site will not be automatically applied to the imported Web page.

TIP Importing a Web Page

To provide your users with access to a Web page not included in your Web site, you can import it directly into your Web site or create a link to that Web page, especially if you do not have the author's permission to add it to your Web site. If you wish to import a Web page with its attached external style sheet(s) or Dynamic Web template, you will need to import all related files. An imported Web page is not automatically added to the navigational structure of the Web site. Therefore, you will need to manually add it as previously explained in this chapter.

Delete a Web Page

After you delete a Web page, it is gone for good, so be certain that you do not need the Web page anymore before deleting it.

When you delete a Web page from a Web site, SharePoint Designer also deletes the related file. To delete a Web page, first click Folder List on the Task Panes menu to display the Folder List task pane if it is not already displayed. Next, right-click the file you want to delete and click Delete on the menu. The Undo command will not retrieve a deleted Web page, and the file related to the deleted Web page will not appear in the Recycle Bin folder. After you delete a Web page, it is gone for good, so be certain that you do not need the Web page anymore before deleting it.

TIP Delete a Web Page Using the Navigation View

To delete a Web page while viewing the Web site navigation structure, in Navigation view, right-click the Web page you want to delete and click Delete on the menu. On the Delete Page dialog box, click Remove page from the navigation structure if you do not want to physically delete the Web page and the related files, or click Delete this page from the Web site if you want to completely delete the Web page and the related files.

Work with Subsites

Web developers often need to group topic-related Web pages to make it easier for visitors to navigate.

A Web site that includes nested subsites is called the **root Web site**.

A Web site nested in another Web site is called a **subsite**.

Web developers often need to group topic-related Web pages to make it easier for visitors to navigate. This strategy also enables you to restrict user access to a group of pages, if necessary, or to apply an external style sheet other than a default external style sheet attached to all Web site pages. Consequently, the best option is to group the related pages into a new Web site within the overall Web site. A Web site nested in another Web site (called the **root Web site**) is called a **subsite**.

The first step in the process of creating a subsite is to create a new folder with a meaningful name. To create a new folder and rename it in Folders view, click the arrow to the right of the New button and click Folder. When the new folder displays in the Folder List task pane, type the new name in the edit box and press Enter.

The second step to creating a new subsite is to move Web pages into the newly created folder. To select more than one file in the Folders List or in Folders view, click the first page and hold down Ctrl while clicking the other pages. After the Web pages are selected, release Ctrl, drag the selected pages over the folder, and release the pages. You may also import Web pages from other Web sites to the new created folder.

After all the related pages are stored in a folder, you create the corresponding subsite by converting the folder into a subsite, as shown in Figure 2.9. A Microsoft Office SharePoint Designer dialog box will appear warning you about the changes that automatically will be made to the Web pages included in the folder that is converted to a subsite. When the conversion is finished, the folder is displayed with the world icon, indicating that it is stored as a Web site (see Figure 2.10).

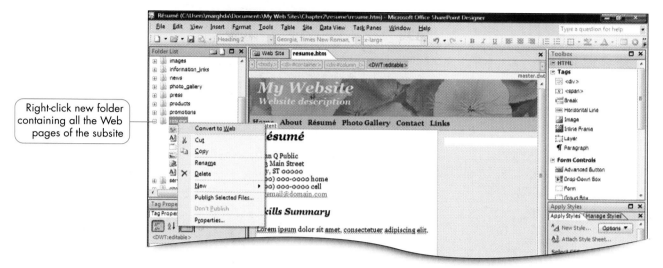

Right-click new folder containing all the Web pages of the subsite

Figure 2.9 Creating a Subsite from a Folder

New subsite

Figure 2.10 Newly Created Subsite in Folders List Pane

(When you convert a folder to a subsite, the new subsite has no navigation structure.)

To open a subsite from the Folder list, double-click the subsite folder. When you convert a folder to a subsite, the new subsite has no navigation structure. If a navigation structure is needed, you can manually create one for the subsite. The first step will be setting a home page, as shown in Figure 2.11. You can format all the pages of a subsite using an external style sheet and a Dynamic Web Template, which will not affect the root Web site, or you can individually format pages.

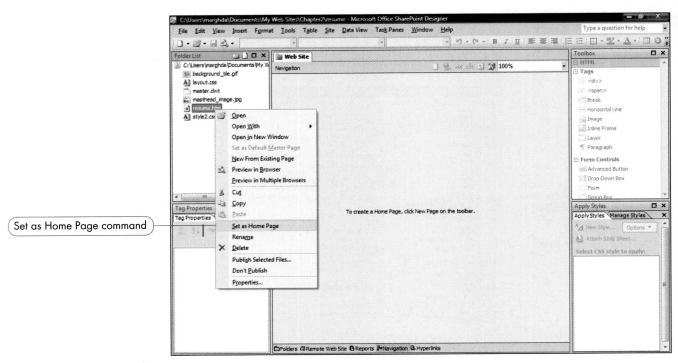

Figure 2.11 Navigation View of a Newly Created Subsite

Publishing SharePoint Designer 2007 Web Sites and Subsites

SharePoint Designer enables you to publish a Web site using the SharePoint Designer Remote Web Site view. You can publish an entire Web site, including all associated subsites, selected subsites, or individual Web pages, to a local or remote Web site.

Web sites published on a server are called *server-based Web sites*.

Web sites stored on your local computer are called *disk-based Web sites*.

A *local Web site* is the initial source Web site that is opened by developers in SharePoint Designer.

A *remote Web site* is the destination site to which you publish your Web site.

After a Web site is built, you need to publish it in order to run specific tests that can be accomplished only after the Web site is published on a Web server and to share it with the intended users. In Chapter 1, you were introduced to servers, Web servers, and publishing a Web site. Web sites published on a server are called *server-based Web sites*. So far you have been working with *disk-based Web sites* that are stored on your local computer hard disk drive.

SharePoint Designer enables you to publish a Web site using the SharePoint Designer Remote Web Site view. You can publish an entire Web site, including all associated subsites, selected subsites, or individual Web pages, to a local or remote Web site. A *local Web site* is the initial source Web site that is opened by developers in SharePoint Designer. It can be located on your computer or on a computer included in a local network. A *remote Web site* is the destination site to which you publish your Web site. It can be located on any of the following locations:

- A local computer.
- A remote computer that hosts your organization's Web server.
- Your organization's intranet server.

- An ISP server where you publish your Web site as a subscriber.
- A freehosting service provider's server that might or might not offer support for SharePoint Services, ASP.NET, or FrontPage Server Extensions.

TIP   Publishing a Web Site on a Remote Web Server

Before you actually publish your Web site on a remote Web server, you must decide which type of remote Web server to use. Although many types of servers are available, many of the more advanced SharePoint Designer features require your Web site to be published on a server that has FrontPage 2002 Server Extensions (there is no 2003 version of the Server Extensions), Microsoft SharePoint Services, or a Web-based Distributed Authoring and Versioning (WebDAV) server. In order to publish a Web site to a remote Web server, you need to have an account on that server with a user name and password for that account. This information can be obtained from your ISP or Web site administrator.

A server that has FrontPage Server Extensions will not be able to supply full functionality for SharePoint Designer Web sites. However, a server that has Microsoft SharePoint Services can supply the most comprehensive level of functionality for FrontPage Web sites. A server that has FrontPage Server Extensions or SharePoint Services enables Web developers to modify Web sites that are located at a remote site without having to publish them again. Among the features that work only with SharePoint Services are those related to the SharePoint Templates. Very useful information about when you can use Microsoft Office FrontPage 2003, Microsoft Windows SharePoint Services, or both to publish your Web site is available at the Microsoft Online Web site at http://office.microsoft.com/en-us/assistance/HA011462111033.aspx.

SharePoint Designer Remote Web Server Types | Reference

SharePoint Designer Remote Web Server Type	Description
Extended Web server running FrontPage Server Extensions from Microsoft or Microsoft SharePoint Services	HTTP servers storing files that have URLs beginning with "http://"
Web-based Distributed Authoring and Versioning (WebDAV) server	WebDAV is an application protocol for creating, editing, and publishing files on a Web server. It enables multiple authors of a Web site to change files and file properties simultaneously without overwriting each other's work. You will not be able to use some components that are supported by FrontPage Server Extensions on a Web site published on a WebDAV–based server.
File Transfer Protocol (FTP) server	FTP is one of the most popular communication protocols, enabling a user to transfer files between remote locations within a network. • Using FTP software application commands, such as listing, renaming, or deleting files and folders, Web developers can easily manage the files on a remote location. • Using an FTP software application outside SharePoint Designer to publish a SharePoint Designer Web site to a remote Web server supporting FrontPage Server Extensions or SharePoint Services can cause serious problems because it might transfer some SharePoint Designer system folders.
Disk-based file system	Remote Web Site view enables you to publish to a remote site, make a backup copy of your entire Web site, or copy selected files and folders by publishing directly to your local file system. This disk-based location can be a floppy disk, a zip disk, or a hard disk on your local machine or any other machine on a network that you can access.

TIP Additional Development Servers

When working on Windows systems, a SharePoint Designer developer can use two additional server types for publishing and testing a Web site: Microsoft ASP.NET Development Server (you learned about it in Chapter 1) and the Internet Information Services (IIS) Web server.

If you require Web server functionality on a desktop operating system, such as Windows XP and Windows Vista, you may consider using the Microsoft IIS Web server. IIS version 5.1 is packaged with Windows 2000, Windows XP Professional, and Windows XP Home Edition, which makes it possible for Web developers to host their own Web site on the Internet. Windows Vista did not ship with a user interface to configure logging into the IIS Server Manager; therefore, you will need to download IIS 7.0 on Windows Vista from the Microsoft Web site (http://www.iis.net/downloads/default.aspx?tabid=3). IIS includes Web and FTP server support and support for Microsoft FrontPage transactions and database connections. Before you can use IIS, you must install it on your hard drive separately after installing Windows on your computer. To learn more about IIS, Windows XP, and Windows Vista visit the Microsoft Internet Information Services Web site (http://www.iis.net/default.aspx).

After you decide which remote Web server type to use, you must select the desired remote Web server type and the remote Web site location. First click the Remote Web Site tab, and then click Remote Web Site Properties at the top of the document window to open the Remote Web site dialog box.

Select the type of Web server under Remote Web server type. Click the Browse button beside the Remote Web site location box to display the New Publish Location dialog box and choose the location of the remote Web site (shown in Figure 2.12), and then click Open. A SharePoint Designer alert message asks you to confirm that you want to create a new Remote Web site. Click OK, then click OK again to close the Remote Web Site Properties dialog box.

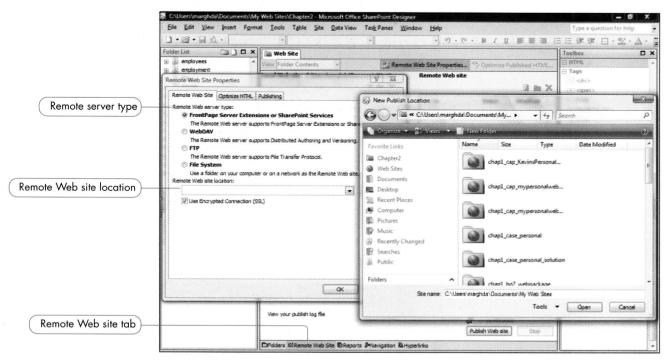

Figure 2.12 Using the Remote Web Site Properties Dialog Box to Create a Remote Web Site

After SharePoint Designer finishes creating the remote Web site, the Remote Web site view displays the Local Web site section and Remote Web site section side by side, as shown in Figure 2.13. Now you can easily publish the local Web site to the remote Web site or vice versa by selecting the Local to Remote or Remote to Local radio button and clicking the Publish Web site button (see Figure 2.13). You can also indicate that you do not want certain files to be published. To indicate the files that you do not want to publish, go to the Local Web site pane and right-click each file that you do not want published. When the shortcut menu appears, click Don't Publish.

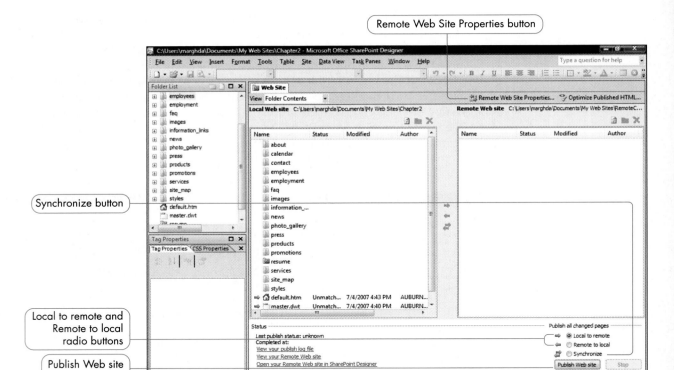

Remote Web Site Properties button

Synchronize button

Local to remote and Remote to local radio buttons

Publish Web site button

Figure 2.13 Remote Web Site View

TIP Publishing Location

After a remote site is created, each local Web site is published at the same remote location until you create another remote location.

TIP Web Components

If Webpages contain Web components that require FrontPage Server Extensions or SharePoint Services and you are publishing your Web site on a server that is not running the FrontPage Server Extensions or SharePoint Services, SharePoint Designer alerts you. You learn more about Web components later in this chapter.

To further customize the publishing process, you can use the Publishing tab of the Remote Web Site Properties dialog box. For example, if your Web site contains subsites that need to be published, make sure that the Includes subsites box is checked, as shown in Figure 2.14.

> When a Web site is developed by a team of people working from different computers or accounts on the same computer, Remote Web Site view can help synchronize the local and remote Web sites.

When a Web site is developed by a team of people working from different computers or from accounts on the same computer, Remote Web Site view can help synchronize the local and remote Web sites, as shown in Figure 2.13. If you click the Changed Pages Only option, you can use the Synchronize option. When you *synchronize* the two versions of a Web site, files are transferred between the two Web sites so that the contents of the Web sites are identical. When a file is not matched up between the two Web sites, SharePoint Designer copies the file from the Web site

You can **synchronize** the local and remote versions of a Web site by transferring files between the two Web sites so that their contents are identical.

The **Optimize HTML** tab of the Remote Web Site Properties dialog box enables you to select the HTML elements that you want to remove from the HTML code of your Web pages while they are being published.

containing the most recent version to the Web site including the out-of-date version. To synchronize the two Web sites, select the Synchronize radio button and click the Publish Web site button.

Using the **Optimize HTML** tab of the Remote Web Site Properties dialog box, you can select the HTML elements that you want to remove from the HTML code of your Web pages while they are being published. The elements that you are allowed to remove using the Optimize HTML tab include, but are not limited to, selective HTML comments, all HTML comments, HTML leading spaces, or HTML white spaces.

Figure 2.14 Publishing Tab of the Remote Web Site Properties Dialog Box

Testing and Validating a Web Site

> The process of testing and validating a Web site is as important as the design and development.

The process of testing and validating a Web site is as important as the design and development. If a Web site does not display and function properly, it can cause more hassles for the Web authors and users than it is worth. As previously discussed in Chapter 1, using the Reports and Hyperlinks views, Web authors can accurately access technical, graphical, and statistical information that they can use to validate, update, and upgrade a Web site.

The process of correcting, updating, and upgrading your Web pages based on the feedback provided by testing and validating tools can be time consuming and annoying if you need to locate the Web page elements that need to be changed manually. The SharePoint Designer Find and Replace feature can assist you in finding and replacing text and in using expressions or HTML rules and tags.

Use Reports View

> Web developers can use SharePoint Designer Reports view to access a comprehensive set of site reports. These reports offer a great way to test and validate a Web site.

Web developers can use SharePoint Designer Reports view to access a comprehensive set of site reports. These reports offer a great way to test and validate a Web site. Click the Reports tab at the bottom of the window, and then select the Site Summary tab at the top of the workspace.

All the SharePoint Designer reports are organized in six categories that can be selected from the Site Summary drop-down menu, shown in Figure 2.15. You can sort all the Site Summary reports by clicking the individual column headers.

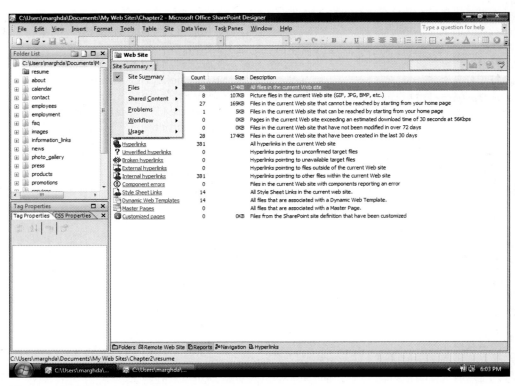

Figure 2.15 Reports View

The **Site Summary** category of reports contains comprehensive overview information about all the Web site's statistics.

Unlinked files are files that cannot be reached by starting from the Web site's homepage.

Slow pages might need more than 30 seconds to be downloaded at a speed of 56 Kbps.

Older files are files that have not been updated within 72 days.

Broken hyperlinks target unavailable files.

1. **Site Summary**—The *Site Summary* set of reports contains comprehensive overview information about all the Web site's statistics, including, but not limited to, the total number and size of the picture files, any *unlinked files* (files that cannot be reached by starting from the Web site's homepage), any *slow pages* (pages that might need more than 30 seconds to be downloaded at a speed of 56 Kbps), any *older files* (files that have not been updated within 72 days), and any *broken hyperlinks* (links targeting unavailable files). The Site Summary category is also the default view that appears when you switch to Reports view. The Name column lists the various Web site elements, such as pictures, linked files, all files, and unlinked files. The Count column displays the number of the items or problems found in the Web site. The Size column indicates the size of the files or other items that were counted. The Description column includes a brief description of the items or reports listed in the Name column.

2. **Files**—The Files report category provides comprehensive information about all files, recently added files, recently changed files, and older files included in the Web site. FrontPage enables you to change the report settings, such as the number of days that SharePoint Designer should consider when preparing these reports.

3. **Shared Content**—The Shared Content report category provides information about Dynamic Web Templates, Master Pages, Customized Pages, and Style Sheet Links.

4. **Problems**—The Problems report category provides information about the different types of problems that can exist in your Web site, such as files included in a Web site that are not linked to any Web page, or Slow Pages (Web pages that take more than 30 seconds to be loaded).

5. **Workflow**—The Workflow report category provides information about the status of the Web site's files (such as publish and review status).

6. **Usage**—The Usage report category includes statistics related to the way your Web site is being accessed on the Internet, such as the browsers and operating systems that your visitors are using. For the usage reports to work, the site must be published to a server that supports Microsoft Windows SharePoint Services 3.0 or a Microsoft Office SharePoint Server 2007. To learn more about the Usage report, see Microsoft Office Online's "View the Usage Summary report" (http://office.microsoft.com/en-us/sharepointdesigner/HA101741361033.aspx?pid=CH100667731033#6).

You can customize the list of files corresponding to each report. For example, to create a custom list in the All Files report, click the drop-down arrow beside one of the All Files report headings (see Figure 2.16), then click (Custom . . .) to open the Custom AutoFilter dialog box (shown in Figure 2.16) and generate the desired filter. If you right-click the generated filtered report, you can choose to arrange and copy it or remove filters.

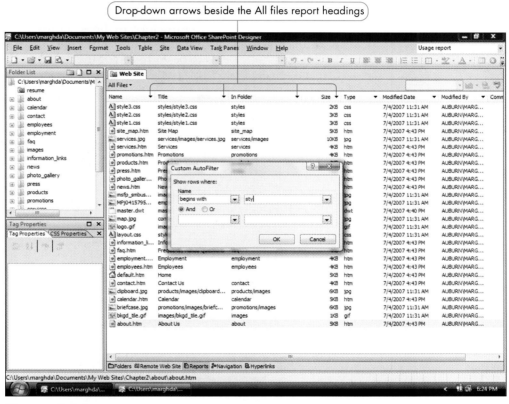

Figure 2.16 Using the Custom AutoFilter Dialog Box

The following reports are the most useful:

- **All Files**—This report enables you to view and sort all the files on your Web site.

- **Unlinked**—This report shows the files on your Web site that visitors cannot access from your home page. These are files the visitors cannot access without knowing the correct URL.

- **Slow Pages**—This report indicates the pages that load slowly in a browser. Slow-loading pages can cause users to get bored and go to other Web sites. The delays could indicate a programming error or large graphics files. When you are working in Page view, you can check the estimated loading time of your Web pages. The loading time based on the speed of your Internet connection is displayed on the right side of the status bar.

- **Older files**—This report indicates files that have not been updated recently. Stale, outdated information can turn off visitors.
- **Broken hyperlinks**—This report provides a list of broken links. When you access this report, you are prompted to let SharePoint Designer test your hyperlinks. When you click Yes, SharePoint Designer generates a full report of any internal and external broken links. When SharePoint Designer checks your links, it errs on the side of caution. Consequently, it almost always indicates more errors than there really are. Because of this, many SharePoint Designer users tend to avoid this report. However, when you are working with a large site, it is always better to check your links than to risk leaving broken links on your site.

Use Hyperlinks View

Hyperlinks view provides a graphical layout of all the hyperlinks included in a Web site.

Hyperlinks view, which helps you test and validate all hyperlinks included in a Web site, is another great tool offered by SharePoint Designer. *Hyperlinks view* provides a graphical layout of all the hyperlinks included in a Web site. Figure 2.17 shows the Hyperlinks view of a Web site with the default.htm home page placed in the middle, links from other pages to the left, links to other pages to the right, a link to an e-mail address, links to pictures, a link to a Dynamic Web Template, and a broken hyperlink. Hyperlinks are represented by lines ending with an arrow. A broken line, such as the line to calendar/calendar.htm, indicates a broken hyperlink, which means that the hyperlink needs to be corrected or the link was made to a page that has not been created yet.

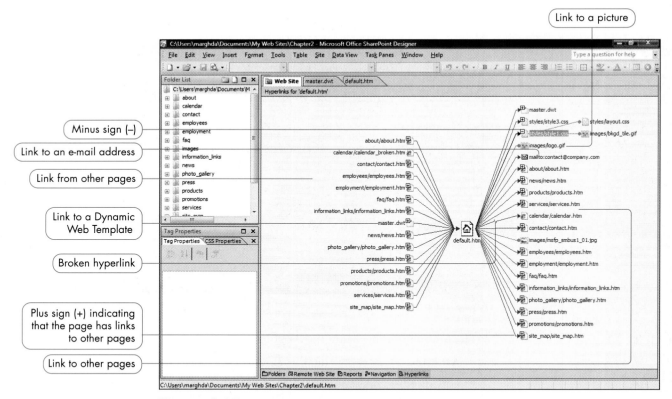

Figure 2.17 Hyperlinks and Extended Hyperlinks Views

A fully developed Web site can include several Web pages, and each Web page might include several hyperlinks. The following features empower Web designers to view, test, and validate a Web site's hyperlinks by collapsing or displaying all links included in a Web page and targeting other Web pages. A plus sign (+) next to a link indicates that the page has links to other pages. If you click the plus sign for a specific Web page, the plus sign is replaced by a minus sign (–) and SharePoint Designer displays all pages linked to that page (see Figure 2.17). To collapse the hyperlinks and display only the linked page, click the minus sign.

TIP Accessibility Guidelines for Hyperlinks

Because text is more usable and accessible than images, to maximize the universal usability of your Web pages, links should be built as text. Also, the text used for links should be as descriptive as possible; hence, they should provide a concise and clear description of the Web page targeted by a link.

Use the Find and Replace Feature

Resolving the issues discovered in the testing and validating process of a Web site can become a complicated task. SharePoint Designer has simplified this task by providing a much improved Find and Replace feature that enables designers to find and replace text using expressions or HTML code.

The ***Find and Replace*** feature enables designers to find and replace text using expressions or HTML code.

Resolving the issues discovered in the testing and validating process of a Web site can become a complicated task. SharePoint Designer has simplified this task by providing a much-improved *Find and Replace* feature that enables designers to find and replace text using expressions or HTML code (see Figure 2.18). The Find and Replace feature includes an HTML rules feature, and you can also search for specific HTML tags, change them, remove them, or add attributes to them (see Figure 2.19). Click Find on the Edit menu to start the Find and Replace feature. To access the HTML rules dialog box (see Figure 2.19), click the HTML tab, click an HTML tag from the Find tag drop-down list, and then click the HTML Rules button to open the HTML Rules dialog box.

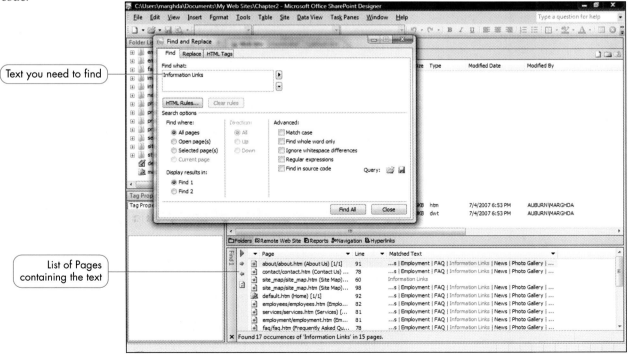

Text you need to find

List of Pages containing the text

Figure 2.18 Find Tab of the Find and Replace Dialog Box

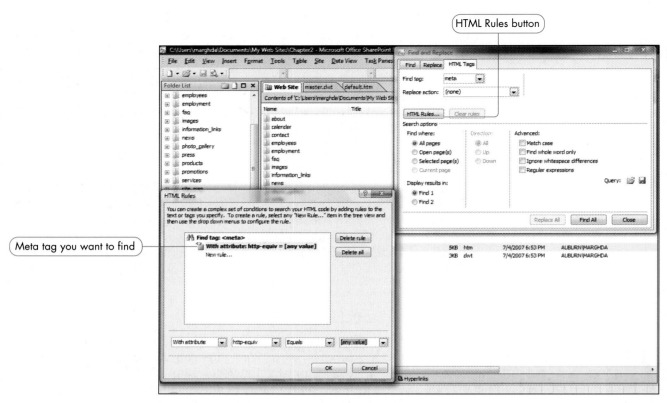

Figure 2.19 Finding an HTML Tag with Rules

To find and replace text, click Replace on the Edit menu to open the Find and Replace dialog box. In the Find what: box, type the text you need to find; type the text you want to replace it with in the Replace with: box. Specify whether to search all pages or selected pages, and click the Find All button (see Figure 2.20) to display a list of pages that include the Find text in the Matched Text column. If you want to find text that appears in the source code, check the Find in Source Code checkbox (see Figure 2.20).

If you decide to replace text in all listed files, right-click any line on the Find and Replace report, then click Find and Replace on the menu to display the Find and Replace dialog box. Click the Find 2 button in order to display the results in a new Find 2 tab (see Figure 2.20). Click All pages (if it is not already selected) and then click the Replace All button. Click Yes on the SharePoint Designer alert box indicating that you will not be able to undo this replace operation. SharePoint Designer enables you to save Find and Replace queries as XML files with an .fpq extension. Click the Save query icon, shown in Figure 2.20, on the Replace tab to save the query for future use. These queries can be opened and used for any other Web site by clicking the Open Query icon on the Find and Replace dialog box.

TIP   Saving and Opening Find and Replace Queries

In Windows XP and Windows Vista, all SharePoint Designer queries are saved, by default, in the C:\Documents and Settings\<user>\Application data\Microsoft\ SharePoint Designer\Queries folder. To enable any other SharePoint Designer user to use one of your saved queries, copy the corresponding .fpq file to the other user's computer in the default folder. The query can then be opened by clicking the Open Query icon on the Find and Replace dialog box (see Figure 2.20).

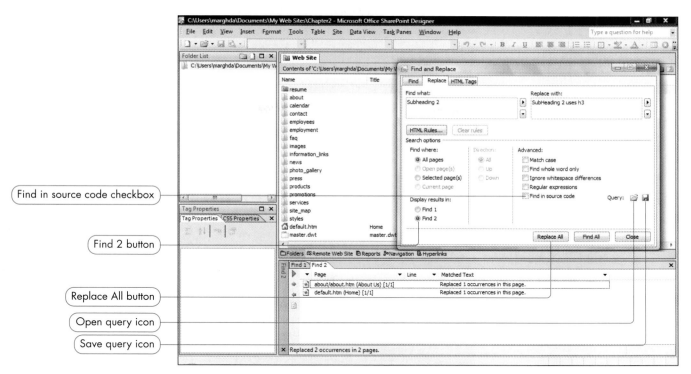

Find in source code checkbox

Find 2 button

Replace All button

Open query icon

Save query icon

Figure 2.20 Working with the Find and Replace Report

The new Find and Replace report is displayed in the Find 2 tab, as shown in Figure 2.20. If you do not want to replace text in all Web pages listed in the Find and Replace report, right-click each item of this report and click Go to Page to open the related page with the found text highlighted. Click the Next Result button to open the next Web page on the report.

Publishing Changes to a Web Site

When only changed Web pages need to be published, SharePoint Designer enables you to synchronize the files on the local and remote Web sites. Alternatively, you can select one of the two available options listed under the Changes section on the Publishing tab of the Remote Web Site Properties dialog box for determining which files have changed since the last time you published.

Designing and developing a Web site can be a never-ending process. Web designers are constantly making improvements and updating the content of their Web pages. When making changes to a Web site, designers can choose to republish only the Web pages that have changed since the last publishing or to republish the entire Web site.

When only changed Web pages need to be published, SharePoint Designer enables you to synchronize the files on the local and remote Web site. Alternatively, you can select one of the two available options listed under the Changes section on the Publishing tab of the Remote Web Site Properties dialog box for determining which files have changed since the last time you published. The Determine changes by comparing source and destination sites option uses SharePoint Designer data records, whereas the Use source file timestamps to determine changes since last publish option compares the time stamps of the files on the local site against those on the remote sites.

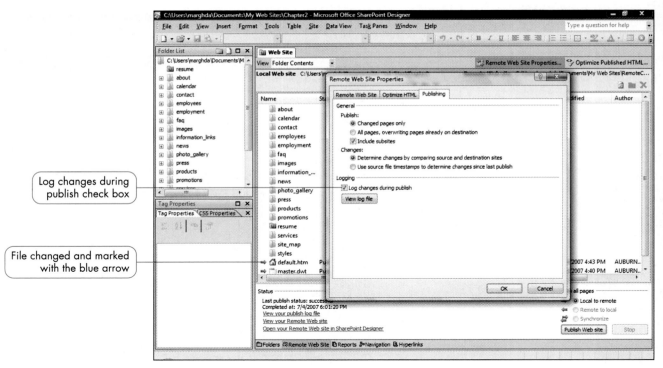

Figure 2.21 Setting the Publishing Properties

If you select the Log changes during publish check box option in the Logging area of the Remote Web Site Properties dialog box (shown in Figure 2.21), SharePoint Designer saves all actions that take place in the publishing process, such as starting and ending the publishing process, creating folders, creating subsites, copying files, and canceling the publishing process. You can view the Publish Log in your Web browser by clicking the View your publish log command in the Status section of the Remote Web site view, and you can save and print the Publish Log while it is open in the Web browser. You can choose to view only selective types of information stored in the log file by using the Show only drop-down list of the Publish Log File command.

After you complete the changes to your Web site, you can publish the changes by clicking the Remote Web Site View tab; then click the Remote Web Site Properties tab to open the Remote Web Site Properties dialog box. Select the appropriate options on the Publishing tab, as shown in Figure 2.21. Select the Log changes during publish check box to record all the changes published in the log file. Click OK to close the Remote Web Site Properties dialog box, and then click the Publish Web site button to publish the changes made to the local Web site. To view the record of your changes, click the View your publish log file link in the Status area (see Figure 2.21). SharePoint Designer displays an alert box if you choose to publish a local Web site without first saving all its Web pages.

Web developers often need to control who can make changes to their Web sites and subsites. They can control this by setting access permissions for such functions, adding and removing users, and changing users' roles. After a Web site is published on a server running, for example, Microsoft FrontPage Server Extensions or Microsoft SharePoint Services, you can use the Administration command on the Site menu to handle these types of requirements. If a Web site is published on a server supporting the FrontPage Server Extensions, on the Site menu point to Administration, and then click Permissions to open the Permissions Web page, as shown in Figure 2.22.

TIP **SharePoint Services 3.0 and SharePoint Server 2007 Site Settings Web site**

If a Web site is published on a server supporting SharePoint Services 3.0 or on a SharePoint Server 2007, on the Site Menu point to Administration Home to open the Site Settings Web site and use the commands under the User and Permissions column.

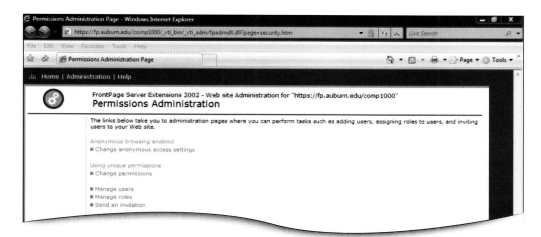

Figure 2.22 SharePoint Designer Permissions Administration Page

TIP **Using Subsites at Administrator Level**

An administrator might need to set unique permissions for a Web site when creating subsites that require different security permissions than the parent Web site does. For example, if a university has a FrontPage server, each major department can have a subsite (also called subweb). The main home page on the parent Web site can provide links between the departmental sites. As you already learned, sub-webs appear below their root Web sites in the Web server's file system. However, depending on the administrator's decision, an author of a Web site does not automatically have permission to edit any of its subwebs, or a user might not be able to browse to a subweb from a parent Web site.

SharePoint Designer Permission
Administration Page | Reference

Permissions Administration Page	Options	Functionalities
Change Anonymous Access Settings		The On and Off radio buttons enable or disable anonymous users from accessing your Web site. Anonymous users do not have an account and usually their access rights are more limited than those of users with accounts.
Change Subweb Permissions		On the Change Subweb Permissions page, you can change the security permissions to your Web site. In the Permissions section of the page, you can select Use same permissions as parent Web site or Use unique permissions for this Web site.
Manage Users	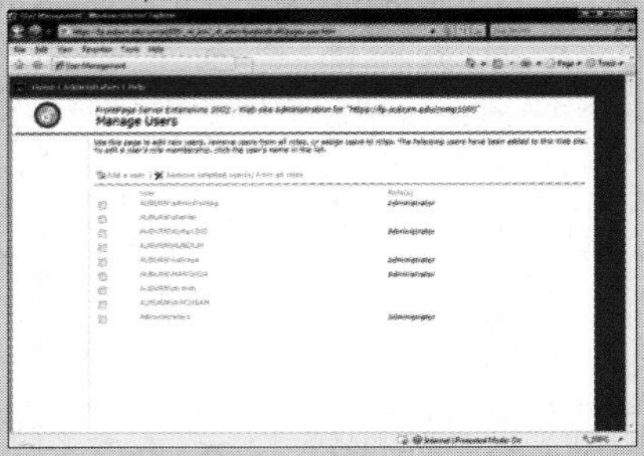 Figure 2.23 Manage Users Page	Using the Manage Users page you can add and remove users. You can also change an existing user's role, as shown Figure 2.23. The user role refers to types of access the user has to all Web pages, files, and folders included on the Web site. For example, a browser user can only view pages and documents, whereas an Administrator user can add, delete, and modify any pages and documents included.
Manage Roles	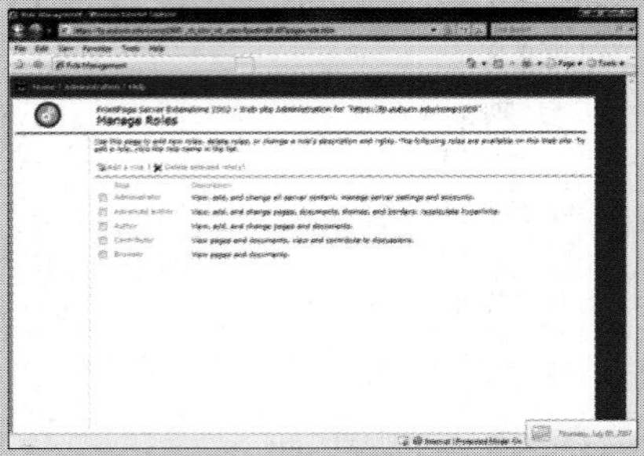 Figure 2.24 Manage Roles Page	On the Manage Roles page, shown in Figure 2.24, you can add new roles, delete roles, or change the description and permissions of an existing role.

TIP — Contributor Settings

SharePoint Designer enables administrators of Web sites published on Web servers supporting SharePoint Services 3.0 or on a Microsoft SharePoint Server 2007 to use the Contributor Settings dialog box. Using the Contributor Settings dialog box, administrators can configure and enable Contributor mode, which is a limited access mode in Microsoft Office SharePoint Designer 2007. Developers who open a Web site for editing in SharePoint Designer 2007 have access to different commands or features depending on which Contributor group they belong to and what editing restrictions have been assigned to that Contributor group. Contributor mode is enabled by default. There is no required setup for the Web site administrator; however, only a Web site administrator can turn Contributor mode on or off. Contributor Settings are applied at the Web site level, and the settings cannot be inherited from a parent site by any subsites. To learn more about Contributor Settings, using the SharePoint Designer Help box, do a search for Contributor Settings.

Hands-On Exercises

1 | Build, Customize, Publish, Test, and Validate a Web Site with Subsites

Skills covered: 1. Start SharePoint Designer, Create a One Page Web Site, and Create Two New Folders. **2.** Import .css and .gif Files, Import a Dynamic Web Template, Attach a Dynamic Web Template to a Web Page, and Open a Dynamic Web Template **3.** Create a Subsite and Modify the Navigation Layout of a Web Site **4.** Publish a Web Site with Subsites **5.** Test and Validate a Web Site with Subsites **6.** Publish Changes to a Web Site

Step 1	Refer to Figure 2.25 as you complete Step 1.

Step 1
Start SharePoint Designer, Create a One-Page Web Site, and Create Two New Folders

Refer to Figure 2.25 as you complete Step 1.

a. Start SharePoint Designer.

You should see the SharePoint Designer default workspace.

b. Point to **New** on the File menu and click **Web site** on the menu.

The Web site tab of the New dialog box should be now be displayed.

c. Click **One Page Web Site** and click **Browse**.

The New Web site Location dialog box should appear.

d. Select the appropriate drive and folder and click **Open** to close the New Web site Location dialog box.

The location of the new Web site now should be displayed in the Specify the location of the new Web site box of the New dialog box.

e. Click at the end of the location in the **Specify the location of the new Web site box** and type **chap2_ho1_solution** to name your Web site folder and click **OK**.

You should see the *chap2_ho1_solution* file in Folders view.

TROUBLESHOOTING: You need to be specific about where you save your Web site. Otherwise, you could have difficulty finding it again.

f. Point to **New** on the File menu and click **Folder** on the menu. Rename the new folder **styles** and press **Enter**.

The styles folder should appear now in Folders view and the Folder List pane.

g. Click the top file location in the **Folder List pane**, point to **New** on the File menu, and click **Folder**. Rename the new folder **images** and press **Enter**.

The images folder should appear now in Folders view and the Folder List pane.

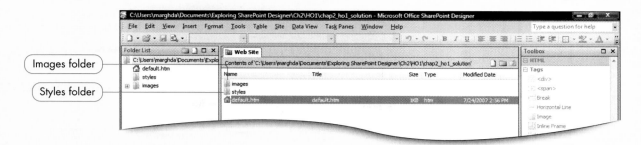

Images folder

Styles folder

Figure 2.25 Create a New Web Site

Step 2

Import .css and .gif Files, Import a Dynamic Web Template, Attach a Dynamic Web Template to a Web Page, and Open a Dynamic Web Template

Refer to Figure 2.26 as you complete Step 2.

a. Double-click the **images folder** in the Folder List pane, point to **Import** on the File menu, and click **File**. Click **Add File** in the Import dialog box and navigate to the chap2_ho1_data folder. Double-click the **chap2_ho1_data folder**, double-click the **images folder**, press and hold **Ctrl**, and click the three **.gif graphic files**. Click **Open** on the Add File to Import List dialog box and click **OK** to close the Import dialog box.

The three .gif graphic files should appear in the Contents of the images window.

b. Double-click the **styles folder** in the Folder List pane, point to **Import** on the File menu, and click **File**. Click **Add File** in the Import dialog box and navigate to the chap2_ho1_data folder located in the Student Data Files folder. Double-click the **chap2_ho1_data folder**, double-click the **styles folder**, press and hold **Ctrl**, and click the four **.css style sheet files**. Click **Open** on the Add File to Import List dialog box, and then click **OK** to close the Import dialog box.

The four .css style sheet files should appear in the Contents of the styles window.

c. Click **default.htm** in the Folder List pane, point to **Import** on the File menu, and click **File**. Click **Add File** in the Import dialog box and navigate to the chap2_ho1_data folder. Click **master.dwt**, click **Open** on the Add File to Import List dialog box, and click **OK** to close the Import dialog box.

The master.dwt file should appear in the Contents window and the Folder List task pane.

d. Double-click **default.htm** in the Folder List pane to open the home page in Design view. Click **Format** on the Menu bar, point to **Dynamic Web Template**, and click **Attach Dynamic Web Template**.

The Attach Dynamic Web Template dialog box should be displayed.

e. Click **master.dwt** and click **Open** to close the Attach Dynamic Web Template dialog box. Click **Close** on the SharePoint Designer alert box. Click the **Save button** on the Common toolbar to save *default.htm*.

TROUBLESHOOTING: Click Yes on the SharePoint Designer alert box asking if you want to continue with the attachment and Close on the SharePoint Designer alert box indicating that (1 of 1) files was updated.

The customized *default.htm* file is now displayed in Design view and the style1.css "screen" should show in the Apply Styles task pane.

TROUBLESHOOTING: Click the Apply Styles tab if not already showing.

f. Click **Format** on the Menu bar, point to **Dynamic Web Template**, and click **Open Attached Dynamic Web Template**.

The *master.dwt* file is now displayed in Design view and the style1.css "screen" should show in the Apply Styles task pane.

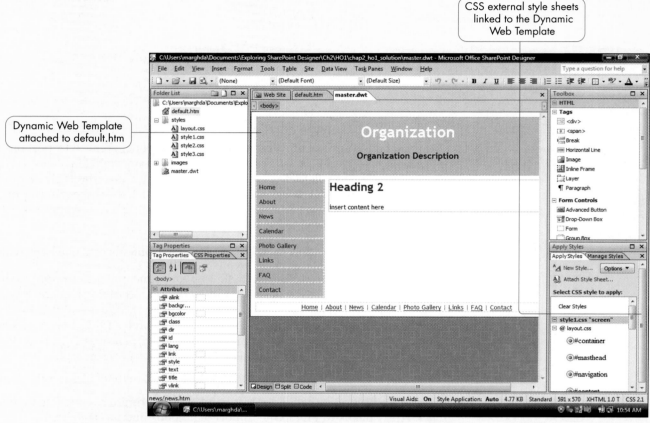

Figure 2.26 Create and Customize a Web Site Using External Style Sheets and Dynamic Web Templates

---

Step 3
Create a Subsite and Modify the Navigation Layout of a Web Site

Refer to Figure 2.27 as you complete Step 3.

a. Click the **Web Site tab**, click **File** on the Menu bar, point to **New**, and click **Folder**. Rename the new folder **about** and press **Enter**.

The about folder should appear now in Folders view and the Folder List task pane.

b. Double-click the **about folder** in the Folder List pane, point to the **Import on File menu**, and click **File**. Click **Add File** in the Import dialog box and navigate to the chap2_ho1_data folder. Double-click the **chap2_ho1_data folder** (if you are not already in this folder), click **about.htm**, click **Open** in the Add File to Import List dialog box, and click **OK** to close the Import dialog box.

The *about.htm* file should appear in the Contents of the about window.

c. Point to the **about folder** in the Folder List pane, right-click, and click **Convert to Web**.

TROUBLESHOOTING: Click Yes on the Microsoft Office SharePoint Designer alert box.

The about subsite folder should be displayed in the Folder List task pane.

d. Click the **Web Site tab** (if it is not already selected) and click the **Navigation button**.

The Navigation view of the Web site should be displayed showing only the default.htm Web page.

e. Click **master.dwt** in the Folder List task pane, drag it below the *default.htm* file, and then drop it.

The master.dwt Dynamic Web Template shows that it is now added to the Web site navigation structure.

f. Click **default.htm** in Navigation view, click the **Add Existing Page button** (see Figure 2.27), double-click the **about subweb**, click **about.htm**, and click **OK** to close the Insert Hyperlink dialog box.

The about.htm Web page shows that it is now added to the Web site navigation structure.

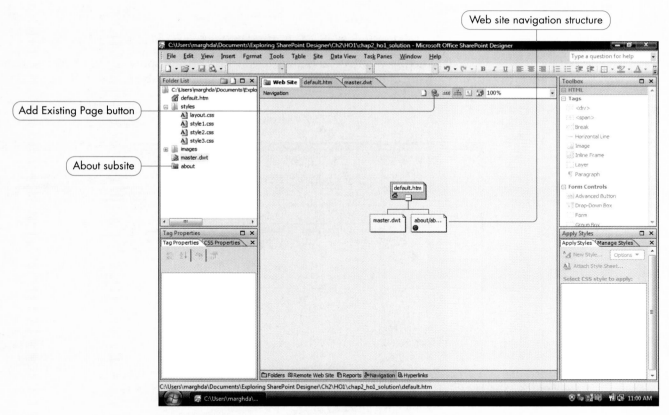

Figure 2.27 Navigation Layout of a Web Site with Subsites

Refer to Figure 2.28 as you complete Step 4.

a. Click the **Web Site tab** (if it is not already selected), click the **Remote Web Site button**, and click the **Remote Web site Properties button**.

The Remote Web Site Properties dialog box should appear.

b. Click **File System** and click **Browse**.

The New Publish Location dialog box should appear.

c. Select the appropriate drive and folder and click **Open** to close the New Publish Location dialog box.

The selected location should now be highlighted in the Remote Web site location: box of the Remote Web Site Properties dialog box.

d. Add **\chap2_ho1_solution_remote** to the end of the path name displayed in the remote Web site location dialog box. Click the **Publishing tab** and, in the *Publish:* section, click **All pages, overwriting pages already on destination sites**, then click the **Includes subsites** check box. Click **OK** to close the Remote Web Site Properties dialog box.

TROUBLESHOOTING: Click Yes in the Microsoft Office SharePoint Designer alert box asking you if you want to create a Web site.

The Local Web site and Remote Web site panes are now displayed.

e. Click the **Publish Web site button**, in the *Publish all pages* section.

All the files, folders, and subsites of the Web site show now in both the Remote Web site and Local Web site pane of the Remote Web Site view.

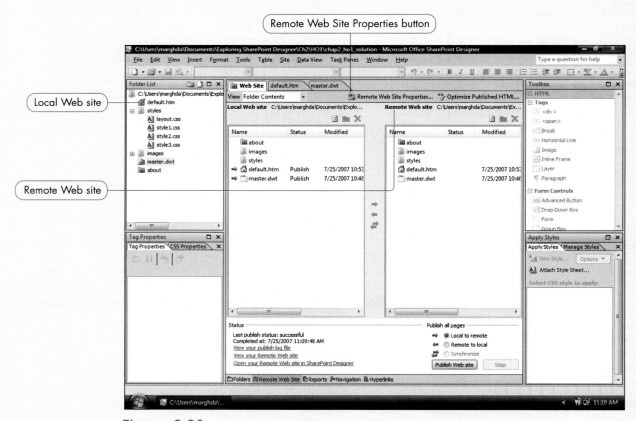

Figure 2.28 Remote Web Site View of a Web Site with Subsites

Refer to Figure 2.29 as you complete Step 5.

a. Click the **default.htm tab** to open default.htm in Design view.

b. Click the **Web Site tab** and click the **Hyperlinks button**.

The Hyperlinks view of the Web site should now be displayed, including a few broken links.

TROUBLESHOOTING: Click View on the Menu bar, then click Refresh if the Hyperlinks view of the Web site including a few broken links is not displayed.

c. Click the **Folders button**, click **File** on the Menu bar, point to **New**, and click **Folder** on the menu. Rename the new folder **news** and press **Enter**.

The news folder should appear now in Folders view and in the Folder List task pane.

d. Double-click the **news folder** in the Folder List task pane, point to **Import** on the File menu, and click **File**. Click **Add File** in the Import dialog box and navigate to the chap2_ho1_data folder. Double-click the **chap2_ho1_data folder**, click **news.htm**, click **Open** in the Add File to Import List dialog box, and click **OK** to close the Import dialog box.

e. Click **default.htm** in the Folder List task pane and click the **Hyperlinks button**.

TROUBLESHOOTING: Click default.htm in the Folder List task pane if you see a message asking you to do this.

The Hyperlinks view of the Web site should now be displayed, and the link to *news/news.htm* no longer shows as broken.

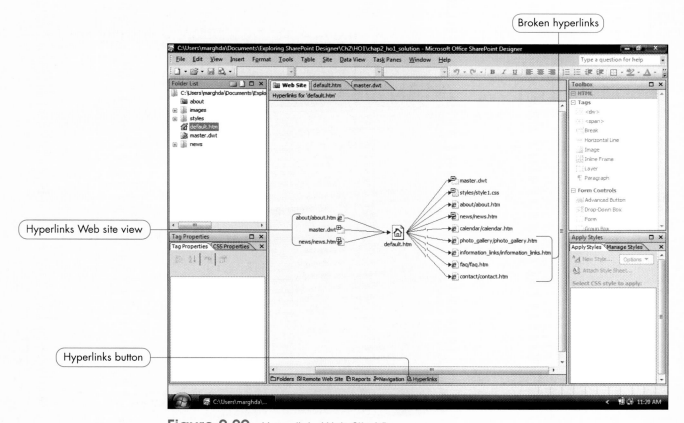

Figure 2.29 Hyperlinks Web Site View

Step 6
Publish Changes to a Web Site

Refer to Figure 2.30 as you complete Step 6.

a. Click **Remote Web Site**, click **Remote Web site Properties**, and click the **Publishing tab**.

The Publishing tab of the Remote Web Site Properties is displayed.

b. Click **Changed pages only** in the *Publish:* section and click **OK**.

c. Click **Publish Web site** in the *Publish all changed pages* section.

d. Click **Open your Remote Web site in SharePoint Designer** in the *Status* section.

The Folders view of the chap2_ho1_solution_remote Web site is now displayed in a new SharePoint Designer window.

e. Click **default.htm** in the Folder List task pane and click **Hyperlinks**.

TROUBLESHOOTING: If the hyperlink to about/about.htm shows as broken, click Site on the Menu bar and click Recalculate Hyperlinks.

The Hyperlinks view of the chap2_ho1_solution_remote Web site should now be displayed and the link to *news/news.htm* no longer shows as broken.

f. Click **File** on the Menu bar and click **Close Site**. Click **File** on the Menu bar and click **Exit** to close the SharePoint Designer window.

The SharePoint Designer window displaying the chap2_ho1_solution_remote Web site should no longer be showing on your screen.

g. Click the **SharePoint Designer tab** on the Windows taskbar, click **File** on the Menu bar, and click **Close Site**. Click **File** on the Menu bar and click **Exit** to close the SharePoint Designer window.

The SharePoint Designer window displaying the chap2_ho1_solution Web site should no longer be showing on your screen.

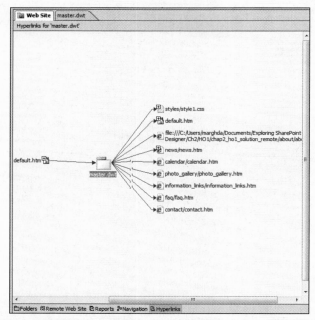

Figure 2.30 Hyperlinks Web Site View of the Remote Web Site

Introduction to Web Page Design and Development

Developing a Web page that makes a positive impact on users and thoroughly communicates your message requires you to come up with appropriate content, suitable two-dimensional design or layout, and appropriate use of multimedia. You also need an understanding of the technical issues related to the Internet and the ways a browser displays information.

In Chapter 1, you were introduced to basic Web page concepts, the basic Web Page elements and the requirements of a good Web page design. You also learned about the SharePoint Designer tools for designing, creating, testing, and validating standard Web pages.

In this section, you will further enrich your knowledge and skills in designing and building a Web page using hyperlinks, tables, and lists, and in enhancing a Web page using graphics, multimedia, and SharePoint Designer Web components.

Designing a Web Page

> It is always wise to take time and think about what you want to do and how you can accomplish it. There is no substitute for planning in the design of a Web page.

It is always wise to take time and think about what you want to do and how you can accomplish it. There is no substitute for planning in the design of a Web page. Here are the major points to consider when designing a Web page:

- Develop a clear statement of purpose for the Web page.
- Identify your audience.
- Identify the material and Web page elements you will use to accomplish your purpose. Focus on the content and the major topics you will provide on the Web page and think about the Web page elements you will use to organize the content.
- Establish the layout style of the Web page.
- Establish the formatting style of the Web page.
- Create a simple navigational layout chart similar to the one shown in Figure 2.2.
- Create a clear design sketch that includes, as much as possible, details about the Web page layout and formatting style, as shown in Figure 2.31.

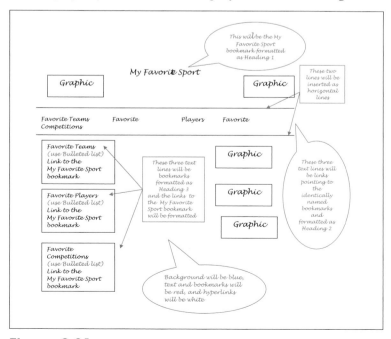

Figure 2.31 Sketch of a Web Page Design

Building a Web Page

If your Web site contains Web components, such as page banners, link bars based on navigation structure, or back and next links, your new Web pages should be added in Navigation view.

SharePoint Designer enables you to quickly and easily add new Web pages to an existing Web site in Page view, Folders view, and Navigation view. In Chapter 1, you became acquainted with how to add a Web page in Page view. The process is identical in Folders view, and earlier in this chapter you learned how to add an existing Web page to a Web site in Navigation view.

If your Web site contains Web components, such as page banners, link bars based on navigation structure, or back and next links, your new Web pages should be added in Navigation view. This enables SharePoint Designer to update these Web components and the navigational structure of the site displayed in Navigation view.

Add a New Web Page to an Existing Web Site

You can add a new Web page to an existing Web site using the Navigation View. Click the Navigation button at the bottom of the workspace to display the navigational structure of your Web site. Right-click the parent Web page of the new Web page, point to New, and then click Page, as shown in Figure 2.32.

A new Web page is added to Navigation view. To see it in the Folder list, switch to Folders view. If the Folder List pane was displayed when you added a new Web page, click View on the Menu bar and click Refresh, as shown in Figure 2.32. The new page appears in the Folder List pane.

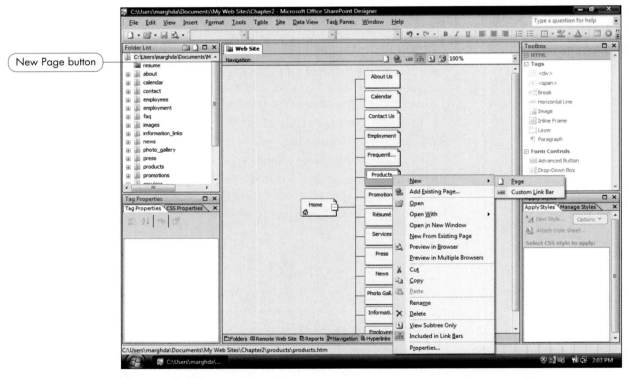

Figure 2.32 Adding a New Web Page to an Existing Web Site in Navigation View

---

TIP Add a New Web Page Using the New Page Button

You can use the New Page button, shown in Figure 2.32, to add a new page to the Web site's navigational structure at the same level as the home page. The new Top Page 1 will be unattached to any of the existing pages. To see the new Top Page 1 in the Folder List as well, click Refresh on the View menu.

Rename a Web Page

(Web page names need to be meaningful and descriptive, clearly suggesting the content of the Web page.)

When a new Web page is created, SharePoint Designer gives it the default title Untitled 1, which corresponds to its default file name untitled_1.htm.

Although Web page names might not seem important for a Web site of only three or four pages, names become crucial when you start adding more Web pages. Web page names need to be meaningful and descriptive, clearly suggesting the content of the Web page. If you add a Web page to the Web site navigation structure before renaming it, SharePoint Designer automatically updates all the references to the Web page when you rename it.

Change the Page Title of a Web Page

The title of a Web page is displayed in the title bar of most browsers. It is also the name that appears in the Favorites lists in Internet Explorer and the Bookmarks lists in Mozilla Firefox® and Netscape® Navigator™. A Web page title should reflect the page's purpose or the name of the person or company represented by that page.

Most designers change page titles in Navigation view; however, you can also use Page or Folders views. In Design view, click Properties on the File menu to display the Properties dialog box, and then use the General tab of the Properties dialog box to change the title of any Web page without changing its file name. Keep in mind that most browsers can display 90 characters in the title bar. However, you should keep your Web page titles as concise as possible while still providing the necessary information.

Change the Page Label of a Web Page

A **_Web page label_** is the name displayed in SharePoint Designer Web component page banners and navigation bars.

When you create a new Web page, SharePoint Designer automatically assigns it a default name, title, and label. The **_Web page label_** is the name displayed in SharePoint Designer Web component page banners and navigation bars (in the Link Bar Based on Navigation Structure shown in Figure 2.113, the News 1, News 2, and News 3 Web page labels are displayed).

The default label of a Web page is the same as the default title: Untitled 1. You can change the label of a Web page without changing its title or file name. You can change the page label in Navigation views: right-click the page and click Rename on the shortcut menu, or double-click the page icon to put the label in edit mode.

TIP   Web Page Title Versus Label

Because the default values of newly created Web page titles and labels are the same (Untiled_1), it is easy to get them confused. However, it is important to remember that they are two different things. The title of a Web page is displayed in the title bar of most browsers, as well as in the Favorites for Internet Explorer or Bookmarks for Mozilla Firefox and Netscape Navigator. Web page labels are displayed in Navigation view and in the page banners and navigation bars that are created by SharePoint Designer. You can change the page title or label without changing the other.

Format a Web Page

Before starting to edit a Web page, you can configure page formatting using the Page Properties dialog box available using the Properties command on the File menu or by right-clicking the Web page. You can configure many page properties using the General, Formatting, Advanced, Custom, and Language tabs.

Use the General tab to add or change the title of a Web page that appears in the title bar of the browser, add a page description that will be seen by users in search results if they search the WWW, add keywords describing the content of your Web page that might be used by search engines, or add a background sound to your Web page.

By default, SharePoint Designer generates the styles corresponding to the formatting changes you make, as shown in Figure 2.33.

You can use the Formatting tab to modify such page elements as Web page background picture, background color, and hyperlink colors. When you use the Formatting tab of the Page Properties dialog box to apply a background picture, by default, a tiling task is launched (the picture is repeated from left to right and downward, covering the entire Web page; see Figure 2.33). It is usually not recommended that you use a tiled background because it will decrease the Web page readability and distract users. By default, SharePoint Designer generates the styles corresponding to the formatting changes you make, as shown in Figure 2.33.

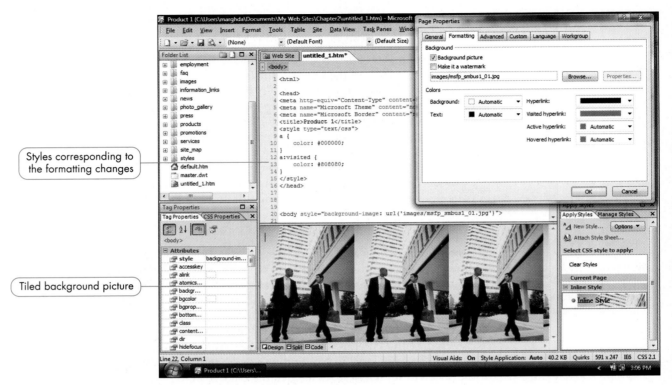

Figure 2.33 Setting Page Properties Using the Formatting Tab

TIP   Style Application Settings

If you wish to save the styles in a new external style sheet, double-click the Style Application Setting indicator to display the Style Application toolbar, select the Manual mode in the Style Application drop-down list, and then click Apply New Style on the Target Rule drop-down list to open the New Style dialog box (see Figure 2.34). When you finish creating the new style sheet, if you click the OK button, you will be prompted to attach the style sheet for the new style. If you click the Yes button, a new Untitled_1.css file that includes the new style is created. The new style created is also shown in the Manage Style pane.

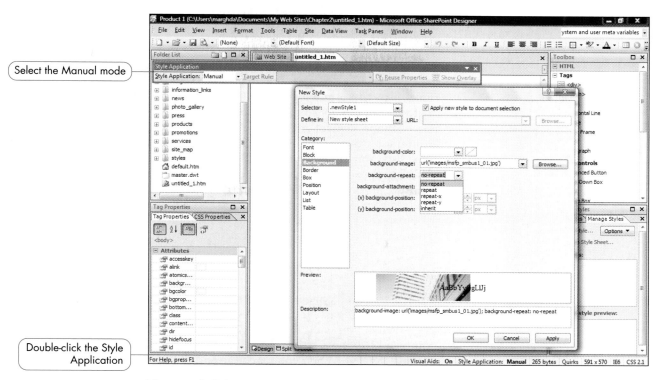

Select the Manual mode

Double-click the Style Application

Figure 2.34 Style Application Settings

Use the Advanced tab to modify Web page margins when, for example, you wish to keep some "clean space" in your Web page. You can further customize and format your Web pages using the Custom tab to add and modify system and user meta variables. (You learn more about system and user meta variables and meta tags in Appendix A.) The Language tab can be used to control page properties, such as the Page language and HTML encoding type. The Workgroup tab can be used to define page properties, such as identifying the work group(s) that have control over the development of the Web page and excluding a Web page from the publishing process of the Web site.

When developing a Web page, you need to format the content that you have added to your Web page. SharePoint Designer's Design view enables you to design, edit, and format a Web page in a way that is similar to word processors and desktop publishing applications.

The benefit of this similarity is that you do not have to become acquainted with a new interface; you can jump right in and begin developing Web content with minimal or no previous knowledge of HTML. However, there are some essential differences between editing in SharePoint Designer Design view and other text-editing applications. For example, in most text-editing applications, the cursor moves down one line when you press the Enter key, whereas, in SharePoint Designer, one blank line will be inserted. This happens because the default <p> tag used for paragraphs requires its own line. If you do not want to begin a new paragraph and just want to move to the next line, you press Shift+Enter, which results in the insertion of a <br> tag.

TIP   Spaces in HTML Code

In contrast with regular text, in HTML code only one blank space between words is recognized. Therefore, if you add more than one space between words in Code view, the Design view and browser view will not be changed. If you need to insert more than one space, you will need to use the non-breaking space character ( ) by simply adding spaces (pressing the Spacebar) in Design view or by manually inserting the non-breaking space character in Code view.

Working with Web Page Content

Now that you know how to add a new Web page to a Web site, you can start working with Web page content. Each Web page has its own individual design and functionality. However, they all use a combination of generic Web page elements, such as text, images, hyperlinks, lists, tables, and forms, to name just a few. All these elements have characteristics that you can modify so that they display and function the way you want them to. The most common element of Web page content is text. In a Web page, text can be used in many different ways, such as normal body text, headings, links, and ordered or unordered lists. You can type text directly in your Web page, import the content of a text file, or copy and paste text from another file. Text can also be edited and formatted to emphasize the purpose of the Web page and enhance its appearance. SharePoint Designer also provides a spelling checker, which you should always use to check the spelling of your Web page text before publishing it. In addition to using the spelling checker, you should also read your Web page text to catch any errors the spelling checker misses.

Add Text

You add text to a Web page in one of the following three ways: type it directly in the Web page, copy and paste it into your page, or insert a previously formatted file into your page. When you want to type text directly onto a Web page, position the insertion point—a blinking vertical bar—where you want the text to appear, and then begin typing the text. When you reach the end of the line, the insertion point is automatically positioned at the beginning of the next line. Press Enter when you want to start a new paragraph.

If you need to insert a character, such as the copyright symbol, that is not available on your keyboard, click Insert on the Menu bar and click Symbol to display the Symbol dialog box. Click the symbol, click Insert to insert the symbol in your page (see Figure 2.35), and click Close to close the dialog box.

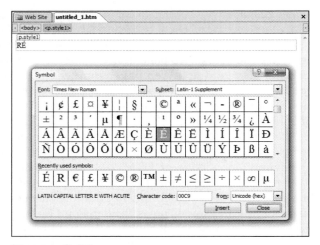

Figure 2.35 Inserting Symbols

TIP Symbols and Cross-Platform Issues

Symbols inserted in SharePoint Designer might not display properly on other computer platforms, such as Macintosh.

You can copy and paste (or move) text from one document to another or within the same page. You can copy and paste text using the Copy and Paste commands on the Edit menu or the Copy and Paste buttons on the Standard toolbar. To move text from one position to another, use the Cut and Paste commands. To copy text from another application, open the source file, highlight the desired text, and click Copy on the Standard toolbar. To paste the copied text in your Web page, open your Web page, click the position where you want to paste the text, and click the Paste button on the Standard toolbar.

When you paste text into a SharePoint Designer file, you see a Paste Options button, as shown in Figure 2.36. This smart tag lets you decide how you want the pasted content to appear in its new location. The available options depend on the type of content you are pasting, the application you copied the content from, and the format of the text surrounding the paste location. Move your mouse pointer over the Paste Option button, click the down arrow, and select an option.

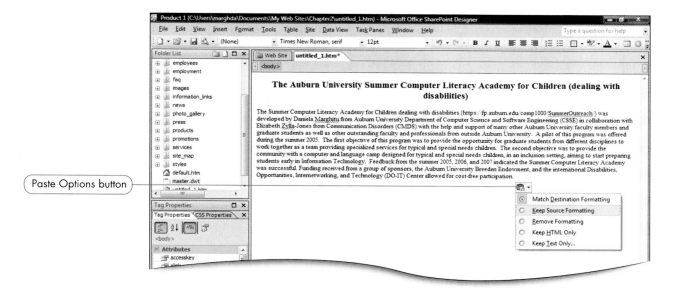

Figure 2.36 Paste Options Smart Tag

When you paste text using the Paste command an excess of tags are included within the text, increasing the risk of creating a Web page with compatibility and accessibility errors. If you need to import text without maintaining any previous formatting, it is highly recommended that you use the Paste Text command included in the Edit menu. If you click the Paste Text command, the Paste Text dialog box opens, as shown in Figure 2.37. Any option displayed will enable you to paste the text without compatibility problems.

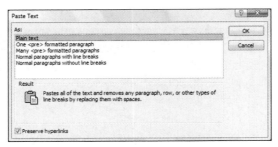

Figure 2.37 Paste Text Dialog Box

Many people work with documents that have already been created in other Microsoft Office applications, such as Word, Excel, or PowerPoint. Instead of recreating these pages, SharePoint Designer automatically converts the contents of these files into HTML when you insert the file into your Web page.

Many people work with documents that have already been created in other Microsoft Office applications, such as Word, Excel, or PowerPoint. Instead of recreating these pages, SharePoint Designer automatically converts the contents of these files into HTML when you insert the file into your Web page. To insert a file into a Web page, position the insertion point where you want to insert the contents of the file. Then select the Insert, File command. Select the location of the file in the Look in box. If you do not see the file you need, select All files *.* in the Files of type box. Double-click the file to insert it into the Web page. If SharePoint Designer displays a dialog box indicating that the file cannot be imported because the specified file format is not installed, you need to install this file format from the Microsoft SharePoint Designer 2007 CD.

TIP Hidden File Extensions

If Windows was configured on your computer to hide file extensions, you cannot see the file extensions in the Select File dialog box. If you want to see the file extensions, in Windows Explorer, use the View tab of the Folder Options dialog box to reconfigure Windows. To open the Folder Options dialog box, launch Windows Explorer, pull down the Tools menu, and click Folder Options.

Edit and Format Text

SharePoint Designer enables you to move, replace, or delete text and change its appearance.

After you have entered text into your Web page, you might need to edit and format it. SharePoint Designer enables you to move, replace, or delete text and change its appearance. Usually all these changes are applied in Design view. In the previous section, you learned how to select, copy, move, and deselect text.

TIP Right-Clicking Selected Text

Right-click selected text to access the shortcut menu commands such as Cut or Copy.

To replace text, select the text and then type the new text. To delete text, select it and press Delete. If you make mistakes while working on your Web page, use the Undo button on the Standard toolbar or press Ctrl+Z. You can undo your 30 most recent consecutive actions. If you accidentally undo the wrong thing, the Redo button on the Standard toolbar (or Ctrl+Y) enables you to reverse the result of the most recent Undo command. Redo is also available for the previous 30 consecutive actions.

TIP Generic Font Families and Fonts

A generic font family defines the general description of a font's appearance. Browsers support five generic fonts: serif (looks more formal and is used mostly for body text), sans-serif (is a less formal font, has no serifs and is used more as a heading font on Web pages), cursive (looks more like handwritten pen or brush writing than printed text), fantasy (looks more decorative), and monospace (all characters have the same width). All five generic font families exist in all CSS implementations (they need not necessarily map to five distinct actual fonts). A specific font is a font actually installed on your computer, such as Arial, Courier, and Times New Roman. To read more about generic font families and specific fonts that fit each generic font family description, see the W3C Web site (go to http://www.w3.org and search the Web site for "CSS2 Fonts"). To read more about Microsoft specific fonts see the Microsoft Fonts Web site (go to http://www.ascendercorp.com and click Microsoft Fonts on the horizontal navigation bar).

As previously discussed in Chapter 1, there are three ways to change the font. You can select the Font command on the Format menu or the shortcut menu, or click the buttons on the Formatting toolbar (or Common toolbar). Using these tools, you can change the font specification properties. You can set up the font that you want to use before the text is actually entered if you position the insertion point where you want to insert the text, then right-click and click Font on the shortcut menu to open the Font dialog box. To apply a font to text already added to the Web page, you first need to highlight (select) the text, then right-click and click Font on the shortcut menu to open the Font dialog box. You can apply a font to the whole Web page if you right-click in any empty space of the Web page body, then right-click and click Font on the shortcut menu to open the Font dialog box.

TIP Change the Default Font Used in Design and Code Views

SharePoint Designer enables you to change the default fonts that you see when you work in Design and Code views. Click Page Editor Options on the Tools menu to open the Page Editor Options dialog box, and then click the Color Coding tab. These settings do not affect the appearance of text in the browser and affect only how SharePoint Designer displays text when you work in a SharePoint Designer window.

The text size can be expressed in HTML and CSS using a rather wide selection of units: keywords, ems, exs, pixels, percentages, picas, points, and even inches, centimeters, and millimeters (see Appendix A to learn more about this selection of units). However, among these measurement units, only pixels, keywords, ems, and percentages are commonly used for sizing text for a computer monitor. When using these four measurement units, the text size is set either by adding to or subtracting from the text size already set on the viewer's browser screen. Hence, if you do not specify a size for text using CSS, Web browsers apply their base font size, which for most browsers is 16 pixels.

TIP   Accessible Text Content

To make sure an uncommon font used your Web page is properly displayed by all browsers, you can create a graphic text (that means you create a graphic file that captures the actual text and insert it in the Web page body). From an accessibility point of view, you should always prefer plain text over graphic text, because graphic text cannot be customized. Plain text using style sheets provides increased flexibility for styling and customizing, such as higher contrast and different combinations of size, color, and typeface.

Font Specification Properties | Reference

Font Specification Property	Description
Font Type	There are five generic font families supported by browsers: sans serif, serif, cursive, fantasy, and monosapce. Arial is probably the best known sans-serif font; Times New Roman, which is also the default SharePoint Designer font, is the best-known serif font; and Courier is the most common monospace font.
Font Style	Font style can be used to enhance text and emphasize its message. The most frequently used font styles are bold and italic. You can apply more than one font style to a selected text. (The most popular combination of styles is bold and italic.)
Font Color	The default font color of a Web page is black. You can alter the font color to emphasize a word or an entire paragraph. SharePoint Designer enables you to create custom colors.
Font Size	In SharePoint Designer, you use the seven CSS keywords (xx-small, x-small, small, medium, large, x-large, and xx-large) to set the text size relative to the baseline text size and the corresponding measure in points.
Text Effects	Some of the better known text effects, other than underline, are superscript and subscript. You can apply text effects from the Font tab of the Font dialog box. To open the Font dialog box, pull down the Format menu and click Font. All available effects are grouped in the Effects section of the Font tab.
Character Spacing	The Character Spacing tab of the Font dialog box enables you to condense (decrease the space between characters) and expand (increase the space between characters) portions of the text. You can also set the position of the text.

Style is a SharePoint Designer feature that enables Web designers to format text using built-in HTML styles.

Another productive SharePoint Designer feature that enables Web designers to format text using built-in HTML styles is called ***Style***. Among the styles included in the Style drop-down list, as shown in Figure 2.38, are headings and some of the more popular styles for formatting lists and alignment. Having these popular styles grouped together this way enables Web designers to give more consistency to their Web page content. There are six levels of headings that you can use in Web design, from Heading 1 to Heading 6. Each heading level has a distinct HTML tag. The <h1> tag creates the largest Heading 1 font, and the <h6> tag creates the smallest. All these heading levels are included in the SharePoint Designer built-in styles and can be accessed by clicking the Style drop-down arrow on the Formatting toolbar, as shown in Figure 2.38.

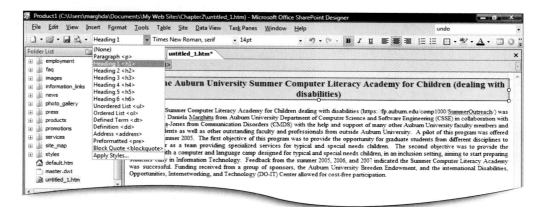

Figure 2.38 Heading 1 Aligned Center

Check the Spelling of Your Text

SharePoint Designer enables you to check the spelling of a highlighted section of a Web page, an entire Web page, a group of selected Web pages, or an entire Web site.

It is always important to check your document for spelling errors. SharePoint Designer enables you to check the spelling of a highlighted section of a Web page, an entire Web page, a group of selected Web pages, or an entire Web site. Open the Spelling dialog box by clicking the Spelling button on the Standard toolbar or by pointing to Spelling on the Tools menu and then clicking Spelling. The Spelling dialog box displays the first misspelled word along with suggestions for correcting it, as shown in Figure 2.39. Choose the best option for correcting the misspelled word or type the word correctly in the Change to box, then click one of the following options:

- Click the Change button to change the selected instance of the word.
- Click the Ignore button to ignore the selected instance.
- Click the Change All button to change every instance of the word.
- Click the Ignore All button to ignore every instance of the word.

After you make your selection, the Spelling dialog box shows the next error on your page.

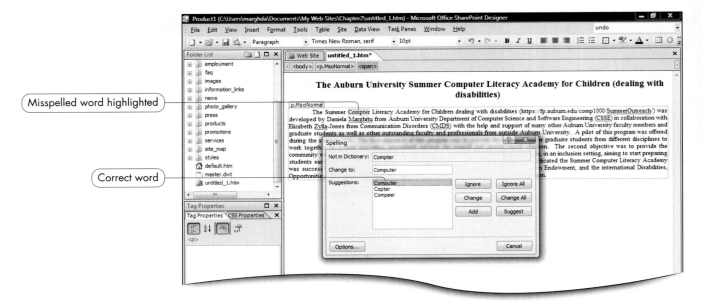

Misspelled word highlighted

Correct word

Figure 2.39 Spelling Dialog Box

Although you can wait until your Web page is finished to check your spelling, SharePoint Designer shows you your mistakes as soon as they occur.

Although you can wait until your Web page is finished to check your spelling, SharePoint Designer shows you your mistakes as soon as they occur. SharePoint Designer uses the Check Spelling as You Type feature to mark each misspelled word with a wavy red line so that you can fix your spelling errors on the spot.

When you find a word on your page with the wavy red line under it, right-click the word to see a selection of possible corrections. From this shortcut menu, you can click one of the word choices, choose to ignore all instances of that particular word, or choose to add the word to a personal dictionary. Alternatively, you can choose to simply click the word in the main text and make your correction there. In addition to using the spelling checker, you should also read your Web page text when it is complete to catch any errors the spelling checker misses.

Using Hyperlinks and Lists in Organizing a Web Page

Nobody likes to explore a cluttered and confusing document. Most people instinctively prefer clear, well-organized, and easy-to-navigate Web pages. Keeping your Web pages clean and organized is an important design consideration. Hyperlinks and lists are two features that can help Web authors achieve these goals.

Hyperlinks can help designers break the contents of a large, difficult-to-navigate Web page into a set of Web pages that are connected. Alternatively, designers can reduce the amount of jumping back and forth between different Web pages by using bookmark links and bookmarks to give users access to their content. Lists are great tools for organizing Web page content in a concise and consistent fashion. You can choose ordered (numbered), unordered (bulleted), and definition lists.

In this section, you learn when and how to use hyperlinks and lists to organize your Web pages. You learn how SharePoint Designer assists you when you are adding, editing, and formatting hyperlinks and lists.

Hyperlinks

> Hyperlinks are not just colored, underlined words that magically take you to another place. Behind each hyperlink, in the HTML code, a URL tells the browser where to go when you click the link.

Hyperlinks are not just colored, underlined words that magi cally take you to another place. Behind each hyperlink, in the HTML code, a URL tells the browser where to go when you click the link. As you recall from Chapter 1, a URL can include an address for a file on the Internet, a file on your computer, a file on a local network, a bookmark within a Web page, or an e-mail address.

An *absolute URL* provides the full path to a Web page or file.

A *relative URL* provides the path to a Web page or a file relative to another file.

There are two different kinds of URLs: absolute and relative (see Figure 2.40). An *absolute URL* provides the full path to a Web page or file, whereas a *relative URL* provides the path to a Web page or a file in relation to another file. The following HTML code shows what typical absolute and relative URLs look like. Notice that relative URLs are shorter than absolute ones are.

```
Absolute URL = http://www.eng.auburn.edu/users/daniela/
Relative URL  = images/phit/daniela_phit_2007.jpg
```

Figure 2.40 Absolute and Relative URL

> SharePoint Designer assists you in creating hyperlinks to existing files or even to files that have not been created yet. You can also decide in which browser window the hyperlink target should display.

Hyperlink target is the file that opens when a hyperlink is clicked.

Absolute URLs are required for files placed outside your Web site. When Web sites include multiple Web pages and many folders and subfolders, they can be confusing and difficult to remember and type correctly; you should use relative URLs. In addition to being shorter, there are other significant advantages to using relative URLs, such as when relocating a Web site to another place on the same Web server or on another Web server.

SharePoint Designer assists you in creating hyperlinks to existing files or even to files that have not been created yet. You can also decide in which browser window the hyperlink target should display. The file that opens when a hyperlink is clicked is called the *hyperlink target*. When you move your mouse pointer over a hyperlink, you can see its target URL in the status bar. To create a hyperlink targeting an existing file, position the insertion point where you want the hyperlink to appear. Then open the Insert Hyperlink dialog box by clicking the Insert Hyperlink button in the Standard toolbar (or Common toolbar) or using the Insert, Hyperlink command. You can choose a file from the Current Folder, Browsed Pages, and Recent Files areas. You can also type an address in the Address text box or locate the desired target file using the Look in drop-down list, the Browse the Web button (which opens a browser window, enabling you to browse the Internet for a Web page), or the Browse for file button (which opens the Link to file dialog box, enabling you to search for a file on your computer or network). You also need to type the display text for the hyperlink in the Text to Display box (see Figure 2.41). Click OK to close the Insert Hyperlink dialog box.

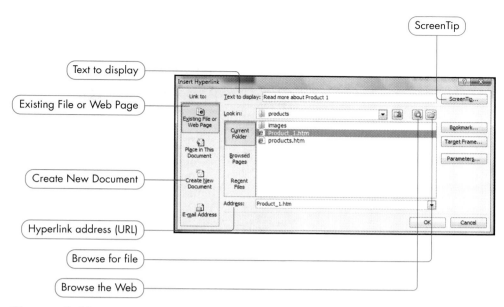

Figure 2.41   Using the Insert Hyperlink Dialog Box to Insert Links into a File

To create a link to a file that has not been created yet, click the Create New Document button, as shown in Figure 2.41. Type the name of the file you want to create in the Name of New Document box, or, if you want to change the path of the new file, click the Change button.

TIP   SharePoint Designer and URLs

If you type a URL (such as http://www.eng.auburn.edu or just www.eng.auburn.edu) in your text, SharePoint Designer automatically converts it into a hyperlink.

A **ScreenTip** is text that displays in the body of the Web page whenever a mouse is moved over the hyperlink.

For all types of links, you can also add a ScreenTip (see Figure 2.42). A **ScreenTip** is text that displays in the body of the Web page whenever a mouse is moved over the hyperlink. To set up a ScreenTip, click the ScreenTip button in the Insert Hyperlink dialog box to open the Set Hyperlink Screen Tip dialog box. Type the desired text in the ScreenTip text box and click OK to close the box (see Figure 2.43). The ScreenTip text displays every time the mouse moves over the link, as shown in Figure 2.42, in Preview view or when viewing the Web page in a browser. Designers use ScreenTip text to provide users with more information about the related hyperlink.

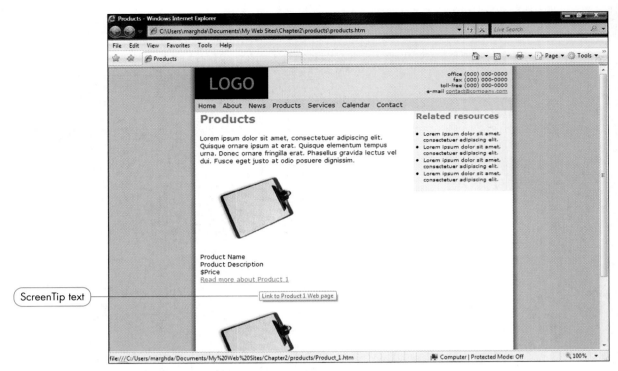

Figure 2.42 Viewing a ScreenTip's Text in the Preview View

ScreenTip text

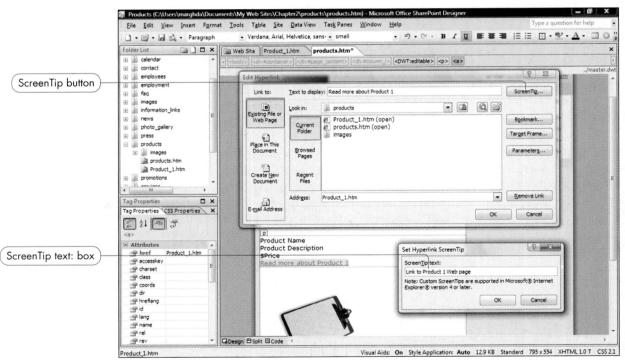

ScreenTip button

ScreenTip text: box

Figure 2.43 Inserting a ScreenTip

If the hyperlink's displayed text has been previously added to the Web page, you can change it by editing the hyperlink. Highlight the text, and then open the Insert Hyperlink dialog box. The selected text is automatically displayed in the Text to Display box.

After a hyperlink has been created, you can change its URL or its text message any time. To edit a hyperlink, position the mouse pointer over it, right-click, and click Hyperlink Properties to open the Edit Hyperlink dialog box. You can also remove the link by clicking the Remove Link button, as shown in Figure 2.44.

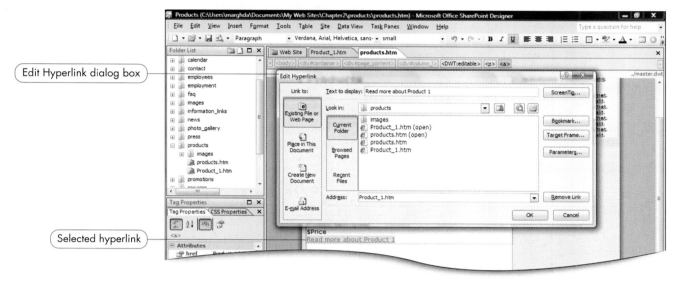

Figure 2.44 Editing a Hyperlink Using the Edit Hyperlinks Dialog Box

You can remove a hyperlink in one of two ways: by deleting the text and the associated link from the page or by keeping the text on the page but removing the associated link. To delete a hyperlink and its text completely from the page, right-click the hyperlink and click Cut. Alternatively, you can select the linked text and press the Delete button. To preserve the hyperlink text on the page but delete the link associated with it, right-click the hyperlink and select Hyperlink Properties to open the Edit Hyperlink dialog box (see Figure 2.44). Click the Remove Link button in the lower right of the dialog box.

A *bookmark link* is a link to a specific position within the same document or another document.

A link to a specific position within the same document or another document is called a *bookmark link*. Bookmark links are helpful navigation tools, especially when you are dealing with long pages, because they replace the slower scrolling (using the vertical and horizontal scrollbars) method of working through the text. Before you can create a bookmark link, you need to create the bookmarks within a page. To create a bookmark, place the insertion point or select the text where the bookmark target will be, click Insert, and then click Bookmark to open the Bookmark dialog box (see Figure 2.45). If you just placed the insertion point, you need to type the bookmark name in the Bookmark name box. If you selected text before opening the Bookmark dialog box, the bookmark text appears in the Bookmark name box. When you have the bookmark name text the way you want it, click OK to close the Bookmark dialog box. You should always use a descriptive name for each bookmark so you can identify it easily when you want to add a link to it.

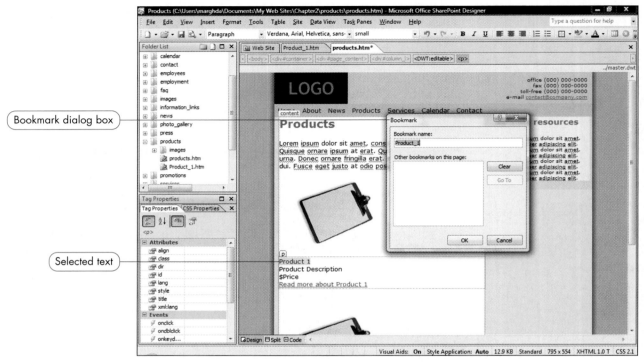

Figure 2.45 Bookmark Dialog Box

Often, it is wise to have one long Web page instead of spreading the content among many Web pages, which forces visitors to jump back and forth among them. When you have a single-page site, you cut down on the time required for users to browse your Web site because they need to load only one page. Bookmarks are the best solution to help visitors navigate a long Web page. After the bookmark is created, the second step is to create the link that points to the bookmark. To accomplish this, open the Insert Hyperlink dialog box, click the Select Place in This Document button to display the list of available bookmarks (as shown in Figure 2.46), and then click the desired bookmark. If you want to display text that is different than the name of the bookmark, type the desired text in the Text to display box and click OK to close the Insert Hyperlink dialog box. Now, when the hyperlink is clicked, the cursor jumps to the bookmarked position, whether it is in the same file or another. If a bookmark is placed in an external file, you need to select the external file in the Insert Hyperlink dialog box before you can select the bookmark to use.

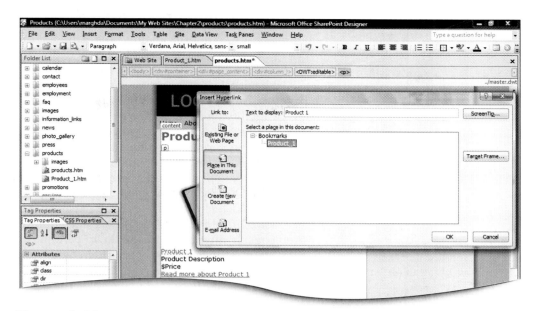

Figure 2.46 Adding a Bookmark Link

Another common type of hyperlink called a ***mailto link*** connects the user to an e-mail address. When users click a mailto link, their default e-mail application opens a new message window, and the target address of the link is already entered in the To address box. You can easily create a mailto link by clicking the E-mail Address button, which is located in the Link To area on the left side of the Insert Hyperlink dialog box. The Insert Hyperlink dialog box displays the mailto options, as shown in Figure 2.47. Type the desired address in the E-mail address field. Observe that SharePoint Designer automatically enters mailto: in the address field preceding the address as you type. If you want, you can also enter a subject for the e-mail. If you type an e-mail address directly in a document, SharePoint Designer automatically formats it as a mailto link.

Figure 2.47 Creating a Mailto Link

The **link attribute** defines the color of hypertext links and corresponds to the a:link {color: #value;} CSS style and Hyperlink color setting in the Page Properties dialog box.

The **vlink attribute** defines the color of links that have been visited by the user and corresponds to the a:visited {color: #value;} CSS style and Visited Hyperlink color setting in the Page Properties dialog box.

The **alink attribute** determines the color of an active hyperlink (a link as it is clicked by the user) and corresponds to the a:active {color: #value;} CSS style and Active Hyperlink color setting in the Page Properties dialog box.

To edit a mailto hyperlink, right-click the hyperlink and click Hyperlink Properties to open the Edit Hyperlink dialog box. After you finish making the appropriate changes, click OK to close the Edit Hyperlink dialog box.

When you create a Web page using a Dynamic Web Template or a CSS external style sheet, the default colors of the active, unvisited, and visited hyperlinks included in your Web page are usually set. As you previously learned in this chapter, these colors can be changed by modifying the Dynamic Web Template or the CSS external style sheet.

In Web pages that do not have an attached template, SharePoint Designer empowers Web designers to format hyperlink colors using the Page Properties dialog box. SharePoint Designer also assists Web designers with adding font effects to hyperlinks in Web pages with or without a CCS external style sheet linked.

SharePoint Designer assists you in setting default colors of active, unvisited, and visited hyperlinks included in your Web page using the Page Properties dialog box. The selected colors are usually distinctive and should blend nicely into the design of your Web page. If, after customizing the hyperlink colors you apply a theme to your Web page, your settings will be overwritten by the theme.

The HTML <a> tag has three attributes for setting the colors of hyperlinks: link, vlink, and alink. The **link attribute** defines the color of hypertext links and corresponds to the a:link {color: #value;} CSS style and Hyperlink color setting in the Page Properties dialog box. The **vlink attribute** defines the color of links that have been visited by the user and corresponds to the a:visited {color: #value;} CSS style and Visited Hyperlink color setting in the Page Properties dialog box. The **alink attribute** determines the color of an active hyperlink (a link as it is clicked by the user) and corresponds to the a:active {color: #value;} CSS style and Active Hyperlink color setting in the Page Properties dialog box.

In SharePoint Designer, you cannot set color effects for a hyperlink if the page uses a Dynamic Web Template. Therefore, the color formatting options are not available in the Page Properties dialog box. However, you can set many color effects on these Web pages by customizing the Dynamic Web Template.

You can set hyperlink colors in Design view using the Formatting tab of the Page Properties dialog box, as shown in Figure 2.48. In the Colors area, you can use the drop-down boxes to select the colors you want to use for the link's background and text and indicate whether the color of a link changes when it is clicked or active. To do so, use the Hyperlink, Visited hyperlink, and Active hyperlink drop-down boxes.

Figure 2.48 Formatting Tab of the Page Properties Dialog Box

You can add rollover effects to hyperlinks so that when a Web site visitor moves the mouse pointer over the hyperlink, the font attribute changes. You can add a hover color effect using the Formatting tab of the Page Properties dialog box (see Figure 2.48). This should help your Web page visitors be aware of the current position of the mouse and add a little dynamic charm to your Web page.

Dynamic HTML (DHTML) is an extension of HTML that adds multimedia, database access, and an object model that programs use to change the styles and attributes of page elements and to replace existing elements with new ones.

Hyperlink rollover effects use *Dynamic HTML (DHTML)*. DHTML is an extension of HTML that adds multimedia, database access, and an object model that programs use to change the styles and attributes of page elements and to replace existing elements with new ones. Some Web browsers might not support this feature, so the rollover effects will not display properly on the user's computer.

To further format hyperlinks (for example, to change the hyperlink text to a smaller, bold, orange font on hover), you can use the New Style dialog box, as shown in Figure 2.49. SharePoint Designer enables you to apply the changes just to the current page, to create a new style sheet, or to add the new style to an existing external style sheet that is also linked to other pages. After you add the new style, you see the style attribute within the external style sheet (see Figure 2.50) and the rollover effect when you view the Web page in a browser (see Figure 2.51).

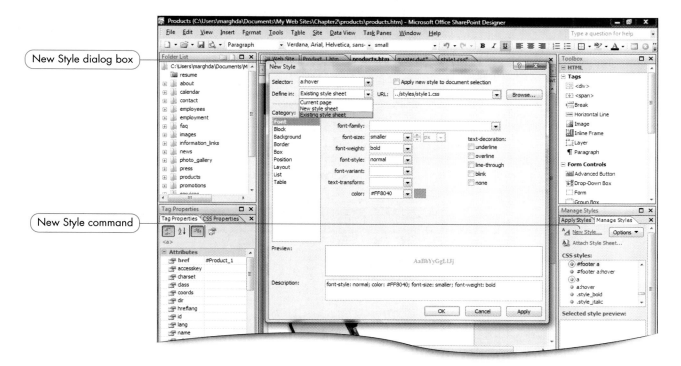

Figure 2.49 Formatting Links with the New Style Dialog Box

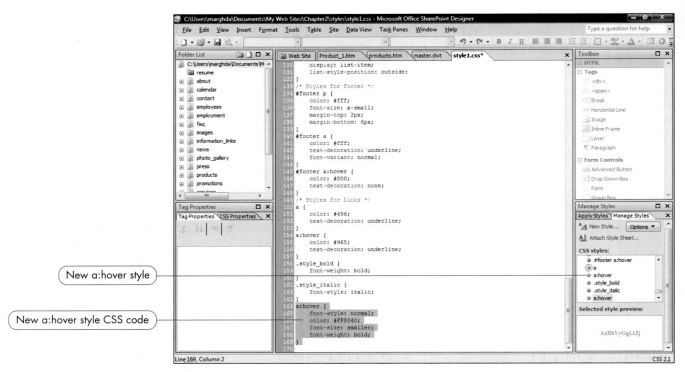

Figure 2.50 Newly Added Style Included in the External Style Sheet

Figure 2.51 Hover Effect Viewed in a Browser

Lists

> The most popular SharePoint Designer list styles are numbered and bulleted. Use a numbered list when the order in which elements appear is important, such as a list of meetings scheduled for a day, or a list of instructions included in a software application tutorial.

The *list* format is a common format seen on many Web pages that helps you organize and present your content in a consistent and concise fashion.

The *list* format is a common format seen on many Web pages. Lists help you organize and present your content in a consistent and concise fashion. The most popular SharePoint Designer list styles are numbered and bulleted. Use a numbered list when the order in which elements appear is important, such as a list of meetings scheduled for a day, or a list of instructions included in a software application tutorial. If the order in which elements appear is not important, use a bulleted list. Figure 2.52 shows an example of text formatted as lists.

In HTML, each line from either type of these lists is included between the pair tags <li> and </li>. The HTML tags for creating lists using picture bullets are the pair tags <ul> and </ul>, whereas the HTML tag for creating lists using numbers are the pair tags <ol> and </ol> (see Figure 2.52).

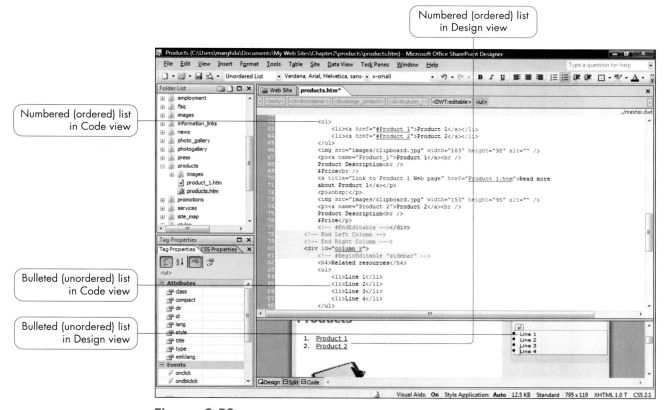

Figure 2.52 Text Formatted as Bulleted (Unordered) and Numbered (Ordered) Lists

Among the elements usually preset in a Web page template or included within a CSS external style sheet are the graphic bullets to be used in bulleted lists. Thus, if a page has an attached template or is linked to a CSS external style sheet, you can create an unordered list that uses the template's preset picture bullets by selecting the text and simply clicking the Bullets buttons on the Formatting toolbar. These buttons apply the list style directly without going through a dialog box (see Figure 2.53).

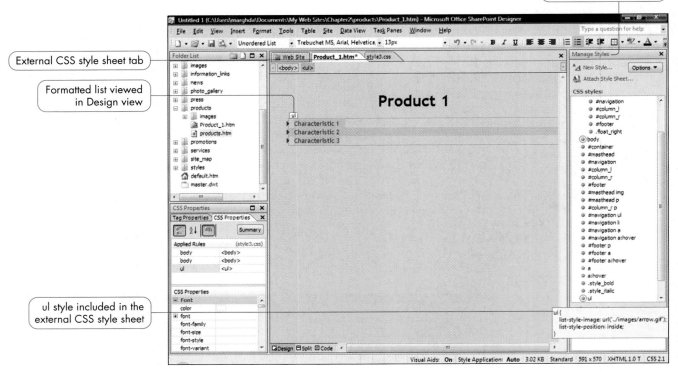

Figure 2.53 Creating a Bulleted List Using Custom Graphic Bullets

> **TIP**   Styling Lists
>
> You can read more about creating and formatting lists using CSS styles from the W3Schools CSS2 Reference (http://www.w3schools.com/css/css_reference.asp#list), as well as in Appendix A.

If your Web page does not have an attached template, you can create a list using the Bullets and Numbering dialog box available from the Format menu. You can use this dialog box to format your list into a numbered list or a bulleted list using either plain bullets or icons. The dialog box contains the following three tabs:

1. **Picture Bullets**—Use the Picture Bullets tab, shown in Figure 2.54, to use a graphic as the bullet. Click Specify Picture in the Picture area, and then click the Browse button to locate and select the desired picture.

Figure 2.54 Picture Bullets Tab

2. **Plain Bullets**—Use the Plain Bullets tab to choose a standard symbol as a bullet. Click the box for the bullet style you prefer from the styles available, as shown in Figure 2.55.

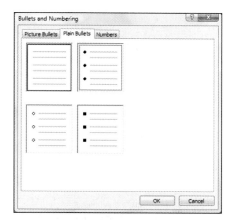

Figure 2.55 Plain Bullets Tab

3. **Numbers**—Use the Numbers tab to create an ordered list. You can choose to use numbers or consecutive letters. Click the box of the numbering style you prefer from the styles available, as shown in Figure 2.56. Use the Start at: list box to set the value of the number or letter you want to use for the first item in the list.

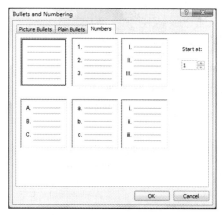

Figure 2.56 Numbers Tab

After you have created a list, you can edit it by right-clicking any line of the list, clicking the List Properties command, and selecting an option from the List Properties dialog boxes discussed previously. Use the Other tab from the List Properties dialog box to create other types of lists such as the Definition list, which is the most often used list.

Nested lists are popular features used by Web designers to emphasize text categories and subcategories. In SharePoint Designer, you can create nested lists, including the same styles or different styles of lists and lists indented under others, as shown in Figure 2.57.

Nested lists are popular features used by Web designers to emphasize text categories and subcategories.

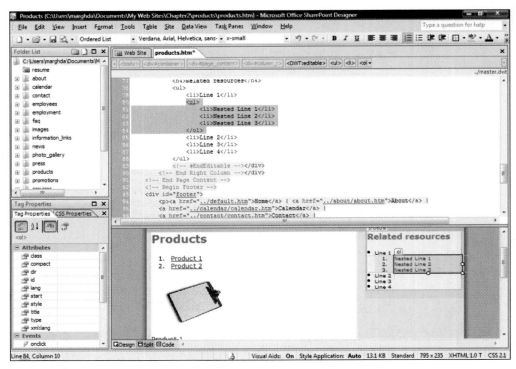

Figure 2.57 Nested Lists

Working with Tables and Layout Tables

(SharePoint Designer provides you with a complete set of tools for working with tables, table-based layouts, layout tables, and cells in Design view, without having to work with HTML or CSS code.)

Standard tables have always been among Web designers' favorite tools for organizing and displaying information, and, although the CSS-based layouts have become more efficient and easier to implement, the table-based layouts continue to be very popular. When using layout tables, you can control the table structure more easily (for example, you are not required to manually modify the rows and columns or merge cells to design the table grid you need, and you can easily draw cell structures). SharePoint Designer provides you with a complete set of tools for working with tables, table-based layouts, layout tables, and cells in Design view, without having to work with HTML or CSS code.

Create a Standard Table

(The fact that tables are supported by all browsers and are similar to the tables used in many other desktop applications makes them attractive to Web designers, from beginners to professionals.)

Tables have always played an important role in Web development. The fact that tables are supported by all browsers and are similar to the tables used in many other desktop applications makes them attractive to Web designers, from beginners to professionals. SharePoint Designer has a comprehensive set of tools for adding and formatting tables. SharePoint Designer offers Web designers a new concept of layout tables and layout cells.

A **table** is a collection of rows having one or more columns.

A **cell** is the intersection of a column and a row.

A **nested table** is a table inserted within a cell of another table.

A *table* is a collection of rows having one or more columns. A *cell* is the intersection of a column and a row. A *nested table* is a table inserted within a cell of another table. Because tables and cells can have 0-pixel borders, they are not necessarily visible when a Web page is displayed in a browser. Therefore, by using tables you can easily position your Web page text, images, Web components, and other Web page elements in a nested table.

Before creating a table you need to consider how many rows and columns you need, the elements that will be placed in the table cells, and the total width and height of the table. SharePoint Designer enables Web designers to establish the size of a table in pixels or as a percentage of the browser window.

In SharePoint Designer Design view, you can create a table by using the Insert Table button from the Standard toolbar or the Insert Table submenu of the Table menu. You can also use the Insert Table button in Code view and Split view.

To create a table using the Insert Table button, click the button to display the Insert Table grid. The ***Insert Table grid*** is a graphical table that enables you to select the number of rows and columns for your table. If the Insert Table grid displays too few rows or columns, you can add more rows and columns by clicking anywhere within the table grid and continuing to move the mouse while keeping the left mouse button pressed. For example, to create a three-row table with three columns, as shown in Figure 2.58, display the Insert Table grid and position the arrow mouse pointer in the third column of the third row. Release the mouse to complete the table.

The ***Insert Table grid*** is a graphical table that enables you to select the number of rows and columns for your table.

Insert Table button

Table grid

A table with three rows and three columns

Figure 2.58   Creating a Table Using the Insert Table Button on the Standard Toolbar

When you copy an Excel or Word table and paste it to a Web page, SharePoint Designer automatically converts it into an HTML table. In Chapter 3, you will learn more about how to integrate Excel and Word tables into a Web page.

Insert Rows and Columns

After inserting a table in a Web page, you might find that you need to add more rows or columns. You can add more rows by positioning the insertion point in the last column of the last row and pressing Tab. You can add more rows and columns anywhere within the table by positioning the insertion point in the desired location within the existing table, clicking Table on the Menu bar, selecting Insert, and then clicking Rows or Columns to display the Insert Rows or Columns dialog box. Click either Rows or Columns, choose the number of rows or columns desired, and then select one of the two options in the Location section—Above selection or Below selection—as shown in Figure 2.59.

Figure 2.59 Insert Rows or Columns Dialog Box

Select and Delete Rows and Columns

As careful as you might be when creating a table or inserting rows or columns into a table, it is only human to make mistakes. Fortunately, you can delete a row or a column from a table at any time. To delete a row, first position the mouse pointer over the left border of the row, and when the mouse pointer changes into a black arrow, click. The row is selected and highlighted, as shown in Figure 2.60. Right-click anywhere within the selected row, point to Delete, and then click Delete Rows to delete the selected row.

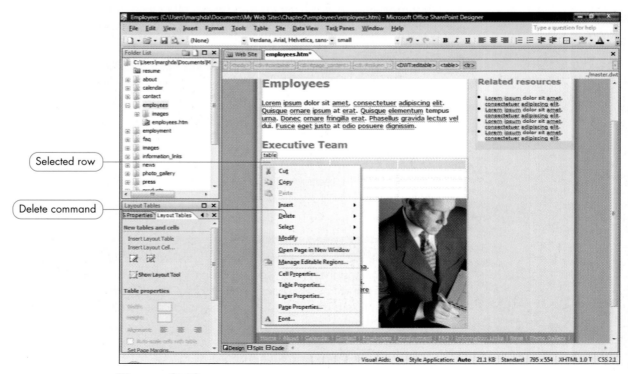

Figure 2.60 Selecting and Deleting a Row

To delete a column, position the mouse over the top border of the column, and when the mouse pointer changes into a black arrow, click. The column is selected and highlighted. Right-click anywhere within the selected column, select Delete, and then select Delete Columns to delete the selected column (see Figure 2.61).

Figure 2.61 Selecting and Deleting a Column

Another method of selecting and deleting rows and columns uses the Table menu. To select a column or a row, position the insertion point anywhere within the row or column, click Table, and point to Delete, as shown in Figure 2.62. To delete the selected row or column, click the Delete Rows or Delete Columns command.

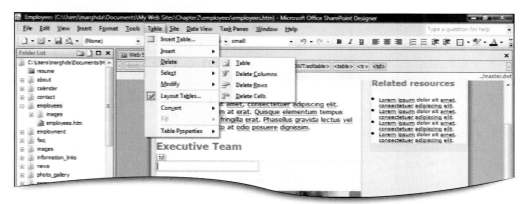

Figure 2.62 Deleting a Row or Column Using the Table Menu

SharePoint Designer enables you to select multiple rows and columns. To select multiple, adjacent, or nonadjacent rows or columns, select a row or column, and then select additional rows or columns while pressing Ctrl. Another method for selecting adjacent rows or columns is to drag along the left border (to select rows) or along the top border (to select columns). After rows and columns have been selected, you can press Delete to delete them. After selecting one or more rows or columns, click anywhere in the Web page body outside the table to deselect the rows or columns.

> ### TIP Using Undo and Redo
>
> One way to eliminate possible errors when working with tables is to use the Undo feature, which enables you to undo as many as 30 past actions. The Redo feature enables you to restore up to the last 30 changes you made. Undo and Redo commands can be used by clicking the Undo and Redo buttons on the Standard toolbar.

Enter Data in a Table

Web designers often prefer to use tables to control the position of the Web page elements, including text. As previously discussed in this chapter, you can add text to a Web page in three ways: by typing directly onto the page, by copying and pasting text into your page, or by inserting a previously formatted file into your page. You can use the same methods for entering text into a table.

When you want to enter text directly in the cell of a table, you first position the insertion point where you want the text to appear, then type the text. Press Enter when you want to start a new paragraph, or click Insert on the Menu bar, click Break, click Normal line break, and click OK to break the line.

To copy and paste text into a table cell, first copy the text from the original location, then position the insertion point in the cell where you want the text to appear, right-click, and click Paste, as shown in Figure 2.63. To insert a previously formatted file, position the insertion point in the cell where you want the text to appear, click Insert, and click File, as shown in Figure 2.64, to open the Select File dialog box.

Figure 2.63 Pasting Text in a Cell

Figure 2.64 Inserting a File into a Cell

Insert an Image

You can insert an image from clip art, a file, or a scanner or camera into the cell of a table using the Picture submenu of the Insert menu. You can also position, resize, and resample an image. Just as with text, images can easily be positioned on a Web page using tables. To insert an image into the cell of a table, position the insertion point in the cell in which you want the image to appear.

To insert a picture from a file, click Insert, point to Picture, and then click the From File command to open the Picture dialog box. Using the Look in drop-down list, navigate the folders until you locate the folder that contains your picture. Click the name of the picture you want and click the Insert button. The image appears in the table cell.

To insert an image from a scanner or camera, after your equipment has been installed, go to the Web page into which you plan to insert your image. Pull down the Insert menu, select Picture, and click the From Scanner or Camera command to open the Insert Picture from Scanner or Camera dialog box. In the displayed Device list, click your specific scanner or camera. After you select the device, click the Custom Insert button to launch the device software, click the picture that you want to add, and click Get Pictures. If you want to add more than one picture, hold Ctrl while clicking all the desired pictures.

To insert a clip art image, pull down the Insert menu, select Picture, and click the Clip Art command to display the Clip Art task pane. In the Search for box, enter a keyword that describes the clip that you are searching for and click the Go button. The results are displayed in the Clip Art task pane, as shown in Figure 2.65. After browsing the results and choosing the clip you want, click the drop-down arrow that appears on its right side, and then click the Insert command from the displayed menu.

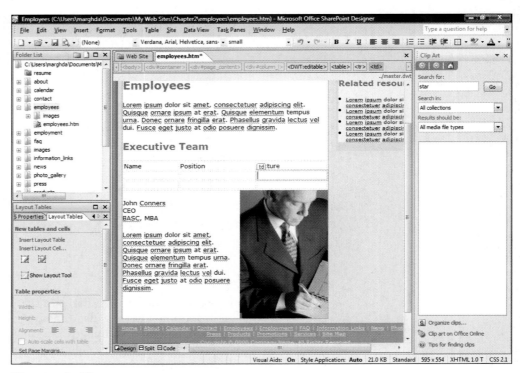

Figure 2.65 Inserting a Clip Art Image into a Cell

TIP   Copy and Paste an Image in a Table

Using a procedure similar to copying and pasting text, you can copy and paste an image into the cell of a table.

Add a Table Caption

A ***caption*** can be a word or a phrase, and, in general, it identifies the content of the table or figure.

SharePoint Designer enables you to add a caption to a table. A ***caption*** can be a word or a phrase, and, in general, it identifies the content of the table or figure. By default, the caption is positioned at the top of the table and centered. However, you can position it at the top or bottom of the table and set the alignment to left, center, right, or justified.

To add a table caption, click anywhere within the table, click Table, point to Insert, click Caption, as shown in Figure 2.66, and then type the caption text. To change the position of the caption, right-click it and click Caption Properties to display the Caption Properties dialog box. Select the Bottom of the table option, and then click OK to close the dialog box and see the caption placed at the bottom of the table. To change the alignment of the caption, click the caption and then click the Align Right, Align Left, Align Center, or Justified button on the Formatting toolbar. To remove a caption, highlight the caption text, right-click, and click Cut.

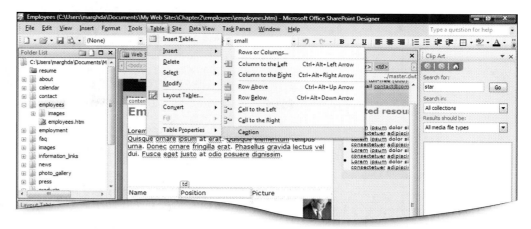

Figure 2.66 Adding a Caption to a Table

It is rather common for a Web designer to change the table and cell properties in the process of developing a Web page. SharePoint Designer makes it easy to modify tables using the Table Properties dialog box. Two other common ways in which Web designers modify the structure of a table and further refine the position of elements within the table are splitting and merging cells, using the Split Cells and Merge Cells commands on the Table menu.

Edit Table Properties

When designing a Web page using SharePoint Designer, you can use the Table Properties dialog box to change a table's properties, affecting the way it is displayed. Among the properties you can modify are the table alignment, width, border size and color, and table background color or background picture, as shown in Figure 2.67.

Figure 2.67 Table Properties Dialog Box

To edit the properties of a table, right-click anywhere within the table, click Table Properties to display the Table Properties dialog box, select the desired properties for your table, and click OK to close the Table Properties dialog box.

Table Properties Dialog Box | Reference

Table Properties Dialog Box Option	Functionality
Layout tools	Enable or disable the layout tools as well as automatically enable layout tools based on table content (layout tools are discussed later in this chapter).
Size	Size is determined by setting the number of rows and columns.
Alignment	A table that is smaller than 100% of the browser window can be aligned left, right, or center. If the default value is selected, the table aligns according to the page content that you place around it.
Float	The way that Web page elements, such as text or graphics, float around a table that is smaller than 100% of the browser window.
Cell padding	In pixels, the amount of empty space surrounding the content of cells.
Cell spacing	In pixels, the amount of empty space between the cells of a table.
Specify width and Specify height	Size of a table, in pixels, or as a percentage of the browser window.
Borders	Size and color properties of the table border and the color of the light and dark table border. If the Collapse table border option is checked, it enables you to collapse the table border. (A collapsed border uses only one line.) The Collapse table border option might not be available depending on the browser compatibility settings.
Background	A color for the table background or a picture for the table background.
Set	You can set your selections to be the default for all new tables.

Edit Cell Properties

> When editing the properties of selected cells, the table-level properties are overridden.

In many tables, you want different cells to have different properties. When editing the properties of selected cells, the table-level properties are overridden. To edit the properties of a cell, right-click within that cell and click Cell Properties to display the Cell Properties dialog box, as shown in Figure 2.68. Select the desired options and click OK to close the Cell Properties dialog box. Using the options included in the Cell Properties dialog box, you can modify a wide range of cell properties.

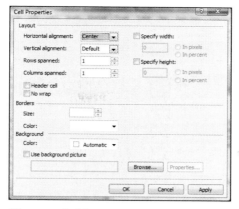

Figure 2.68   Cell Properties Dialog Box

Cell Properties Dialog Box | Reference

Cell Properties Dialog Box Selected Option	Functionality
Horizontal alignment	Determines the horizontal alignment of the cell contents (Left, Right, Center, and Justified).
Vertical alignment	Determines the vertical alignment of the cell contents (Top, Middle, Baseline, and Bottom).
Rows spanned	Sets the number of rows the cell will span (without deleting any cell), as shown in Figure 2.69.
Columns spanned	Sets the number of columns the cell will span (without deleting any cell), as shown in Figure 2.69.
Specify width and Specify height	Specifies the width and the height of the cell in pixels or in percentage of the table's total width and height.
Header cell	Automatically applies a bold and centered format to any text typed within the cell, as shown in Figure 2.69.
No wrap	Prevents cell contents from wrapping, which results in the cell expanding to fit the contents inserted in the cell.
Borders color	Defines the color of the cell borders, including Light border and Dark border settings.
Background color	Changes the background color of a cell (the default background color is white).
Use background picture	Enables you to use a picture as the cell background.

Cell spanning two columns and two rows

Figure 2.69 Setting Cell Properties

Split and Merge Cells

> Web designers commonly choose to split or merge cells to further refine the positioning of elements within a table.

Web designers commonly choose to split or merge cells to further refine the positioning of elements within a table. Theoretically, you can split a cell into as many distinct cells as needed. Likewise, you can merge as many distinct cells as needed into one combined cell. To split a cell, move the mouse pointer over it, right-click, point to Modify, and then click Split Cells to display the Split Cells dialog box, as shown in Figure 2.70. Click the Split into columns or Split into rows option, as needed, and then choose the number of rows or columns to split. Click OK to close the Split Cells dialog box.

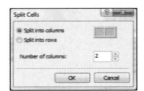

Figure 2.70 Split Cells Dialog Box

TIP Split Multiple Cells

To simultaneously split more than one cell, position the mouse in the first cell, click the Table menu, point to Select, point to Cell, and press Ctrl and keep it pressed while clicking the rest of the cells to be split. After you have selected all the necessary cells, right-click, point to Modify, and click Split cells to display the Split Cells dialog box.

For a more precise positioning of Web page elements within a table, SharePoint Designer enables you to merge adjacent table cells. To merge cells, click and drag the mouse across the cells to be merged. Then right-click, point to Modify, and click Merge cells, as shown in Figure 2.71, to merge all the selected cells.

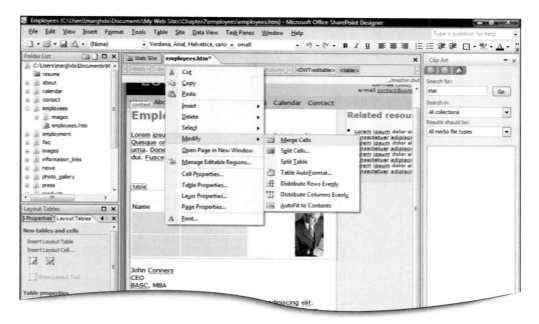

Figure 2.71 Merging Cells

Nested Tables

Nested tables are used by Web designers to further refine the position of elements within a Web page. Theoretically, you can insert a nested table in any cell of a table, but in reality you should not add more than one or two nested levels of tables. To insert a nested table, first position the insertion point in the desired location (cell) and follow the regular procedure for creating a table.

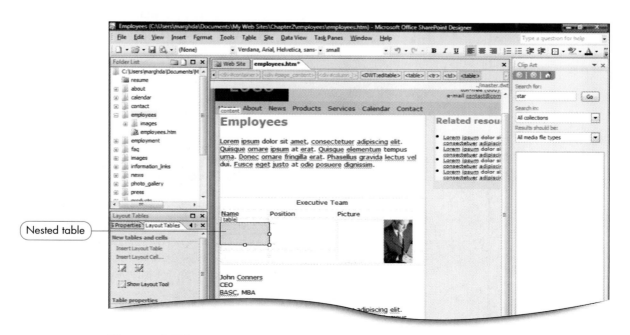

Figure 2.72 A Two-Row by Two-Column Nested Table

Select and Delete Tables

To select a table, click anywhere within the table, click Table on the Menu bar, point to Select (shown in Figure 2.73), and then click Table. All the table's cells are automatically highlighted (selected), including any nested tables.

TIP Dragging a Table

After a table is selected, you can click and hold the mouse anywhere on the table and drag it anywhere you want within the Web page.

If you click within a nested table, only the nested table is selected. If you want to delete the entire outer table, right-click within the selected table, point to Delete, and then select Table, or click Table on the Menu bar, point to Delete, and then click Delete Table, as shown in Figure 2.73.

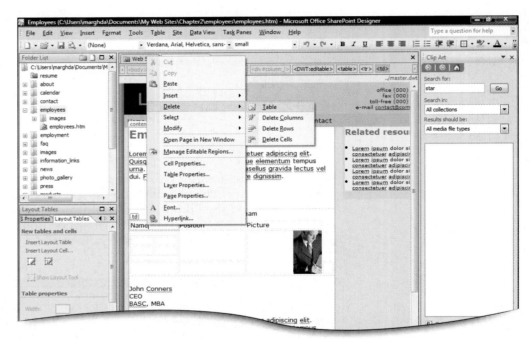

Figure 2.73 Deleting a Table

TIP Quick Tag Selector Toolbar

You can also select a table, row, cell, or nested table using the Quick Tag Selector toolbar. When you click a tag on the Quick Tag Selector toolbar, its color automatically changes, depending on the color scheme, and the corresponding table, row, cell, or nested table is selected. Click the down arrow, situated at the right of each tag as you point to it, and click the Tag Properties command on the drop-down list that is displayed to change the properties of the element that correspond to that tag, as shown in Figure 2.74.

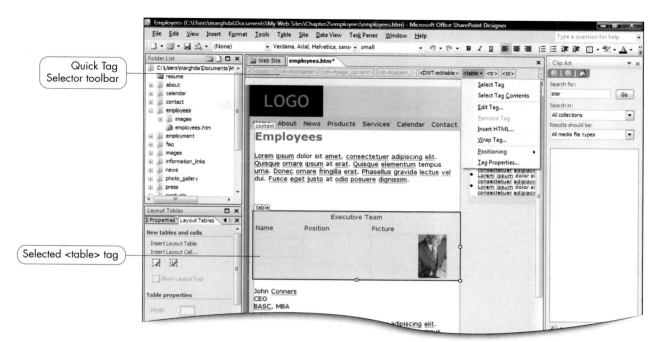

Figure 2.74 Using the Quick Tag Selector Toolbar

Quick Tag Selector toolbar

Selected <table> tag

TIP Accessible Tables

There are two major requirements for building accessible tables in compliance with the W3C requirements: Identify row and column headers by placing them in the first row and first column and use the <th> tag for all header cells. To read more about building accessible tables, visit the W3C Web site (go to http://www.w3.org and search the Web site for "accessible tables").

Use the Tables Toolbar

Another great tool provided by SharePoint Designer for creating tables and cells is the Tables toolbar. To display the Tables toolbar, click View on the Menu bar, point to Toolbars, and then click Tables. The Tables toolbar, shown Figure 2.75, provides many of the options included in the Insert Table, Table Properties, and Cell Properties dialog boxes, as well as some other useful options.

Figure 2.75 Tables Toolbar

Tables Toolbar | Reference

Button Name	Description	Icon
Show Layout Tool	Turns on and off the Layout tool. (This tool is discussed later in this chapter.)	Show Layout Tool
Draw Layout Table	Enables you to develop a layout table.	
Draw Layout Cell	Enables you to develop a layout cell.	
Row Above Row Below	Assists you in adding rows to a table.	
Column to Left Column to Right	Assists you in adding columns to a table.	
Delete Cells	Assists you in modifying a table by deleting one or more cells.	
Merge Cells	Assists you in modifying a table by merging selected cells.	
Split Cells	Assists you in modifying a table by splitting selected cells.	
Align Top, Center Vertically, and Align Bottom	Enables you to position the content of a cell.	
Distribute rows evenly Distribute columns evenly	Enables you to equally divide the table space among rows and columns.	
AutoFit to Contents	Automatically sizes a cell to fit the contents.	
Fill Color	Sets the fill color of the selected cell.	
Table AutoFormat Combo	Enables you to select one of the SharePoint Designer built-in styles to format a table.	None
Table AutoFormat	Displays the Table AutoFormat dialog box (shown in Figure 2.75).	

> The SharePoint Designer 2007 Layout Tables task pane provides Web designers with a more sophisticated and exact way to create a Web page layout.

Layout tables are Web page layout frameworks that consist of a regular one-cell table to which SharePoint Designer attaches an identification tag.

Layout cells are the building bricks for Layout tables.

A **spacer image** is a transparent GIF image that you can use to control spacing in autostretch tables; it consists of a single-pixel transparent image, outstretched to represent a specified number of pixels in width.

The SharePoint Designer 2007 Layout Tables task pane provides Web designers with a more sophisticated and exact way to create a Web page layout. **Layout tables** can be defined as Web page layout frameworks that consist of a regular one-cell table to which SharePoint Designer attaches an identification tag, as shown in the code sample included in Figure 2.76. To draw a layout table, position the insertion point in the desired location and click the Insert Layout Table command on the Layout Tables task pane. A layout table includes regions built using the Layout Cell feature. Consequently, **layout cells** can be defined as the building bricks for Layout tables.

When the Layout tool is activated by clicking the Insert Layout Tool command on the Layout Tables task pane, tabs indicate the exact size (in pixels) of all the layout tables and layout cells included on the Web page. When you click the drop-down arrow displayed to the right of any tab displaying a row or column size, you can define the row or column properties, as shown in Figure 2.76. Use one of the three options displayed on the drop-down list: Change Column (or row) Width, Make Column (or row) Autostretch, and Use Column Spacer Image. You can apply the Autostretch option to only one row or column in a layout table, whereas the other rows or columns in the layout table must be set at a fixed width or height. When you use the Autostretch option for a column, by default, SharePoint Designer adds a spacer image. A **spacer image** is a transparent GIF image that you can use to control spacing in autostretch tables; it consists of a single-pixel transparent image, outstretched to represent a specified number of pixels in width. Because browsers cannot display a table column narrower than the widest image contained in a cell within that column, using a spacer image in a layout table column forces browsers to maintain the column at least as wide as the spacer image.

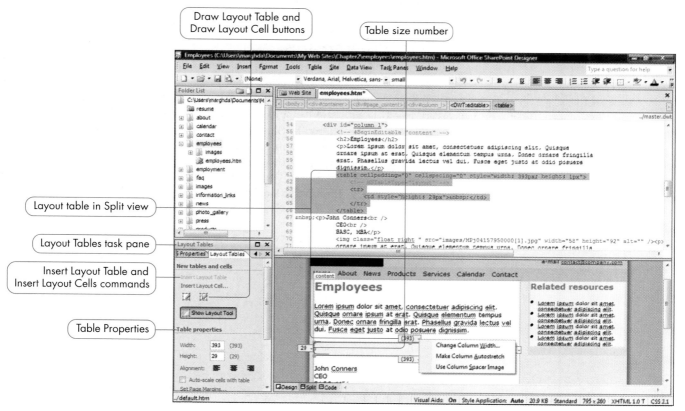

Figure 2.76 Working with a Layout Table

Click the Insert Layout Table command in the Layout Tables task pane to start developing a table layout for your Web page. (If the Layout Tables task pane is not displayed, click the Task Panes menu and click Layout Tables.) You can insert a layout cell by clicking the Insert Layout Cell command in the same section to display the Insert Layout Cell dialog box. Select the desired options and click OK to close the dialog box, as shown in Figure 2.77. To modify the size of the table and change its alignment, use the options included in the Table properties section of the Layout Tables task pane. It includes features such as Auto-scale cells with table and Set Page Margins.

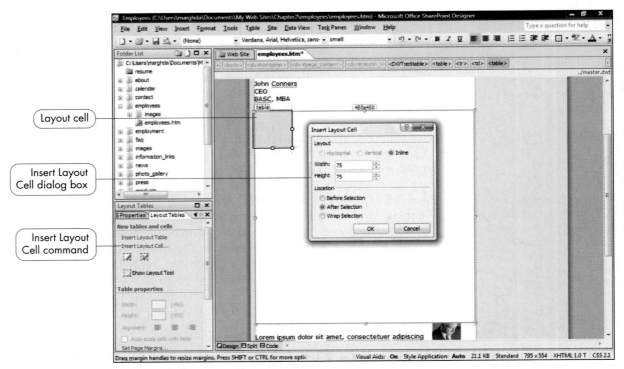

Figure 2.77 Inserting a Layout Cell Using the Insert Layout Cell Dialog Box

If a Web page does not have a Dynamic Web Template attached, you can use one of the Table layout templates offered by SharePoint Designer to build a table layout for your Web page. These templates are available in the Table layout section of the Layout Tables task pane. You just need to scroll down and click the desired template. SharePoint Designer automatically attaches it to your Web page, as shown in Figure 2.78. If there is content on the Web page, SharePoint Designer inserts the layout below the content. If a layout table was previously selected, the template is applied to it instead.

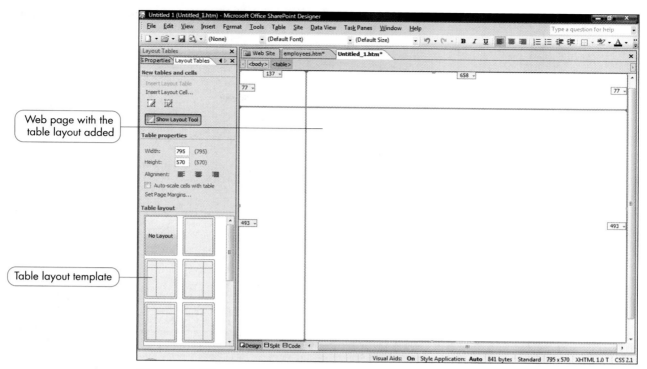

Web page with the table layout added

Table layout template

Figure 2.78 Inserting a Layout Table Using a Table Layout Template

Layout Tables and Cell Formatting

> The Table Properties and Cell Properties dialog boxes empower you with a complete set of tools to further refine your layout tables.

Although the Layout Tables task pane enables you to fully develop a layout table or cell and to customize the table and cell properties, the Table Properties and Cell Properties dialog boxes empower you with a complete set of tools to further refine your layout tables.

To format a layout cell, you first need to click one of its borders to select it (when a cell is selected, the control handles show) and right-click the layout cell to display the Cell Properties dialog box, shown in Figure 2.79. You can select specific borders to modify, and then choose the width and color of the borders. The cell shown in Figure 2.79 is a header cell, centered, with an orange background color and navy borders 2 pixels in width.

To format a layout table, right-click anywhere within the layout table to display the Table Properties dialog box. A new formatting style of a layout table does not override the formatting style of an included layout cell, as shown in Figure 2.80.

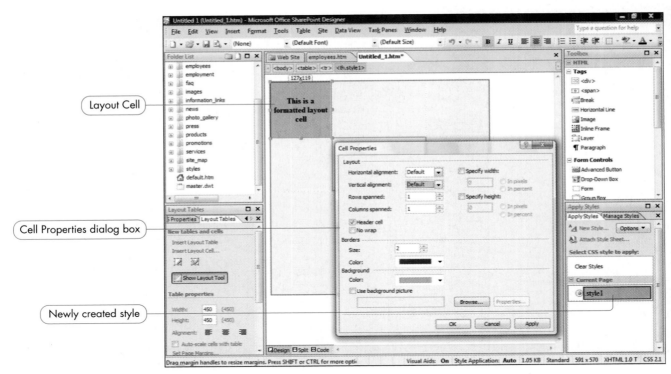

Figure 2.79 Formatting a Layout Cell

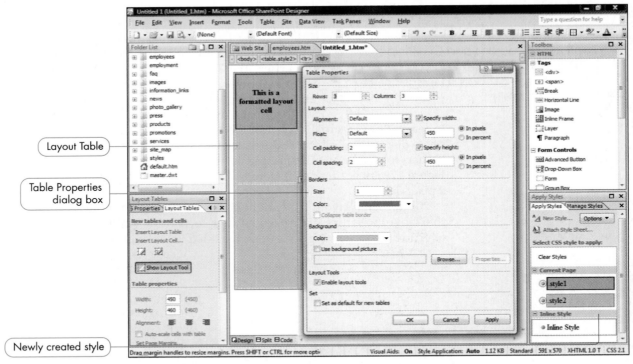

Figure 2.80 Formatting a Layout Table

Enhancing a Web Page Using Graphics, Multimedia, and Web Components

Chapter 1 covered the basic principles of good Web page design, and in this chapter you have been already introduced to more principles of good Web site design. Now, you will continue to apply these principles while learning how to enhance a Web page using graphics, multimedia, and SharePoint Designer Web components. Figure 2.81 contains a sample of some of these elements.

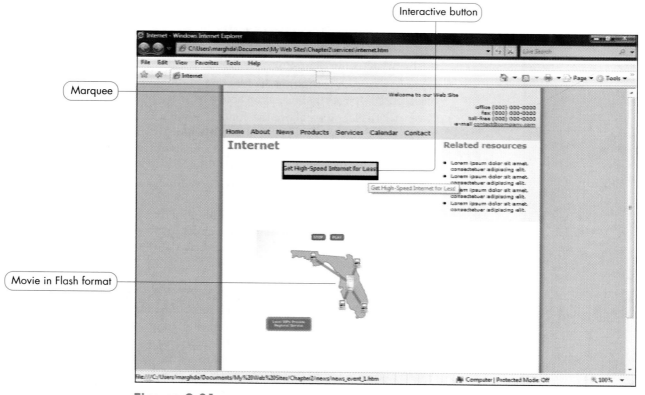

Figure 2.81   Enhancing a Web page

> To be a great Web developer you need good computer knowledge, practical skills, the imagination of Picasso, and the clear vision of Leonardo DaVinci.

To be a great Web developer you need good computer knowledge, practical skills, the imagination of Picasso, and the clear vision of Leonardo DaVinci. Web designers need to balance the demanding requirements of developing highly technical, usable, accessible, and attractive Web pages.

SharePoint Designer empowers Web designers to increase the attractiveness of their Web sites by using graphics and multimedia elements and to enrich the content and improve the usability of their Web pages by using more advanced design elements, such as the SharePoint Designer Web components. (Appendix A includes the top ten dos and don'ts of Web design, along with references to a few great Web sites that synthesize these tips.) When combining these elements, Web designers should follow a set of Web style guidelines including, but not limited to, the following recommendations:

- Use graphic, audio, and video files only when they support your Web page's message. Overusing such files makes your Web pages cumbersome and difficult to navigate.
- As a general rule, audio files should not be used as background sound for your Web pages. Sound irritates the majority of Web page visitors.
- Provide captions or transcripts of relevant audio content.
- Provide text or audio descriptions for relevant video content.
- When using graphics, keep in mind that people with different visual impairments might not be able to see every graphic. Consider including brief paragraphs describing the information that the graphics convey, as recommended by Access Board Section 508 standards (http://www.access-board.gov/508.htm). For image maps, consider assigning text to each hot spot.
- Avoid graphic animations that run continuously because they distract and irritate Web site visitors.
- Some SharePoint Designer Web components are not fully supported by all browsers or older browser versions. In addition, some components are not properly displayed if used in Web pages published on a server that does not support FrontPage server extensions, SharePoint Services, or SharePoint Server 2007.
- Development teams should not use some SharePoint Designer Web components, such as those based on the Web site navigational structure, unless all members of the team are using SharePoint Designer.
- Do not include large multimedia files on your main page. Larger files should appear on secondary pages that users can access from the main pages of your site.
- Give users a clear idea about the content of your multimedia files before they begin to download them. Main pages should include descriptive information about the multimedia files with previews such as still shots from the video. Provide the run time for media and the file size for materials that users can download.
- Clearly explain any software requirements for accessing the multimedia files and provide a download link.
- Store audio and video files on a streaming media server, which is a server that ensures high quality when delivering audio and video files via the Internet. Such servers enable users to quickly load and play these files in a browser.

TIP | Microsoft Windows Media Services 9 Series

The Windows Media Services 9 Series is one of the most powerful streaming media servers available and is known for the high-quality audio and video content it delivers via the Internet. Windows Media Services 9 Series is distributed as part of the Microsoft Windows 2003 server and can be downloaded from http://www.microsoft.com/windows/windowsmedia/9series/server.aspx.

At the time this manuscript was being developed, Windows Media Services was also available for the Windows Server 2008 Beta 3.

Add Graphics to a Web Page

Now that you know how to create a Web site and a Web page, you are ready to learn how to enhance a Web site using clip art and images from files, scanners, or cameras; position and format the images using the Picture toolbar; add links to images; create thumbnails and image maps; and insert AutoShape drawing objects. As discussed in Chapter 1, the following two image file formats are supported by most Web browsers:

The **Graphics Interchange Format (GIF)** supports transparent colors, is most often used to create animated images, can display only 256 colors, and has large file sizes compared, for example, with the Joint Photographic Experts Group (JPEG) format.

Animated GIFs combine several images and display them one after the other in rapid succession.

Joint Photographic Experts Group (JPEG) does not support animation and transparent colors, displays all 17.6 million colors that are available in the color palette, and uses an image compression algorithm.

Portable Network Graphics (PNG) format supports transparent colors, can be used for animated graphics, can display all 17.6 million colors available in the color palette, but is not yet fully supported by all browsers.

Interlacing is a technology used for displaying images in stages.

Adobe Flash is a popular application used to create Flash animated graphics

1. *GIF (Graphics Interchange Format)*—GIF files are most often used for drawn graphics and are still the preferred standard. You can easily create *animated GIFs* by combining several images and displaying them one after the other in rapid succession. You can create these animations using most graphic applications, including many of the graphic and animation programs that can be downloaded from the Internet for free. GIFs support transparent colors, which you can use to simulate motion and display slide shows. However, there are some drawbacks to using GIFs. They can display only 256 colors and they have large file sizes. The large file size can increase the time required to display GIFs in a browser.

2. *JPEG (Joint Photographic Experts Group; also JPG)*—JPEGs can display all 17.6 million colors that are available in the color palette and are most often used for photographs. JPEGs also use an image compression algorithm. Although increasing the degree of compression can considerably reduce the file size, it often reduces the quality of the image. Another drawback of JPEGs is that they do not support animation and transparent colors.

A more recent figure file format, called *Portable Network Graphics (PNG)*, is becoming more and more popular and might eventually replace GIF. PNGs can be used for animated graphics. They support transparent colors and can display all 17.6 million colors available in the color palette. Unfortunately, older browsers do not support the new PNG format, which causes some compatibility problems.

Interlacing is a technology used for displaying images in stages. For example, every third line of the image is displayed, then every fifth line, followed by every sixth line, and so on until the whole image is displayed. This technology can be used with GIF, JPG, and PNG files on the Internet, which enables users (especially those with a slow connection) to get a general idea of what the image is going to look like before it is fully displayed.

Another popular option for displaying graphics is Adobe® Flash®. More and more Web sites include Adobe Flash, or simply Flash, multimedia content, usually involving animated graphics. *Adobe Flash* is a popular application used to create Flash animated graphics. To view a Flash animated graphic, the user needs the Flash player, which can be downloaded free of charge from the Adobe Web site (http://www.adobe.com/products/flashplayer). As indicated in Chapter 1, SharePoint Designer supports these files.

TIP   BMP, XPM, and XBM Images and Browsers

BMP, XPM, and XBM images can cause some cross-browser problems. Of these three graphic file formats, Internet Explorer can display graphic files only in the BMP format. Consequently, they are not commonly used in Web design.

Images affect the content, style, and online performance of your Web page. When choosing images that you want to add to a Web page, never forget that each image you add increases the amount of time required for your Web page to display on your visitors' browsers. The Insert Picture command displays a submenu through which you can insert a clip art image, or an image from a file, scanner, or camera.

The **Clip Art task pane** provides you with a wide variety of media files, generically called *clips*, stored in a comprehensive group of collections.

Office Collections includes media files stored in the Office Collections folder when SharePoint Designer was installed.

Web Collections includes media files downloaded from the Web and stored in the Web Collections folder.

My Collections includes your personal collection of media files.

Using the SharePoint Designer **Clip Art task pane**, you can insert a wide variety of media files, generically called *clips*. These clips are stored in a comprehensive group of collections that include the **Office Collections** (media files stored in the Office Collections folder when SharePoint Designer was installed), the **Web Collections** (media files downloaded from the Web and stored in the Web Collections folder), and your personal collection of media files (**My Collections**). Click Insert, point to Picture, and click the Clip Art command to display the Clip Art task pane that you can use to insert a clip. Enter a keyword that describes the clip that you are searching for in the Search for box and click the Go button. The results are displayed in the Clip Art task pane. After browsing the results and choosing the clip you want, click the down arrow that appears on the left side, and then click the Insert command from the displayed drop-down menu. If the Accessibility Properties dialog box is displayed, as shown in Figure 2.82, type a concise descriptive text in the Alternate text box and click OK to close the dialog box.

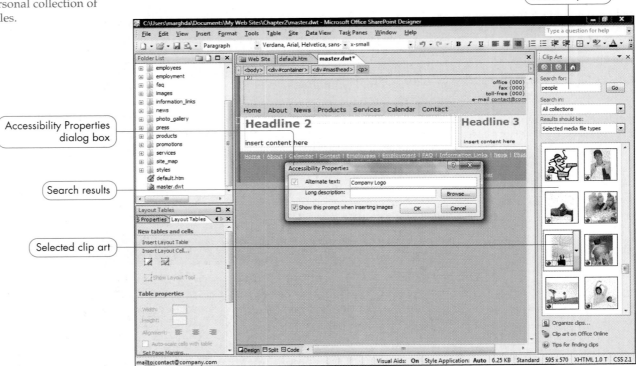

Figure 2.82 Clip Art Task Pane

The **Microsoft Clip Organizer** can simplify your searches by cataloging all the clips available to you.

The **Microsoft Clip Organizer** can simplify your searches by cataloging all the clips available to you. To access the Microsoft Clip Organizer (see Figure 2.82), click the Organize clips link near the bottom of the Clip Art task pane. The Microsoft Clip Organizer enables you to search for and add new clips and collections or to reorganize the current collections.

In addition to clip art images, you can use pictures that have been captured and stored in files. To insert a picture from a file, click Insert, point to Picture, and click the From File command to open the Picture dialog box. Using the Look in drop-down list, navigate until you locate the folder that contains your picture. Click the name of the picture you want and click the Insert button (shown in Figure 2.83). If the Accessibility Properties dialog box is displayed, type a concise descriptive text in the Alternate text box and click OK to close the dialog box. The image appears in the body of your Web page.

Figure 2.83   Picture Dialog Box

If you have a scanner, you can scan and insert pictures directly into your SharePoint Designer Web pages. You can also copy pictures from a digital camera to your Web page (either directly from SharePoint Designer or by using a camera-specific software application). To use images from these sources, you need to install your scanner or camera in Windows.

Most recent cameras and scanners are plug and play, which means that Windows can automatically detect and install them as soon as they are plugged into your computer. After your equipment has been installed, go to the Web page in which you plan to insert your image. Click Insert, point to Picture, and click the From Scanner or Camera command to open the Insert Picture from Scanner or Camera dialog box, shown in Figure 2.84. In the displayed Device list, click your specific scanner or camera. After you select the device, click the Custom Insert button to launch the device software, click the picture that you want to add, and click Get Pictures. If you want to add more than one picture, hold Ctrl while clicking all the desired pictures.

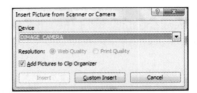

Figure 2.84   Insert Picture from Scanner or Camera Dialog Box

An image that has been included in a Web page can be characterized by the size it is when displayed in the Web page and by its actual physical size (the size of the file that stores the picture). SharePoint Designer enables you to modify the display size of each picture (*resize* it) and to modify the physical size of the picture in the file (*resample* it). When you click a picture that has already been added to a Web page, a set of sizing *handles* is displayed. The sizing handles look like little squares evenly distributed around the picture, as shown in Figure 2.85. You can resize the picture by dragging one of the corner handles to another position. The cursor changes to a double arrow when you click the sizing handles. If you click and drag one of the side handles, only the width of the picture changes. Similarly, if you click and drag on a top or bottom handle, only the height of the picture changes.

To **resize** a picture means to modify its display size.

To **resample** a picture means to modify its physical size.

Sizing **handles** look like little squares evenly distributed around the picture; they enable you to resize the picture.

Figure 2.85   Resizing a Picture Using Handles

The **Keep aspect ratio** check box enables you to maintain the aspect ratio of the picture as you resize it.

Another feature you can use to resize a picture is the Picture Properties dialog box. To access this dialog box, right-click the image, and then click the Picture Properties command on the shortcut menu. Click the Appearance tab and use the options in the Size area to change the width and height of the picture. To maintain the aspect ratio of the picture—the width versus the height of the picture—as you resize it, select the **Keep aspect ratio** check box, as shown in Figure 2.86.

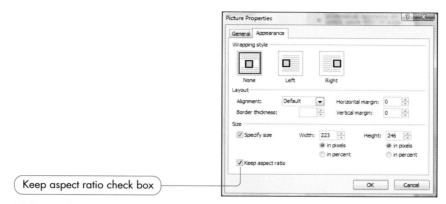

Figure 2.86   Resizing a Picture Using the Picture Properties Dialog Box

The two options described so far change only the way the picture appears on the Web page without affecting the physical size of the picture itself. The only way to change the size of the file that stores the picture itself is to resample the original picture file so that it is the size you want it to appear on the page. To resample the image, adjust the physical appearance of the image on your page, click the Picture Actions icon, and then click the Resample Picture to Match Size radio button, shown in Figure 2.87.

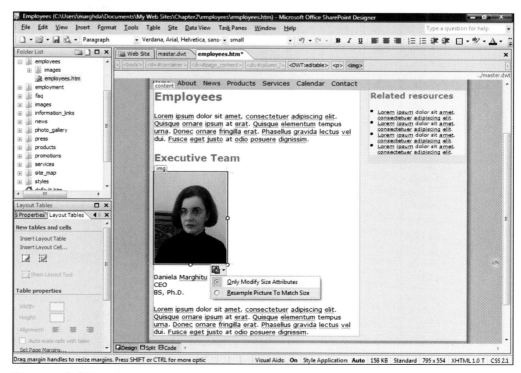

Figure 2.87   Resampling a Picture Using the Picture Actions Icon

> The SharePoint Designer Pictures toolbar includes a collection of buttons that give you access to a comprehensive set of features.

Modifying an image goes beyond resizing and resampling it. The SharePoint Designer Pictures toolbar includes a collection of buttons that give you access to a comprehensive set of features for creating thumbnails, rotating images, controlling the contrast and brightness of images, cropping images, adding hotspots to images, and more.

As you learned in Chapter 1, you can display the Pictures toolbar shown in Figure 2.88 by clicking View on the Menu bar, pointing to Toolbar, and then clicking the Pictures command. Another method is to right-click a picture, and then click the Show Pictures Toolbar command from the shortcut menu that displays.

If you want to use only a portion of the picture and remove the rest of the picture, you do so by using the Crop button from the Pictures toolbar. With the Pictures toolbar displayed, right-click the picture. Click the Crop button on the Pictures toolbar to display a dashed cropping box with its own set of handles that appears within your picture, as shown in Figure 2.88. Drag the handles to position the dashed box over the area that you want to keep. When you are satisfied with the position of the box, click the Crop button or double-click one of the crop box handles to complete the cropping process. Any part of the picture that was outside the dashed box is deleted. The cropped picture now displays on the Web page.

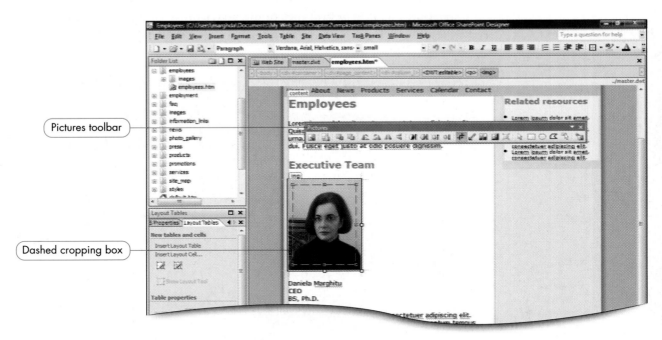

Pictures toolbar

Dashed cropping box

Figure 2.88 Cropping a Picture

SharePoint Designer has useful features that enable you to adjust the appearance of an image by improving the contrast and brightness of your image, by changing a picture to black and white only, and by making it appear washed out. To adjust the contrast of an image, click the More Contrast button or Less Contrast button until the desired contrast is reached. To adjust the brightness of a picture, click the More Brightness button or the Less Brightness button. You can change a picture to black and white or make it appear washed out by clicking the Color button and then clicking the Grayscale command or the Washing Out command from the displayed shortcut menu.

Using the *Set Transparent Color* button, shown in Figure 2.89, you can change the background color of the picture (or any specific color within the picture) to be transparent. When a picture has a transparent color, the Web page background color or image becomes visible within the picture.

The *Set Transparent Color* button enables you to change the background color of the picture (or any specific color within the picture) to be transparent.

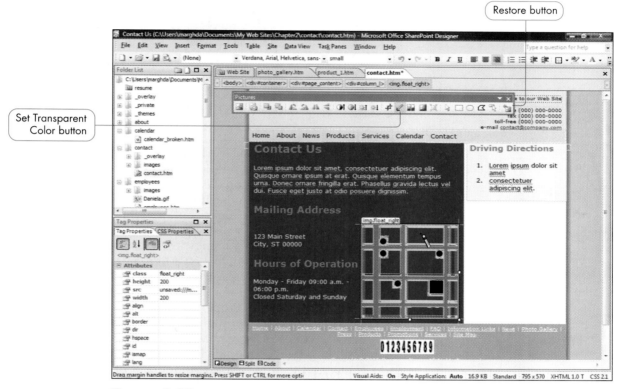

Figure 2.89 Using the Set Transparent Color Button

TIP   Transparent Picture

If you try to make a .jpg format picture transparent, SharePoint Designer will alert you about the fact that it will first need to convert it into a .gif format picture.

It is not unusual to be unhappy with the look of a picture after you have made a number of changes to it. The good news is that you can reverse the changes you made to a picture (including resizing, cropping, and applying colors, but excluding resampling) by clicking the Restore button (see Figure 2.89).

After adding images to a Web page, saving a Web page that includes newly embedded files requires a few more steps. When you click the Save button to save a Web page that includes embedded images, the Save Embedded Files dialog box displays, as shown in Figure 2.90. The Save Embedded Files dialog box displays a list of all the embedded files, a picture preview of the first (or selected) file, and the following buttons:

- **Rename**—Enables you to rename the embedded picture.
- **Change Folder**—Enables you to save the embedded picture in a different folder.
- **Set Action**—Enables you to maintain the previous copy of the picture or overwrite it.
- **Picture File Type**—Enables you to convert the picture to another format.

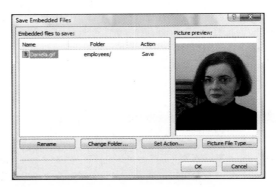

Figure 2.90 Save Embedded Files Dialog Box

> When you need to use a large image and you are concerned that the size of the file will make your page load too slowly, SharePoint Designer has an Auto Thumbnail option that creates a thumbnail of the image to appear on your page.

As you work with your Web page, you might want to change the position of an image on the page. You can reposition any image on the vertical axis by clicking and dragging the picture. When the mouse is where you want the image to appear, release the mouse button. While being dragged, the picture is followed by a small icon shaped like a square. You can align a picture horizontally by clicking it and then clicking the Center, Right Align, or Left Align button on the Formatting toolbar. SharePoint Designer also enables you to decide how a picture should be positioned in relation to the text. You can decide this by double-clicking the picture to open the Picture Properties dialog box. Click the Appearance tab, if necessary, and click None, Left, or Right in the Wrapping style area.

When you need to use a large image and you are concerned that the size of the file will make your page load too slowly, SharePoint Designer has an option for you. The *Auto Thumbnail* feature creates a thumbnail of the image to appear on your page. You can then add the necessary HTML code so that when the user clicks the thumbnail, the image is loaded in its true size.

Auto Thumbnail creates a thumbnail of the image to appear on your page.

- Before creating an auto thumbnail, you can set its properties using the AutoThumbnail tab of the Page Options dialog box. To access this dialog box, click the Tools menu and click Page Editor Options to open the Page Editor Options dialog box. Click the AutoThumbnail tab, shown in Figure 2.91, choose from the options there, and then click OK to close the Page Options dialog box.

  o To change the size of the thumbnail, use the Set drop-down list: Select the desired width, height, shortest side, or longest side settings, and use the Pixel box to specify the size.

  o To create a thumbnail border, check the Border Thickness check box and set the thickness of the border using the Pixel box.

  o To create a beveled effect for the thumbnail, check the Beveled edge check box.

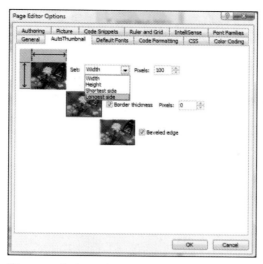

Figure 2.91 Setting the AutoThumbnail Properties

If you do not change the AutoThumbnail properties, they will be used every time you create a thumbnail. To create a thumbnail image, click the picture, and then click the AutoThumbnail button on the Picture toolbar, shown in Figure 2.92.

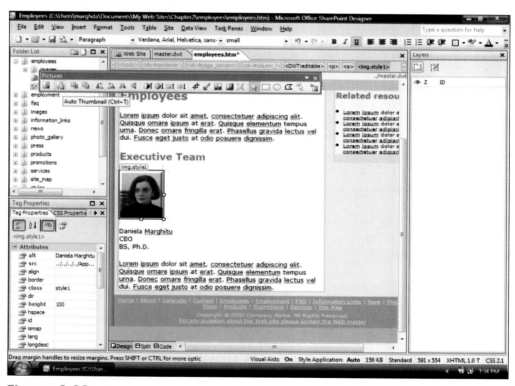

Figure 2.92 Creating an AutoThumbnail

As discussed in Chapter 1, you can add a hyperlink to an image. To do so, right-click the image to open the Picture Properties dialog box and click the General tab, as shown in Figure 2.93. In the Location box of the Hyperlink section, type the URL of the hyperlink, and then click OK to close the Picture Properties dialog box.

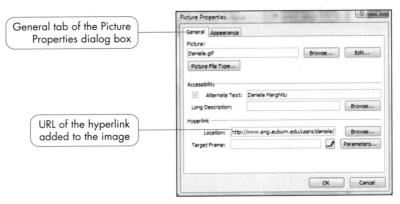

General tab of the Picture Properties dialog box

URL of the hyperlink added to the image

Figure 2.93 Adding a Hyperlink to an Image Using the Picture Properties Dialog Box

Another method for adding a hyperlink to an image is to click Insert on the Menu bar and click the Hyperlink command to display the Insert Hyperlink dialog box, as shown in Figure 2.94. In the Address box, type the URL of the hyperlink and click OK to close the Insert Hyperlink dialog box.

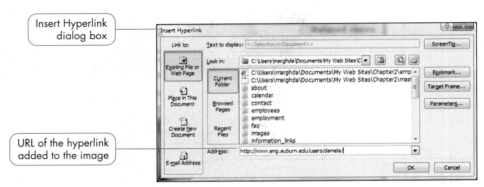

Insert Hyperlink dialog box

URL of the hyperlink added to the image

Figure 2.94 Adding a Hyperlink to an Image Using the Insert Hyperlink Dialog Box

To better arrange Web page content, after including images, it is highly recommended that you use CSS styles. Let us use the Web page shown in Figure 2.95 to learn more about images and Web page layout. In the highlighted section of the Web page, the text is too close, and it is unevenly wrapped around the picture.

To better position the image in the layout, you can float the image to the right or left of the adjacent content using the float property. In Design view, using the HTML command from the Insert menu, insert a <div> tag just above the selected section. Then, keeping the mouse button pressed, drag and drop the selected section within the <div> </div> (see Figure 2.95). Select the image and click New Style in the Apply Styles task pane to open the New Style dialog box.

Figure 2.95 Creating a <div> Section

TIP   The <div> tag

The <div> tag is commonly used in Web design to define Web page document sections. A unique ID is given to each <div> tag to which you can apply styles. These styles will apply to all Web page elements contained within the section.

To create a new class style, type .floatimageleft in the Selector box. To save the new class style in the style sheet already linked to the Web page, select Existing style sheet in the Define inbox. Click the Browse button to locate the existing style sheet and check the Apply new style to document selection in order to automatically apply the new style to the selected image. In the Category list, select Layout, and in the float list select left, then click OK to close the dialog box (see Figure 2.96). Now drag the image before the first word of the adjacent text and observe how text now wraps around the right side of the image but too close to the picture's right edge.

Figure 2.96 Creating a Floating Layout

Padding increases the space between any element content and its borders, whereas margins represent the space outside the element's borders.

To further refine the layout of your page, you can apply padding and margins to the image as well as visible borders. *Padding* increases the space between any element content (the image in our case) and its borders, whereas margins represent the space outside the element's borders. To add visible borders to the image, right-click the .floatimageleft style in the Manage Styles task pane and select Modify Style to open the Modify Style dialog box. Click Border in the Category list and select the values for the Border styles (see Figure 2.97). Click Box in the Category list, select the values for the image padding and margins (see Figure 2.98), and click OK to close the Modify Style dialog box.

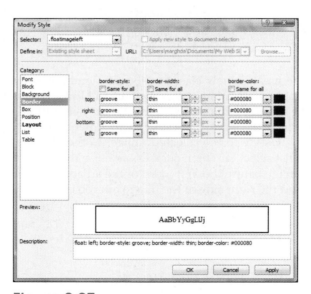

Figure 2.97 Adding Borders to an Image

Figure 2.98 Adding Padding and Margins to an Image

Select the <div> tag that contains the image and in the Tag Properties type team_member as a value of the id attribute. In the Manage Styles task pane, click New Style to open the New Style dialog box. Type .team_member in the Selector box and Current page in the Define in box. Check the Apply new style to document selection check box. Click Font in the Category list and select the values for the font-family and color. Click Apply to see the changes made to the <div> tag, and then click OK to close the Modify Style dialog box. If you wish to further edit the newly created style, right-click the team_member style in the Manage Styles task pane and select Modify Style to open the Modify Style dialog box (see Figure 2.99).

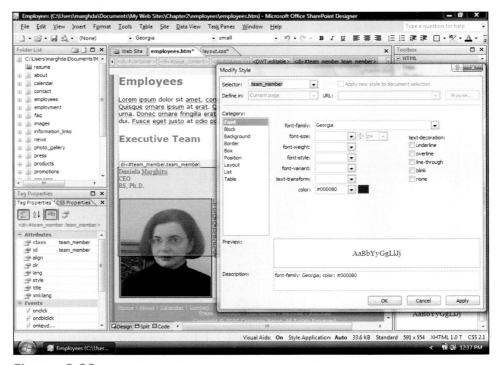

Figure 2.99 Creating a Class Style for the <div> Tag

Work with Multimedia Files

Using sound and video is another way Web designers enhance their Web pages. If you choose to add audio and video elements to your Web sites, you can make them available in two formats. You can incorporate sound and video files that can be downloaded and played, or create streaming audio and video files that enable users to hear and view these files while they are downloading. A streaming video file contains a sequential set of images that are sent in compressed form via the Internet and displayed as they arrive. If your Web page is stored on a Web server that cannot stream the content of audio and video files, your visitors must completely download them before they can see or listen to them.

TIP   Using Sounds

Just because you can add sounds to your Web page does not mean you should. Like graphic files, audio files can increase the size of your Web page and the time required to load your Web page in a browser.

A *plug-in* is a software application that can be an integral part of a browser or can give the browser additional multimedia capabilities.

Today's technology still requires the use of programs called plug-ins to interact with (view or play) some of these multimedia files. A *plug-in* is a software application that can be an integral part of a browser or can give the browser additional multimedia capabilities. Plug-ins need to be downloaded from the software developer's Web site (usually at no charge) and installed. Table 2.1 shows the audio and video file types that SharePoint Designer supports.

Table 2.1 Audio and Video File Types Supported by SharePoint Designer

File type	Description
Windows video files (*.avi)	The standard audio and video file format for Microsoft Windows.
Windows media files (*.wmv, *.wma, *.asf)	The file formats used with the Windows Media Player. Users need to download the Windows Media Player plug-in: http://www.microsoft.com/windows/windowsmedia/default.mspx. The only differences between ASF files and WMV or WMA files are the file extensions and the Multipurpose Internet Mail Extension (MIME) types. The MIME type for a WMV file is video/x-ms-wmv, and for WMA it is audio/x-ms-wma. The MIME type for ASF is video/x-ms-asf. The basic internal structure of the files is identical.
Motion picture experts group (*.mpg, *.mpeg)	The audio and video format used with Windows Media Player and Real Networks RealPlayer. Users need to download the Windows Media Player plug-in or the Real Audio plug-in.
RealAudio® files (*.ram, *.ra)	The audio file format used with RealNetworks® RealPlayer®. Users need to download the Real Audio plug-in: http://www.real.com.
Apple® QuickTime® (*.mov, *.qt)	Apple's audio and video file format. Windows users need to download the QuickTime plug-in: http://www.apple.com/quicktime/products/qt.
Flash files (*.swf)	Adobe's audio and video. Users need to download the Adobe Flash Player plug in: http://www.adobe.com/downloads.

TIP Multipurpose Internet Mail Extension (MIME) Types

Multipurpose Internet Mail Extension (MIME) types enable the exchange of different kinds of files on the Internet. Usually browsers have their MIME types set automatically, but in some cases you might have to set them manually. For Microsoft Windows Media files and live broadcasts to stream properly, both Web browsers and Web servers must have their MIME types configured to recognize Windows Media file types. MIME types usually have to be configured manually on a Web server. To learn more about MIME types, see the Microsoft Web page MIME Type Settings for Windows Media Services (http://support.microsoft.com/kb/288102).

SharePoint Designer enables you to add a link to an audio file on your Web page or to place an audio file on your Web page. To insert a link to an audio file, click Insert on the Menu bar and click the Hyperlink command. In the Insert Hyperlink dialog box, type the text of the link you want to display and choose the audio file. Click OK to close the Insert Hyperlink dialog box and see the link added to your Web page (see Figure 2.100). You will need to use the Plug-In Web component in order to place an audio file on your Web page (you will learn more about this later in the chapter).

> SharePoint Designer enables you to add a link to an audio file on your Web page or to place an audio file on your Web page.

Figure 2.100 Adding a Link to an Audio File

TIP User-Friendly Web Design

Whenever you include audio or video files on your Web page, it is a good practice to add a link to the Web site that contains the download for the plug-in that your visitors need to play those media files.

SharePoint Designer enables you to add a background sound to a Web page. A *background sound* is an audio file that plays for as long as a Web page is open in a browser or for a limited number of loops, or cycles, depending on the designer's preference. To add a background sound to your Web page, click File on the Menu bar, click Page Properties, and click the General tab, as shown in Figure 2.101. Enter the name of the audio file you want to use as a background sound or click the Browse button to locate it, select the number of loops, and then click OK.

> *Background sound* is an audio file that plays for as long as a Web page is open in a browser or for a limited number of loops, or cycles, depending on the designer's preference.

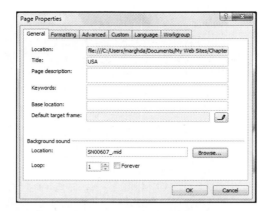

Figure 2.101 Adding a Background Sound to a Web Page

For the past few years, the technology of video streaming has developed and improved. Powerful companies, such as Microsoft and RealNetworks, are investing in research dedicated to improving the performance standards for Web-based video. The popularity of Web-based video is also driven by the reduction in the prices of digital video cameras, which enables more people and businesses to create their own digital video clips and post them on the Web. However, the size of video files is still rather large and the quality of delivery is not always the best. Table 2.1 shows the types of video files that are supported by SharePoint Designer.

As with audio, the main ways to use video on your Web page are to insert a link to a video file or to place a video file directly onto your Web page as streaming media. In SharePoint Designer, you can also add links to Flash movies to your Web page by dragging them from the Folders List to your Web page, as shown in Figure 2.102. To insert a link to a video file on your Web page, click the Hyperlink command on the Insert menu to open the Insert Hyperlink dialog box. Type the hyperlink text, choose the video file, and click OK to close the Insert Hyperlink dialog box. When the dialog box closes, the link is displayed on the Web page. You will need to use the Plug-In Web component in order to place a video file on your Web page (you will learn about this later in the chapter).

> As with audio, the main ways to use video on your Web page are to insert a link to a video file or to place a video file directly onto your Web page as streaming media.

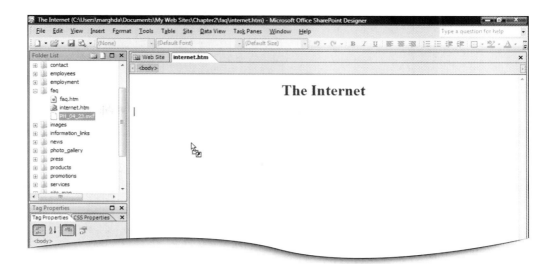

Figure 2.102 Dragging a Video File to a Web Page

Use Web Components

Web components represent
another great collection of
SharePoint Designer features
that you can use to enhance
content and improve navigation on your Web site.

Web components represent another great collection of SharePoint Designer features that you can use to enhance the content and improve the navigation on your Web site. SharePoint Designer enables you to add Web components to your Web pages using the Insert Web Component dialog box, shown in Figure 2.103. After you add a Web Component to your Web page, you can edit it at any time by double-clicking the component to open its Properties dialog box, such as the one shown in Figure 2.104.

TIP Microsoft Expression Web and Web Components

Microsoft Expression Web does not provide you with the set of Web Components discussed in this section. However, it allows you to modify the properties of these Web Components.

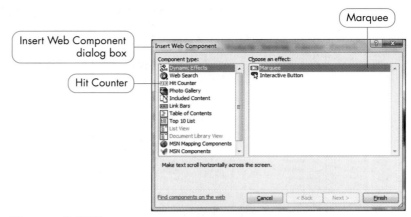

Figure 2.103   Inserting Web Components

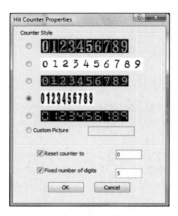

Figure 2.104   Hit Counter Properties Box

Not all Web components are fully supported by all browsers, especially old versions of browsers. When designing a Web page using Web components, you should remember the following:

• Some Web components will not work unless the Web page is published on a server that supports FrontPage Server Extensions or SharePoint Services.

• Some Web components are supported only by Internet Explorer.

• Some Web components are not supported by older versions of many browsers, including Internet Explorer. (Most Web components require Internet Explorer version 4.0 or higher to function properly.)

If keeping track of the number of people visiting your Web site is important to you, you should consider inserting the SharePoint Designer Web component called a *hit counter*. SharePoint Designer provides five primary styles of hit counters (see Figure 2.104). You can also use a custom picture instead of the five styles, reset the counter to a specific value, and choose the number of digits used to display the number of hits.

To add a hit counter to your Web page, pull down the Insert menu and click the Web Component command to open the Web Component dialog box (see Figure 2.103). In the Component type area of the box, click Hit Counter. In the Choose a Counter style area of the dialog box, click a style, and then click the Finish button to close the Insert Web Component dialog box and open the Hit Counter Properties dialog box. In the Counter Style area, choose the appropriate values for the Reset counter to and Fixed number of digits options, and then click OK to close the Hit Counter Properties dialog box and see the hit counter inserted in your Web page (see Figure 2.104).

TIP   Hit Counter Custom Picture

If you want to use a custom picture for your hit counter, you need to create a custom picture in GIF format. See the Microsoft How to create a custom image for the hit counter by using SharePoint Designer 2007 or FrontPage 2003 Web page (http://support.microsoft.com/kb/825549).

The Hit Counter Web component is supported by Internet Explorer version 2.0 and higher and Mozilla Firefox version 5.0 or higher. Figure 2.105 shows how the hit counter appears in Internet Explorer. Figure 2.106 shows how the hit counter appears in Mozilla Firefox. As you can see, the hit counter improperly displays almost exactly the same in both browsers.

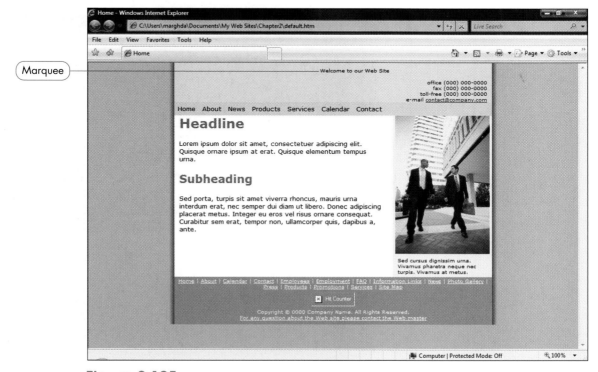

Figure 2.105   Hit Counter and Marquee Displayed in Internet Explorer

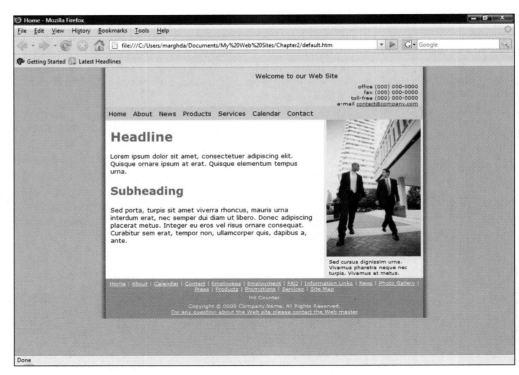

Figure 2.106 Hit Counter and Marquee Displayed in Mozilla Firefox

> A Hit Counter will not display properly in Web pages that are published on servers without the FrontPage Server Extensions or SharePoint Services.

A Hit Counter will not display properly in Web pages that are published on servers without the FrontPage Server Extensions or SharePoint Services, as shown in Figures 2.105 and 2.106. Once Web pages are published on a Web server supporting the FrontPage Server Extensions or SharePoint Services, they will be properly displayed, as shown in Figure 2.107.

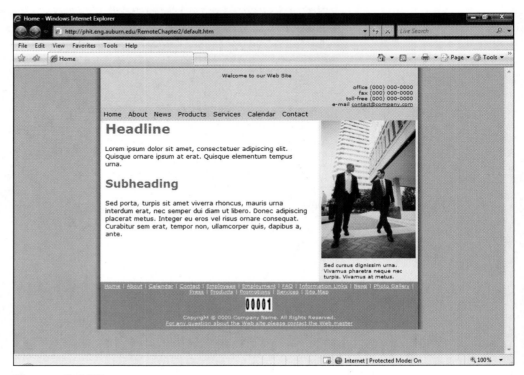

Figure 2.107 Web Page Published on a Web Server Supporting the SharePoint Services

A *marquee* is an attractive Web component that looks much like the tickers that you see at the bottom of your TV set when you watch news channels.

A *marquee* is an attractive Web component that looks much like the tickers that you see at the bottom of your TV set when you watch news channels, such as CNN, FOX News, or CNBC. It is an easy way to add a dynamic effect to your Web page. It is often used to display news or updated information related to the Web page's topic.

To add a marquee to your Web page, pull down the Insert menu and click the Web Component command to open the Web Component dialog box (see Figure 2.103). In the Component type area, click Dynamic Effects. In the Choose an effect area, click Marquee, and then click the Finish button. In the Marquee dialog box, type the text you want to scroll across your page and choose the appropriate options, such as the direction of the text movement (Left or Right), the speed of the movement, the behavior of the movement (Scroll, Slide, Alternate), the size and background color, and the type of repetition (Continuously or Fixed). Click OK to close the dialog box and see the marquee inserted in your Web page.

The Marquee Web component is supported by Internet Explorer version 2.0 and higher, as shown in Figure 2.105, and Mozilla Firefox version 5.0 or higher, as shown in Figure 2.106. You can insert a marquee in Web pages published on servers without the FrontPage Server Extensions or SharePoint Services.

Interactive buttons are buttons that change in appearance when users click them or hover over them with the mouse.

Interactive buttons are buttons that change in appearance when users click them or hover over them with the mouse, as shown in Figures 2.108 and 2.109. You can also attach a hyperlink to an interactive button. You can use interactive buttons to build navigation bars and tables of contents. You can also use them in forms. (You will learn about forms later in this chapter.)

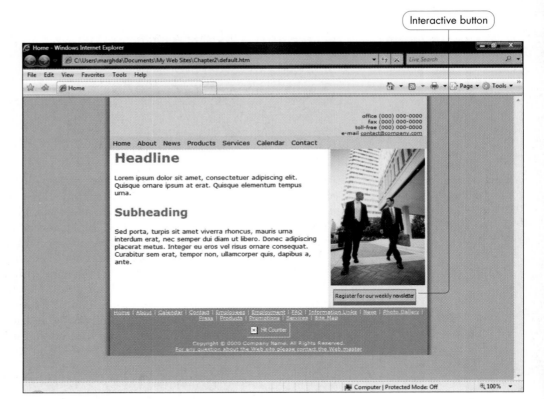

Figure 2.108 Interactive Button

Figure 2.109 Interactive Button as the Mouse Hovers Over It

To insert an interactive button in your Web page, click Insert on the Menu bar and click the Web Component command to open the Web Component dialog box. In the Component type area, click Dynamic Effects, and in the Choose an effect area, click Interactive Button, then click Finish to close the Web Component dialog box. The Interactive Buttons dialog box opens. It has three tabs (Button, Font, and Image). Click the various tabs and apply the desired options. If you want to add a hyperlink to the button, click the Button tab of the Interactive Buttons dialog box, type or browse for the correct location of the Web page or file you want to link to, and click OK to close the Interactive Buttons dialog box. The Interactive Button Web component is supported by Internet Explorer version 2.0 and higher and Mozilla Firefox version 5.0 and higher. You can use interactive buttons on Web pages published on servers without the FrontPage Server Extensions or SharePoint Services.

> ## TIP   Changing an Interactive Button's Properties
>
> To change an interactive button's properties, double-click the button in Design view and apply the appropriate changes in the three tabs of the Interactive Buttons dialog box. The Button tab options enable you to use a custom image for the button, to modify the label of the button, and to attach a link to it. The Font tab option enables you to set the font, font style, and font size of the button label. You can also set the original font color, hover font color, and pressed font color of the button. You can set the horizontal and vertical alignment of the button. With the Image tab, you can edit the image properties used to create the button, such as width and height, for any graphic file, such as JPEG or GIF.

Link bars can be extremely helpful navigational components of a Web site; they can contain custom links or links based on the Web site's navigational structure.

Link bars can be extremely helpful navigational components of a Web site. Link bars can contain custom links or links based on the Web site's navigational structure. To insert a link bar into your Web page, pull down the Insert menu and click the Web Component command to open the Web Component dialog box. In the Component type area, click Link bars, and in the Choose a bar type area, click one of the listed bar types. The first step in inserting any of the listed bar types is to choose a bar style from the list of available themes or from one of eight listed text styles. Next, decide whether you want to apply a vertical or horizontal alignment to the bar. Then click the Finish button to open the Link Bar Property dialog box to set the specific properties:

The ***Bar with custom links*** option includes links and text.

- *Bar with custom links*—Use this option to assign links and text to the link bar. The Link Bar Properties dialog box for this option is shown in Figure 2.110 and a bar with custom links is shown in Figure 2.111.

Figure 2.110 Link Bar Properties Dialog Box

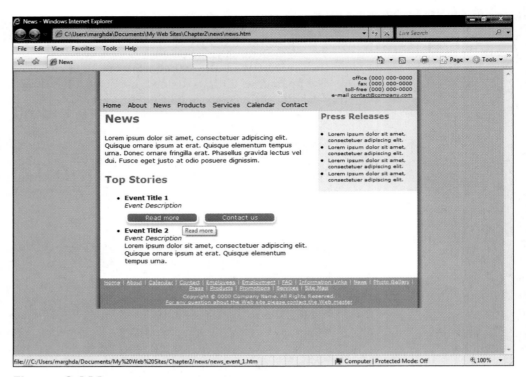

Figure 2.111 Link Bar with Custom Links

The ***Bar with back and next links*** option includes only Back and Next buttons.

- ***Bar with back and next links***—Use this option to create a link bar that includes only Back and Next buttons, as shown in Figure 2.112. The Link Bar Properties dialog box for this option prompts you to assign the links to the link bar. Although it is not displayed on the link bar, you are required to add a link to the current page.

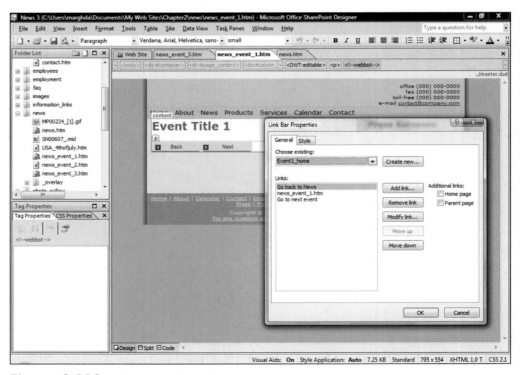

Figure 2.112 Link Bar with Back and Next Links

The **Bar based on navigation structure** option is built upon the navigational structure of your Web site.

- *Bar based on navigation structure*—This option enables you to create a link bar that is built upon the navigational structure of your Web site, as shown in Figure 2.113. The Link Bar Properties dialog box provides you with six radio buttons for choosing the type of page links you want to use on the bar. You also have the option to add two additional pages (a Home page and Parent page) by clicking their corresponding check boxes, as shown in Figure 2.113.

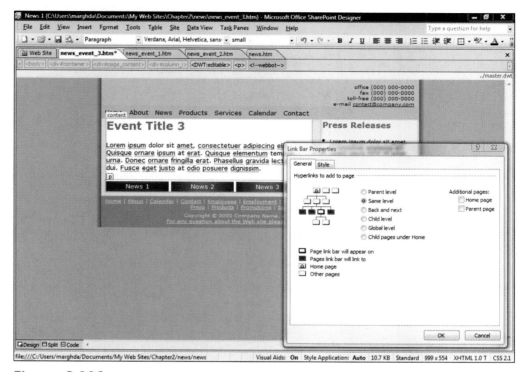

Figure 2.113   Building a Link Bar Based on Navigation Structure

Advanced controls enable Web designers to add more advanced components to their Web pages, such as Java applets, audio and video files, Plug-In, and Active-X.

Advanced controls enable Web designers to add more advanced components to their Web pages. Some of the most popular Advanced controls are Java™ applets, audio and video files (including the Flash format that you learned about earlier in this chapter), Plug-In, and Active-X. A Java applet is normally used by Web designers to add animation and music or to send and retrieve information to and from a database. Java applets, Plug-In, and Active-X are supported by Internet Explorer version 2.0 and higher and Mozilla Firefox 2.0.0.4 and higher. These components can also be used with Web pages published on servers without the FrontPage Server Extensions or SharePoint Services.

The Plug-In advanced control makes it easier to insert a browser plug-in into your Web page. The Active-X control assists you by providing all the data needed to support an Active-X advanced control, such as a radio button or check box, on your Web site. Active-X controls are not supported by Netscape and Mozilla Firefox browsers.

For example, to insert a video file in Flash format (.swf), click Insert on the Menu bar and click Web Component to open the Insert Web Component dialog box. In the Component type area, click Advanced Controls. In the Choose a Control area, click Plug-In. Then click Finish to close the Insert Web Component dialog box and open the Plug-In Properties dialog box, which you can use to locate and select the video or audio file you want to insert in your Web page. Click Insert to close the dialog box. SharePoint Designer places an icon on your Web page to help you locate the Flash file, as shown in Figure 2.114.

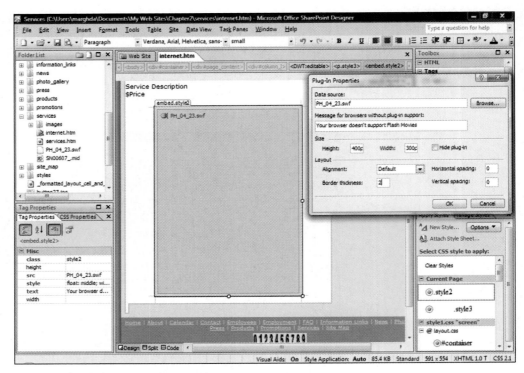

Figure 2.114 Inserting a Movie in Flash Format Using the SharePoint Designer Plug-In Advanced Control

If you decide to make a change to the properties of a movie in Flash, double-click the icon and make the desired changes in the Movie in Flash Format Properties dialog box. For example, to create the Web page shown in Figure 2.115, the border thickness was set to size 2.

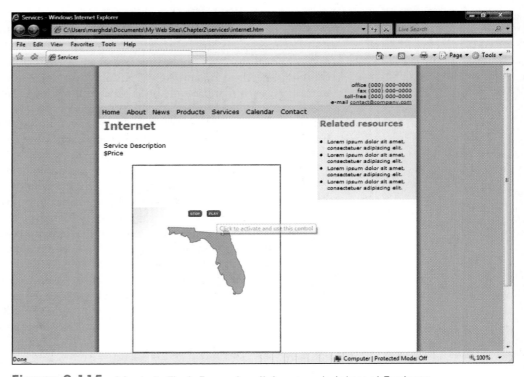

Figure 2.115 Movie in Flash Format as It Appears in Internet Explorer

To view the Flash movie in Preview in Browser view using the Mozilla Firefox browser, you first need to install the Adobe Flash Player, which is available free of charge (http://www.adobe.com/downloads). See also Figure 2.116.

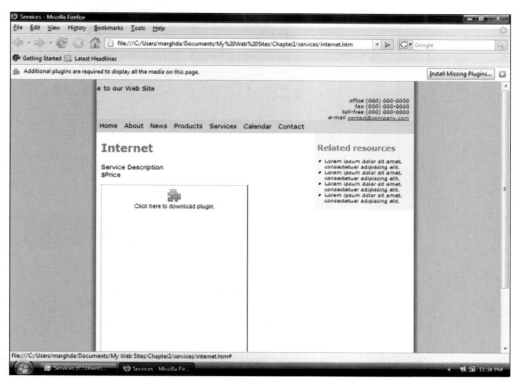

Figure 2.116   Movie in Flash Format as It Appears in Mozilla Firefox Browser When Missing the Adobe Flash Player

An applet is a Java program that can be embedded in your Web page. When the Web page loads in a browser, the applet downloads and executes. Java applet Web components are supported by Internet Explorer version 2.0 and higher and Mozilla version 5.0 and higher. You can also insert applets in Web pages published on servers without the SharePoint Designer extensions. To view a Web page including a Java applet in Internet Explorer 7.0, you first need to install a Java virtual machine on your computer. For more information, visit the Microsoft Web page on Java virtual machine support (http://www.microsoft.com/java). To view a Web page including a Java applet in Mozilla Firefox, you first need to install Java Runtime Environment on your computer. For more information, visit Sun© Microsystem's Java Plug-in Technology Web page (http://java.sun.com/products/plugin).

To insert a Java applet, click Insert on the Menu bar and click the Web Component command to open the Insert Web Component dialog box. In the Component type area, click Advanced Controls. In the Choose a Control area, click Java Applet, and then click Finish. The Insert Web Component dialog box closes and the Java Applet Properties dialog box opens, requiring the following information (see Figure 2.117):

- In the Applet source box, type the name of the Java applet source file. (Java applet source files typically have a .class file extension.)

- In the Applet base URL box, type the URL of the folder containing the Java applet file if the Web page is in a different folder than the Java applet file.

- In the Message for browsers without Java support box, type alternate text to display in Web browsers that do not support Java applets.

Click OK to close the dialog box and insert the Java applet in the Web page. If you decide to change the properties of a Java applet component, double-click it and make the appropriate changes in the Java Applet Properties dialog box.

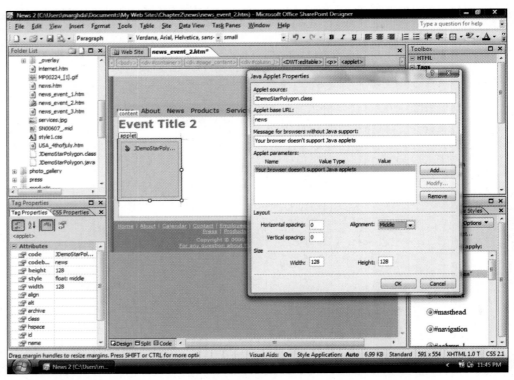

Figure 2.117 Inserting a Java Applet Advanced Control as It Appears in Page View

---

TIP   Freeware Java Applets

SharePoint Designer does not provide a collection of applets; thus, the Java applet file must be imported to the Web folder first. Sun Microsystem's Applets Web page (http://java.sun.com/applets) is a great source of applet samples and resources.

Included Content represents an extremely helpful and popular set of Web components that enable you to include different types of components, such as Web page configuration variables, another Web page, and a picture or Web page, based on a predefined time schedule.

A *comment* is text that can be seen only in Design, Split, and Code views, but that is not visible in Preview in Browser view.

Included Content represents an extremely helpful and popular set of Web components that enable you to include different types of components, such as Web page configuration variables, another Web page, or a picture, based on a predefined time schedule. All Included Content components are supported by Internet Explorer version 4.0 and higher, and Mozilla Firefox version 5.0 and higher. To add included content, click the Insert menu and click Web Component to open the Insert Web Component dialog box. In the Component type section, click Included Content, and then, in the Choose a type of component section, choose one of the following components:

- *Comment*—This component is the counterpart of the New Comment Review feature available in all Microsoft Office 2007 applications—a text section that can be seen only in Design, Split, and Code views (see Figure 2.118), but that is not visible in Preview in Browser view (see Figure 2.119).

The **Date and Time** option opens the Date and Time dialog box and includes a few options about when to update the date and time and how to format each.

The **Substitution** component inserts a page configuration variable, such as author, description, modified by, and page URL, into your Web site.

The **Page** component inserts an entire page into a Web page so that any changes made and saved in the inserted page's original file appear in all pages where this page was inserted as a page component.

The **Page Banner** component displays the page titles as they appear in Navigation view and will not be displayed on the Web page unless the page is included in the navigation structure.

- *Date and Time*—This component opens the Date and Time dialog box. It includes a few options about when to update the date and time and how to format each (see Figures 2.118 and 2.119).

- *Substitution*—This component inserts a page configuration variable, such as author, description, modified by, and page URL, into your Web site. To insert a substitution component, click Substitution component to display the Substitution Properties dialog box. Click the drop-down arrow on the right of the Substitute with box and click the desired option. Then click OK to close the dialog box. Figures 2.118 and 2.119 show the Modified by variable inserted on a Web page in Design and Preview in Browser views.

- *Page*—This component inserts an entire page into a Web page. Any changes made and saved in the inserted page's original file appear in all pages where this page was inserted as a page component. To add a page component, click Page Component and click Finish. In the Include Page Properties dialog box that displays, type the URL for the desired Web page or click the Browse button to locate the desired Web page, and then click OK. Figures 2.118 and 2.119 show an included Page component in Design and Preview in Browser views.

- *Page Banner*—This component displays the page titles as they appear in Navigation view. A page banner will not be displayed on the Web page unless the page is included in the navigation structure. To add a page banner, click Page Banner to open the Page Banner Properties dialog box. Select one of the two options for displaying the page banner: as a picture or as text. If the Web page was not formatted with CSS styles, the Page Banner displays as simple text, which you can format later. If the Web page was formatted with CSS styles, you can choose to display the Page Banner as simple text or as a picture. The picture used is dictated by the CSS styles. However, you can still format the page banner later. Figures 2.118 and 2.119 show a Page Banner in Design and Preview in Browser views.

TIP Changing the Text of a Page Banner

If you change the way a page title reads in Navigation view, the default text of the Page Banner is automatically updated.

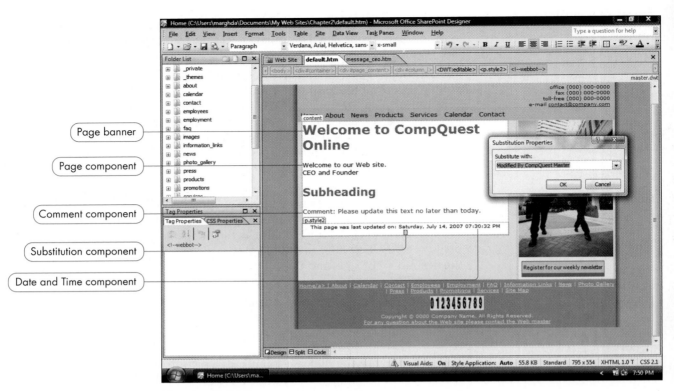

Page banner

Page component

Comment component

Substitution component

Date and Time component

Figure 2.118 Included Content Components Displayed in Design View

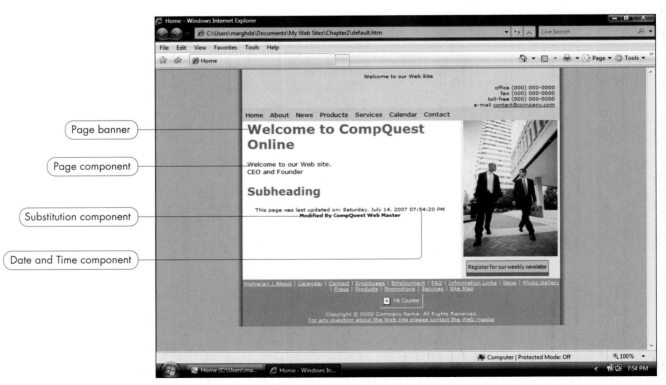

Page banner

Page component

Substitution component

Date and Time component

Figure 2.119 Included Content Components Displayed in Preview in Browser View

- *Page Based on Schedule*—This component enables you to add an entire separate page to your Web page at regularly scheduled intervals. This feature enables Web designers to update the content of a Web page on a predefined schedule. Any changes made in the page used as the Page Based on Schedule Component are updated in all Web pages in which the modified page was included. To add a page based on schedule component, click Page Component and click Finish. In the Scheduled Include Page Properties dialog box that displays, type the URL for the desired Web page or click the Browse button to locate the desired Web page, select the starting and ending time of the display period, and then click OK to close the dialog box. Figure 2.120 shows a Page Based on Schedule component.

- *Picture Based on Schedule*—This component is similar to the Page Based on Schedule component and enables you to insert a picture in a Web page at regularly scheduled intervals. To add a Picture Based on Schedule component, click Page Component and click Finish. In the Scheduled Picture Properties dialog box that displays, type the address of the picture you want to display or click the Browse button to locate the picture, select the starting and ending time of the display period (see Figure 2.121), and then click OK.

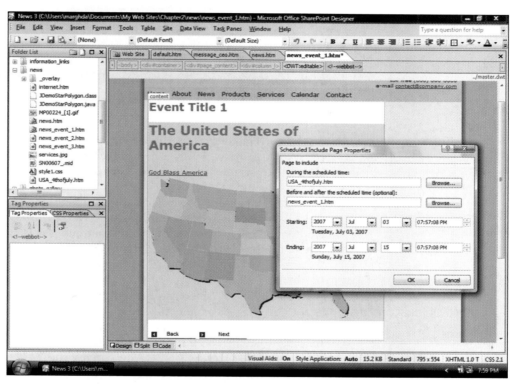

Figure 2.120   Page Based on Schedule Added to a Web Page

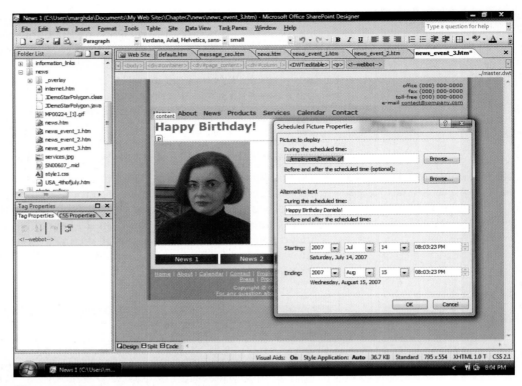

Figure 2.121 Picture Based on Schedule Added to a Web Page

A ***site map*** is a hierarchical outline of a Web site's sections, which provides a Web site overview to help users locate the Web page they are looking for in the Web site architecture.

Users dislike Web sites where they have a hard time finding what they are seeking. A ***site map***, which is a hierarchical outline of a Web site's sections, provides a Web site overview to help users locate the Web page they are looking for in the Web site architecture.

The SharePoint Designer Table of Contents Web component enables you to quickly create a site map. In the Insert Web Component dialog box, select Table of Contents. Under Choose a table of contents, select For This Web Site and click the Finish button. The Table of Contents Properties dialog box is displayed. In the Page URL for starting point of table, enter or browse for the path of the Web page that you wish to select as the root of the site map, select, as desired, the other options of the site map, and click OK. A generic site map appears on the Web page, including default headings (see Figure 2.122). To modify the options of the site map, double-click on the generic site map to display the Table of Contents Properties dialog box (see Figure 2.122). After saving the Web page, click Preview in Browser using Internet Explorer (see Figure 2.123). The Table of Contents component is fully supported by Mozilla Firefox 2.0.0.4 and higher; it is not necessary to publish it on a server supporting FrontPage Server Extensions or SharePoint Services.

> The SharePoint Designer Table of Contents Web component enables you to quickly create a site map.

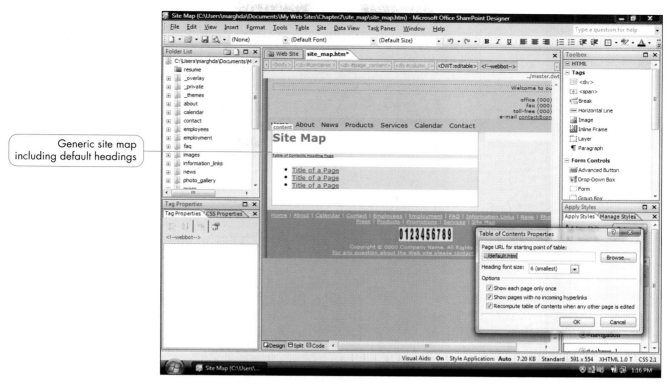

Generic site map including default headings

Figure 2.122 Site Map in Design View

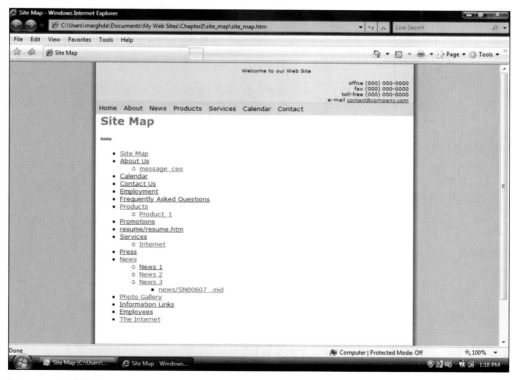

Figure 2.123 Site Map in Preview in Browser View

One of the most popular SharePoint Designer Web components is the ***Photo Gallery***, which arranges your photos in one of four predesigned layouts.

> SharePoint Designer automatically creates thumbnails of your images, and, depending on the selected layout option, descriptive text or caption text for each image can be displayed.

One of the most popular SharePoint Designer Web components is the ***Photo Gallery***, which arranges your photos in one of the four predesigned layouts, displayed under Choose a Photo Gallery Option (see Figure 2.124).

SharePoint Designer automatically creates thumbnails of your images, and, depending on the selected layout option, descriptive text or caption text for each image can be displayed. In the Insert Web Component dialog box, click Photo Gallery, select a Photo Gallery Option, and click Finish to display the Photo Gallery Properties dialog box. The Pictures tab enables you to add, edit, or remove images from the gallery, modify the thumbnail size, customize the font, and add a caption or text description for each image (see Figure 2.125). The Layout tab enables you to choose a layout and select the number of pictures per row (when this option is available). When you save the Web page, the Save Embedded Files dialog box will be displayed. Figure 2.126 shows a Photo Gallery Web component with Horizontal Layout, five pictures per row, and caption added for the first picture. To modify the options of a Photo Gallery Web component, double-click the Web component in Design view to display the Photo Gallery Properties dialog box.

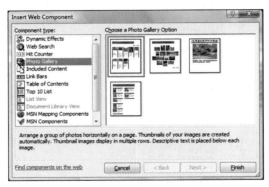

Figure 2.124   Using the Insert Web Component Dialog Box to Add a Photo Gallery to a Web Page

Figure 2.125 Pictures Tab of the Photo Gallery Properties Dialog Box

Figure 2.126 Photo Gallery Displayed in Preview in Browser View

Printing a Web Page

To print a Web page, use the File, Print command. The Print dialog box appears, as shown in Figure 2.127, providing you with many different print options. After you have made your selections, click OK to print. These selections become the default print settings used when you click the Print button from the Standard toolbar. The dialog box is divided into three areas where you can make selections:

- **Printer**—Select the printer you want to use from the Name list. Click the Properties button to set up the printer the way you want to use it. Choose from properties such as Orientation (Portrait or Landscape), Print on Both Sides, Pages per Sheet, and Tray selection.

- **Print range**—Select to print all pages or specify the exact pages to print.
- **Copies**—Determine the number of copies you want and whether you want the copies to be collated.

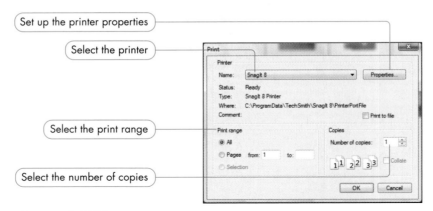

Figure 2.127   Printing a Web Page Using the Print Dialog Box

> It is becoming a standard practice to help visitors print Web pages by creating a printer-friendly version that is accessible through a text link, such as Printer-friendly version.

If you provide information on your Web pages that people might want to print, you need to make sure that your pages will print well. As Web design becomes more and more sophisticated, it is becoming standard practice to help visitors print Web pages by creating a printer-friendly version that is accessible through a text link, such as Printer-friendly version. To create a printer-friendly version of a Web page, consider the following actions:

- Remove any links.
- Remove all graphics or any unessential graphics, including the background image.
- Remove banners.
- Make sure there is a good contrast between the background and text colors.

Depending on how many Web page elements you need to remove or reformat, it might actually be easier to create a simple text version of the Web page first and then save it as your printer-friendly option.

To see how the page will appear when printed, click File on the Menu bar, then click Print Preview. You can see that there are differences between this preview and the view from a Web browser. The *Print Preview* feature paginates and assigns page numbers, whereas Web browsers do not.

Print Preview allows you to see how a Web page will appear when printed; this feature paginates and assigns page numbers, whereas Web browsers do not.

TIP   Creating a Printer-Friendly Version of a Web Page

The following article provides additional guidelines for creating a printer-friendly version of a Web page: http://webdesign.about.com/cs/printerfriendly/a/aa041403a.htm.

Hands-On Exercises

2 | Creating and Enhancing a Web Page in SharePoint Designer 2007

Skills covered: 1. Start SharePoint Designer, Open a Web site, Create a New Folder, Add a New Web Page in Navigation View, and Format the New Web Page **2.** Add Text Content to a Web Page and Format Text Using CSS Inline Styles and External Style Sheets **3.** Organize a Web Page Using Hyperlinks and Format Hyperlinks Using CSS Styles **4.** Organize a Web Page Using Lists and Format Lists Using CSS Styles **5.** Insert a Standard Table, Format a Standard Table, and Add Content to a Standard Table **6.** Add Graphics to a Web Page and Create an Auto Thumbnail **7.** Add a Plug-In Web Component to a Web Page, Add a Page Banner Web Component to a Dynamic Web Template, and Add a Marquee Web Component to a Dynamic Web Template

---

Step 1
Start SharePoint Designer, Open a Web Site, Create a New Folder, Add a New Web Page in Navigation View, and Format the New Web Page

Refer to Figure 2.128 as you complete Step 1.

a. Start SharePoint Designer. Click **File** on the Menu bar, click **Open Site**, navigate to the chap2_ho2_website Web site folder, click it, and then click the **Open button**. Create a backup **chap2_ho2_website_solution** Web site folder using the Remote Web Site view.

You should see the chap2_ho2_website Web site folder and the chap2_ho2_website_solution Web site folder in Remote Web Site view.

b. Click the **Open your Remote Web site in SharePoint Designer hyperlink** in the *Status* section of the Remote Web Site view.

You should see the *chap2_ho2_website_solution* Web site in *Folders* view.

TROUBLESHOOTING: You should still see on the Windows task bar the tab of the SharePoint Designer application open from step a; right-click that tab and click Close on the shortcut menu to close it.

c. Point to **New** on the Menu bar and click **Folder**. Rename the new folder **faq** and press **Enter**.

The faq folder should now appear in Folders view and the Folder List task pane.

d. Click the **Navigation button** to view the Web site in Navigation view. Click **default.htm** and click the **New Page button** in Navigation view. Click **View** on the Menu bar and click **Refresh**.

The *untitled_1.htm* file now shows in the Folders List task pane and navigation structure of the Web site.

e. Click **untitled_1.htm** in the Folders List task pane, and then click again. In the edit text box, type **faq.htm** and press **Enter**.

The file name of the newly created Web page is now showing in the Folders List task pane.

f. Right-click **Untitled 1** in Navigation view and click **Rename** on the menu. In the edit text box, type **Frequently Asked Questions** and press **Enter** to change the label of the newly created Web page.

The label of the newly created Web page is now showing in Navigation view.

g. In the Folder List task pane, click **faq.htm**, drag it over the faq folder, and drop it. Click the **plus sign** showing now to the left of the faq folder. Double-click the file name **faq.htm** in the Folders List task pane to open the Web page in Design view.

h. Right-click the body of the Web page and click **Page Properties** on the menu.

The Page Properties dialog box is now displayed.

i. Click the **General tab**, if it is not already displayed, and see that *Frequently Asked Questions* is displayed in the Title box.

j. Click the **Formatting tab**, click the **drop-down arrow** to the right of the Background box, and click the **Fuchsia** color. Click **OK** to close the Page Properties dialog box. Click the **Save button** on the Common toolbar.

The faq.htm Web page with Fuchsia background color should now be displayed in Design view. The new inline style should also be displayed in the Apply Styles and CSS Properties task panes.

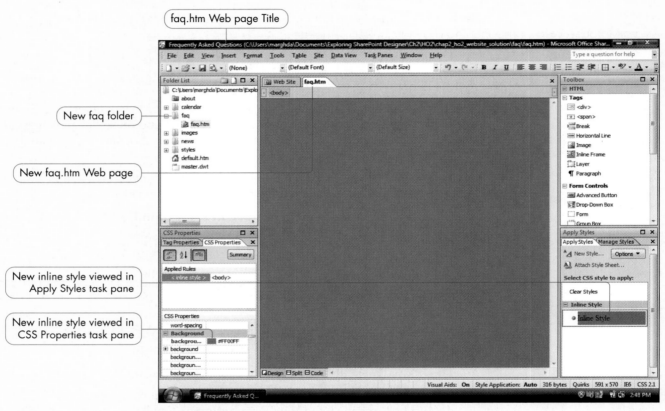

Figure 2.128 Adding and Formatting a New Web Page

Refer to Figure 2.129 as you complete Step 2.

Step 2

Add Text Content to a Web Page and Format Text Using CSS Inline Styles and External Style Sheets

a. Click the **Split tab** and position the insertion cursor between the <body> </body> pair tags, in Code view.

b. Click **Insert** on the Menu bar, point to **HTML**, and click **<div>**. In the *Attributes* section of the Tag Properties task pane, click **id** and press **Tab**. Type **container** and press **Enter**.

<div#container> shows now in Design view and <div id="container"> </div> shows in Code view.

c. Position the insertion point, in Design view, within the div#container section (or in Code view between the <div id="container"> </div> tag pair) and, repeating the procedure presented in paragraph b, insert a <div id="masthead"> </div> pair and a <div id= "navigation" > </div> section. Position the insertion point, in Code view, just below the <div id="container"> </div> pair and insert a <div id="content" > </div> pair. Position the insertion point, in Code view, just below the <div id="content"> </div> pair and insert a <div id="footer"> </div> section.

d. Position the insertion point, in Design view, within the <div#masthead> section. Click the **drop-down arrow** to the right of the Style box on the Common toolbar and click **Heading 1 <h1>** on the menu. Type **Young Women Journalists**.

e. Position the insertion point, in Design view, within the <div#content> section. Click the **drop-down arrow** to the right of the Style box on the Common toolbar and click **Heading 2 <h2>** on the menu. Type **Frequently Asked Questions** and press **Enter**.

f. Click the **drop-down arrow** to the right of the Style box on the Common toolbar and click **Heading 4 <h4>** on the drop-down list. Type **Topic 1** and press **Enter**. Click the **drop-down arrow** to the right of the Style box on the Common toolbar and click **Heading 4 <h4>** on the menu. Type **Topic 2** and press **Enter**. Click the **drop-down arrow** to the right of the Style box on the Common toolbar and click **Heading 4 <h4>** on the menu. Type **Topic 3** and press **Enter**. Click the **drop-down arrow** to the right of the Style box on the Common toolbar and click **Heading 4 <h4>** on the drop-down list. Type **Topic 4** and press **Enter**.

g. Position the insertion point, in Design view, within the <div#navigation> section. Right-click **Horizontal Line** in the *HTML* task pane and click **Insert**. Right-click **Horizontal Line** in the HTML task pane and click **Insert**. Click between the two <hr> tags, in Code view. Click the **drop-down arrow** to the right of the Style box on the Common toolbar and click **Heading 3 <h3>** on the menu. Type **Topic 1** and press **Tab**. Type **Topic 2** and press **Tab**. Type **Topic 3** and press **Tab**, and then type **Topic 4**.

The text for the four hyperlinks that need to be included in the <div#navigation> section are now showing.

h. Position the insertion point within the <div#footer> section in Design view. Right-click **Horizontal Line** in the *HTML* task pane, click **Insert**, and repeat. Click between the two <hr> tags, in Code view. Click the **drop-down arrow** to the right of the Style box on the Common toolbar and click **Heading 3 <h3>** on the menu. Type **Topic 1** and press **Tab**. Type **Topic 2** and press **Tab**. Type **Topic 3** and press **Tab**, and then type **Topic 4**.

The text for the four hyperlinks that need to be included in the <div# footer> section are now showing.

i. Double-click the **Style Application Settings indicator** on the Status toolbar to display the Style Application toolbar. Click the **drop-down arrow** to the right of the Style Application box, click **Manual**, and then click **Apply New Style** on the Target Rule drop-down list.

The New Style dialog box is now open.

j. Click **h1** on the Selector drop-down list, click **New style sheet** on the Define in drop-down list, click **Arial, Helvetica, sans-serif** on the font-family drop-down list, and type **Trebuchet MS** in the font-family text box just before *Arial, Helvetica, sans-serif*. Click **Block** in the *Category* section and click **center** in the text-align drop-down list. Click **OK** to close the New Style dialog box, click **Yes** on the alert box, and click the **Close button** on the Style Application toolbar to close it.

The Untiled_1.css tab is showing.

k. Click the **Save button** to save the *faq.htm* file.

The Save As dialog box is now open showing *Untitled_1.css* in the File name box.

l. In the Save As dialog box, double-click the **styles folder**, in the File name box type **faq.css**, and click **Save**.

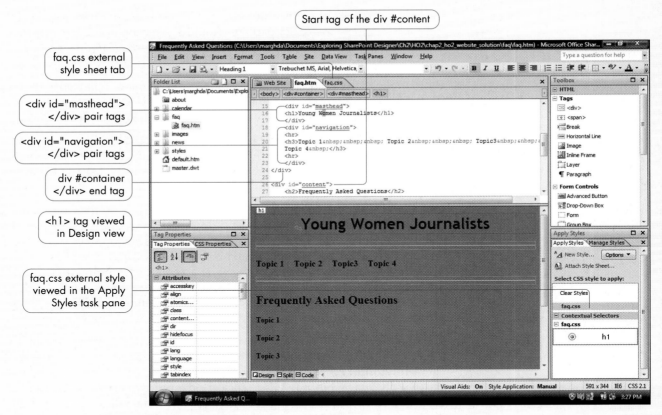

Figure 2.129 Adding and Formatting Text Content for a Web Page

Step 3

Organize a Web Page Using Hyperlinks and Format Hyperlinks Using CSS Styles

Refer to Figure 2.130 as you complete Step 3.

a. Highlight, in Design view, the *Young Women Journalists* text line designated to become a bookmark. Click **Insert** on the Menu bar, click **Bookmark**, and, because the name of the Bookmark appears in the Bookmark name box, you just need to click **OK**.

b. Highlight each text line, in the *<div#content>* section, designated to become bookmarks (see *chap2_ho2_sketch1_data.pdf*), and follow the same steps included in paragraph a.

c. Highlight the *Topic 1* text line in the <div#navigation> designated to become a bookmark link, and right-click and select **Hyperlink**.

The Hyperlink dialog box should be displayed.

d. Click the **Place in this Document button** and click the related bookmark, **Topic 1**, in the Bookmarks list. Click the **ScreenTip button**, type an appropriate text describing the bookmark targeted in the ScreenTip text box, and click **OK**. In the Set Hyperlink dialog box, click **Topic_1**, then click **OK** in the Insert Hyperlink dialog box.

The Topic 1 bookmark link is now showing.

e. Repeat the procedures included in paragraphs c and d for each text line designated to become a bookmark link.

f. Click **New Style** in the Apply Styles task pane.

The New Style dialog box is now showing.

g. Click **a** in the Selecto*r* box, click the **Purple color box** on the color drop-down list, and click **OK** to close the New Style dialog box.

h. Click the **Save button** to save the *faq.htm*. Click **OK** on the Save Embedded Files dialog box to save the *faq.css* attached style sheet.

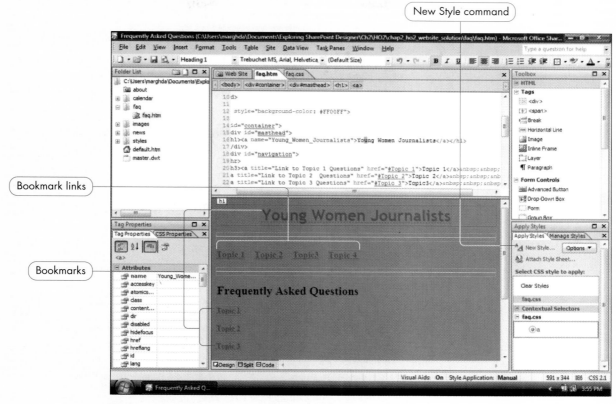

Figure 2.130 Organizing a Web Page Using Hyperlinks

Step 4
Organize a Web Page Using Lists and Format Lists Using CSS Styles

Refer to Figure 2.131 as you complete Step 4.

a. Highlight the four bookmarks within the *<div#content>* section and click the **Bullets button** on the Common toolbar.

The bulleted list is now displayed.

b. Click **New Style** in the Apply Styles task pane.

The New Style dialog box is now showing.

c. Click **ul** in the Selector box and click **List** in the *Category* section. Click **square** on the list-style-type drop-down list, click **inside** on the list-style-position drop-down list, and then click **OK** to close the New Style dialog box.

d. Click **New Style** in the Apply Styles task pane. Type **.topic** in the Selector box, click **Current Page** in the Define in drop-down list, and click **Font** in the *Category* section. Click **italic** on the font-style drop-down list and click **OK** to close the New Style dialog box.

The new topic style is now showing the *Current Page* section of the Manage Styles task pane.

e. Highlight the four lines of the <ul> list, click the **Apply Styles tab**, click the **drop-down arrow** to the right of the .topic style, and click **Apply Style** on the drop-down list.

The four lines of the <ul> list are now italicized.

f. Click the **Save button** to save *faq.htm*. Click **OK** on the Save Embedded Files dialog box to save the *faq.css* attached style sheet.

The Web page should look similar to the screen capture displayed in Figure 2.131.

g. Click **File** on the Menu bar and click **Close** to close *faq.htm*. Click **File**, on the Menu bar, and click **Close** to close *faq.css*. Click **Task Panes** on the Menu bar and click **Reset Workspace Layout**.

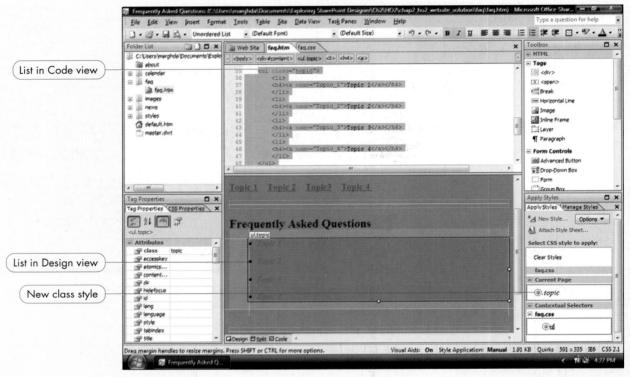

Figure 2.131 Organizing a Web Page Using Lists

Step 5

Insert a Standard Table, Format a Standard Table, and Add Content to a Standard Table

Refer to Figure 2.132 as you complete Step 5.

a. Click the **Design view button** at the bottom of the workspace. Double-click the **calendar folder** in the Folder List task pane. Double-click the **calendar.htm file** in the Folder List task pane to open it in Design view.

b. Position the insertion point at the end of the text line *Highlights* and press **Enter**.

c. Click the **Insert table button** on the Common toolbar, move the mouse over the **Insert Table grid** to create a table with three rows and three columns, and then click on the highlighted area of the Insert Table grid.

The new table is now showing.

d. Position the insertion point in row one, column one, click, then click on the **remaining two cells in the first row** while keeping **Ctrl** pressed. Right-click and click **Cell Properties** on the menu. Click the **Header cell check box** and click **OK** to close the Cell Properties dialog box.

The cells of the first row are now header cells.

e. Position the insertion point in row one, column one, click, and then press **Shift** and click in row three, column three. Click **Table** on the Menu bar, point to **Modify**, and click **Distribute Columns Evenly**. Click **Table** on the Menu bar, point to **Table Properties**, and click **Table** to open the Table Properties dialog box. In the *Layout* section, click the **In percent option**, and then click **OK** to close the Table Properties dialog box.

f. Click **Table** on the Menu bar, point to **Insert,** and click **Caption**. Click anywhere within the heading, *Highlights*, click the **<h3> tab**, right-click, and click **Cut** on the shortcut menu. Position the insertion point in the caption, right-click, and click **Paste** on the shortcut menu.

g. Position the insertion point in row one, column one, click, type **Event Title**, and press **Tab**.

The insertion point is now in the row one, column two cell.

h. Type **Event Description** and press **Tab**. Type **Media Coverage** and press **Tab**.

i. Position the insertion point in row two, column one, and type **Pitchfork Music Festival**.

The Web page should look similar to the screen capture displayed in Figure 2.132.

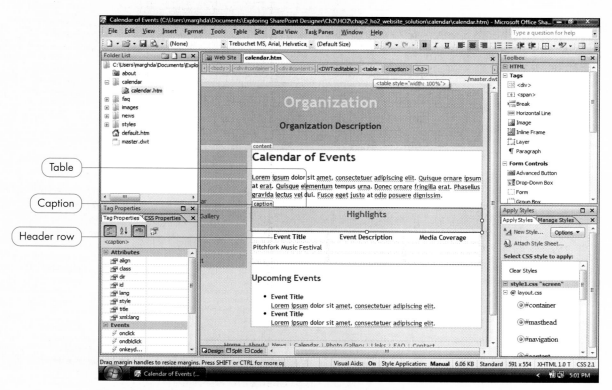

Figure 2.132 Insert a Standard Table, Format a Standard Table, and Add Content to a Standard Table

Refer to Figure 2.133 as you complete Step 6.

a. Place the insertion point in row one, column three. Click **Insert** on the Menu bar, point to **Picture**, and click **From File** on the menu.

The Picture dialog box is now displayed.

b. Double-click the **image folder**, click **pmf_banner.jpg**, and click **Insert** in the Picture dialog box.

The Accessibility Properties dialog box is now displayed.

c. Type **Pitchfork Music Festival Banner** in the Alternate text box and click **OK** to close the Accessibility Properties dialog box.

d. Click **View** on the Menu bar, point to **Toolbars**, and click **Pictures** on the menu. Click the **Auto Thumbnail button** on the Pictures toolbar, and then click the **Close button** on the upper-right corner of the Pictures toolbar to close it.

The thumbnail picture is now showing.

e. Right-click the **<td> tab** to open the Cell Properties dialog box. In the *Layout* section, click **Center** on the Horizontal alignment drop-down list, click **Middle** on the Vertical alignment drop-down list, click the **In Percent button**, and type **33** in the Specify width box. Then click **OK** to close the Cell Properties dialog box.

f. Click the **Save button** and click **OK** in the Save Embedded Files dialog box.

The Web page should look similar to the screen capture displayed in Figure 2.133.

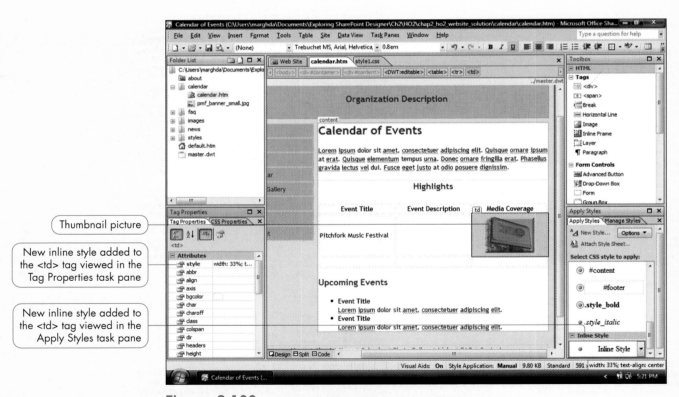

Thumbnail picture

New inline style added to the <td> tag viewed in the Tag Properties task pane

New inline style added to the <td> tag viewed in the Apply Styles task pane

Figure 2.133 Insert a Graphic File Within a Table

Step 7

Add a Plug-In Web Component to a Web Page, Add a Page Banner Web Component to a Dynamic Web Template, and Add a Marquee Web Component to a Dynamic Web Template

Refer to Figure 2.134 as you complete Step 7.

a. Place the insertion point in row two, column two. Click **Insert** on the Menu bar and click **Web component**.

The Insert Web Components dialog box is now displayed.

b. Click **Advanced Controls** in the *Component type* section, click **Plug-in** in the *Choose a control* section, and click **Finish**.

The Plug-In Properties dialog box is now displayed.

c. Click the **Browse button** and navigate to the Exploring folder, locate the *pmf.wav* file, click, and click **OK** to close the Select Plug-In Data Source dialog box. Type **Sorry, your browser doesn't support this audio plug-in . . .** in the Message for browsers without plug-in support box, then click **OK** to close the Plug-In Properties dialog box.

The plug-in is now displayed.

d. Click the **Save button** and click **OK** to close the Save Embedded Files dialog box.

e. Click **Format** on the Menu bar, point to **Dynamic Web Template**, and click **Open Attached Dynamic Web Template** on the menu.

The *master.dwt* file should now be open in Design view.

f. Double-click the **Organization Heading 1 text line**, right-click, and click **Cut**. Click **Insert** on the Menu bar and click **Web Component**.

The Insert Web Component dialog box is now displayed.

g. Click **Included Content** in the *Component type* section, click **Page Banner** in the *Choose a control* section, and click **Finish**. In the Page Banner Properties dialog box, click the **Picture button**, highlight **master.dwt** in the Page banner text box, and type **Young Women Journalists**. Click **OK** to close the Page Banner Properties dialog box.

h. Highlight the **Organization Description Heading 3 text line**, right-click, and click **Cut**. Click **Insert** on the Menu bar and click **Web Component**. Click **Dynamic Effects** in the *Component type* section and click **Marquee** in the *Choose a control* section, if they are not already selected, and then click **Finish**. Type **An international membership organization connecting, mobilizing, and promoting young women journalists** in the Text box of the Marquee Properties dialog box, click the **Thistle color box** in the *Document Colors* section of the Background Color drop-down list, and click **OK** to close the Marquee Properties dialog box.

The marquee should now be displayed below the page banner.

i. Click the **Save button** on the Common toolbar, click **Yes** in the alert box (asking if you wish to update the two files attached to *master.dwt*), and click **Close** on the next alert box.

j. Click the **calendar.htm tab** to open the calendar.htm Web page. Double-click the **Page Banner**, type **Young Women Journalists** in the Page banner text box, and click **OK**. Click the **Save button**.

TROUBLESHOOTING: You can also change the banner text in the calendar.htm by changing the Page Label in Navigation view.

The SharePoint Designer workspace should look like the one displayed in Figure 2.134.

k. Click **File** on the Menu bar, point to **Preview in Browser**, and click **Windows Internet Explorer 7.0**.

TROUBLESHOOTING: If the Internet Explorer Information bar appears at the top of your screen, click it and then click Allow Blocked Content. . . . Click Yes on the Security Warning box (if it is displayed). If you want to preview this Web page in Mozilla Firefox browser, you may need to download the Apple QuickTime plug-in.

The *pmf.wav* audio clip should automatically play, and if you click the thumbnail picture you should see the picture in its original size.

l. Click **File** on the Menu bar and click **Close Site**.

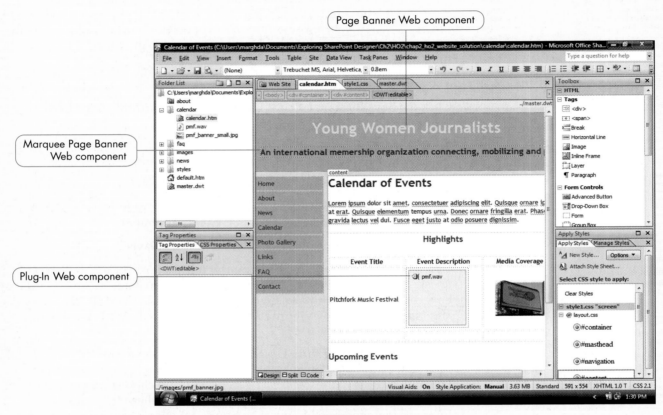

Figure 2.134 Adding Web Components to a Web Page

Summary

1. **Design a Web site.** You should always create a sketch of a Web site's navigational layout before starting to build a Web site. SharePoint Designer's Navigation view enables you to build and modify the Web site's navigational structure, toggle between viewing the navigational structure in Portrait and Landscape mode, zoom the navigational structure, and view only sections (called subtrees) of the Web site's navigational structure.

2. **Build a Web site.** After you have your navigational layout sketched, there are three ways in which you can develop a SharePoint Designer Web site: by using an appropriate General template, an empty Web site, or a Web site containing only one Web page to which, one by one, you add, import, and modify Web pages or import the content of a Personal Web Package; by importing a preexisting Web site using the Import Web Site Wizard; or by using an appropriate template, creating a Personal Web Package or SharePoint Template. When using a Dynamic Web Template to build and maintain your Web site pages, it is highly recommended that you link an external style sheet to the Dynamic Web Template instead of linking it to each Web page. Subsites enable you to restrict user access to a group of Web pages, or to apply that you this group of Web pages an external style sheet other than a default external style sheet attached to all Web site pages.

3. **Publish SharePoint Designer Web sites and subsites.** After a Web site is built, you need to publish it. SharePoint Designer enables you to publish a Web site using the SharePoint Designer Remote Web Site view. You can publish an entire Web site, including all associated subsites, selected subsites, or individual Web pages to a local or remote Web site. A local Web site is the source Web site that is opened by developers in SharePoint Designer. It can be located on your computer or on a computer included in a local network. A remote Web site is the destination site to which you publish your Web site. It can be located on any of the following locations: a local computer, a remote computer that hosts your organization's Web server, your organization's intranet server, an ISP server where you publish your Web site as a subscriber, or a free hosting service provider's server that might or might not offer support for FrontPage Server Extensions or SharePoint Services.

4. **Test and validate a Web site.** Using the Reports and Hyperlinks views, you can accurately access the technical, graphical, and statistical information that you can use to validate, update, and upgrade a Web site. The process of correcting, updating, and upgrading your Web pages based on the feedback provided by testing and validating tools can be time consuming and annoying if you need to manually locate the Web page elements that need to be changed. The SharePoint Designer Find and Replace feature can assist you in finding and replacing text, and in using expressions or HTML rules and tags.

5. **Publish changes to a Web site.** Designing and developing a Web site can be a never-ending process. Web designers are constantly making improvements and updating the content of their Web pages. When making changes to a Web site, designers can choose to republish only the Web pages that have changed since the last publishing or to republish the entire Web site.

6. **Design a Web page.** There is no substitute for planning and designing a Web page. When designing a Web page you should always develop a clear statement of purpose for the Web page, identify your audience, identify the material and Web page elements you will use to accomplish your purpose (focus on the content and the major topics you will be providing on the Web page and think about the Web page elements you will use to organize the content), establish the adequate layout style of the Web page, establish the adequate formatting style of the Web page, create a simple navigational layout chart, and create a clear design sketch that includes, as much as possible, details about the Web page layout and formatting style.

7. **Build a Web page.** SharePoint Designer enables you to quickly and easily add new Web pages to an existing Web site in Page view, Folders view, and Navigation view. SharePoint Designer also provides you with a set of tools for formatting a Web page.

8. **Work with Web page content.** When building a Web page in SharePoint Designer, text can be used in many different ways, such as normal body text and headings and in ordered or unordered lists. You can type text directly into your Web page, import the content of a text file, or copy and paste text from another file. Text also can be edited and formatted to emphasize the purpose of the Web page and enhance its appearance. SharePoint Designer also provides a spelling checker that you should always use to check the spelling of your Web page text before publishing it.

...continued on Next Page

9. **Use hyperlinks and lists in organizing a Web page.** Hyperlinks can help designers break up the contents of a large, difficult-to-navigate Web page into a set of Web pages that are connected. Alternatively, designers can reduce the amount of jumping back and forth between different Web pages by using bookmark links and bookmarks to give users access to their content. Lists are great tools for organizing Web page content in a concise and consistent fashion. You can choose ordered (numbered), unordered (bulleted), and definition lists. SharePoint Designer assists you in adding, editing, and formatting hyperlinks and lists.

10. **Work with tables and layout tables.** Standard tables have always been among Web designers' favorite tools for organizing and displaying information, and, although the CSS-based layouts have become more efficient and easier to implement, the table-based layouts continue to be very popular. When using layout tables, you can easily control a table structure (for example, you are not required to modify manually the rows and columns or merge cells to design the table grid you need, and you can easily draw cell structures). SharePoint Designer provides you with a complete set of tools for working with tables, table-based layouts, layout tables, and layout cells in Design view, without having to work with HTML or CSS code.

11. **Enhance a Web page using graphics, multimedia, and Web components.** SharePoint Designer empowers Web designers with features to increase the attractiveness of their Web sites by using graphics and multimedia elements such as pictures and audio and video files. SharePoint Designer also provides a great set of Web components that you can use to enrich the content and improve the usability of your Web pages. Some of the most popular Web components include, but are not limited to, the hit counter, the marquee, the page banner, the link bars, and the photo gallery.

12. **Print a Web page.** If you provide information on your Web pages that people might want to print, you need to make sure that your pages will print well. As Web design becomes more and more sophisticated, it is becoming standard practice to help visitors print Web pages by creating a printer-friendly version of a Web page that is accessible through a text link, such as Printer-friendly version. Depending on how many Web page elements you need to remove or reformat, it might actually be easier to create a simple text version of the Web page first and then save it as your printer-friendly option. To see how the page will appear when printed, you should use the SharePoint Designer Print Preview tool. You can see that there are differences between this preview and the view from a Web browser. The Print Preview feature paginates and assigns page numbers, whereas Web browsers do not.

Key Terms

Multiple Choice

1. Which of the following items is not a SharePoint Designer 2007 tool for creating Web sites?

   (a) Personal Web Package
   (b) Customer Support Web Site template
   (c) Empty Web Site template
   (d) One Page Web Site template

2. Which of the following items is a SharePoint Designer 2007 wizard?

   (a) Import Web site
   (b) Corporate Presence
   (c) Table of Contents
   (d) Discussion Web Site

3. It is correct to say that:

   (a) You can create a Dynamic Web Template.
   (b) All Dynamic Web Templates have a CSS layout style sheet.
   (c) Newly exported Personal Web Packages are automatically saved in the SharePoint Designer My Templates folder.
   (d) An imported Web page is automatically attached to the Dynamic Web Template applied to all other Web pages.

4. In SharePoint Designer you cannot do which of the following?

   (a) Customize a Dynamic Web Template and save it under the same original name.
   (b) Link a CSS external style sheet theme to only selected Web pages in a Web site.
   (c) Remove the link to a CSS external style sheet within any Web page.
   (d) Modify within a Web page the noneditable regions of its attached Dynamic Web Template.

5. Using SharePoint Designer, you cannot publish a Web site on which of the following servers?

   (a) A WebDav Web server
   (b) An ASP Development server
   (c) A SQL2000 server
   (d) An FTP server

6. Which of the following statements about publishing a SharePoint Designer Web site is not true?

   (a) Web sites published on an ASP Development server or a personal Web server are placed on a unique location on your local hard disk.
   (b) Before publishing a Web site, you must specify a remote Web server.
   (c) You create a subsite by grouping related Web pages in a new folder and converting it to a site.
   (d) You cannot publish the subsites of a Web site using the Remote Web site view.

7. The five categories of Reports view reports do not include:

   (a) Files reports
   (b) Accessibility reports
   (c) Usage
   (d) Workflow

8. Hyperlinks view provides information about:

   (a) Broken hyperlinks
   (b) Unverified links
   (c) Style Sheet links
   (d) All of the above

9. Which of the following is not true regarding the title of a Web page?

   (a) The title and the label of a Web page are always identical.
   (b) The title of a Web page is displayed in Bookmarks (for Netscape Navigator).
   (c) The title of a Web page is displayed in Favorites (for Internet Explorer).
   (d) The title of a Web page is usually displayed in the title bar.

10. Which of the following is not true regarding hyperlinks?

   (a) A hyperlink can link to a file.
   (b) A bookmark link can have only a relative URL.
   (c) A hyperlink can link to an e-mail address.
   (d) A hyperlink can link to a bookmark.

11. Which of the following is true about editing hyperlinks?

    (a) The URL of a hyperlink can be edited.
    (b) The font of a hyperlink can be edited.
    (c) The color of a hyperlink can be edited.
    (d) All of the above.

12. You cannot organize the text of your Web pages using:

    (a) A hierarchical list
    (b) A numbered list
    (c) Nested lists
    (d) A bulleted list

13. What happens when you select a table and use table properties to change some of its properties?

    (a) The changes are not applied to cells of the nested tables.
    (b) Cell properties that were set using the Cell Properties dialog box do not override the changes made at table level.
    (c) The changes cannot be automatically reproduced for all new tables.
    (d) The changes will not affect other tables included in the same Web page.

14. Which of the following statements about table cells is not true?

    (a) A cell can be spanned.
    (b) A group of cells can be merged.
    (c) When you right-click a selected table and click Delete cells, the cells of a nested table will not be deleted.
    (d) A deleted cell can be restored using the Undo command.

15. In the Table Properties dialog box, you cannot:

    (a) Set the size of the table in pixels.
    (b) Remove rows or columns from a table.
    (c) Set the properties selected as default for all new tables.
    (d) Choose to collapse the table border.

16. Using the Tables toolbar you cannot:

    (a) Draw a layout table or a layout cell.
    (b) Distribute rows and columns evenly.
    (c) Merge cells of the table.
    (d) Format a layout cell.

17. A layout table:

    (a) Cannot be formatted using the Table Properties dialog box
    (b) Cannot be formatted using the Table AutoFormat Combo box
    (c) Cannot be formatted using the Page Properties dialog box
    (d) Cannot be nested in another table

18. Which of the following commands cannot be performed on an image?

    (a) Resizing
    (b) Resampling
    (c) Condensing
    (d) Cropping

19. Which of the following statements about hit counters SharePoint Designer Web components is not true?

    (a) Hit counters are Web components.
    (b) Hit counters can be properly displayed when published on any Web server.
    (c) Hit counters keep track of the number of people who visit your Web site.
    (d) Hit counters are supported by Internet Explorer browser version 4.0 and higher.

20. Which of the following statements about marquees SharePoint Designer Web components is not true?

    (a) Marquees look like a news ticker on your Web page.
    (b) Marquees can be inserted on a predefined schedule.
    (c) Marquees can be properly displayed when published on any Web server.
    (d) Marquee properties can be changed.

21. If your Web site does not already have a navigational structure, which of the following can you still insert in your Web page?

    (a) Java applet
    (b) Bar with back and next links
    (c) Bar based on navigation structure
    (d) Page banner

Practice Exercises

1 Creating an Investment Management Company E-Business Web Site

Your e-business course semester project consists of developing a Web site for an investment management company. Dan King, your e-business professor, is providing you with a generic investment management company SharePoint Designer Dynamic Web Template that you can use to develop the Web site. The Dynamic Web Template file is also accompanied by its linked CSS external style sheet files. You will import the Dynamic Web Template and the styles folder, including all CSS external style sheet files, and you will attach the Dynamic Web Template to the home page. Using the Broken Hyperlinks Report, Folders view, and Navigation view, you will add all the required folders and Web pages, and start adding Web pages to the root Web site navigation structure. Then you will create a subsite, create the navigation structure of the subsite, and link the subsite to the root Web site navigation structure. The navigation structure of the root Web site and its subsite is shown in Figure 2.135. Proceed as follows:

a. Start SharePoint Designer. Locate and open the *chap2_pe1_ebusiness* Web site. Using the Remote Web Site view, create a **chap2_pe1_ebusiness _solution** Web site backup. Click the **Open your Remote Web site in SharePoint Designer link** to open the chap2_pe1_ebusiness_solution Web site folder.

b. Point to **Import** on the File menu and click **File** to open the Import dialog box. Click **Add File** in the Import dialog box to open the Add File to Import List dialog box. Locate and double-click to open the **master.dwt Dynamic Web Template** in the Student Data Files folder. Then click **OK** in the Import dialog box to close the Import dialog box.

c. Point to **Import** on the File menu and click **File** to open the Import dialog box. Click **Add Folder** in the Import dialog box to open to File Open dialog box. Locate and click the **styles folder**, then click **Open** in the File Open dialog box. Then click **OK** in the Import dialog box to close the Import dialog box.

d. Double-click **default.htm** in the Folder List task pane to open the home page in Design view. Point to **Dynamic Web Template** on the Format menu and click **Attach Dynamic Web Template** to open the Attach Dynamic Web Template dialog box. Locate and double-click **master.dwt**. Click **OK** on the SharePoint Designer alert box and click **Close** on the SharePoint Designer update box if necessary.

e. Point to **Reports** on the Site menu and click **Site Summary** to display the Site Summary included report. Click the **Hyperlinks report**. Carefully review the report and make a note of all the broken hyperlinks.

f. Click the **root folder** in the Folder List task pane, point to **New** on the File menu, and click **Folder**. Rename the newly created folder **about**.

g. Repeat the procedure in step f to create the following ten new folders: **accounts**, **calendar**, **cash**, **contact**, **faq**, **market_research**, **news**, **services**, **site-map**, and **trade**.

h. Click the **Navigation tab** to display the Navigation view of the Web site.

i. Click the **New Page button** on the Navigation bar to add a new *Untitled_1* Web page beneath *default.htm*. Right-click **Untitled_1** and click **Rename** on the menu. Type **about** on the highlighted text. Click **Refresh** on the View menu if you do not see the about.htm file name in the Folder List task pane. Click **about.htm** in the Folder List task pane, drag it over the about folder, and then drop it to include *about.htm* in the about folder.

j. Point to **New** on the File menu and click **HTML**. Click the **Save button** on the Common Toolbar to open the Save As dialog box. Double-click **about** in the Save As dialog box and type **privacy_security.htm** in the File name box. Click the **Change Title button** in the Save As dialog box to open the Set Page Title dialog box. Type **Privacy and Security** in the Page title box and click **OK** to close it. Then click **Save** on the Save As dialog box to close it.

k. Click the **Web Site tab** (click the **Reports tab** if the Hyperlinks report is not showing) to see that now there is no listed broken link toward the about folder.

l. Click the **Navigation tab** to display the Navigation view of the Web site. Click the **about Web page** and type **About Us** to change the title and the label of the *about.htm* Web page. Click **privacy_security.htm** in the Folder List task pane, drag it beneath *About Us* in Navigation view, and then drop it.

m. Repeat the procedure from step j to create the following new HTML documents contained within the services folder:

...continued on Next Page

- **services.htm** with **Services** as page title
- **agreements_disclosure.htm** with **Agreements and Disclosure** as page title
- **feedback.htm** with **Feedback** as page title
- **customer_services.htm** with **Customer Services** as page title
- **web_accessibility.htm** with **Web Accessibility** as page title

n. Click the **Web Site tab** (click the **Reports tab** if the Hyperlinks report is not showing) to see that now there is no listed broken link toward the services folder. Click the **Navigation tab** to display the Navigation view of the Web site. Double-click **services** in the Folder List task pane (click **Refresh** on the View menu if you do not see all the files created in step m in Folder List).

o. Right-click the **services folder** in the Folder List task pane and click **Convert to Web**. Click **Yes** on the SharePoint Designer alert box.

p. Right-click **default** in Navigation view and click **Add Existing Page** to open the Insert Hyperlink dialog box. Locate the **services Web folder** and double-click. Click **services.htm**, and then click **OK** to close the Insert Hyperlink dialog box.

q. Double-click the **services Web folder**, in the Folders List task pane, to open it in a new SharePoint Designer window. Right-click **services** in the Folder List task pane and click **Set as Home Page**. Click the **Navigation tab** to view the services subsite in Navigation view.

r. Click in the Folder List task pane, then drag and drop beneath *default.htm* (having *Services* as a label) the other four Web pages created in step m: **agreements_ disclosure.htm**, **customer_services.htm**, **feedback.htm**, and **web_accessibility.htm**.

s. Click **Close Site** on the File menu to close the services subsite, and then click **Exit** on the File menu to close the second SharePoint Designer window.

t. Click **Close Site** on the File menu to close the *chap2_pe1_ebusiness_solution* root Web site.

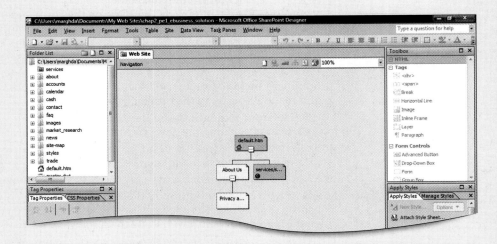

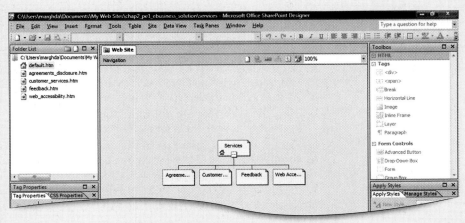

Figure 2.135 Creating an Investment Management Company E-Business Web Site

Dan King, your e-business professor, is providing you with more information about new Web page elements for the home page and new Web pages he wishes to include in the e-business Web site that you created. You will enhance the home page using tables, images, hyperlinks, and Web Components, as shown in Figure 2.136. You will also create a site map for the Web site using the Table of Contents Web Component (also shown in Figure 2.136). Proceed as follows:

a. Start SharePoint Designer. Locate and open the *chap2_pe2_ebusiness* Web site. Using the Remote Web Site view, create a **chap2_pe2_ebusiness_solution** Web site backup. Click the **Open your Remote Web site in SharePoint Designer link** to open the *chap2_pe2_ebusiness_solution* Web site folder. Double-click **default.htm** in the Folder List task pane to open it in Design view.

b. Position the insertion point to the left of the *Headline 2* text line. Click **Table** on the Menu bar and point to **Insert Table** to display the Insert Table dialog box. In the *Size* section of the Insert Table dialog box, select **2** in the Rows drop-down box and **2** in the Columns drop-down box. Within the *Layout* section, in the Alignment drop-down list click **Left**, in the Cell padding drop-down list click **1**, and in the Cell spacing drop-down list click **0**. In the Specify width box, type **50** and select the *In percent* option. Then in the Specify height box, type **100** and select the *In percent* option. Click **OK** to close the Insert Table dialog box.

c. Press **CTRL** and click on the cell in the second row and first column. Then right-click, point to **Modify**, and click **Merge Cells**. The two cells of the first column are now merged.

d. Point to **Picture** on the Insert menu and click **From File** to open the Picture dialog box. Locate and double-click the **images folder**. Double-click the **MPj04157950000[1].jpg file**, type **Chief Investment Strategist Richard Ball** in the Alternate text box of the Accessibility Properties dialog box, and click **OK** to close the Accessibility Properties dialog box.

e. Double-click the picture entered in step d to open the Picture Properties dialog box, click the **Appearance tab**, and type **100** in the Height box. Then click **OK** to close the Picture Properties dialog box.

f. Position the insertion point in row one, column two, and type **New Strength for Large Caps**. Highlight the entered text and click **Heading 4 <h4>** on the Style drop-down list.

g. Position the insertion point in row two, column two, and type **From the Chief Investment Strategist Richard Ball Learn More**. Highlight the entered text and click **Heading 4 <h4>** on the Style drop-down list. Position the insertion point before the word *Learn*, right-click **Break** in the HTML pane, and click **Insert**.

h. Highlight *Learn More*, right-click, and click **Hyperlink** to open the Insert Hyperlink dialog box. Locate and click the **market_research folder**. In the Address box, type **large_cap_growth.htm** and click **OK** to close the Insert Hyperlink dialog box and to add a hyperlink to a Web page not created yet in the market_research folder.

i. Click **Format** on the Menu bar, point to **Dynamic Web Template**, and click **Open Attached Dynamic Web Template** to open *master.dwt* in Design view. Position the insertion point before the word *Copyright* in the document footer and type **Last time edited:** (include a space after the colon). Click **Insert** on the Menu bar and click **Web Component** to open the Insert Web Component dialog box. Click **Included Content** in the *Component type* section, click **Date and Time** in the *Choose a type of content* section, and click **Finish** to open the Date and Time dialog box.

j. In the Date and Time dialog box, select the **Date this page was last edited option** in the Date Format drop-down box select the Date format similar to *Saturday, August 25, 2008*, and click **OK** to close the Date and Time dialog box. Press **Enter**.

k. Click the **Save button** on the Common toolbar to save the changes made to the *master.dwt* file. Click **Yes** on the first alert box and **Close** on the second alert box displayed.

l. Click the **default.htm tab** to open *default.htm* in Design view. Click the **Save button** on the Common toolbar to save the changes made to the *default.htm* file and its attached Dynamic Web Template.

...continued on Next Page

m. Highlight the *Headline 2* text line and type **Today's Headlines**. Highlight the *insert content here* paragraph placed beneath the text you just entered and type **Investing with Taxes in Mind**.

n. Highlight the *Headline 3* text line and type **Highlights**. Highlight the *insert content here* paragraph placed beneath the text you just entered and type **Global Research Highlights**. Click the **Save button** on the Common toolbar to save the changes made to the *default.htm* file.

o. Click the **New Document button** on the Common toolbar to create a new *Untitled_1.htm* document. Click the **Save button** on the Common toolbar to save **Untitled_1.htm**. In the Save As dialog box, locate the site_map folder and click. In the File name box, type **site_map.htm**. Click the **Change title button** to open the Set Page Title dialog box. Type **Site Map** in the Page title box and click **OK** to close the Set Page Title dialog box. Click **Save** to close the Save As dialog box.

p. Click **Insert** on the Menu bar and click **Web Component** to open the Insert Web Component dialog box. Click **Table of Contents** in the *Component type* section, click **For This Web Site** in the *Choose a type of content* section, and click **Finish** to open the Table of Contents Properties dialog box. Click the **Recompute table of contents when any other page is edited check box** and click **OK**. Click the **Save button** on the Common toolbar.

q. Click the **default.htm tab**. The SharePoint Designer workspace should look as shown in Figure 2.136. Click **File** on the Menu bar and click **Close Site**.

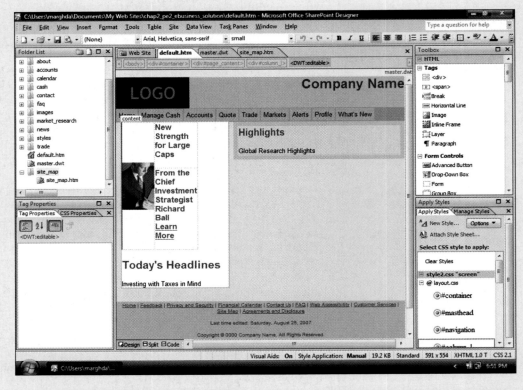

Figure 2.136 Develop and Enhance Web Pages of an Investment Management Company E-Business Web Site

Dan King, your e-business professor, is providing you with more information about a new Global Research Highlights Web page he wishes to include in the e-business Web site that you created. You will enhance the new Web page using audio files and Web Components, as shown in Figure 2.137. Proceed as follows:

a. Start SharePoint Designer. Locate and open the *chap2_pe3_global* Web site. Using the Remote Web Site view, create a **chap2_pe3_global_solution** Web site backup. Click the **Open your Remote Web site in SharePoint Designer link** to open the *chap2_pe3_global_solution* Web site folder.

b. Point to **New** on the File menu and click **Create from Dynamic Web Template**. Locate and double-click, in the Attach Dynamic Web Template dialog box, **master.dwt**. Click the **Close button** on the Microsoft SharePoint Designer alert box.

c. Click the **Save button** on the Common toolbar to open the Save As dialog box. Double-click **market_research** in the Save As dialog box and type **global.htm** in the File name box. Click the **Change Title button** in the Save As dialog box to open the Set Page Title dialog box. Type **Global Research Highlights** in the Page title box and click **OK** to close it. Then click **Save** on the Save As dialog box to close it.

d. Highlight the *Headline 2* text line and type **Global Research Highlights**. Highlight the *insert content here* paragraph placed beneath the text you just entered and press **Enter** four times.

e. Highlight the *Headline 3* text line and type **Global Research Highlights Today**. Highlight the *insert content here* paragraph placed beneath the text you just entered, click **Table** on the Menu bar, and click **Insert Table** to display the Insert Table dialog box. In the *Size* section of the Insert Table dialog box, select **1** in the Rows drop-down box and **2** in the Columns drop-down box. Within the *Layout* section, in the Alignment drop-down list click **Center**, in the Cell padding drop-down list click **1**, and in the Cell spacing drop-down list click **0**. In the Specify width box, type **80** and select the *In percent* option. Then, in the Specify height box, type **80** and select the *In percent* option. Click **OK** to close the Insert Table dialog box.

f. Click **Insert** on the Menu bar and click **Web Component** to open the Insert Web Component dialog box. Click **Advanced Controls** in the *Component type* section of the Insert Web Component dialog box, click **Plug-In** in the *Choose a control* section of the Insert Web Component dialog box, and click the **Finish button** to open the Plug-In Properties dialog box.

g. Click the **Browse button** to open the Select Plug-In Data Source. Locate and double-click **global.wma** (in the market-research folder). In the *Message for browsers without plug-in support*, type **A text transcript of the Global Research Highlights Today audio report is available as well.** Type **45** in the Height box and type **200** in the Width box. Click **Absmiddle** on the Alignment drop-down list. Type **5** in the Horizontal spacing box, type **5** in the Vertical spacing box, and click **OK** to close the Plug-In Properties dialog box.

h. Position the insertion point in the second column of the table and type **Download the report transcript**. Highlight the typed text, right-click, and click **Hyperlink** on the menu to open the Insert Hyperlink dialog box. Double-click the **market_research folder** in the Insert Hyperlink dialog box and click **global.rtf** to close the Insert Hyperlink dialog box. Click the **ScreenTip button** to open the Set Hyperlink ScreenTip dialog box. Type **Download the report transcript** in the ScreenTip text box, click **OK** to close the Set Hyperlink ScreenTip dialog box, and then click **OK** to close the Insert Hyperlink dialog box. Click the **Save button** on the Common toolbar (or Standard toolbar). The SharePoint designer workspace should now look similar to the one shown in Figure 2.137.

i. Click **File** on the Menu bar, point to **Preview in Browser**, and click **Internet Explorer 7.0**. The SharePoint designer workspace should now look similar to the one shown in Figure 2.137.

j. Click **File** on the Menu bar, click **Close Site** to close the *chap2_pe3_global_solution* Web site.

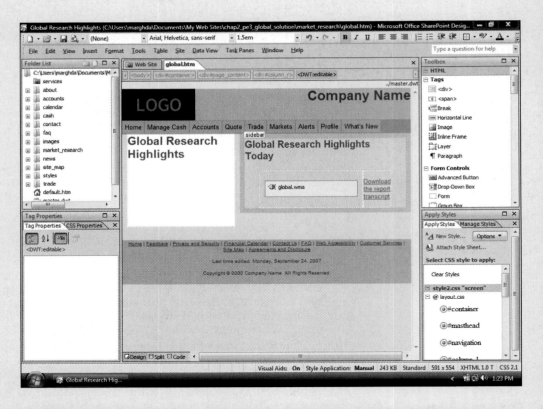

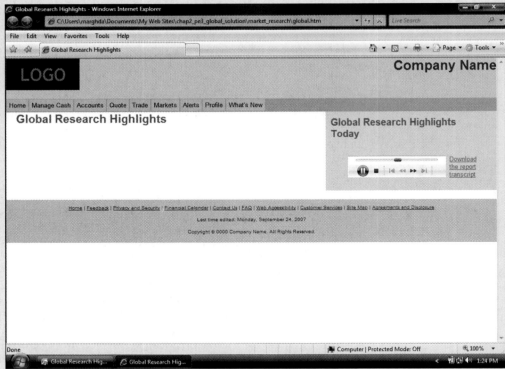

Figure 2.137 Global Research Highlights Web Page

Mid-Level Exercises

1 Enhancing the Home Page of the "Help Katrina & Rita Hurricane Victims" Initiative Web Site

As part of their "Help Katrina & Rita Hurricane Victims" initiative, the members of your sorority/fraternity have asked you to start creating a Web site dedicated to helping the hurricane victims. Visitors can use this Web site to stay updated with the aftermath of the two hurricanes, to donate money and needed items, or to volunteer their time and energy for helping the devastated communities. You will enhance the home page of the Web site using lists and Web components. Figure 2.138 shows the completed stage two of the Web site. Use this figure as a guide.

a. Start SharePoint Designer. Locate and open the *chap2_mid1_katrina* Web site. Using the Remote Web Site view, create a **chap2_mid1_katrina_solution** Web site backup. Click the **Open your Remote Web site in SharePoint Designer link** to open the *chap2_mid1_katrina_solution* Web site folder. Open *default.htm.* in Design view.

b. Use the drop-down Style list to format as an Unordered List <ul> the eight hyperlinks placed beneath the *Hurricanes Katrina & Rita* text line.

c. Highlight the unordered list created in step b; click the **New Style link** in the Apply Styles task pane to open the New Style dialog box. Create a new element style for the li selector in the current page and *List* category. Click the **Browse button** to the right of the list-style-image drop-down box, navigate to the images folder, and double-click **BD21365_.gif**. Click **OK** to close the New Style dialog box. Save *default.htm.*

d. Place the insertion point beneath the *New Orleans after Hurricane Katrina* text line and insert a Dynamic Effects Marquee Web component that scrolls continuously from right to left that reads, **Thank you for helping the Katrina hurricane victims!** The background color of the marquee is identified by rgb(143, 188, 143).

e. Save *default.htm* using the **Save button**, switch to Design view, and compare your SharePoint Designer workspace to Figure 2.138.

f. Close the Web site and exit SharePoint Designer.

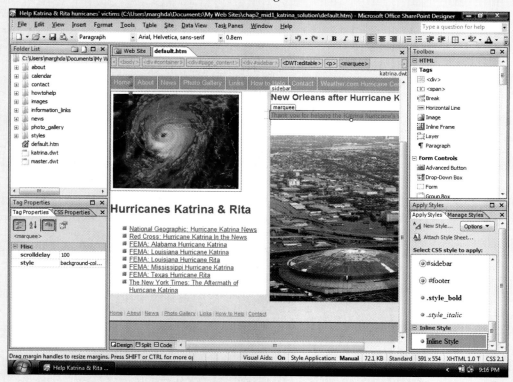

Figure 2.138 Enhancing the Home Page of the Help Katrina & Rita Hurricane Victims Web Site

...continued on Next Page

You have to develop a subsite of the Starbright Children's Foundation Web Site dedicated to the International Children's Day. Figure 2.139 shows the completed subsite. Use this figure as a guide.

a. Start SharePoint Designer. Locate and open the *chap2_mid2_website_org* Web site. Using the Remote Web Site view, create a **chap2_mid2_website_org_solution** Web site backup. Click the **Open your Remote Web site in SharePoint Designer link** to open the *chap2_mid2_website_org_solution* Web site folder. Create a new **children_day** folder in Folders view.

b. Click the **New Document button** to create a new HTML document and click the **Save button** to save it as **children_day_home.htm** in the children_day folder.

c. Click the **Format menu**, point to **Dynamic Web Template**, and click **Attach Dynamic Web Template** to attach the *master.dwt* Dynamic Web Template to *children_day_home.htm*. Right-click the **children_day folder** and click **Convert to Web**. Double-click the new **subweb folder** in the Folder List task pane to open it in a new SharePoint Designer window. Double-click **children_day_home.htm** to open it in Design view.

d. Highlight the *Heading 2* text line and type **Starbright Observes Children's Day All Over the World**.

e. Start Microsoft Word, then locate and open *ChildrensDay.doc*. Click **Select** in the Editing module of the ribbon and click **Select All** to select all text. Click the **Copy button** on the Clipboard module of the ribbon. Click the **SharePoint Designer tab** on the Windows taskbar, highlight the *insert content here* text line beneath the text typed in step d, right-click, and click **Paste** on the shortcut menu. Click **Remove Formatting** on the Paste Option drop-down list.

f. Highlight, one by one, and format as Heading 4 <h4> the three subtitles of the text pasted.

g. Highlight the *Heading 3* text line and type **Children Around the World**. Highlight the *insert content here* text line beneath the text you just typed. Open the Insert Web Component dialog box, click **Photo Gallery**, click **Horizontal Layout**, and click **Finish** to open the Photo Gallery Properties dialog box. Click the **Add button** and click **Pictures from Files** to open the File open dialog box. Locate the **images folder** and press **Shift** while clicking on the range of **.jpg files**. Then click the **Open button**. Click **OK** to close the Photo Gallery Properties dialog box. Click the **Layout tab** and click **2** on the Number of pictures per row drop-down list. Click **OK** to close the Photo Gallery Properties dialog box.

h. Click **OK** on the SharePoint Designer alert box. Click the **Save button** to save *children_day_home.htm* and the embedded files.

i. Position the insertion point just before the text of the International Children's Day paragraph, click **Insert**, and click **Web Component** to display the Insert Web Component dialog box. Click **Included Content**, **Picture Based on Schedule**, and then click **Finish** to close the Insert Web Component dialog box and open the Scheduled Picture Properties dialog box. Select to display the **j0284916.jpg thumbnail** within the photogallery folder starting May 28, 2008, and ending June 3, 2008. Type **International Children's Day June 1, 2008** in the During the scheduled time text box, and then click **OK** to close the Scheduled Picture Properties dialog box.

j. Save the *children_day_home.htm* Web page. The SharePoint Designer workspace should look like the one shown in Figure 2.139.

k. Close the *children_day* subsite and close the SharePoint Designer window. Close the *chap2_mid2_website_org_solution* Web site and close the SharePoint Designer window. Close the Microsoft Word Window.

...continued on Next Page

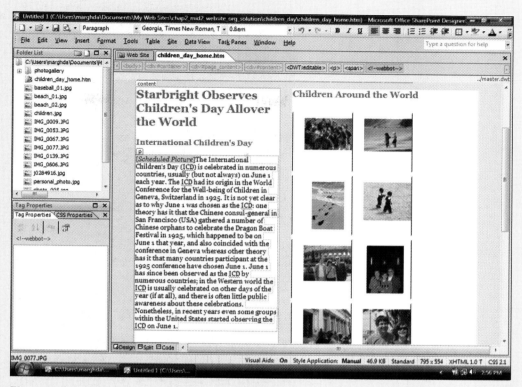

Figure 2.139 Home Page of the Subsite Dedicated to Children's Day

3 Enhancing the Design and Accessibility of the Subsite of the Starbright Children's Foundation Web Site Dedicated to the Children's Day

You have to further enhance the design and check for accessibility of the subsite of the Starbright Children's Foundation Web Site dedicated to the Children's Day using the Find and Replace and Accessibility checker tools. Figure 2.140 shows how the SharePoint Designer workspace should look at the end of this exercise. Use this figure as a guide.

a. Start SharePoint Designer. Locate and open the *chap2_mid3_website_org* Web site. Using the Remote Web Site view, create a **chap2_mid3_website_org_solution** Web site backup. Click the **Open your Remote Web site in SharePoint Designer link** to open the *chap2_mid3_website_org_solution* Web site folder.

b. Open the *children_day* subsite and open the *children_day_home.htm* Web page in Code view. Click the **Photo Gallery Web Component** in the Design view window and see in Code view the highlighted Photo Gallery Web component including the path to the *real.htm* file. Close *children_day_home.htm*.

c. Open the photogallery folder, and then open the photogallery00022877 folder. Open *real.htm* and *real_p.htm*.

d. Open the Find and Replace dialog box and display the HTML Tags tab:
   • Click **td** in the Find tag drop-down list.
   • Click **Remove attribute** in the Replace action drop-down list.
   • Click **Style** in the Attribute drop-down list.
   • Click the **Open page(s) option** in the *Find where* section.
   • Click the **Replace all button**.
   • Review and then close the Find 1 pane.
   • Save **real.htm** and **real_p.htm**.

e. Open the Accessibility Checker dialog box:
- Check **Open page(s)** in the *Check where* section.
- Check **all three check boxes** in the *Check for* section.
- Check the **Errors check box** in the *Show* section.
- Click the **Check button**.

f. Review the Accessibility pane content. It should include 28 accessibility problems found in *real.htm*. Save **real_p.htm**.

g. Click the **picture** placed in row 1 and column 1 of the *real_p.htm* layout table. Open the Picture Properties dialog box, select the *Alternate Text* check box in the General tab, and type a meaningful text in the Alternate Text box, such as **Girls' Baseball Team**. Then click the **OK button**.

h. Repeat the actions in step g for all pictures included in *real_p.htm*, and then save **real_p.htm**.

i. Repeat again the actions from step e. Review the Accessibility pane content. It should now include 14 accessibility problems found in *real.htm*. Repeat the actions included in step g for all pictures included in *real.htm*, and then save **real.htm**.

j. Repeat again the actions from step e. Review the Accessibility pane content. It should include 0 accessibility problems found in *real.htm*. Save **real_p.htm**.

k. Open *children_day_home.htm* in Design view. Figure 2.140 shows how the SharePoint Designer workspace should look at this point.

l. Close the *children_day* subsite and exit SharePoint Designer. Close *chap2_mid3_website_org_solution* and exit SharePoint Designer.

Figure 2.140 Enhanced Home Page of the Subsite Dedicated to Children's Day

Capstone Exercise

The Personal Computer Applications course Web site was developed three years ago by a graduate student as part of his Master's in Computer Software Engineering project, using FrontPage 2003 as a Web authoring tool. He did an excellent job, and you have now been hired to start building a new and enhanced version of the Web site using SharePoint Designer as the Web authoring tool. Your faculty supervisor is providing you with a Dynamic Web Template and the external style sheets used to develop the Dynamic Web Template.

Start Creating a New Web Site Using a SharePoint Designer General Template and a Dynamic Web Template

You will create a new Web site using a SharePoint Designer General template and a Dynamic Web Template.

a. Create a new *chap2_cap_IT_course* Web site using the One Page Web Site General template.

b. Locate and import the **styles_cap folder** and the *master_cap.dwt* Dynamic Web Template. Rename *master_cap.dwt* **master.dwt**. Rename *styles_cap* **styles**.

c. Open the *default.htm* home page and attach the *master.dwt* Dynamic Web Template.

d. Save **default.htm**.

Develop an Information Technology Course Web Site Using the Hyperlinks View

You will use Hyperlinks view to add the required folders and Web pages to a Web site. You will customize the Dynamic Web Template of the Web site.

a. Display the Hyperlinks view of the Web site showing all the broken hyperlinks from *default.htm*.

b. Create all the folders and Web pages as shown in the Hyperlinks view.

c. Display again the Hyperlinks view of the Web site and make sure there are no broken hyperlinks.

d. Open the *master.dwt* Dynamic Web Template. Replace the three headlines contained in the

<div #masthead> section (use the Quick Tag Selector bar) with your university, department, and course.

e. Save the **master.dwt** Dynamic Web Template and update the attached file. Save **default.htm**.

Enhance Web Pages of an Information Technology Course Web Site Using Web Components

You will enhance the Web site home page using Date and Time and Page Based on Schedule Web Component.

a. Create a New Document and type within its body **MyITLab Windows Vista Quiz is scheduled on February 4 & 5, 2008**. Save the new document as **myitlab_windows_quiz.htm** in the course_info folder.

b. Create a New Document and type within its body **No announcements**. Save the new document as **no_announcements.htm** in the course_info folder.

c. Open *default.htm*. Replace the *Heading 2* text line with **Announcements**. Position the insertion point beneath the text line and insert a **Date and Time Web Component**. Make sure you select the *Date this page was last automatically updated* option on the Date and Time dialog box.

d. Position the insertion point beneath the Date and Time Web Component and insert a **Page Based on Schedule Web Component** that will display the *myitlab_windows_quiz.htm* during the scheduled time (starting January 31, 2008, and ending February 6, 2008), and *no_announcements.htm* before and after the scheduled time (for testing purposes you can adjust the starting and ending times).

e. Save **default.htm**, close the *chap2_cap_IT_course* Web site, and exit SharePoint Designer.

Mini Cases

Use the rubric following the case as a guide to evaluate your work. However, keep in mind that your instructor may have additional grading criteria or use a different standard to evaluate your work.

Maximize the Usability and Accessibility of the Information Technology Lab Web Site

GENERAL CASE

You finalized your work on the capstone exercise, and you now want to further improve the usability and accessibility of the Information Technology Course Web site and build a site map. Open the *chap2_mc1_IT_course* Web site and create a **chap2_mc1_IT_course_solution** backup Web site. Carefully review the Hyperlinks view of the Web site. Change the Web page labels to reflect their purpose and create the Web site navigation structure using the Navigation View. Figure 2.141 shows a sample solution of the Web site navigational structure. Attach *master.dwt* to *sitemap.htm* and create a site map using the SharePoint Designer Table of Contents Web Component.

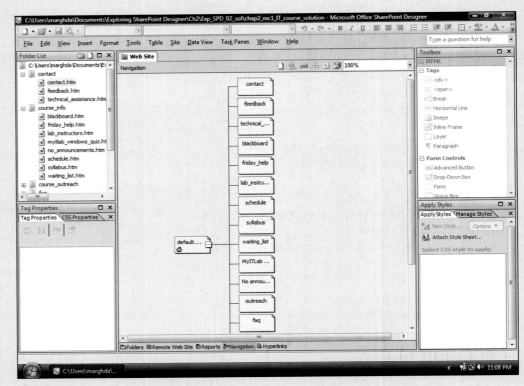

Figure 2.141 Information Technology Course Web Site Navigation View

Performance Elements	Exceeds Expectations	Meets Expectations	Below Expectations
Create the backup Web site	Successfully creates the backup Web site.	Successfully creates the backup Web site.	Fails to create the backup Web site.
Create the Web site navigation structure	Modifies all Web page labels and includes all Web pages and related documents.	Includes all Web pages and related documents.	Fails to include Web pages or related documents.
Create the site map	Attaches master.dwt and inserts the Table of Contents.	Inserts the Table of Contents.	Fails to insert the Table of Contents.

Real Estate Market Analysis

RESEARCH CASE

As a result of the turmoil in the real estate market, DestinQuest has decided to develop a mortgage subsite of its DestinQuest Web site to provide its current and prospective customers with up-to-date information and assistance toward making the best decision in buying or selling real estate. Search the Web for real estate Web sites that provide mortgage calculators and tools to make the most informed decisions, keeping in mind that core decision factors should include the following:

• Buying or refinancing a home.

• Moving up or downsizing.

• How much house one can afford.

• Choosing a broker.

• Selecting a mortgage.

• Making the offer.

• Closing the deal.

Open the *chap2_mc2_realestatemarket* Web site and create a **chap2_mc2_realestatemarket_ solution** Web site. Create a mortgage subsite. Using the *master.dwt* Web site Dynamic Web Template create a home page for the subsite and create a Web page for each core decision factor. Add relevant content to each Web page, based on the sources of information you identified. Add a Home Buyer's Guide to Mortgages hyperlink leading to the home page of the mortgage subsite, placed in the sidebar editable region of the DestinQuest Web site home page. Check the home page of the mortgage subsite for compatibility with XHTML 1.0 Strict and CSS 2.0 options. Eliminate all compatibility problems and generate and save the Compatibility Report.

Performance Elements	Exceeds Expectations	Meets Expectations	Below Expectations
Creating the mortgage subsite and adequate Web pages for all core factors	Creates the subsite and creates Web pages for all core factors with adequate file names and page titles.	Creates the subsite and creates Web pages for all core factors with adequate file names.	Creates the subsite and creates Web pages just for some core factors.
Emphasize in the subsite home page the core decision factors	Uses headings, lists, and hyperlinks to lay out and format the home page content.	Uses headings and hyperlinks to lay out and format the home page content.	Uses hyperlinks to lay out and format the home page content.
Identify and add to the mortgage subsite home page links to financial calculators	Identifies and properly adds to the mortgage subsite home page links to financial calculators.	Identifies financial calculators.	Uses no financial calculator content.
Check for compatibility the home page of the mortgage subsite with XHTML 1.0 Strict and CSS 2.0 options	Checks the home page of the mortgage subsite for compatibility and eliminates all errors.	Checks the home page of the mortgage subsite for compatibility and eliminates some errors.	Checks the home page of the mortgage subsite for compatibility.

Creating an Accessible Alternative Web Page

DISASTER RECOVERY

Open the *chap2_mc3_katrinanews* Web site and create a **chap2_mc3_katrinanews_solution** backup Web site. Open the *news.htm* Web page and run the Accessibility Reports tool. Make sure the Warnings check box on the Accessibility Checker is selected. Save the Accessibility Report and carefully review the WCAG accessibility problems related to programmatic objects. Create a news_alt.htm copy of the news.htm Web page, remove the Calendar Web Component, and save the Web page. In news.htm, double-click the Calendar. Click the Object Tag tab on the Active-X Control Properties dialog box and type **<a href="news_alt.htm">Alternative Accessible Web Page </a>** in the HTML box.

Performance Elements	Exceeds Expectations	Meets Expectations	Below Expectations
Check the Accessibility	Properly runs the Accessibility Checker and identifies all accessibility problems related to programmatic objects.	Properly runs the Accessibility Checker.	Fails to properly run the Accessibility Checker.
Create the news_alt.htm alternative Web page for the Calendar Web Component Object	Creates the news_alt.htm Web page and properly adds it as an alternative Web page for the Calendar Web Component Object.	Creates the news_alt.htm Web page.	Fails to create the news_alt.htm Web page and properly add it as an alternative Web page for the Calendar Web Component Object.

Microsoft Office 2007 Documents and Web Forms

Integrating Microsoft Office 2007 Documents and Adding Interactive Web Forms to Microsoft Office SharePoint Designer 2007 Web Sites

Objectives

After you read this chapter, you will be able to:

1. Work with Word 2007 documents in SharePoint Designer 2007 **(page 260)**.

2. Work with PowerPoint 2007 Presentations and SharePoint Designer 2007 **(page 265)**.

3. Work with Excel 2007 spreadsheets in SharePoint Designer 2007 **(page 275)**.

4. Work with Access 2007 databases in SharePoint Designer 2007 **(page 282)**.

5. Design a Web form **(page 297)**.

6. Create a Web form with SharePoint Designer 2007 **(page 300)**.

7. Work with Web forms and scripts in SharePoint Designer 2007 **(page 316)**.

Hands-On Exercises

Exercises	Skills Covered
1. INTEGRATE MICROSOFT OFFICE 2007 AND SHAREPOINT DESIGNER 2007 (page 288) **Case Study–Related** **Open:** chap3_ho1_solution_word, chap3_ho1_solution_ppt, chap3_ho1_solution_excel, chap3_ho1_solution_access, web_design_tutorial.docx, impressionist_paintings.pptx, population_solution.xlsx, and nationalbank.accdb **Save as:** chap3_1_solution_word_solution, chap3_ho1_solution_ppt_solution, chap3_ho1_solution_excel_solution, chap3_ho1_solution_access_solution, and web_design_tutorial.pdf	• Start SharePoint Designer, Open a Web Site, Start Word, Copy and Paste Word Content, Import a PDF File, and Add a Hyperlink to the Imported PDF File • Open a Web Site, Start PowerPoint, Save a PowerPoint Slide as JPG File Interchange Format (*.jpg), Save a PowerPoint Presentation as a Web Page *(*.htm; *html), Add a *.jpg File to a Web Page, Add a Hyperlink to a PowerPoint Presentation Saved as a Web Page *(*.htm; *html), and View a PowerPoint Presentation Saved as a Web Page *(*.htm; *html) in Internet Explorer 7.0 • Open a Web Site, Start Excel, Save an Excel Workbook as an XPS Document (*.xps), Save an Excel Workbook as a Web Page *(*.htm; *html), View an Excel Workbook Saved as an XPS Document (*.xps) in Internet Explorer 7.0, and View an Excel Workbook Saved as a Web Page *(*.htm; *html) in Internet Explorer 7.0 • Open a Web Site, Start Access, Export an Access Object as an XPS Document (*.xps), Export an Access Object as an HTML Document, View an Access Object as an XPS Document (*.xps) in Internet Explorer 7.0, and View an Access Object as an HTML Document in Internet Explorer 7.0
2. DEVELOP WEB FORMS WITH SHAREPOINT DESIGNER 2007 (page 322) **Case Study–Related** **Open:** chap3_ho2_solution_forms **Save as:** chap3_ho2_solution_forms_solutions	• Start SharePoint Designer, Open a Web Site, Create a New Blank Web Page, Insert a Layout Table, Insert an <h1> Line Text and an Image in the Cells of the Table, Insert Form Controls Within the Table Container Dotted Line, and Save the Web Page • Modify the Properties of a Drop-Down Box and Modify the Properties of a Text Box • Customize a Push Button Using JavaScript and the Behavior Task Pane, and View and Test a Form in Internet Explorer 7.0

CASE STUDY

Enhancing the DestinQuest Company Web Site Using Microsoft Office Documents and Web Forms

Stefania, Nadia, Emily, and Codi are four intelligent and enthusiastic best friends who, as soon as they graduated from college three years ago, decided to build their own successful real estate company, named DestinQuest, based in Destin, Florida.

Initially they planned to provide services related to buying, selling, and renting properties situated in the little paradise surrounding the Destin area. They now own their business headquarters building, which is well placed in Destin's business district. They have also opened two more offices in Vail, Colorado, and Catalina Island, California. Three years ago, they hired Melissa to help

Case Study

them develop a FrontPage Web site to promote, publicize, and manage their company. Thanks to their efforts and Melissa's skills, they have a functional Web site, and their DestinQuest company is constantly expanding, making a lot of progress in the Destin, Vail, and Catalina Island real estate business. Melissa did an excellent job in upgrading their previous Frontpage 2003 e-business Web site using SharePoint Designer 2007. DestinQuest extended her work contract so she can add new customer support and marketing Web pages to their e-business Web site. Because DestinQuest employees are Microsoft Office 2007 power users, Melissa also needs to integrate Microsoft Word, Excel, PowerPoint, and Access content into the upgraded e-business Web site.

Your Assignment

- Read the chapter, paying special attention to Hands-On Exercises 1 and 2, which help you grasp skills for integrating Microsoft Office 2007 and SharePoint Designer, and get acquainted with designing Web forms, creating Web forms with SharePoint Designer, and working with Web forms and scripts in SharePoint Designer 2007.
- You will put yourself in Melissa's place and open the *chap3_case_DestinQuest* Web site folder, which contains the partially completed Web site, and create a **chap3_case_DestinQuest_solution** backup Web site folder.
- Study the structure of the Web site, the Dynamic Web Template, and the home page content.
- Open the *register_destinquest_newsletter.htm* Web page, in the promotions folder. Open *NewsletterAndPromotions.pdf* included in the data_files folder. Add a form for signing up for the DestinQuest Newsletter and Promotions, as shown in NewsletterAndPromotions.pdf.
- Use the Accessibility Reports tool to make sure the *register_destinquest_newsletter.htm* Web page has no accessibility problems against the Web Content Accessibility Guidelines (WCAG) and Accessibility Board Section 508 Guidelines.
- In Word, open the *DestinQuestRealEstateListings.docx* document included in the data_files folder and save it as **DestinQuestRealEstateListings.xps** within the same data_files folder.
- In Excel, open the *DestinQuestCondoRates.xlsx* file included in the *data_files folder* and publish it as the **DestinQuestCondoRates.htm** Web page (make sure the AutoRepublish every time this book is saved checkbox is checked).
- In PowerPoint, open the *DestinQuest.pptx* presentation included in the data_files folder and save it as **DestinQuest.htm**. Make sure you click the Publish button in the Save As dialog box, type or click the Browse button, and save the DestinQuest.pptx as DestinQuest.htm.
- Use the Site Summary reports and the Hyperlinks View to check and make sure there are no broken hyperlinks in the DestinQuest Web site.
- Close the DestinQuest Web site and exit SharePoint Designer.

Integrate Microsoft Office 2007 and SharePoint Designer 2007

(SharePoint Designer makes it easy to integrate Microsoft Office 2007 files, as well as Microsoft Office 2003 files, into your Web site.)

SharePoint Designer makes it easy to integrate Microsoft Office 2007 files, as well as Microsoft Office 2003 files, into your Web site. Microsoft Office 2007 introduces new file formats that are based on XML called *Microsoft Office open XML formats*. These formats apply to Microsoft Office Word 2007, Microsoft Office Excel 2007, and Microsoft Office PowerPoint 2007. By default, documents, worksheets, and presentations that you create in the 2007 Office release are saved in XML format with new file name extensions that add an *x* or an *m* to the file name extensions with which you are already familiar. An *x* signifies an XML file that has no macros, and an *m* signifies an XML file that does contain macros.

Portable Document Format (PDF) and *XML Paper Specification (XPS)* are two fixed-layout electronic file formats that preserve document formatting and enable file sharing. The PDF and XPS formats ensure that when the file is viewed online or printed, it retains exactly the format that you intended, and that data in the file cannot be easily changed. The PDF format is also useful for documents that will be reproduced by using commercial printing methods.

Microsoft Office open XML formats are new Microsoft Office 2007 file formats that are based on XML and that apply to Microsoft Office Word 2007, Microsoft Office Excel 2007, and Microsoft Office PowerPoint 2007.

Portable Document Format (PDF) is a fixed-layout electronic file format that preserves document formatting, enables file sharing and is also useful for documents that will be reproduced by using commercial printing methods.

XML Paper Specification (XPS) is a fixed-layout electronic file format that preserves document formatting and enables file sharing.

TIP   Microsoft Office Files Compatibility

The 2007 Office release allows you to save files in the new Office XML formats, as well as in the file format of earlier versions of Office. When you save a document in Word, the file now uses the .docx file name extension by default, rather than the .doc file name extension. When you save a file as a template, you see the same kind of change. The template extension used in earlier versions is there, but it now has an x or an m on the end. If your file contains code or macros, you must save it by using the new macro-enabled XML file format, which adds an m for macro to the file extension. The 2007 Office release includes both compatibility checkers and file converters to facilitate file sharing between different versions of Office. The 2007 Office compatibility checker ensures that you have not introduced a feature that an earlier version of Office does not support. When you save the file, the compatibility checker reports those features to you and then allows you to remove them before continuing with the save.

TIP   More About Microsoft Office 2007, PDF, and XPS

To read more about the new Microsoft XPS format, see Microsoft's XML Paper Specification: Overview Web site (http://www.microsoft.com/whdc/xps/default .mspx) or visit the XPS Team Blog on XML Paper Specification and the Open Packaging Conventions (http://blogs.msdn.com/xps). In order to save and export work to PDF and XPS format in Microsoft Office 2007, you need to download and install on your computer additional software from the Microsoft Download Center (http://www.microsoft.com/downloads) called 2007 Microsoft Add-in: Microsoft Save as PDF or XPS. In order to view files in PDF format you will also need to download the Adobe® Reader® software (http://www.adobe.com/products/reader). In order to view files in XPS format, you might also be required to install additional software on your computer; see the Microsoft View and Generate XPS Web page (http://www.microsoft.com/whdc/xps/viewxps.mspx).

In this section, you will learn how you can work in SharePoint Designer with Microsoft Word, Power Point, Excel, and Access documents.

Working with Word 2007 Documents in SharePoint Designer 2007

Microsoft Word is probably one of the most popular word processors available. As with all the Microsoft Office suite applications, Word enables integration with other applications. Its capability to create documents that can be cut and pasted into Web pages or even to create documents ready to be published on the World Wide Web (WWW) has consistently improved in the past few years. Additionally, when you use SharePoint Designer, you can add Word content, import a Word document into a Web site, and edit Word content and files.

Add Word Content to a Web Page

You can take advantage of the Microsoft Word and SharePoint Designer content integration features and use content created in Word in your Web pages. The easiest way to add Word content to a SharePoint Designer Web page is by using the traditional Cut and Paste commands. (In the Add Text section of Chapter 2, you learned how to use the traditional Cut and Paste commands and the Paste Options button; you also learned how to use the Cut and Paste Text commands.)

You can also use the Clipboard Task pane to copy and paste text from Word to SharePoint Designer. To do so, launch Microsoft Word and open the document containing the content you want to use. Highlight the section of the document you want to copy, right-click, and then click Copy, as shown in Figure 3.1. The highlighted section is copied to the Clipboard.

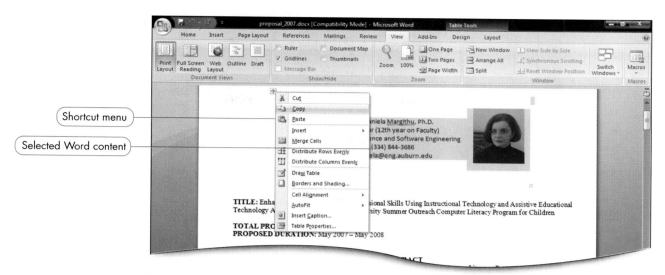

Shortcut menu

Selected Word content

Figure 3.1 Copying Word Content

After you have copied the Word content, launch SharePoint Designer and create a new Web page or open an existing one. Click Clipboard on the Task Panes menu and you will see the copied text on the Clipboard task pane. Position the insertion point in the body of the Web page where you want the Word content to appear, click the drop-down arrow to the right of the copied text, and click Paste. SharePoint Designer automatically converts the Word content into HTML, as shown in Figure 3.2. Using the Paste Options drop-down list (see Figure 3.2), you can format the pasted text in different ways. If you click Keep Text Only, the Paste Text dialog box opens.

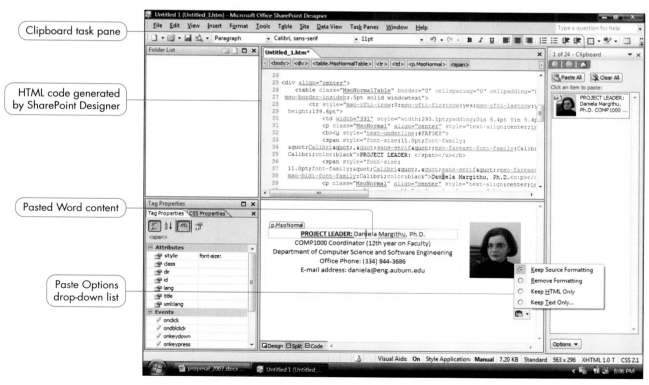

Clipboard task pane

HTML code generated by SharePoint Designer

Pasted Word content

Paste Options drop-down list

Figure 3.2 Pasting Word Content in a SharePoint Designer Web Page

Add Word Documents to a Web Site

Microsoft Word enables users to create a new regular Word document (.docx file format), a Web page (.htm file format), or an XML file (.xml file format). It also empowers users with three options for saving a Word document as a Web page: Single File Web page; Web page; and Web page, Filtered. Starting with Microsoft Word 2007 you can also save and export a Word document as a PDF (.pdf file format) or XPS Document (.xps file format). When you are creating a Web page in Word, you should work in the Web Layout view because it gives you a good idea of how the document will look when it is viewed in a Web browser.

The **Single File Web page** option saves the entire document as a single .mht-format file, which is supported only by Internet Explorer version 4.0 and higher. The **Web page** option saves the document as an .htm file with a set of files (grouped in a folder having the same name as that of the .htm file), which enables you to rebuild the original Word document (for example, but not limited to, all graphic files included in the original Word document and .xml files defining the color scheme used by the original Word document). Word metadata include information about the document, such as the full name, path, smart tags, hyperlinks, tracked changes, comments, hidden text, and the last ten authors. The **Web page, Filtered** option saves the document in an .htm file format with an additional set of files grouped in a folder, but it filters and removes all the Word-specific metadata.

SharePoint Designer enables you to import any Word file format. To import a Word document, click File on the Menu bar, point to the Import command, and click File to open the Import dialog box. Click the Add file button to open the Add File to Import List dialog box, as shown in Figure 3.3. Click the desired .docx document, click the Open button to close the Add File to Import List dialog box, and then click OK to close the Import dialog box. From a developer's point of view, the process of importing a document saved as a PDF document, XPS document, or Single File Web page is identical. When you are working with a document saved as a Web page or as a Web page, Filtered, the supporting files are not automatically imported for you by SharePoint Designer from the filename_files folder. Therefore, you will need to import this folder as well. To import a filename_files folder, click File on the Menu bar, point to the Import command, and click File to open the Import dialog box. Click the Add Folder button to open the File Open dialog box. Click the desired filename_files folder, click the Open button to close the File Open dialog box, and then click OK to close the Import dialog box. If you choose to delete this folder, SharePoint Designer will display an alert window indicating that you will need to delete its related document.

The **Single File Web page** option saves the entire document as a single .mht-format file, which is supported only by Internet Explorer version 4.0 and higher.

(SharePoint Designer enables you to import any Word file format.)

The **Web page** option saves the document as an .htm file with a set of files grouped in a folder that enables you to rebuild the original Word document.

The **Web page, Filtered** option saves the document in an .htm file format with an additional set of files grouped in a folder, but it filters and removes all the Word-specific metadata.

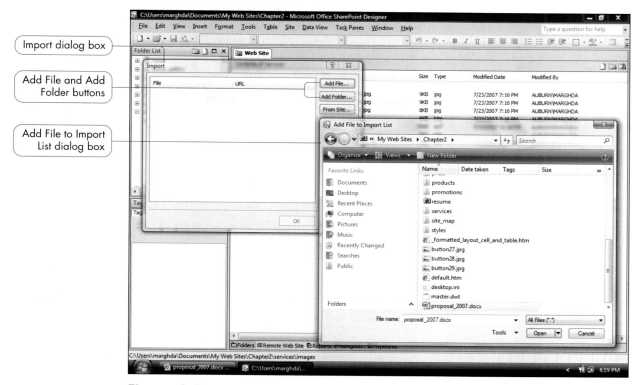

Figure 3.3 Importing a Word Document into a SharePoint Designer Web Site

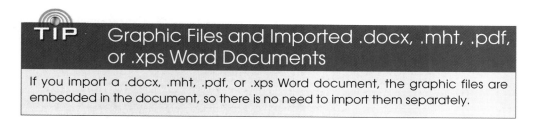

TIP Graphic Files and Imported .docx, .mht, .pdf, or .xps Word Documents

If you import a .docx, .mht, .pdf, or .xps Word document, the graphic files are embedded in the document, so there is no need to import them separately.

Edit Word Documents in SharePoint Designer 2007

When you open any Word document in SharePoint Designer, your document is opened in Word by default. You can overwrite this default option using the Configure Editors tab of the Application Options dialog box, as shown in Figure 3.4 (click Application Options on the Tools menu to display the dialog box). To open in SharePoint Designer an HTML document created in Word, right-click the file in the Folder list, point to Open With, and click SharePoint Designer (Open as HTML).

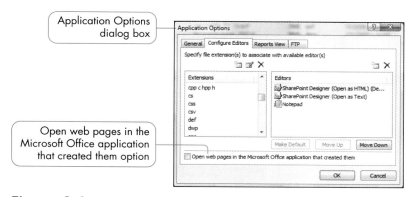

Figure 3.4 Opening a Word Document in SharePoint Designer

To open an imported .pdf or .xps file in SharePoint Designer, double-click these files in the Folder List task pane. The .pdf file will be displayed in an Adobe Reader window (see Figure 3.5), and the .xps file will be displayed in an XPS Viewer window (see Figure 3.6).

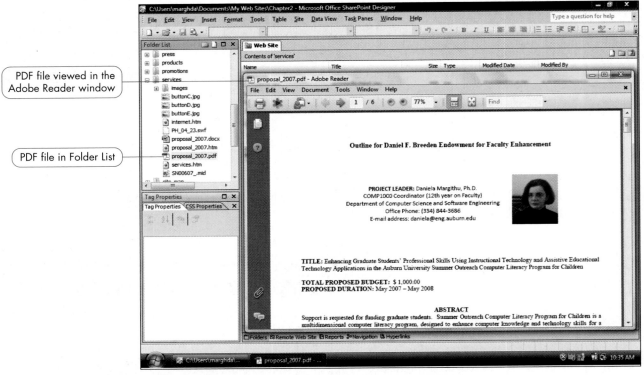

Figure 3.5 Opening a PDF Document in SharePoint Designer

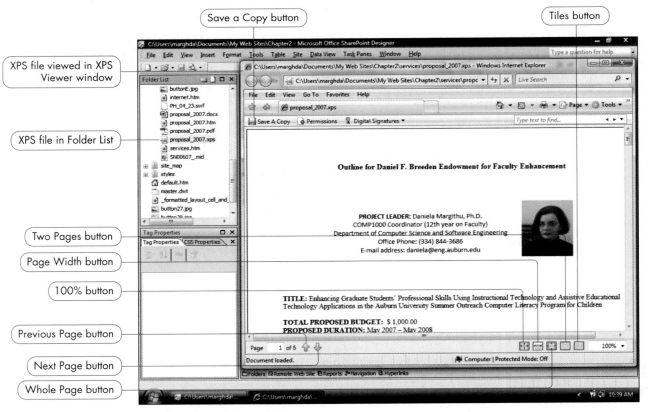

Figure 3.6 Opening an XPS Document in SharePoint Designer

If you need to modify any imported Web page created in the Word .htm or .mht file formats, you should edit the original .docx source file of the Web page in Word, save it again as an .htm or .mht file, and then import the updated file into your Web site, replacing the existing files. You can also edit these files in SharePoint Designer with the Word editor and save them directly to the Web site, replacing the existing files. Edit these files directly in SharePoint Designer only if there is no other option because you will not be able to use all the tools in the Word editor, such as the Reviewing toolbar.

If you need to modify any imported Web page created in the Word .pdf or .xps file formats, you should edit the original .docx source file of the Web page in Word, save it again as a .pdf or .xps file, and then import the updated file into your Web site, replacing the existing files.

Working with PowerPoint 2007 Presentations and SharePoint Designer 2007

PowerPoint is another popular Microsoft Office application. It is so versatile that a nine-year-old child could use it to prepare a show-and-tell school presentation, a Ph.D. candidate could use it to prepare his or her thesis, or a corporate tycoon could use it to prepare a company's annual report. You can use SharePoint Designer to make content from PowerPoint or entire presentations available on a Web page. From copying and pasting PowerPoint components to a Web page, to inserting an entire presentation into a Web page, saving a presentation for use on the Web, and publishing a PowerPoint presentation on a Web server, SharePoint Designer can assist Web developers in achieving their goals.

Add PowerPoint Presentations to a Web Site

The easiest way to include the content of a PowerPoint presentation on your Web page is to use the copy-and-paste method. You select any or all elements included in a PowerPoint slide, copy them, and paste them to a Web page.

To copy the content from a PowerPoint slide and paste it to a SharePoint Designer Web page, you open the slide in PowerPoint, press and hold Ctrl, click the blocks included in the slide, right-click, and then click Copy to copy the selected block including text and image as shown in Figure 3.7. Next, create or open a SharePoint Designer Web page, position the insertion point in the desired location, right-click, and click Paste. The block will be, by default, pasted as an <img> tag, as shown in Figure 3.8. The Paste Options drop-down list provides you with two options for further formatting the image (see Figure 3.8).

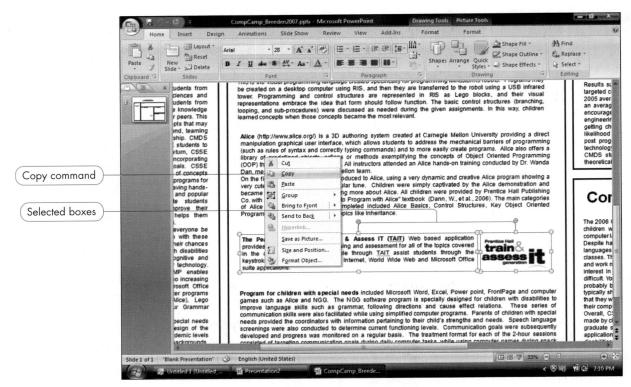

Figure 3.7 Copying Content Blocks from a PowerPoint Slide

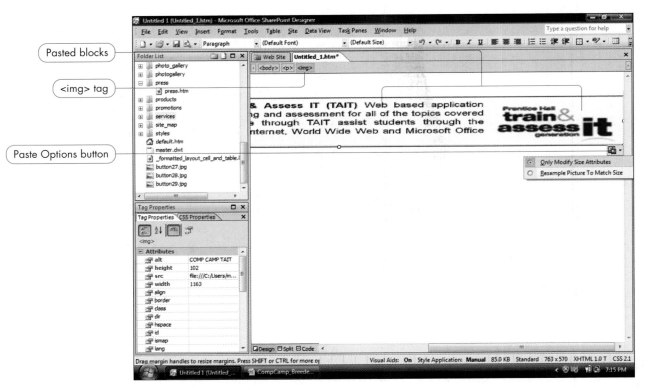

Figure 3.8 Content Blocks Pasted from a PowerPoint Slide Translated into an <img> Tag

If you just highlight the text included in the block shown in Figure 3.8, SharePoint Designer enables you to format the pasted text by using the Paste Options drop-down list, shown in Figure 3.9, which includes the following four options:

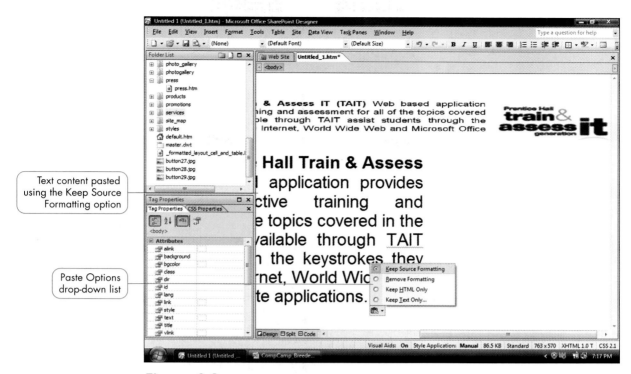

Figure 3.9 Pasted Content Using the Keep Source Formatting Option

1. **Keep Source Formatting**—makes no changes to the format of the contents (see Figure 3.9) and adds Vector Markup Language (VML) image files to the content. To learn more about VML visit the W3C Vector Markup Language (VML) Web page (http://www.w3.org/TR/NOTE-VML).

2. **Remove Formatting**—converts the pasted contents into text content using the SharePoint Designer Default Font and Default Size (see Figure 3.10). You can further modify the text as you learned previously.

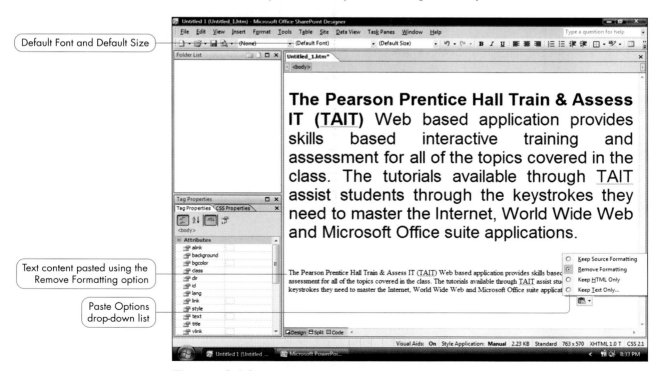

Figure 3.10 Pasted Content Using the Remove Formatting Option

3. **Keep HTML Only**—Keep all the HTML code, as shown in Figure 3.11.
4. **Keep Text Only**—Opens the Paste Text dialog box and enable you to paste contents using different text formatting options, as shown in Figure 3.11.

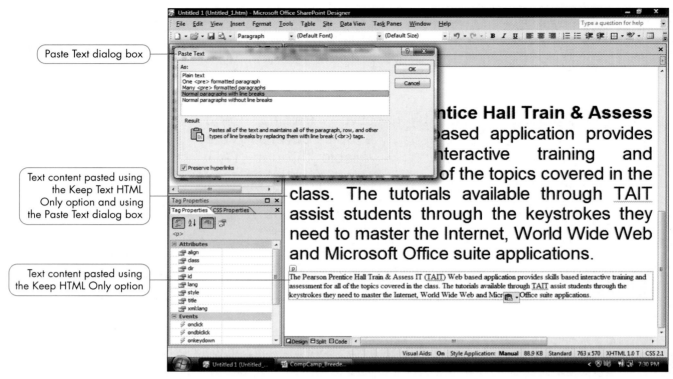

Figure 3.11 Pasted Content Using the Keep HTML Only and Keep Text Only Options

When a visitor clicks a link to a PowerPoint presentation, the presentation that is saved in the original PowerPoint format (.pptx) or the PowerPoint Slideshow format (.ppsx) opens in PowerPoint.

If you want to copy an image from a PowerPoint slide and paste it into a SharePoint Designer Web page, the process is identical to the copy-and-paste process for any other image file. However, make sure images are in a format that is supported by newer versions of Internet Explorer, Mozilla Firefox®, and Netscape®.

As a Web developer, you can make an entire PowerPoint presentation accessible via a Web page. Internet Explorer versions 4.0 and higher have a built-in PowerPoint player that enables users to read and play PowerPoint presentations with or without having the PowerPoint application installed on their computers. When a visitor clicks a link to a PowerPoint presentation, the presentation that is saved in the original PowerPoint format (.pptx) or the PowerPoint Slideshow format (.ppsx) and a dialog box open, as shown in Figure 3.12, enabling you to open or save the presentation.

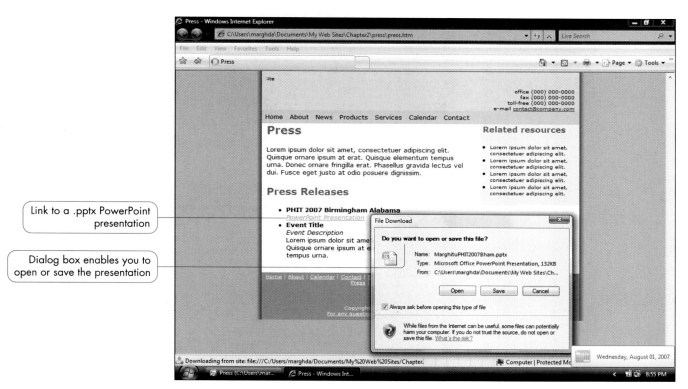

On the left side, with callouts:

Link to a .pptx PowerPoint presentation

Dialog box enables you to open or save the presentation

Figure 3.12 PowerPoint Presentation Viewed in the Internet Explorer Browser

TIP Cross-Browser Issues

Netscape and Mozilla Firefox browsers cannot read or play PowerPoint presentations saved in .pptx or .ppsx formats. However, if your viewers have PowerPoint already installed on their computers, the PowerPoint presentations automatically open in PowerPoint. If they do not have PowerPoint, they can download a freeware PowerPoint Viewer 2007 from the Microsoft Download Center Web site (http://www.microsoft.com/downloads/search.aspx?displaylang=en).

To insert a link to a PowerPoint presentation in your Web page, you first need to import the presentation into your Web site. The process of importing a .pptx file is identical to the process of importing a Word file as explained in previous sections of this chapter. After importing the presentation's .pptx file to your Web site, create a hyperlink to the .pptx file on your Web page, as shown in Figure 3.13.

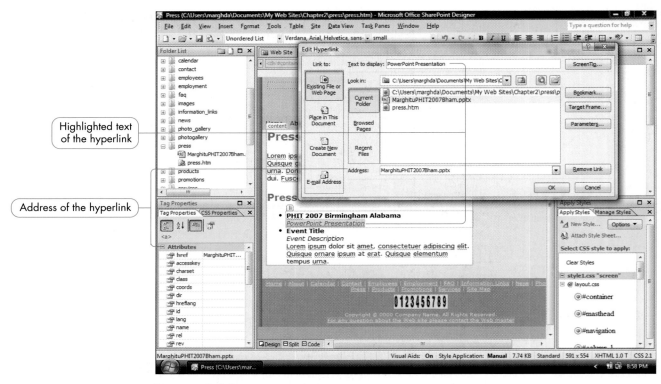

Figure 3.13   Inserting a Hyperlink into a PowerPoint Presentation

Create Web Page Content Using PowerPoint Slides

Microsoft PowerPoint enables its users to save any or all of the slides of a presentation in a variety of formats. If you choose to save all the slides in a presentation in one of the available graphic formats, shown in Figure 3.14, each slide is saved as a separate file (in the graphic format selected) in a folder. If you choose this solution, you need to develop a Web page in which you display the graphic files corresponding to each

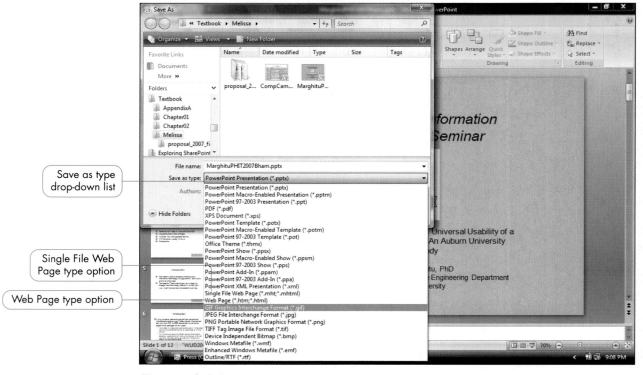

Figure 3.14   Saving a PowerPoint Presentation as a Graphic File

slide. This means that you need to create a Web page and include or add links to the graphic files that correspond to each slide.

You can also save a PowerPoint presentation directly as a Web page or as a Single File Web page, as shown in Figure 3.14. As when saving a Word document as a Web page, when you save a PowerPoint file as a Web page, the whole presentation is saved as a collection of files in a folder. When you choose to save a PowerPoint presentation as a Single File Web page, the whole presentation is saved as a single .mht or .mhtml file that can be viewed only in Internet Explorer version 4.0 or higher.

If you elect to save your PowerPoint presentation as a Web page or as a Single File Web page, the Publish button appears in the Save As dialog box. Click this button to display the Publish as Web Page dialog box, as shown in Figure 3.15, which enables you to prepare the presentation and publish it to the desired server location.

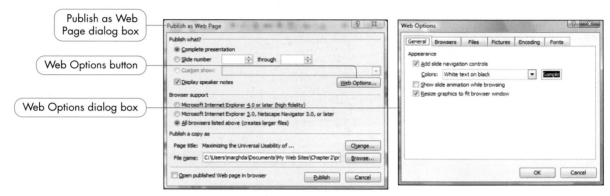

Figure 3.15 Publishing a PowerPoint Presentation as a Web Page

In the Publish what? section of the Publish as Web Page dialog box you can select to publish the complete presentation or a selected range of slides. The Browser support section includes three useful options for addressing potential cross-browser issues:

1. **Microsoft Internet Explorer 4.0 or later (high fidelity)**—This option creates a Web page supported only by Internet Explorer version 4.0 or higher.

2. **Microsoft Internet Explorer 3.0, Netscape Navigator 3.0, or later**—This option creates two versions of the PowerPoint presentation supported by the different versions of Microsoft Internet Explorer and Netscape browsers.

3. **All browsers listed above (creates larger files)**—This option includes HTML code that checks to see which browser the visitor is using and directs the browser to the files needed to display the Web page.

The Publish a copy as section of the Publish as Web Page dialog box enables you to change the title of the Web page and to select the location to which to publish it. After a PowerPoint presentation is published as a Web page, you can preview it in a browser window, as shown in Figure 3.16, or in SharePoint Designer by right-clicking the file in the Folders view, selecting Open With, and clicking one of the available browsers.

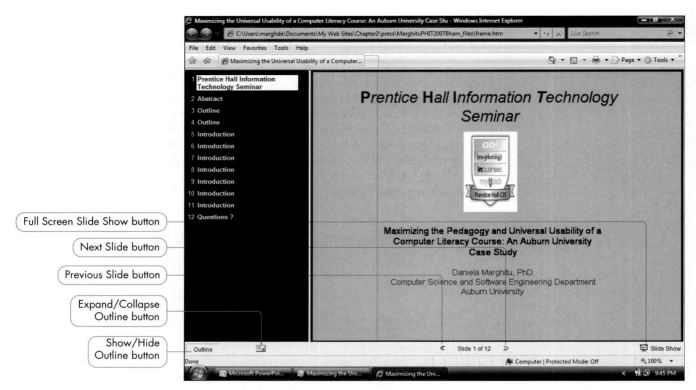

Figure 3.16 PowerPoint Presentation Saved as a Web Page and Viewed in Internet Explorer 7.0

The following labels appear to the left of the figure:

- Full Screen Slide Show button
- Next Slide button
- Previous Slide button
- Expand/Collapse Outline button
- Show/Hide Outline button

When you are working with a PowerPoint presentation saved as a Web Page or as a Web Page, Filtered, the supporting files are not automatically imported for you by SharePoint Designer from the filename_files folder, where filename_files is the folder containing the supporting PowerPoint files. Therefore, you will need to import this folder as well. To import a filename_files folder, click File on the Menu bar, point to the Import command, and click File to open the Import dialog box. Click the Add Folder button to open the File Open dialog box. Click the desired filename_files folder, click the Open button to close the File Open dialog box, and then click OK to close the Import dialog box. SharePoint Designer will display an alert window if you choose to delete this folder, indicating that you will need to delete its related file.

Edit PowerPoint Contents in SharePoint Designer 2007

A PowerPoint presentation that has been included in a SharePoint Designer Web site can be edited in PowerPoint or SharePoint Designer. If you double-click the PowerPoint presentation file in the Folder List task pane or in Folders view, it opens in PowerPoint. To edit a PowerPoint presentation in SharePoint Designer, right-click the file in Folders view, select Open With, and click SharePoint Designer (Open as HTML). If you choose the SharePoint Designer (Open as HTML) option instead of the SharePoint Designer (Open as Text) option, the HTML source of the Web page is displayed, enabling you to edit the HTML code. It is strongly recommended that you edit the original PowerPoint source file and then save it as a Web page rather than edit PowerPoint presentations directly in SharePoint Designer.

> A PowerPoint presentation that has been included in a SharePoint Designer Web site can be edited in PowerPoint or SharePoint Designer.

PowerPoint 2007 introduces three new options for integrating PowerPoint content with SharePoint Designer Web sites. You can save PowerPoint slides as a PDF or XPS file, or you can save slides to be reused. To save PowerPoint slides as a PDF or XPS file, click PDF (*.pdf) or XPS Document (*.xps) on the Save as type drop-down list in the Save As dialog box (see Figure 3.14). Click the Options button to open the Options dialog box, which enables you to select the range of slides you wish to publish and offers you more options regarding what to publish and how to publish the slides (see Figure 3.17).

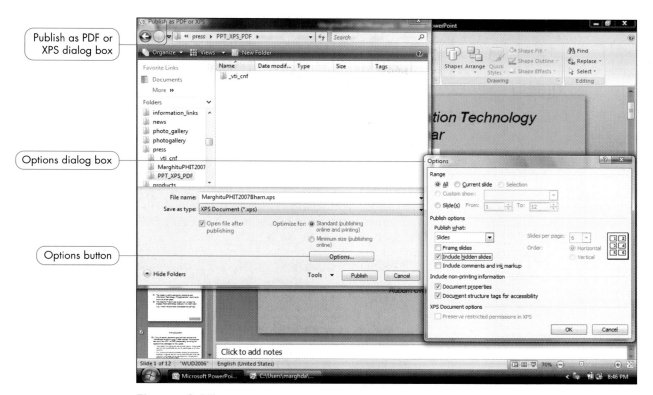

Figure 3.17 Saving a PowerPoint Presentation as a PDF (*.pdf) or XPS Document (*.xps)

To integrate a PowerPoint presentation saved as a PDF (*.pdf) or XPS document (*.xps) into a SharePoint Designer Web site you will first need to import the files into the Web site; then you can add a link to these files. Figure 3.18 shows a PowerPoint presentation saved as an XPS document (*.xps), viewed in Internet Explorer 7.0.

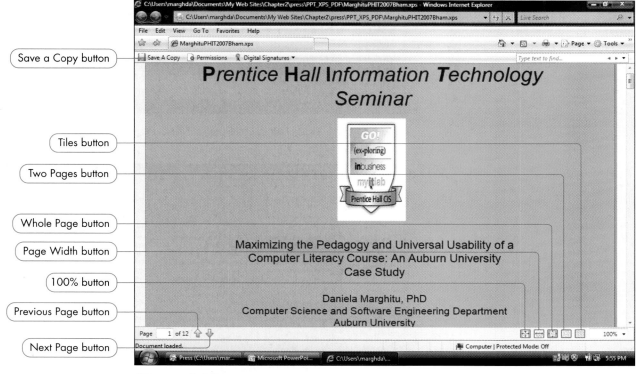

Figure 3.18 PowerPoint Presentation Saved as an XPS document (*.xps) and Viewed in Internet Explorer 7.0

You can also store slides or even entire presentations so that they will be available for use in any presentation using the Publish Slides command. Launch PowerPoint, point to Publish, and then click Publish Slides to open the Publish Slides dialog box, shown in Figure 3.19. In the Publish Slides dialog box, select the check box for the slide you wish to store. In the Publish To box, type the path (or URL) or click the Browse button to locate the SharePoint Designer Web site, and then click Publish. Each slide will be stored as a separate file (see Figure 3.20).

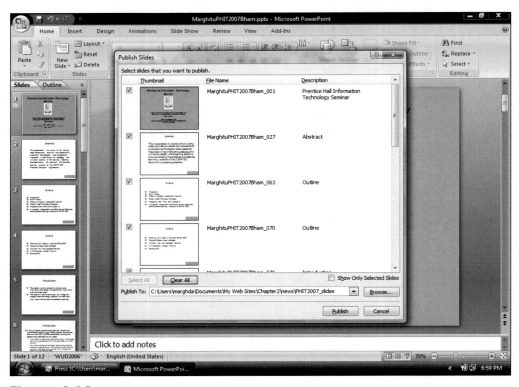

Figure 3.19 Storing Slides Using the Publish Slides Dialog Box

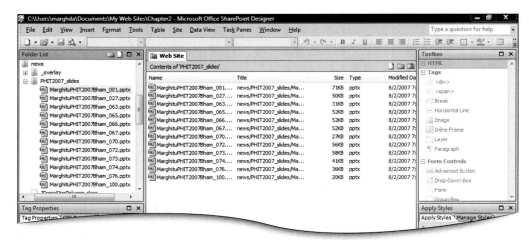

Figure 3.20 Slides Published into a SharePoint Web Site Using the Publish Slides Dialog Box

Working with Excel 2007 Spreadsheets in SharePoint Designer 2007

Excel is one of the most in-demand Microsoft applications. Its versatility enables students from second grade through college, home and business owners, or scientists to fulfill a wide variety of tasks. With its friendly user interface and comprehensive set of features, Excel can assist you in building a spreadsheet for keeping track of your household expenses or sophisticated business and scientific statistical studies and charts.

Excel enables integration with other applications. Its capability to create spreadsheets that can be cut and pasted into Web pages or even to create spreadsheets ready to be published on the World Wide Web has consistently improved in the past few years. Additionally, when you use SharePoint Designer you can add Excel content or import an Excel spreadsheet into a Web site and then edit Excel content and files.

> Excel enables integration with other applications. Its capability to create spreadsheets that can be cut and pasted into a Web page or even to create a spreadsheet ready to be published on the World Wide Web has consistently improved in the past few years. Additionally, when you use SharePoint Designer you can add Excel content or import an Excel spreadsheet into a Web site and then edit Excel content and files.

Add Excel Content to a Web Page

You can take advantage of the Microsoft Excel and SharePoint Designer content integration features and use content created in Excel in your Web pages. A *spreadsheet* is the computerized version of a ledger; it consists of rows and columns of data. A *worksheet* is a single spreadsheet consisting of a grid of columns and rows that can contain descriptive labels, numeric values, formulas, functions, and graphics. A *workbook* is a set of related worksheets contained within a file.

A *spreadsheet* is the computerized version of a ledger; it consists of rows and columns of data.

A *worksheet* is a single spreadsheet consisting of a grid of columns and rows that can contain descriptive labels, numeric values, formulas, functions, and graphics.

A *workbook* is a set of related worksheets contained within a file.

The easiest way to add Excel content to a SharePoint Designer Web page is by using the traditional Copy and Paste commands. (In the Add Text section of Chapter 2, you learned how to use the traditional Cut and Paste commands and the Paste Options button; you also learned how to use the Cut and Paste Text commands.)

You can also use the Clipboard task pane to copy and paste content from an Excel worksheet to SharePoint Designer. To do so, launch Microsoft Excel and open the spreadsheet containing the content you want to use. Click the first cell in the cell range you want to copy and drag the mouse pointer over the remaining cells you want to select. Right-click, and then click Copy, as shown in Figure 3.21. The selected cell range is copied to the Clipboard.

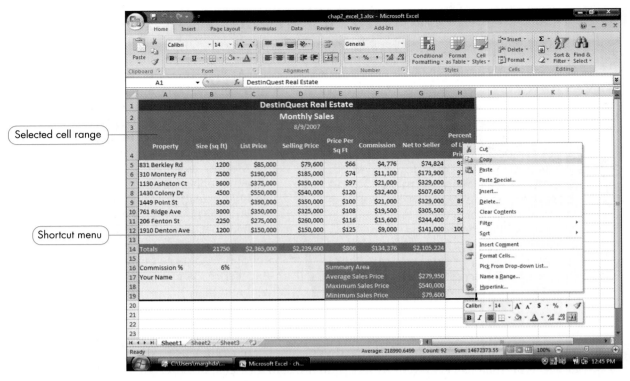

Figure 3.21 Copying Excel Content

After you have copied the Excel content, launch SharePoint Designer and create a new Web page or open an existing one. Click Clipboard on the Task Panes menu and you will see the copied content on the Clipboard task pane. Position the insertion point in the body of the Web page where you want the Excel content to appear, click the drop-down arrow to the right of the copied content, and click Paste. SharePoint Designer automatically converts the Excel content into HTML. Using the Paste Options drop-down list (see Figure 3.22), you can format the pasted content in different ways. If you click the Keep Text Only button, the Paste Text dialog box opens.

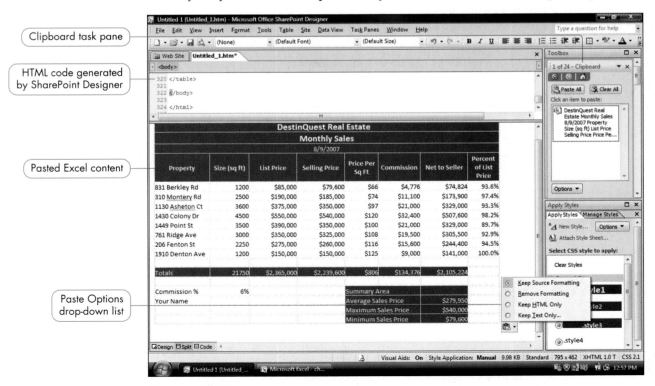

Figure 3.22 Pasting Excel Content in a SharePoint Designer Web Page

Paste Options | Reference

Paste Option	Pasted content		Description
Keep Source Formatting	Clipboard task pane / HTML code generated by SharePoint Designer / Apply Styles task pane / Pasted Excel content	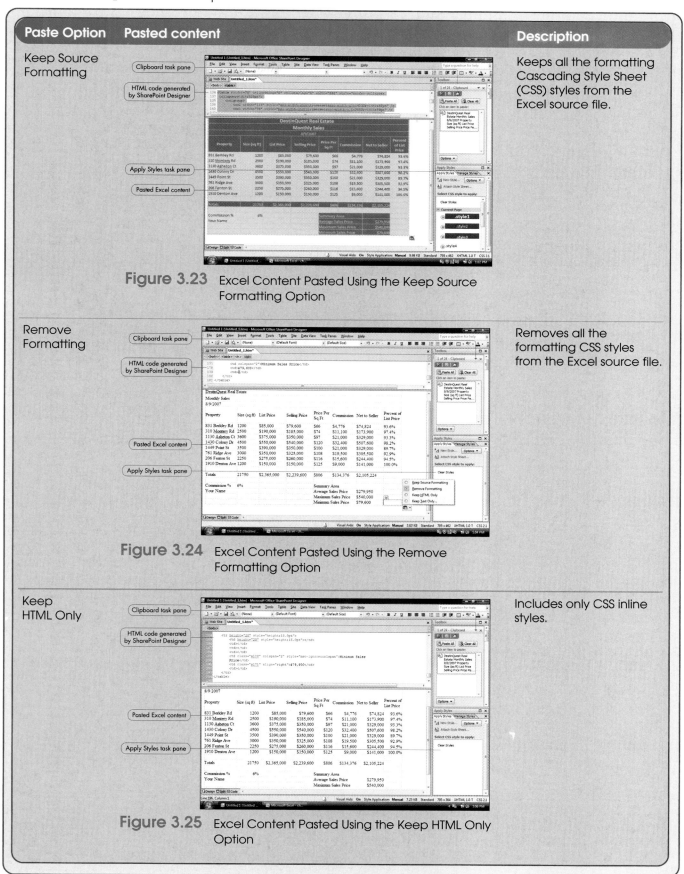	Keeps all the formatting Cascading Style Sheet (CSS) styles from the Excel source file.

Figure 3.23 Excel Content Pasted Using the Keep Source Formatting Option

| Remove Formatting | Clipboard task pane / HTML code generated by SharePoint Designer / Pasted Excel content / Apply Styles task pane | | Removes all the formatting CSS styles from the Excel source file. |

Figure 3.24 Excel Content Pasted Using the Remove Formatting Option

| Keep HTML Only | Clipboard task pane / HTML code generated by SharePoint Designer / Pasted Excel content / Apply Styles task pane | | Includes only CSS inline styles. |

Figure 3.25 Excel Content Pasted Using the Keep HTML Only Option

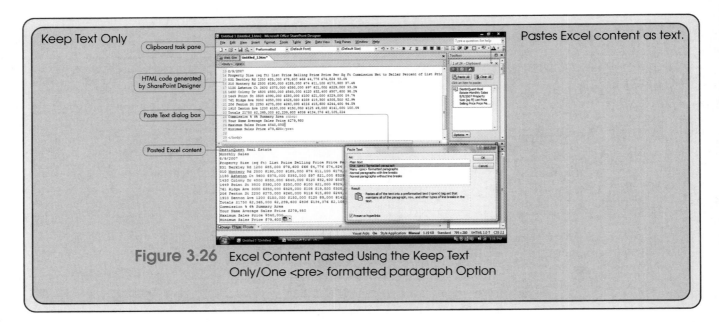

Figure 3.26 Excel Content Pasted Using the Keep Text
Only/One <pre> formatted paragraph Option

Add Excel Spreadsheets to a Web Site

Microsoft Excel 2007 enables users to create new XML formats such as Excel workbook files (*.xlsx). It also empowers users with three options for saving or exporting an Excel file in an Excel Binary Workbook XML (*.xlsb) format, or as a Web Page (*.htm; *.html) or Single File Web Page (*mht; *.mhtml). Starting with Microsoft Excel 2007 you can also save or export an Excel file as a PDF (*.pdf) or XPS Document (.xps). When you are creating a Web page in Excel, you should work in the Web Layout view, because it gives you a good idea of how the document will look when it is viewed in a Web browser.

The Single File Web page option saves the entire spreadsheet into a single .mht format file, which is supported only by Internet Explorer version 4.0 and higher. If you use the Web page option, the spreadsheet is saved as an .htm or .html file with a set of files grouped in a filename_files folder that includes Excel metadata that enable you to rebuild the original Excel spreadsheet. Excel metadata include information about the spreadsheet, such as the full name, path, smart tags, hyperlinks, tracked changes, comments, hidden text, and the last ten authors. When you save an Excel spreadsheet as a Single File Web page or Web page, you can choose to save the Entire Workbook or a Selection: Sheet (the active Worksheet). When you click the Publish button, the Publish as Web Page dialog opens, enabling you to select the AutoRepublish every time this workbook is saved check box (see Figure 3.27).

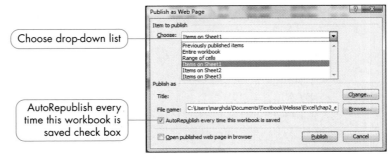

Figure 3.27 Publish as Web Page Dialog Box

When you save an Excel file as a PDF or XPS file, click the Options button to open the Options dialog box (see Figure 3.28). Within the sections of this dialog box, you can select the Page range to publish or whether to publish the active sheet(s), the entire workbook, or just a selection (cell range) within a worksheet.

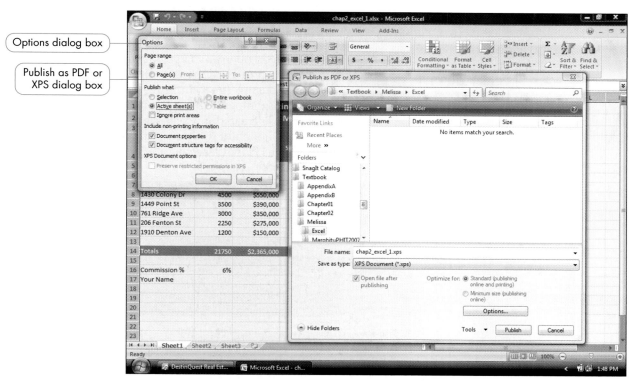

Options dialog box

Publish as PDF or XPS dialog box

Figure 3.28 Saving an Excel File as a PDF or XPS File

TIP   Saving an Excel File as a PDF or XPS File

If the Excel table is so wide that it occupies two pages, try using the Landscape Orientation in the Excel Page Setup dialog box.

SharePoint Designer enables you to import any Excel file format.

SharePoint Designer enables you to import any Excel file format using a procedure similar to the one used to import a Word file (see Figure 3.3). To import an Excel file, click File on the Menu bar, point to the Import command, and click File to open the Import dialog box. Click the Add File button to open the Add File to Import List dialog box. Click the desired .xlsx file, click the Open button to close the Add File to Import List dialog box, and then click OK to close the Import dialog box. From a developer's point of view, the process of importing an Excel file saved as a PDF or XPS file or as a Single File Web page or Web page is identical. When you are working with a spreadsheet saved as a Web page, the supporting files are not automatically imported for you by SharePoint Designer from the filename_files folder. Therefore, you will need to import this folder as well. If you first import the .xlsx file into the Web site and save it as a Web page within the same Web site, you will no longer need to import the filename_files folder.

TIP   Graphic Files and Imported .xlsx, .mht, .pdf, or .xps Excel Spreadsheets

If you import an .xlsx, .mht, .pdf, or .xps Excel spreadsheet, the graphic files are embedded in the file, so there is no need to import them separately.

Edit Excel Documents in SharePoint Designer 2007

When you open any Excel spreadsheet in SharePoint Designer, your file is opened in Excel by default. You can overwrite this default option using the Configure Editors tab of the Application Options dialog box.

When you open any Excel file in SharePoint Designer, your file is opened in Excel by default. You can overwrite this default option using the Configure Editors tab of the Application Options dialog box. To open in SharePoint Designer an .htm or .html file created in Excel, right-click the file in the Folder List task pane, point to Open With, and click SharePoint Designer (Open as HTML); see Figure 3.29.

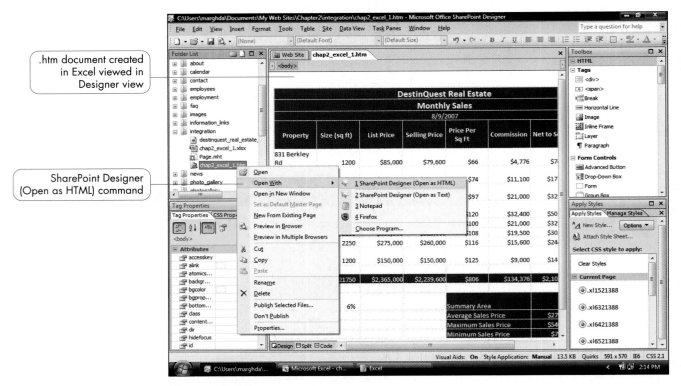

.htm document created in Excel viewed in Designer view

SharePoint Designer (Open as HTML) command

Figure 3.29 Opening an .htm File Created in Excel

TIP Opening a Single File Web Page in SharePoint Designer

If you double-click, in the Folder List task pane, a Single File Web page spreadsheet created in Excel, the spreadsheet will open as plain text. You cannot open this type of file using the SharePoint Designer (Open as HTML) command, but you can open it with the SharePoint Designer (Open as Text) command.

To open imported .pdf or .xps files in SharePoint Designer, double-click these files in the Folder List task pane. A .pdf file will be displayed in an Adobe Reader window (see Figure 3.30), and an .xps file will be displayed in an XPS Viewer window (see Figure 3.31).

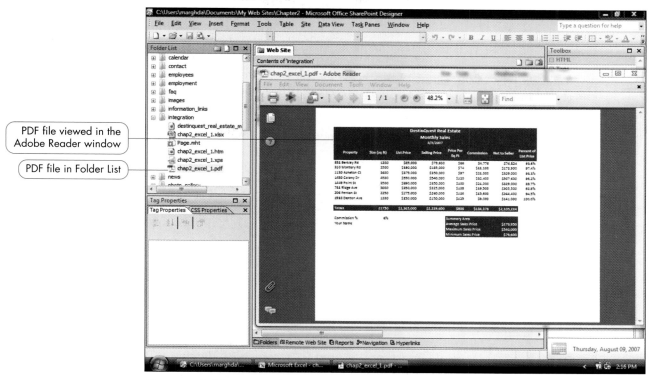

Figure 3.30 Opening a PDF File in SharePoint Designer

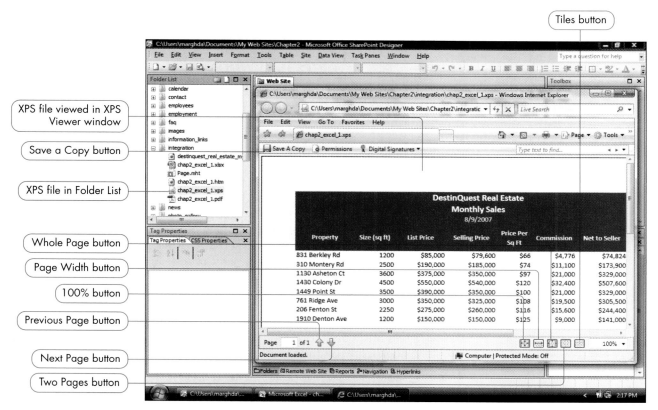

Figure 3.31 Opening an XPS File in SharePoint Designer

If you need to modify any imported Web page created in the Excel .htm or .mht file formats, you should edit the original .xlsx source file of the Web page in Excel. If you select the AutoRepublish every time this workbook is saved check box on the Publish as a Web Page dialog box, the work will be republished when you save it. You can also edit these files in SharePoint Designer with the Excel editor and save them directly to the Web site, replacing the existing files, but this is not recommended.

Working with Access 2007 Databases in SharePoint Designer 2007

In response to the boom of the Internet applications built on real-time access to databases for e-commerce and e-trading, in recent years the SharePoint Designer database capabilities have been upgraded. Microsoft Access is one of the most in-demand database applications. Its versatility enables students from middle school through college, home and business owners, or scientists to fulfill a wide variety of academic, business, or scientific tasks. With its friendly user interface and comprehensive set of features, Access can, for example, assist you in keeping track of financial and academic records stored in a university database. Profit and nonprofit organizations use databases to keep track of their employees, volunteers, events, sales, and acquisitions.

Access enables integration with other applications. Its capability to create databases that can be copied and pasted into Web pages or even to create databases ready to be published on the World Wide Web has consistently improved in the past few years. Additionally, when you use SharePoint Designer, you can add Access content, import an Access database into a Web site, and edit Access content and files.

Add Access Content to a Web Page

A **database** consists of fields, records, and tables.

A **field** is a single piece of information represented as a column.

A **record** is one complete set of fields represented as a row.

A **database table** is a collection of records.

You can take advantage of the Microsoft Access and SharePoint Designer content integration features and use content created in Access in your Web pages. A **database** consists of fields, records, and tables. A **field** is a single piece of information represented as a column. A **record** is one complete set of fields represented as a row. A **database table** is a collection of records. Databases can contain many tables.

The easiest way to add Access content to a SharePoint Designer Web page is by using the traditional Cut and Paste commands. (In the Add Text section of Chapter 2, you learned how to use the traditional Cut and Paste commands and the Paste Options button; you also learned how to use the Cut and Paste Text commands.)

You can also use the Clipboard task pane to copy and paste content from Access to SharePoint Designer. To do so, launch Microsoft Access and open an Access file database containing the content you want to use. In the Navigation pane, double-click the desired Access Object, such as a Table, a Query, a Form, or a Report. If, for example, you wish to copy the whole content of an Access Table Object, click the Select button on the Find Group. If you wish to copy only a selection from the Access Table Object, click the row selector to highlight the first record, navigate to the last record, press Shift, and click the row selector, as shown in Figure 3.32. Then right-click and click Copy on the shortcut menu. The highlighted section is copied to the Clipboard.

Figure 3.32 Copying Access Content

After you have copied the Access content, launch SharePoint Designer and create a new Web page or open an existing one. Click Clipboard on the Task Panes menu and you will see the copied text on the Clipboard task pane. Position the insertion point in the body of the Web page where you want the Access content to appear, click the drop-down arrow to the right of the copied Access content, and click Paste. SharePoint Designer automatically converts the Access content into HTML (see Figure 3.33). Using the Paste Options drop-down list (identical to the one shown in Figure 3.22), you can format the pasted content in different ways. If you click the Keep Text Only button, the Paste Text dialog box opens.

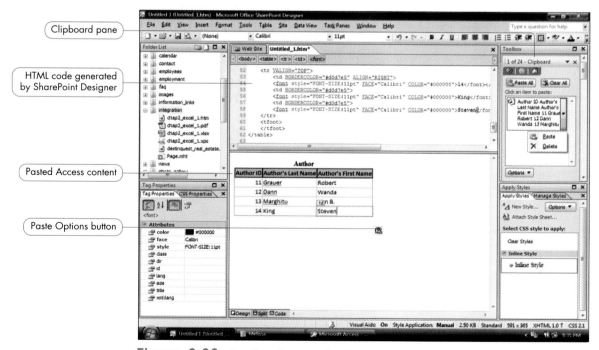

Figure 3.33 Pasting Access Content in a SharePoint Designer Web Page

Add Access Databases to a Web Site

Microsoft Access enables users to create a new regular Access XML file format (.accdb). It also empowers users with options to export Access Objects in other formats (see Figure 3.34), such as an Excel XML file format, Word RTF file, PDF (.pdf file format) or XPS Document (.xps file format), Access Database, Text File (.txt), XML File (.xml), ODBC Database, and HTML Document (.html).

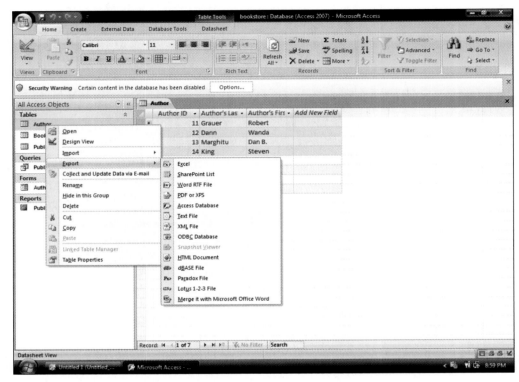

Figure 3.34 Exporting an Access Object

When you export an Access database as an HTML Document (.html), the Export-HTML Document dialog box enables you to specify export options (see Figure 3.35). When you click the OK button, the HTML Output Options dialog box opens, enabling you to select an HTML Template as well as the encoding you wish to use for saving the file (see Figure 3.35). When you click OK on the HTML Output Options dialog box, the Export - HTML Document dialog box opens, enabling you to select the Save export steps check box that will make any further export of the file easier (see Figure 3.35).

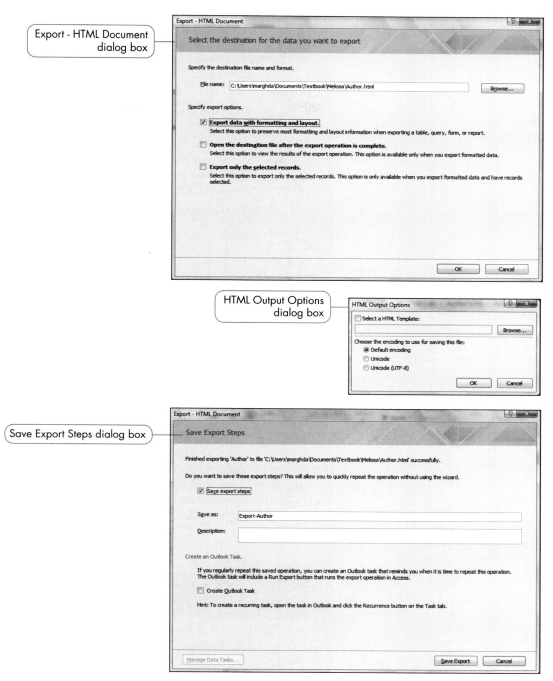

Export - HTML Document dialog box

HTML Output Options dialog box

Save Export Steps dialog box

Figure 3.35 Exporting an Access Object as an HTML Document (.html)

When you export an Access Object as a PDF or XPS Document, click the Options button to open the Options dialog box (see Figure 3.36). Within the sections of this dialog box, you can select the page range to publish or whether to publish all records, selected records, or selected pages. You can also choose to select or clear the *Document structure tags for accessibility* check box. This check box is selected by default so that the file created is more accessible to users with special needs. If you clear this check box, for example, data are not included in the file that enable your readers using screen readers to more easily navigate through the file.

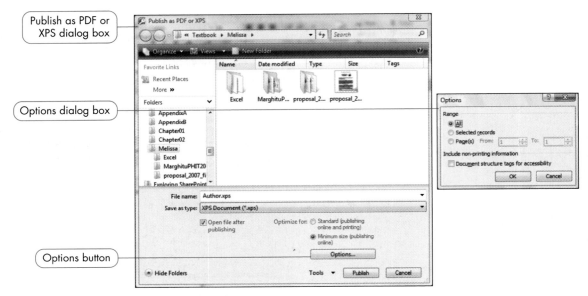

Publish as PDF or XPS dialog box

Options dialog box

Options button

Figure 3.36 Exporting an Access Object as an XPS Document (.xps)

When you open any .accdb Access database in SharePoint Designer, your database is opened in Access by default. You can overwrite this default option using the Configure Editors tab of the Application Options dialog box.

Access metadata include information about the database, such as the full name, path, smart tags, hyperlinks, tracked changes, comments, hidden text, and the last ten authors. SharePoint Designer enables you to import any Access file format. To import an Access database, click File on the Menu bar, point to the Import command, and click File to open the Import dialog box. Click the Add file button to open the Add File to Import List dialog box (as previously shown in Figure 3.3). Click the desired .accdb database, click the Open button to close the Add File to Import List dialog box, and then click OK to close the Import dialog box. From a developer's point of view, the process of importing an Access database saved as a PDF, XPS, or HTML document is identical.

TIP Graphic Files and Imported .accdb, .html, .pdf, or .xps Access Databases

If you import an .accdb, .html, .pdf, or .xps Access database, the graphic files are embedded in the file, so there is no need to import them separately.

If you need to modify any imported Web page created in the Access HTML Document format, you should edit the original .accdb source file of the Web page in Access, export it again in HTML Document format, and then import the updated file into your Web site, replacing the existing files.

Edit Access Databases in SharePoint Designer 2007

When you open any .accdb Access database in SharePoint Designer, your database is opened in Access by default. You can overwrite this default option using the Configure Editors tab of the Application Options dialog box. To open in SharePoint Designer Design view an HTML file created in Access, right-click the file in the Folder List task pane, point to Open With, and click SharePoint Designer (Open as HTML). To open the source of the .html file, click SharePoint Designer (Open as Text).

To open an imported .pdf file in SharePoint Designer, double-click this file in the Folder List task pane. The .pdf file will be displayed in an Adobe Reader window. To open an imported .xps file in SharePoint Designer, right-click this file in the Folder List task pane, point to Open With, and click XPS Viewer. The .xps file will be displayed in an XPS Viewer window.

If you need to modify any imported Web page created in the Access HTML Document format, you should edit the original .accdb source file of the Web page in Access, export it again in HTML Document format, and then import the updated file into your Web site, replacing the existing files. You can also edit these files in SharePoint Designer and save them directly to the Web site, replacing the existing files. Edit these files directly in SharePoint Designer only if there is no other option because you will not be able to use all the tools in the Access editor.

Hands-On Exercises

1 | Integrate Microsoft Office 2007 and SharePoint Designer 2007

Skills covered: 1. Start SharePoint Designer, Open a Web Site, Start Word, Copy and Paste Word Content, Import a PDF File, and Add a Hyperlink to the Imported PDF File **2.** Open a Web Site, Start PowerPoint, Save a PowerPoint Slide as JPG File Interchange Format (*.jpg), Save a PowerPoint Presentation as a Web Page (*.htm; *.html), Add a *.jpg File to a Web Page, Add a Hyperlink to a PowerPoint Presentation Saved as a Web Page (*.htm; *.html), and View a PowerPoint Presentation Saved as a Web Page (*.htm; *.html), in Internet Explorer 7.0 **3.** Open a Web Site, Start Excel, Save an Excel Workbook as an XPS Document (*.xps), Save an Excel Workbook as a Web Page (*.htm; *.html), View an Excel Workbook Saved as an XPS Document (*.xps) in Internet Explorer 7.0, and View an Excel Workbook Saved as a Web Page (*.htm; *.html), in Internet Explorer 7.0 **4.** Open a Web Site, Start Access, Export an Access Object as an XPS Document (*.xps), Export an Access Object as an HTML Document, View an Access Object as an XPS Document (*.xps) in Internet Explorer 7.0, and View an Access Object as an HTML Document in Internet Explorer 7.0

Step 1
Start SharePoint Designer, Open a Web Site, Start Word, Copy and Paste Word Content, Import a PDF File, and Add a Hyperlink to the Imported PDF File

Refer to Figure 3.37 as you complete Step 1.

a. Start SharePoint Designer. Click **Task Panes** on the Menu bar and click **Clipboard**. Click **File** on the Menu bar and click **Open Site**. Navigate to the chap3_ho1_solution_word Web site folder, click, and then click the **Open button**. Create a backup **chap3_ho1_solution_word _solution Web site folder** using the Remote Web Site view.

You should see the the chap3_ho1_solution_word Web site folder and the chap3_ho1_solution_word_solution Web site folder in Remote Web Site view.

b. Click the **Open your Remote Web site in SharePoint Designer hyperlink** in the *Status* section of the Remote Web Site view.

You should see the chap3_ho1_solution_word _solution Web site in Folders view.

TROUBLESHOOTING: You should still see on the Windows taskbar the SharePoint Designer tab opened in step a; right-click that tab and click Close on the shortcut menu to close it.

c. Double-click **default.htm** in the Folder List task pane.

The *default.htm* file should now be opened in Design view.

d. Start Microsoft Word. Click the button to the right of the Clipboard, on the Ribbon.

You should see the Word workspace including the Clipboard task pane, and *Document1* should show.

e. Click the **Office button** and click **Open**. Navigate to the *web_design_tutorial.docx* file, click, and then click the **Open button**.

The *web_design_tutorial.docx* file should now be opened.

f. Highlight the *Designing a Web site* text on the first page, right-click, and click **Copy** on the shortcut menu. Scroll down to page 3, highlight the three introductory paragraphs, shown in Figure 3.37, right-click, and click **Copy** on the shortcut menu.

The copied text now shows on the Clipboard task pane.

TROUBLESHOOTING: In order to save and export work in PDF and XPS formats in Microsoft Office 2007, you need to download and install on your computer additional software from the Microsoft Download Center (http://www.microsoft.com/downloads) called 2007 Microsoft Add-in: Microsoft Save as PDF or XPS.

g. Click the **Office button**, point to **Save As**, and click **PDF or XPS**.

The Save As dialog box is now showing.

TROUBLESHOOTING: In order to view files in PDF format you will also need to download the Adobe Reader software (http://www.adobe.com/products/reader).

h. On the Save as type drop-down list, click **PDF (*.pdf)** and click the **Save button**.

The *web_design_tutorial.pdf* document now shows in the Adobe Reader window.

i. Click the **SharePoint Designer tab** on the Windows Taskbar and click the **Paste All button** on the Clipboard task pane.

TROUBLESHOOTING: The default.htm file needs to be open in order to see the Paste All button as active.

The copied text now shows in the SharePoint Designer document window.

j. Double-click the **word_documents folder** in the Folder List task pane, click **File** on the Menu bar, point to **Import**, and click **File**.

The Import dialog box should now show.

k. Click the **Add File button** to open the Add File to Import dialog box, navigate to *web_design_tutorial.pdf*, and double-click. Click **OK** to close the Import dialog box.

The *web_design_tutorial.pdf* file is now showing in the Folder List task pane.

l. Click somewhere on the *default.htm* page, click **Insert** on the Menu bar, point to **Picture**, and click **From File**. Navigate to the word_documents folder and double-click **pdf.gif**. In the Alternate Text box of the Accessibility Properties dialog box, type **PDF Graphic Icon** and click **OK** to close the Accessibility Properties dialog box.

The picture is now displayed.

m. Press the **Space bar** two times and type **PDF version (653KB)**. Highlight the text, right-click, and click **Hyperlink** on the shortcut menu. In the Insert Hyperlink dialog box, navigate to the imported *web_design_tutorial.pdf* file and click. Click the **ScreenTip button** and type **Hyperlink to the PDF version of the Designing a Web Site brochure**. Then click **OK** two times to close the two open dialog boxes.

The link to *web_design_tutorial.pdf* is now displayed.

n. Position the insertion point to the right of the link added in step m, press the **Space bar** ten times, and type **Get Acrobat Reader**. Highlight the text, right-click, and click **Hyperlink** on the shortcut menu. In the Address box of the Insert Hyperlink dialog box, type **http://www.adobe.com/products/acrobat/readstep2.html**. Click the **ScreenTip button** and type **Download Acrobat Reader**. Then click **OK** two times to close the two open dialog boxes.

The link to http://www.adobe.com/products/acrobat/readstep2.html is now displayed, and the SharePoint Designer workspace should look similar to the one shown in Figure 3.37.

o. Click the **Save button** on the Common toolbar to save the *default.htm* homepage, click **Task Panes** on the Menu bar, and click **Reset Workspace Layout**. Then click **File** on the Menu bar and click **Close Site**. Close the Word and Adobe Reader windows.

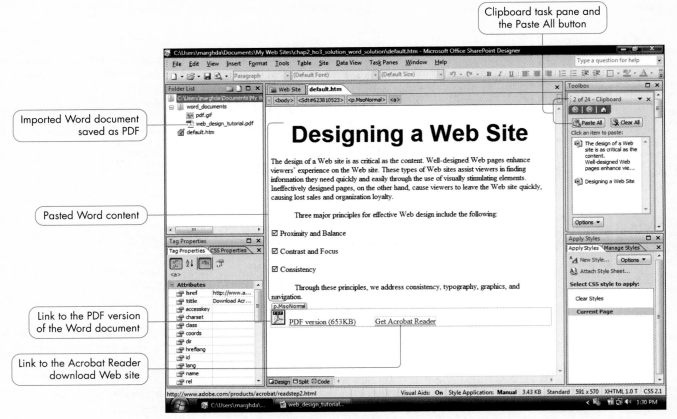

Clipboard task pane and
the Paste All button

Imported Word document
saved as PDF

Pasted Word content

Link to the PDF version
of the Word document

Link to the Acrobat Reader
download Web site

Figure 3.37 Integrating Microsoft Word and SharePoint Designer

Step 2

**Open a Web Site, Start
PowerPoint, Save a
PowerPoint Slide as
JPG File Interchange
Format (*.jpg), Save
a PowerPoint
Presentation as a Web
Page (*.htm; *.html),
Add a *.jpg File to
a Web Page, Add a
Hyperlink to a
PowerPoint
Presentation Saved
as a Web Page
(*.htm; *.html), and
View a PowerPoint
Presentation Saved
as a Web Page
(*.htm; *.html) in
Internet Explorer 7.0**

Refer to Figure 3.38 as you complete Step 2.

a. Click **File** on the Menu bar and click **Open Site**. Navigate to the chap3_ho1_solution_ppt Web site folder, click, and then click the **Open button**. Create a backup **chap3_ho1_solution_ppt _solution** Web site folder using the Remote Web Site view.

You should see the chap3_ho1_solution_ppt Web site folder and the chap3_ho1_solution_ppt_solution Web site folder in Remote Web Site view.

b. Click the **Open your Remote Web site in SharePoint Designer hyperlink** in the *Status* section of the Remote Web Site view. Double-click **default.htm** in the Folder List task pane.

The *default.htm* file should now be opened in Design view.

TROUBLESHOOTING: You should still see on the Windows taskbar the SharePoint Designer tab opened in step a; right-click that tab and click Close on the shortcut menu to close it.

c. Start Microsoft PowerPoint. Click the **Office button** and click **Open**. Navigate to the *impressionist_paintings.pptx* file, click, and then click the **Open button**.

You should see the PowerPoint workspace, and the *impressionist_paintings.pptx* file should show.

d. Click the **Office button**, point to **Save As**, and click **Other Formats**.

The Save As dialog box is now showing.

e. Navigate to the ppt_folder folder contained in the *chap3_ho1_solution_ppt_solution* Web site folder. On the Save as type drop-down list, click **JPEG File**

Interchange Format (*.jpg) and click the **Save button**. On the Microsoft Office PowerPoint alert box, click **Current Slide Only**.

f. Click the **Office button**, point to **Save As**, and click **Other Formats**. Navigate to the ppt_folder folder contained in the chap3_ho1_solution_ppt_solution Web site folder. On the Save as type drop-down list, click **Web Page (*.htm; *html)** and click the **Publish button**. In the *Browser support* section of the Publish as Web Page dialog box, click the **All browsers listed (creates larger files) check box**. In the *Publish a copy as dialog* section, click **Browse** and navigate to the ppt_folder folder contained in the chap3_ho1_solution_ppt_solution Web site folder. Click **OK** to close the Publish As dialog box and click **Publish**.

g. Click the **SharePoint Designer tab** on the Windows Taskbar and double-click **ppt_folder** in the Folder List task pane.

The *impressionist_paintings.htm* and *impressionist_paintings.jpg* files now show in SharePoint Designer in the Folder List task pane.

TROUBLESHOOTING: If the impressionist_paintings.htm and impressionist_paintings. jpg files do not show, click View on the Menu bar, and then click Refresh.

h. Click the **default.htm tab**, click **Insert** on the Menu bar, point to **Picture**, and click **From File**. Navigate to the ppt_folder folder and double-click **impressionist_paintings.jpg**. In the Alternate Text box of the Accessibility Properties dialog box, type **Impressionist Paintings** and click **OK** to close the Accessibility Properties dialog box.

The picture is now displayed.

i. Right-click **impressionist_paintings.jpg** within the Design view of *default.htm* and click **Auto Thumbnail** on the shortcut menu.

The Auto Thumbnail now shows in the Design view of *default.htm*.

j. Place the insertion point after the thumbnail, press the **Space bar** two times, and type **HTML version**. Highlight the text, right-click, and click **Hyperlink** on the shortcut menu. In the Insert Hyperlink dialog box, navigate to the imported *impressionist_painting.htm* and click. Click the **ScreenTip button** and type **Hyperlink to the HTML version of the Impressionist Paintings presentation**. Then click **OK** two times to close the two open dialog boxes.

The link to *impressionist_painting.htm* is now displayed.

k. Click the **Save button** on the Common toolbar to save the default.htm home page, click **Change Folder** on the Save Embedded Files dialog box, navigate to the ppt_folder folder on the Change Folder dialog box, double-click, and click **OK** two times to close both open dialog boxes.

The *impressionist_paintings_small.jpg* file is now displayed within the ppt_folder folder in the Folder List task pane.

l. Click **File** on the Menu bar, point to **Preview in Browsers**, and **click Windows Internet Explorer 7.0**.

The *default.htm* file is now displayed in the Internet Explorer 7.0 window.

m. Point the mouse to **Thumbnail image**.

The value of the Thumbnail image alt attribute (Impressionist Paintings) should now be displayed.

n. Point the mouse to the **HTML version hyperlink**.

The ScreenTip hyperlink to the HTML version of the Impressionist Paintings presentation should now be displayed.

o. Click the **HTML version hyperlink**.

> **TROUBLESHOOTING:** If the yellow Information bar is displayed at the top of the Internet Explorer window, click where it displays Click here for options, and then click Allow Blocked Content.

Your screen should look like the one shown in Figure 3.38.

p. Close the Internet Explorer 7.0 and PowerPoint windows. Then click **File** on the Menu bar and click **Close Site**.

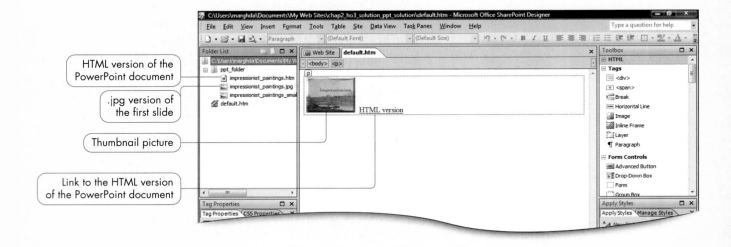

HTML version of the PowerPoint document

.jpg version of the first slide

Thumbnail picture

Link to the HTML version of the PowerPoint document

HTML version of the PowerPoint document viewed in Internet Explorer 7.0

Figure 3.38   Integrating Microsoft PowerPoint and SharePoint Designer

Open a Web Site, Start
Excel, Save an Excel
Workbook as an XPS
Document (*.xps),
Save an Excel
Workbook as a Web
Page (*.htm; *.html),
View an Excel
Workbook Saved as an
XPS Document (*.xps)
in Internet Explorer 7.0,
and View an Excel
Workbook Saved as a
Web Page
(*.htm; *.html) in
Internet Explorer 7.0

Refer to Figure 3.39 as you complete Step 3.

a. Click **File** on the Menu bar and click **Open Site**. Navigate to the chap3_ho1_solution_excel Web site folder, click, and then click the **Open button**. Create a backup **chap3_ho1_solution_excel_solution** Web site folder using the Remote Web Site view. Click the **Open your Remote Web site in SharePoint Designer hyperlink** in the *Status* section of the Remote Web Site view.

TROUBLESHOOTING: You should still see on the Windows taskbar the SharePoint Designer tab opened in step a; right-click that tab and click Close on the shortcut menu to close it.

You should see the chap3_ho1_solution_excel_solution Web site in Folders view.

b. Start Microsoft Excel. Click the **Office button** and click **Open**. Navigate to the *population_solution.xlsx* file, click, and then click the **Open button**.

You should see the Excel window, and the *population_solution.xlsx* workbook should show.

c. Click the **Office button**, point to **Save As**, and click **Other Formats**. Navigate to the excel_documents folder. On the Save as type drop-down list, click **XPS Document (*.xps)**. Click the **Option button** and click the **Entire workbook option** in the *Publish what* section of the Options dialog box. Click **OK** to close the Options dialog box and then click **Save** to close the Save As dialog box.

d. Click the **Office button**, point to **Save As**, and click **Other Formats**. Navigate to the excel_documents folder. On the Save as type drop-down list, click **Web Page (*.htm;*html)**, click **Entire workbook** in the *Save* section of the Save As dialog box, and then click the **Publish button**.

The Publish as Web Page dialog box should now display.

e. Click **Entire workbook** on the Choose drop-down list and click the **Publish button**. Click the **SharePoint Designer tab** on the Windows taskbar and double-click the **excel_documents folder** in the Folder List task pane.

The *population_solution.xps* and *population_solution.htm* files now show in SharePoint Designer in the Folder List task pane.

TROUBLESHOOTING: If the population_solution.xps and population_solution.htm files do not show, click View on the Menu bar, and then click Refresh.

f. Double-click **population_solution.htm** in the Folder List task pane.

The *population_solution.htm* file is now displayed in SharePoint Designer Design view.

g. Click **File** on the Menu bar, point to **Preview in Browsers**, and click **Windows Internet Explorer 7.0**.

The *population_solution.htm* file now shows in the Internet Explorer 7.0 window, and the *Population Density* spreadsheet is displayed.

h. Click the **Region Chart tag** on the lower-left side of the screen.

The *Region Chart* spreadsheet is now displayed, as shown in Figure 3.39.

i. Close the Internet Explorer 7.0 window.

j. Right-click **population_solution.xps** in the Folder List task pane, point to **Open With**, and click **XPS Viewer**.

The *population_solution.xps* file now shows in XPS Viewer, and the *Region Chart* spreadsheet is now displayed.

k. Click the **Two Pages button**.

The *Region Chart* spreadsheet and *Population Density* spreadsheet are now displayed, as shown in Figure 3.39.

l. Close the Internet Explorer 7.0 and Excel windows. Then click **File** on the Menu bar and click **Close Site**.

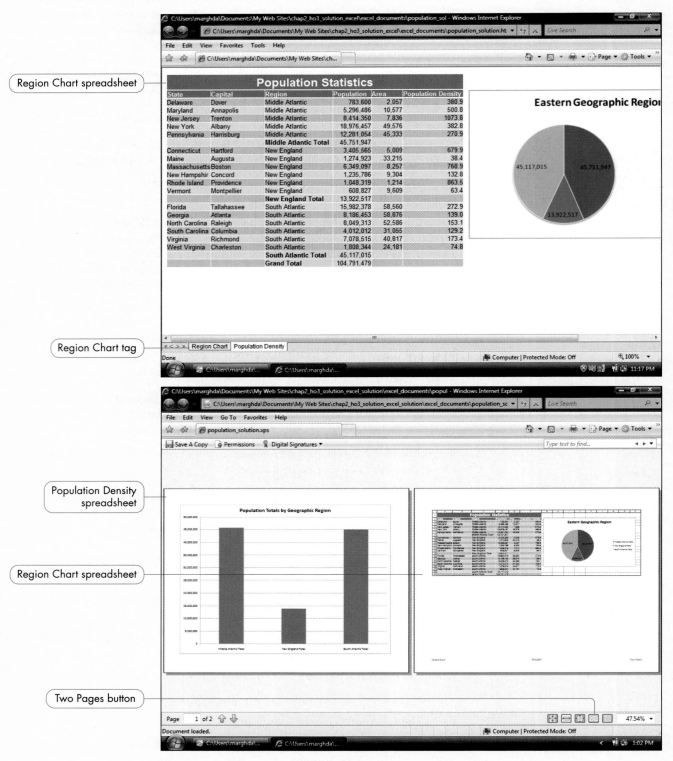

Figure 3.39 Integrating Microsoft Excel and SharePoint Designer

Step 4

Open a Web Site, Start Access, Export an Access Object as an XPS Document (*.xps), Export an Access Object as an HTML Document, View an Access Object as an XPS Document (*.xps) in Internet Explorer 7.0, and View an Access Object as an HTML Document in Internet Explorer 7.0

Refer to Figure 3.40 as you complete Step 4.

a. Click **File** on the Menu bar and click **Open Site**. Navigate to the chap3_ho1_solution_access Web site folder, click, and then click the **Open button**. Create a backup **chap3_ho1_solution_access_solution** Web site folder using the Remote Web Site view. Click the **Open your Remote Web site in SharePoint Designer hyperlink** in the *Status* section of the Remote Web Site view.

TROUBLESHOOTING: You should still see on the Windows taskbar the SharePoint Designer tab open in step a; right-click that tab and click Close on the shortcut menu to close it.

You should see the chap3_ho1_solution_access_solution Web site in Folders view.

b. Start Microsoft Access. Click the **Office button** and click **Open**. Navigate to the *nationalbank.accdb* file, click, and then click the **Open button**.

You should see the Access window, and the *nationalbank.accdb* file should be showing.

TROUBLESHOOTING: Make sure All Access Objects is displayed in the Access Navigation pane so you can see all Access Objects included in the national-bank.accdb file.

c. Right-click the **Your Name Payments Received Access Report Object**, point to **Export**, and click **PDF or XPS**.

The Publish as PDF or XPS dialog box opens.

d. Navigate to the access_documents folder. On the Save as type drop-down list, click **XPS Document (*.xps)** and click the **Publish button**. Click **Close** on the Export - XPS dialog box.

e. Right-click the **Your Name Payments Received Access Report Object**, point to **Export**, and click **HTML document**.

The Export - HTML Document dialog box opens.

f. Click the **Browse button**, navigate to the access_documents folder, and click the **Save button** to close the File Save dialog box. Click **OK**.

The HTML Output Options dialog box should now be displayed.

g. Click **OK** to close the HTML Output Options dialog box and click **Close** on the Export - HTML Document dialog box.

h. Click the **SharePoint Designer tab** on the Windows taskbar and double-click the **access_documents folder** in the Folder List task pane.

The *Your Name Payments Received.xps*, *Your Name Payments Received.htm*, *Your Name Payments ReceivedPage2.htm*, and *Your Name Payments ReceivedPage3.htm* files now show in SharePoint Designer in the access_documents Folder List task pane.

TROUBLESHOOTING: If the Your Name Payments Received.xps, Your Name Payments Received.htm, Your Name Payments ReceivedPage2.htm, and Your Name Payments ReceivedPage3.htm files do not show, click View on the Menu bar, and then click Refresh.

i. Double-click **Your Name Payments Received.html** in the Folder List task pane.

The *Your Name Payments Received.html* file is now displayed in Design view.

j. Click **File** on the Menu bar, point to **Preview in Browsers**, and click **Windows Internet Explorer 7.0**.

The *Your Name Payments Received.html* file now shows in the Internet Explorer 7.0 window.

k. Click the **Next link** at the bottom of the Web page, as shown in Figure 3.40, to see *Your Name Payments ReceivedPage2.htm*. Click the **Next link** again to see *Your Name Payments ReceivedPage3.htm*.

l. Right-click **Your Name Payments Received.xps** in the Folder List task pane, point to **Open With**, and click **XPS Viewer**.

The *Your Name Payments Received.xps* file now shows in XPS Viewer.

m. Click the **Two Pages button**.

The first two pages of the *Your Name Payments Received.xps* are now displayed.

n. Click the **Next Page button**.

The third page of the *Your Name Payments Received.xps* is now displayed.

o. Close the Internet Explorer 7.0 and Access windows. Then click **File** on the Menu bar and click **Close Site**.

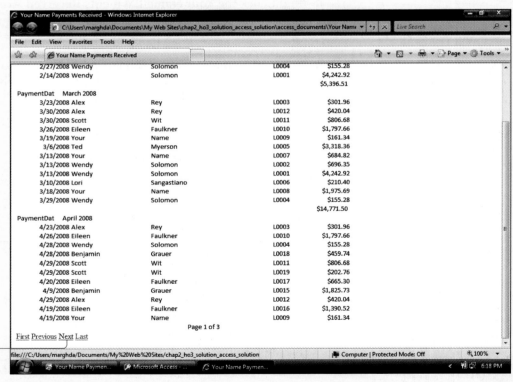

Figure 3.40 Integrating Microsoft Access and SharePoint Designer

Develop Web Forms with SharePoint Designer 2007

(SharePoint Designer enables you to insert and modify forms and form fields such as text boxes, check boxes, option buttons, group boxes, drop-down boxes, text areas, push buttons, and advanced buttons.)

Online forms are slowly but surely replacing many of the paper forms we all used to fill in, from the simple marketing survey to the mighty IRS 1040 form, from a sketchy request for information form to complicated mortgage application forms. SharePoint Designer offers Web developers a comprehensive set of features for developing and customizing forms.

SharePoint Designer enables you to insert and modify forms and form fields such as text boxes, check boxes, option buttons, group boxes, drop-down boxes, text areas, push buttons, and advanced buttons.

Designing a Web Form

When designing a form, all the key factors of good Web page design discussed in Chapter 1, such as usability, navigation, compatibility, accessibility, consistency, validity, and attractiveness, need to be taken into consideration. What are the characteristics of good form design, and how can SharePoint Designer assist you in designing and developing forms? This section addresses these questions and the skills required.

A *form* can be defined as a set of form fields used to collect information from visitors for additional processing.

A *form field* is the basic form element that enables visitors to supply information.

A *form* can be defined as a set of form fields used to collect information from visitors for additional processing. A *form field* is the basic form element that enables visitors to supply information. Table 3.1 includes the most popular and most frequently used form fields, which are also shown in Figure 3.41.

Table 3.1   Key SharePoint Designer Form Fields

Form Field	SharePoint Designer Forms Control	Description	Requirements
Text box	Input (Text)	Enables visitors to enter up to 500 alphanumeric characters. If no character is entered, only the text box name is sent to the server.	None
Text area	Text Area	Enables visitors to enter up to 999 columns and 999 rows of text in a scrolling text box.	None
Check box	Input (Checkbox)	Enables visitors to check or clear one or more boxes from a group of boxes representing a set of options.	None
Option button (or radio button)	Input (Radio)	Enables visitors to check only one option button from a group of option buttons.	None
Drop-down box (or Menu)	Drop-Down Box	Enables visitors to select one or more options from a list of options.	None
Push button	Input (Button)	Enables visitors to submit the information entered in a form (the Submit button), to clear form fields by resetting the form (the Reset button), or to run a custom script attached to the button.	None
Advanced button	Advanced Button	Enables visitors to use all the functionalities provided by a push button; provides Web developers with more control over form functionality and button display.	Netscape Navigator 4.0 and earlier do not display advanced buttons.
Label	Label	A word or short phrase that provides relevant information about the type of data required for an associated form field.	None

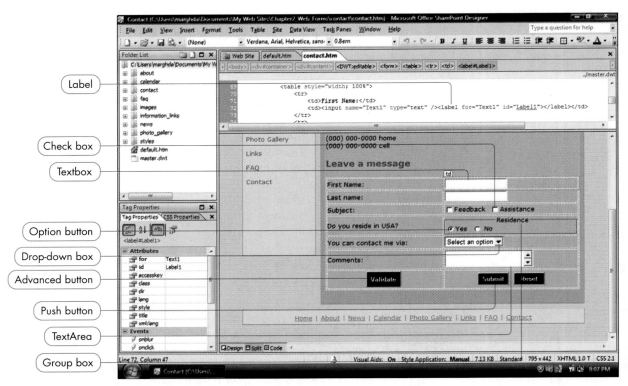

Figure 3.41 Common Form Fields

Labels in figure: Label, Check box, Textbox, Option button, Drop-down box, Advanced button, Push button, TextArea, Group box

Sometimes Web designers need to include certain information on a Web page form that visitors do not need to see. By limiting the information that your Web site visitors see to only what they really need, you can avoid confusion. A *hidden form field* is a form field that does not appear on the visitors' view of the Web page; thus they cannot make changes to it. You might want to use hidden form fields in the following situations:

- You need to store information from one Web page on another page so that your Web site visitors do not need to reenter identical data on each page.

- You need to pull additional data, such as a login name, from your Web site visitors.

- You need to indicate the e-mail address of the person who will receive the data entered by the Web site visitors as a form field value.

Although visitors cannot see the hidden fields, the data in hidden form fields are not secure. Visitors can read hidden information if they view the source code of a Web page in a Web browser.

Usually, a form incorporates a set of form fields and a Submit and Reset button. The *Submit button* enables visitors to submit the information to a Web server for further processing. The *Reset button* enables visitors to return the contents of the form fields to their default status. When a visitor clicks the Submit button, a form handler is executed. A *form handler* is a program residing on a Web server that processes the information the visitor submitted.

When the visitor clicks the Submit button, the data that visitor entered or selected in the form are sent as ASCII text using a name-value format for each form field, where *name* indicates the field name and *value* indicates the value assigned by the visitor to the field. If the visitor used spaces within the value, the spaces are converted to plus signs (+). Each name-value pair is separated by an ampersand (&). Figure 3.42 is an example of the form handler string of data that would be sent from a form that contains two text box fields (first_name and last_name).

A *hidden form field* is a form field that does not appear on the visitors' view of the Web page; thus they cannot make changes to it.

The *Submit button* enables visitors to submit the information to a Web server for further processing.

The *Reset button* enables visitors to return the contents of the form fields to their default status.

A *form handler* is a program residing on a Web server that processes the information the visitor submitted.

> Although visitors cannot see the hidden fields, the data in hidden form fields are not secure. Visitors can read hidden information if they view the source code of a Web page in a Web browser.

Coding Example
first_name=Ashley&last_name=Wachs+Broun

Figure 3.42 Example of String of Data Sent from a Form

(Usually, a form incorporates a set of form fields and a Submit and Reset button.)

The first step in designing a form is to analyze the type of information to be included on the form. As previously discussed in this chapter, it is always wise to start by creating a sketch of a new Web page including the form, as shown in the example in Figure 3.43.

Here are some other tips for increasing the usability of a form:

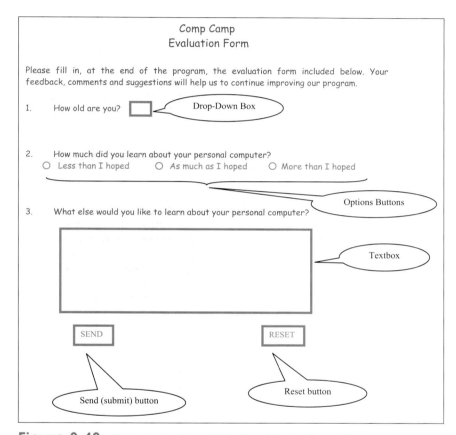

Figure 3.43 Sketch of a New Web Page Including a Form

- Use clear and meaningful labels for each of your form fields.
- Use option buttons instead of drop-down lists whenever possible and when you are not restricted by limited space. Option buttons take more space than drop-down lists because visitors can see all of their options at once.
- Provide an alternative option, such as "None," "N/A," or "Don't know," in case the visitor chooses not to make a selection.
- Provide comprehensive options for the user to select by including the "Other" option, supplemented, if necessary, by a type-in field.
- Provide a default option whenever visitors must make a selection (such as when using option buttons and drop-down boxes).
- Use a vertical layout when combining groups of option buttons or check box form elements to avoid any confusion about which option is associated with which option button or check box.

Creating a Web Form with SharePoint Designer 2007

(In SharePoint Designer, the Toolbox pane enables you to create a form and to insert form fields.)

The first step in creating a form is to insert a form container. In SharePoint Designer, the Toolbox pane enables you to create a form and to insert form fields. To create a form, position the insertion point where you wish to create the form, right-click Form in the Form Controls section of the Toolbox pane, and click Insert (you can also just double-click Form in the Form Controls section). When creating forms in SharePoint Designer, it is essential to keep all the form fields within the dotted line that indicates the form container (see Figure 3.44). Any form field placed outside of the lines is not recognized by SharePoint Designer as part of the form and will not be included in the form results.

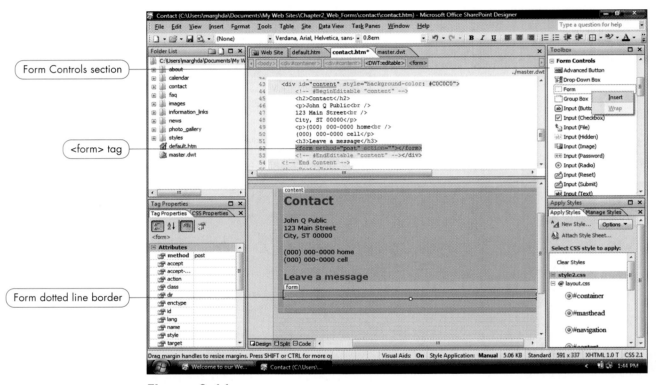

Figure 3.44 Creating a Form

(One way to ensure that all form fields stay within the dotted line surrounding the form is to use a table as a layout guide.)

One way to ensure that all form fields stay within the dotted line is to use a table as a layout guide. To insert a layout table inside the form, click inside the dotted line surrounding the form, click Table on the Menu bar, and click Insert Table to open the Insert Table dialog box. Then select the number of rows and columns for the table depending on the number of form fields and their desired position within the layout of the Web page. Because the new table is inserted within the dotted line surrounding the form, SharePoint Designer will not create a new form each time you add a new form field to the form. After you click OK to close the Insert Table dialog box, the table is displayed within the form, as shown in Figure 3.45. As specified in Appendix B, using a table as a layout guide for forms is also a good practice for building accessible forms because it enables Web developers to place form fields in the same cell as an explicit label, as required in paragraph n of Section 508.

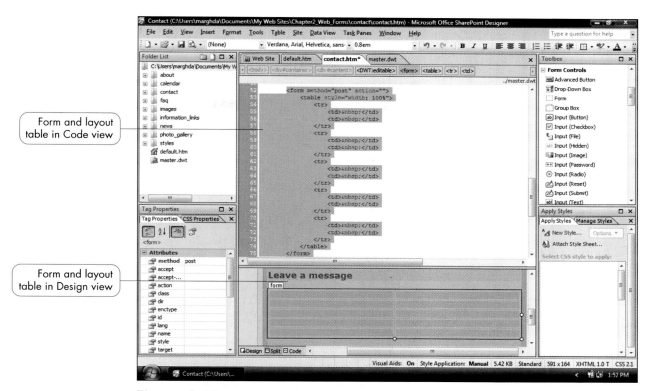

Figure 3.45 Form with a Layout Table

After creating your form, you can add more form fields to it and modify its properties.

After creating your form, you can add more form fields to it and modify its properties. From the Toolbox task pane, drag the desired form field into a table cell inside the form container, as shown in Figure 3.46.

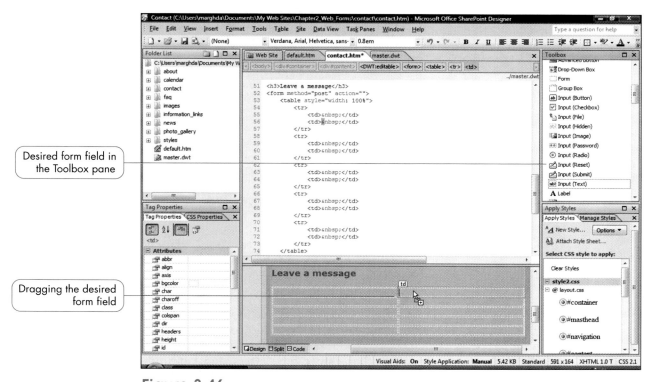

Figure 3.46 Adding a Form Field to a Form

To modify the properties of a form field, right-click the field, and then click Form Field Properties. The corresponding properties dialog box for each form field element opens, enabling you to select the appropriate options. When modifying the properties of a form field, remember that form field names cannot include spaces and are case sensitive.

Another good practice for making forms accessible and usable is to assign keyboard shortcuts (*accesskey* attributes) to form fields. This enables visitors who need to use a keyboard instead of a mouse to navigate the page more easily using two keys (Alt+key) instead of the mouse.

The *accesskey* form field attribute enables visitors to use a keyboard instead of the mouse to navigate between form fields.

Insert a Text Box Form Field and Modify Its Properties

(Text boxes are used to obtain textual information from visitors.)

Text boxes are used to obtain textual information from visitors. Web designers can control the properties of a text box field using the Text Box Properties dialog box. To insert a new text box field within the form, position the insertion point in the desired location, type the text prompt to be associated with the new text box field, press tab to place the insertion point in the adjacent cell of the same row, double-click Input (Text) in the Toolbox task pane, and click Insert. Figure 3.47 shows a form with a text box field added.

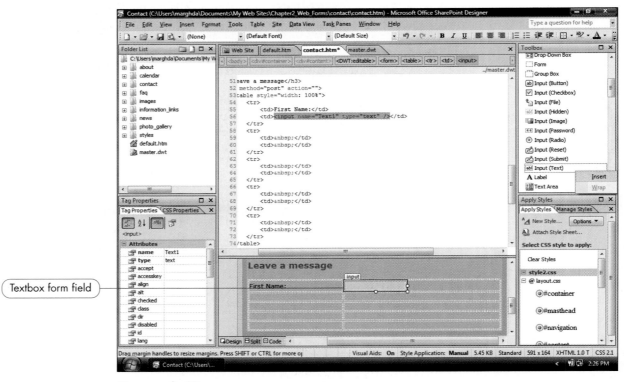

Textbox form field

Figure 3.47 Inserting a Text Box Form Field

To modify the properties of a text box, right-click the text box field and click Form Field Properties (or double-click the text box field) to open the Text Box Properties dialog box, shown in Figure 3.48. This dialog box includes the following options for controlling visitor input:

- **Name**—The default value of the first text box is Textbox1, followed by Textbox2, Textbox3, and so on, in the order in which they are added to the form. The Name value can be modified. The first character must be a letter or underscore, and subsequent characters can be letters, digits, or underscores. SharePoint Designer alerts you if you try to use a character that is not allowed.

- **Initial value**—This option enables you to assign a default value for the text box field.

- **Width in characters**—This option is used to set up the total length of the text box (in number of characters). However, a user can type more characters than the indicated width.

- **Tab order**—This option indicates the order in which fields are accessed by visitors if they are using the Tab key to navigate. You can change the tab order by assigning a number to each field, representing the order in which it should be selected.

- **Password field**—This option can be set to Yes if you want visitors to type a password in the text box. The data typed in a password field will be concealed, but not encrypted.

- **Validate button**—This option can be used to open the Text Box Validation dialog box, which enables you to set validation rules for the data visitors type in the text box, as shown in Figure 3.48. For example, if a text box field requests that visitors enter their full names, the validation rule should be set to restrict the characters entered to only text and spaces.

Figure 3.48 Working with Text Box Fields

Insert and Modify the Properties of a Check Box Form Field

Check boxes are typically used to enable a visitor to provide more than one answer to a specific question. For example, if you want to build a Leave a Message online form, one of the questions would likely be about the subject. This type of question can have more than one answer—for example, feedback or request for assistance. Using a group of check boxes minimizes the amount of text visitors need to type and restricts the number of possible answers, which simplifies your analysis. To insert a group of check boxes, type the text prompt/question and press tab. Then double-click Input (Checkbox) and click Insert. Press ➡, type the answer choice associated with that specific check box, and press the space bar one or more times, as you wish. You need to repeat these actions for each answer. Figure 3.49 shows examples of check boxes.

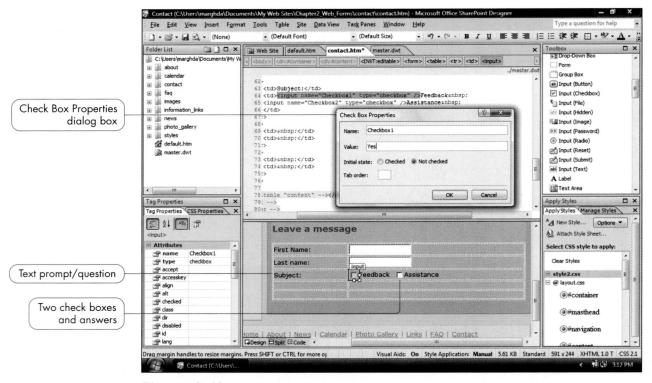

Figure 3.49 Working with a Check Box Form Field

You can modify the properties of any check box form field to better suit your needs. First, double-click the check box to open the Check Box Properties dialog box, shown in Figure 3.49. In the Check Box Properties dialog box, you need to enter a name and a value because these two options create the name and value pair used to submit data. Use the following options to control visitor input:

- **Name**—The default value of the first check box is Checkbox1, followed by Checkbox2, Checkbox3, and so on, in the order in which they are added to the form. The Name can be modified, but the first character must be a letter or underscore, and subsequent characters can be letters, digits, or underscores. SharePoint Designer alerts you if you try to use a character that is not allowed.

- **Value**—The default value for a check box is ON, indicating that it is an active field within the form.

- **Initial state**—This option enables you to preselect a check box as the default answer to a question on your form.

- **Tab order**—This option indicates the order in which fields will be accessed by visitors if they are using the Tab key. You can change the tab order by assigning a number to each field, representing the order in which it should be selected.

Insert an Option Button Form Field and Modify Its Properties

> Option buttons are used when visitors are allowed to choose only one option out of a group of available options.

SharePoint Designer refers to the classic radio button as an *option button*. Option buttons are used when visitors are allowed to choose only one option out of a group of available options. For example, you might want to add a question about your customer's location in or out of the United States to the

Leave a Message online form. By using a group of option buttons, you minimize the amount of text visitors need to type and restrict the possible answers.

To insert a group of option buttons into your form, type the text prompt/question, shown in Figure 3.50, and press Tab. Then right-click Input (Radio) on the Toolbox task pane and click Insert. Press ➡ and type the answer option associated with that specific option button. You need to repeat these actions for each answer option that you make available.

Similar to other form fields, you can modify the properties of an option button form field. First, double-click the option button to open the Option Button Properties dialog box, as shown in Figure 3.50. You can choose from the following options to control visitor input:

(You can modify the properties of an option button form field.)

- **Group name**—The Group name has to be the same for all option buttons in a group of answers that are related to the same question. As with other kinds of form fields, the first character must be a letter or underscore, and subsequent characters can be letters, digits, or underscores. SharePoint Designer alerts you if you try to use a character that is not allowed. In the example shown in Figure 3.50, the group name is USA.

- **Value**—If this option is selected, the value of each option button is sent to the form handler for further processing. When using option buttons, only one name-value pair is sent to the form handler. In the example shown in Figure 3.50, the USA-Yes pair would be sent for further processing because the Yes option is selected.

- **Initial state**—This option enables you to preselect an option button as the default. If you decide to set an initial state, you should preselect the option button that has a highest probability of being selected by visitors.

- **Tab order**—This option indicates the order in which fields will be accessed by visitors if they are using the Tab key. You can change the tab order by assigning a number to each field, representing the order in which it should be selected.

- **Validate button**—This option can be used to open the Option Button Validation dialog box. From this dialog box, you can select the Data required check box, which requires visitors to select an option button. In the Display name box, you can type the group name or some other message to the visitor about selecting an option in the group.

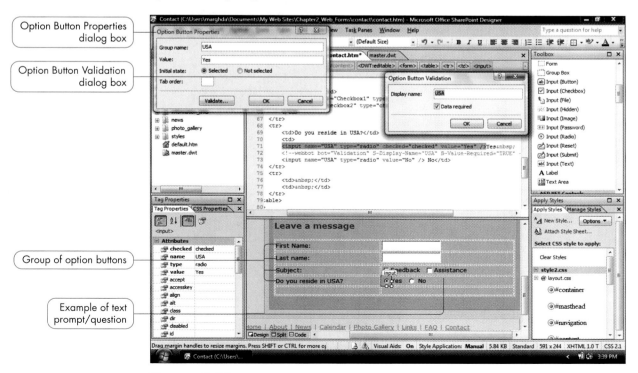

Figure 3.50 Working with an Option Button Form Field

A ***group box*** is a titled border placed around a group of related fields.

Forms can become complex, and Web developers often need to improve the usability of a form by grouping related form fields in group boxes. A ***group box*** is a titled border placed around a group of related fields.

To insert a group box, right-click Group Box on the Toolbox task pane and click Insert. After the group box is created, right-click anywhere within its border and click Group Box Properties to display the Group Box Properties dialog box, as shown in Figure 3.51. You should add a meaningful label to the group box, such as the group name of the option buttons it contains, and select the appropriate alignment for the group box from the Align drop-down list.

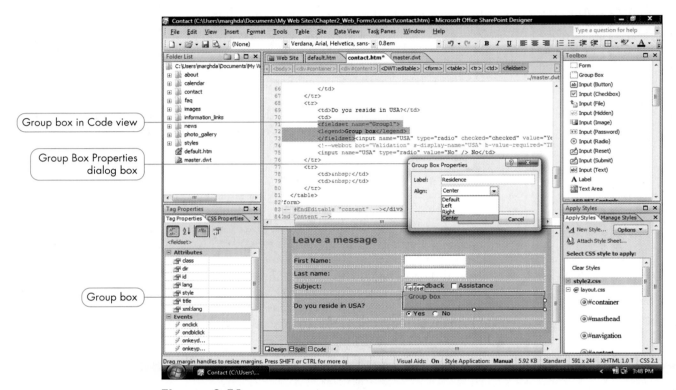

Group box in Code view

Group Box Properties dialog box

Group box

Figure 3.51 Working with the Group Box Form Field

TIP   Groups of Option Buttons

You should always include option buttons within a group box even when you have only one group of option buttons. The titled border of a group box provides a useful hint to the visitor that the option buttons are related. If you have already inserted the group of option buttons, you can highlight them, right-click, and click Cut on the shortcut menu, as shown in Figure 3.52. Then place the insertion point where the group will be (for example, after the </legend> and </fieldset> tags as shown in Figure 3.52), right-click, and click Paste.

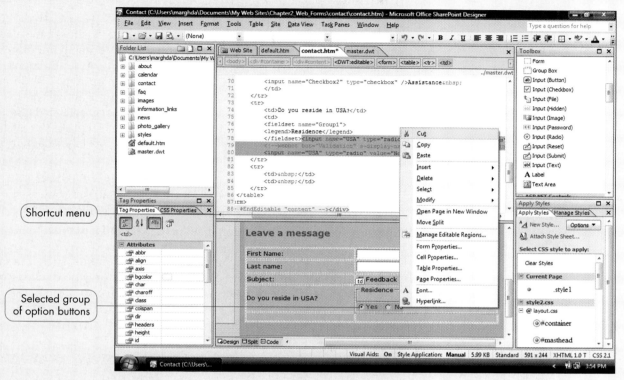

Figure 3.52 Pasting Option Buttons into a Group Box Form Field

The drop-down box is one of the most versatile form fields that you can use. It enables visitors to select one or more options using a small fraction of the form space.

Insert a Drop-Down Box Form Field and Modify Its Properties

The drop-down box is one of the most versatile form fields that you can use. It enables visitors to select one or more options using a small fraction of the form space. The options listed in the drop-down box usually appear in alphabetical order or in the order visitors are most likely to select them. You can also set a default choice that will be submitted to the form handler if the visitor makes no selection.

TIP   Using a Drop-Down Box Versus Groups of Option Buttons and Check Boxes

The drop-down list box is usually more efficient than groups of option buttons or check boxes when there are many choices.

To insert a drop-down box, right-click Drop-Down Box on the Toolbox task pane and select Insert. To type the list of options and modify properties, double-click the drop-down box. The Drop-Down Box Properties dialog box is displayed, as shown in Figure 3.53, enabling you to modify the following properties:

- **Name**—This option is initially set to a default value of Select1 and should be replaced with a new meaningful name.

- **Height**—This option indicates the number of options that will be visible in the box without clicking an arrow button. If the Height is equal to the number of choices, the choices appear in a simple list box without drop-down and scroll arrows.

- **Allow multiple selections**—This option indicates whether visitors can select more than one option from the list. If you select the Yes button, SharePoint Designer creates a list box with scroll arrows instead of a drop-down menu. The Drop-Down Box Validation dialog box has two additional options: Minimum Items, indicating the minimum number of options a visitor is allowed to select, and Maximum Items, indicating the maximum number of options a visitor is allowed to select. Selecting the No button and setting the Height to 1 creates a typical drop-down box. If the Disallow first choice check box is selected, it prevents the first choice from being selected by visitors.

- **Tab order**—This option indicates the order in which fields will be accessed by visitors if they are using the Tab key. You can change the tab order by assigning a number to each field, representing the order in which it should be selected.

- **Validate button**—Selecting this button displays the Drop-Down Box Validation dialog box. To require visitors to make a selection from the drop-down box, select the Data required check box. Type an appropriate display name, such as a message to "Select an option" in the text box. If the Disallow first choice check box is selected, the first choice in the drop-down list is descriptive, and thus, visitors cannot select it.

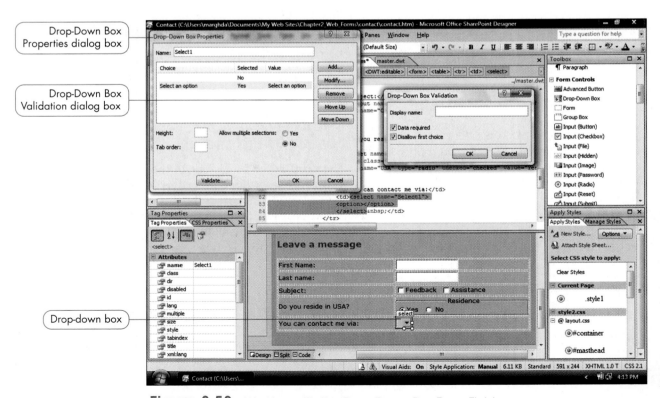

Figure 3.53 Working with the Drop-Down Box Form Field

To add choices to an existing drop-down list, double-click the drop-down list box to open the Drop-Down Box Properties dialog box and click the Add button to open the Add Choice dialog box. The Add Choice dialog box includes the following options, as shown in Figure 3.54:

- **Choice**—This text box should include the text for each option.
- **Specify Value**—It is optional to assign a value to a choice, but if the form results require submitting data other than what is in the choice box, select Specify value and type the value in the box.
- **Initial state**—You can use this option to preselect an option as the default for the drop-down list.

After all appropriate options have been selected, click the OK button to close the Add Choice dialog box and see the new choice added to the form. Click the Add button to continue adding choices. When you have finished adding choices to the list, click the OK button.

Figure 3.54 Adding Choices to a Drop-Down Box Form Field

Insert a Text Area Form Field and Modify Its Properties

> The text area form field is extremely useful when visitors might need to type more than one line of text or their answers are too variable to be easily grouped in a list. It also provides visitors with a better way to review the text before submitting it.

The text area form field is extremely useful when visitors might need to type more than one line of text or their answers are too variable to be easily grouped in a list. It also provides visitors with a better way to review the text before submitting it. To insert a text area form field right-click Text Area on the Toolbox task pane and click Insert. To modify the properties of a text area form field, double-click the form field to open the TextArea Box Properties dialog box, as shown in Figure 3.55, which contains the following options:

- **Name**—This text box contains the name assigned to the form field. The default value is TextArea1, TextArea2, and so on depending on the order in which the text area was added to the form.

- **Initial value**—This option indicates the default value, if any, that should be displayed in the form field. Type the text you want to display, which can be edited by visitors who fill in the field.

- **Width**—This option indicates the total number of characters that can be included in a line of the text area form field.

- **Number of lines**—This option represents the number of lines of text that will display in the form field on screen. A scrollbar becomes active if the visitor types more lines than this, allowing the visitor to scroll up and down to review the contents of the text area before submitting the form.

- **Validate**—Selecting this button displays the Text Box Validation dialog box, as shown in Figure 3.55, which includes the display name of the form field and options that you can use to control visitor input, such as Data type, Text format, Data length, and Data value.

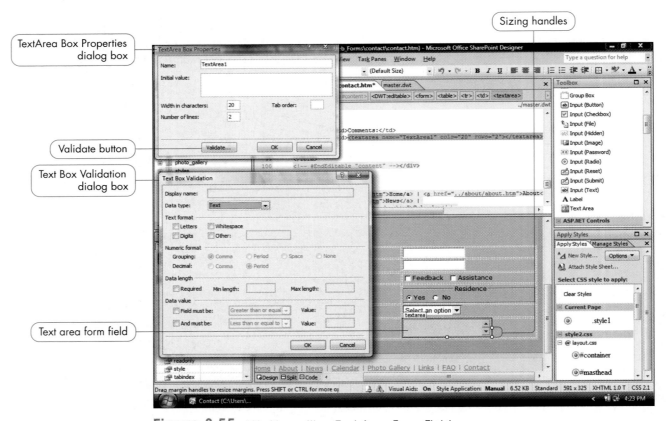

Figure 3.55 Working with a Text Area Form Field

When you are finished selecting the desired options in the Text Box Validation dialog box, click OK twice to close all open dialog boxes. You can resize a text area by clicking the text area box and then dragging the sizing handles shown in Figure 3.55 until it reaches the desired size.

Insert a Push Button Form Field and an Advanced Button Form Field and Modify Their Properties

A regular push button initially displays a button default label in a form. You can attach a custom script to the push button that will be launched whenever a visitor clicks the button. The Submit button is a push button used to submit all input from the form to

> You can attach a custom script to a push button that will be launched whenever a visitor clicks the button.

the server processing the data. The Reset button is a push button used to reset all the input fields from the form to their original values. As described in Table 3.1, SharePoint Designer also enables you to insert a highly customizable advanced button. An advanced button enables you to attach a script to the button, giving you more control over form functionality and enabling you to use more customizing features, such as size, color, fonts, and even tables.

> **TIP** Validating Form Fields Using JavaScript® in SharePoint Designer
>
> One of the main purposes for attaching a custom script to a push button or advanced button is to validate form fields. To learn more about how you can validate form fields using JavaScript and, in general, how to use custom scripts with buttons, visit the W3Schools JavaScript Tutorial Web site (http://www.w3schools.com/js/default.asp).

> An advanced button enables you to attach a script to the button, giving you more control over form functionality and enabling you to use more customizing features, such as size, color, fonts, and even tables.

To insert a push button form field, position the insertion point in the desired location, right-click Input (Button) on the Toolbox task pane, and click Insert. After the button is inserted, double-click it to open the Push Button Properties dialog box, as shown in Figure 3.56. Replace the default text in the Name text box, Button1, with the name that you want displayed in the form. The default Value/label, button, should be replaced with a meaningful label that suggests the button's function. The Button type section of the dialog box enables you to choose the type of button required depending on its predetermined function. If you want to assign this button a function other than submitting or resetting the form, select the Normal type, as shown in Figure 3.56.

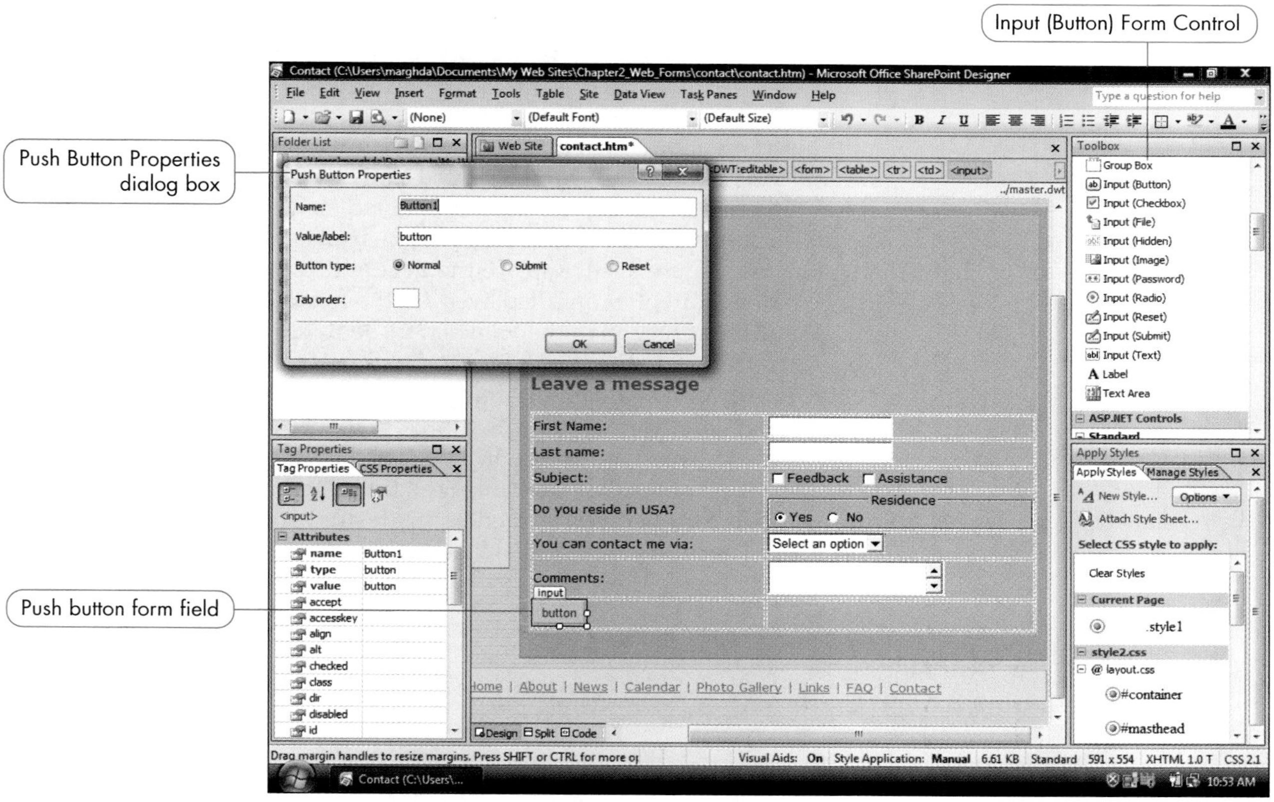

Figure 3.56 Working with the Push Button Form Field

If you click New Style in the Apply Styles task pane, as shown in Figure 3.57, you can customize the button using the Modify Style dialog box. You can save the specific style as a CSS class, as shown in Figure 3.57, or CSS ID. (See Appendix A for more information.) If you click Apply, the modified button is displayed with the new style, as shown in Figure 3.57. If you then click OK, the new style will be saved in the Current page and it will show in the Apply Styles and Manage Styles task panes (see Figure 3.57). If you right-click the newly created class, the commands included in the displayed shortcut menu will enable you to further customize it.

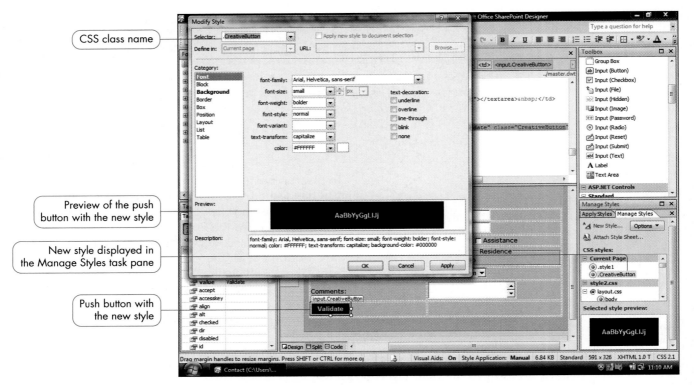

Figure 3.57 Modifying a Push Button Using the Modify Style Dialog Box

To insert an advanced button, right-click Advanced Button on the Toolbox task pane and click Insert. The button is added to the form. If you double-click the button, you can type the correct label in the highlighted area, as shown in Figure 3.58. Right-click and click Advanced Button Properties to display the Advanced Button Properties dialog box (see Figure 3.58). Replace the default text in the Name text box, Abutton1, with the name that you want displayed on the form. Type meaningful text that suggests the button's function in the Value box. The Button Type section of the dialog box enables you to choose the type of button required depending on its predetermined function. If you want to assign this button a function other than submitting or resetting the form, select the Normal type, as shown in Figure 3.58. The Button Size section of the dialog box enables you to precisely resize the button. As previously discussed in this section, you can further customize the button by applying a CSS style. Click the button's border to select it, right-click the desired style (see Figure 3.59), and click Apply Style. The button will be displayed with the new style.

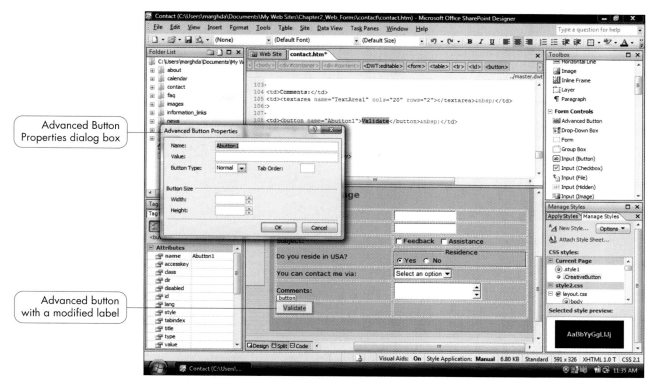

Figure 3.58 Working with the Advanced Button Form Field

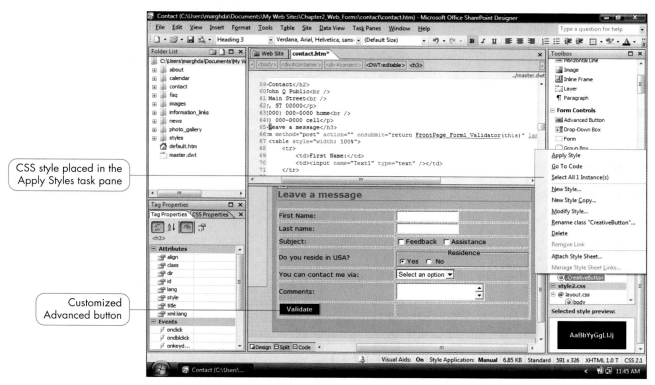

Figure 3.59 Applying a CSS Class Style to an Advanced Button Form Field

The methodology for inserting and modifying the properties of a Submit or Reset button are very similar to the methodology used for the generic push button corresponding to the Input (Button) Form Control (see Figure 3.60). If you wish to insert a Submit or Reset push button you can also use the Input (Submit) or the Input (Reset) Form Control. To modify the properties of these buttons, right-click and click Form Field Properties on the shortcut menu to display the Push Button Properties dialog box. To apply a new style to a Submit or Reset button, click anywhere within its area to select it, right-click the desired style in the Apply Styles task pane, and click Apply Style on the shortcut menu.

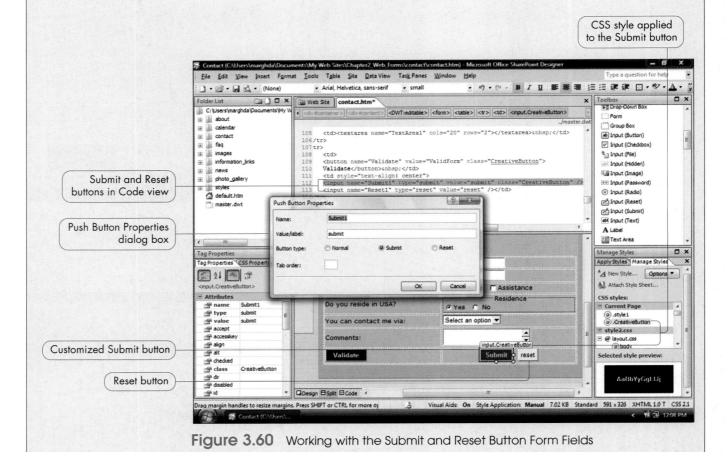

Figure 3.60 Working with the Submit and Reset Button Form Fields

Assign a Label to a Form Field

As required by paragraph n of Section 508 (subsection 1194.22), all form elements must have adjacent labels (placed in the same table cell if a table is used as a layout guide for a form). The W3C HTML 4.01 specifications (http://www.w3.org/TR/REC-html40) enable Web developers to include a <label> tag associated with a form element to create the needed label. You can use the <label> tag in two distinctive ways: as explicit labels or as implicit labels. (See Appendix B for more information.) However, most developers use the explicit label because the majority of assistive technology applications work extremely well with explicit labels.

SharePoint Designer enables you to add an explicit label to a form field. Just position the insertion point within the same cell as the form field, right-click the

> As required by paragraph n of Section 508 (subsection 1194.22), all form elements must have adjacent labels (placed in the same table cell if a table is used as a layout guide for a form). You can use the <label> tag in two distinctive ways: as explicit labels or as implicit labels.

Label command on the Toolbox task pane, and click Insert. SharePoint Designer automatically adds an implicit label, as shown in Figure 3.61. To modify the label into an explicit label, click it in the Code View, click the down arrow at the right of the label tag on the Quick Tag Selector, which is showing when you point your mouse to the label tag on the Quick Tag Selector, and click Edit Tag. Press the Space bar, type *for*, and then press the Space bar again. Type the name of the form field between the quotation signs and click the Enter button, as shown in Figure 3.61.

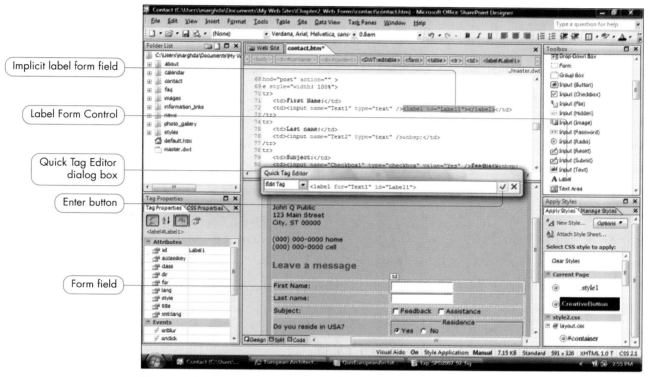

Figure 3.61   Adding an Explicit Label to a Form Field

TIP   Using the Tag Properties Task Pane

You can also add a value to the for attribute of the implicit label using the Tag Properties pane.

Insert Hidden Form Fields

As previously discussed, Web designers often need to hide form fields from visitors—in other words, create fields that will not be displayed in the browser window. To hide any field in a Microsoft SharePoint Designer form, right-click within the form in Design view, and then click Form Properties to open the Form Properties dialog box.

In the Form Name text box, type a valid name for the form. Click Advanced to open the Advanced Form Properties dialog box, and then click Add to open the Name/Value Pair dialog box, as shown in Figure 3.62. Type the name of the new hidden field in the Name box. In the Value box, type the value to be sent to the form handler and then click OK. Click OK twice to close all open dialog boxes. Save the Web Page and click Preview in Browser on the File menu to verify that the new field is not displayed (see Figure 3.63). However, remember that visitors who look at the source code will see the hidden fields.

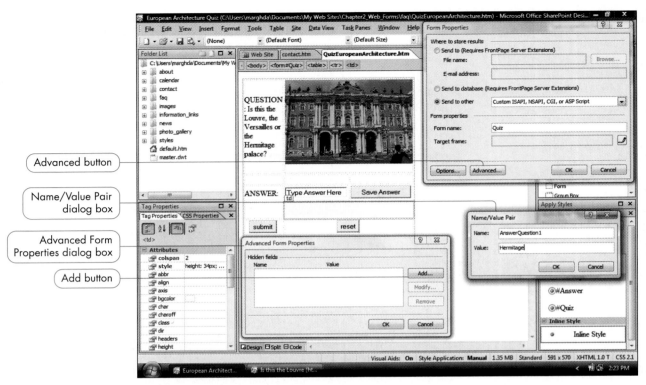

Figure 3.62 Inserting a Hidden Form Field

- Advanced button
- Name/Value Pair dialog box
- Advanced Form Properties dialog box
- Add button

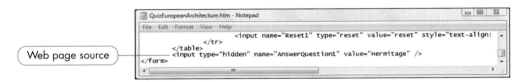

Web page source

Figure 3.63 Using a Hidden Form Field

In the Web page shown in Figure 3.63, the hidden field is used for storing the correct answer to an online quiz. The answer is not displayed in the browser, but is used to grade the question. How can you do that? The next section will teach you just that.

Working with Web Forms and Scripts in SharePoint Designer 2007

> SharePoint Designer also enables you to use scripts not included in Share-Point Designer Server Extensions and SharePoint Services to search the Internet; retrieve, validate, and process the data entered by visitors via a form; modify databases; or change the information on the screen. These scripts can be embedded in a Web page or in an external file.

As discussed in Chapter 1, SharePoint Services and FrontPage Server Extensions are collections of programs and scripts that provide you with features required to create Web pages able to search the Internet; retrieve, validate, and process the data entered by visitors via a form; modify databases; or change the information on the screen. SharePoint Designer also enables you to use scripts not included in SharePoint Designer Server Extensions and SharePoint Services for these tasks. These scripts can be embedded in a Web page or in an external file. You can use any combination of embedded script code and scripts placed in an external file. You can also use scripts to create your own customized functions. Functions can be embedded in a Web page or in an external file as well. Scripts embedded in a Web page are placed between the <script> . . . </script> tags.

An *event* causes a Web browser to trigger a script. When an event occurs, your script executes the code that responds to that particular event.

An *event handler*, or *action*, is scripting code that executes in response to a specific event.

An *event* causes a Web browser to trigger a script. When an event occurs, your script executes the code that responds to that particular event. Code that executes in response to a specific event is called an *event handler* or *action*. You can include code for an event handler as an attribute of the HTML element that initiates the event. In JavaScript, for example, the syntax of an event handler within an element is <element event_handler ="JavaScript code">. Event handler names are the same as the name of the event itself, plus a prefix, such as "on." For example, the event handler for the load event is onload: <body onLoad="alert('Welcome to my Web site!');">.

TIP Events

The most common events are actions that users take, such as clicking a button. A common use of an event is to run some sort of code in response to a user request. User-generated events, however, are not the only types of events scripts monitor. Events that are not direct results of user actions, such as the load event, are also monitored. The load event, which is triggered automatically by a Web browser, occurs only when an HTML document finishes loading in a Web browser. To learn more about scripting see the Microsoft Scripting Web site (http://msdn2.microsoft.com/en-us/library/ms950396.aspx).

In SharePoint Designer, the best way to add a custom script to an advanced button is to use the Behaviors task pane, shown in Figure 3.64. To display this task pane click Task Panes on the Menu bar and click Behaviors. Click the border of the advanced button to select it, click the Insert button in the Behaviors task pane, and then click Call Script, as shown in Figure 3.65, to open the Call Script dialog box.

> In SharePoint Designer, the best way to add a custom script to an advanced button is to use the Behaviors task pane.

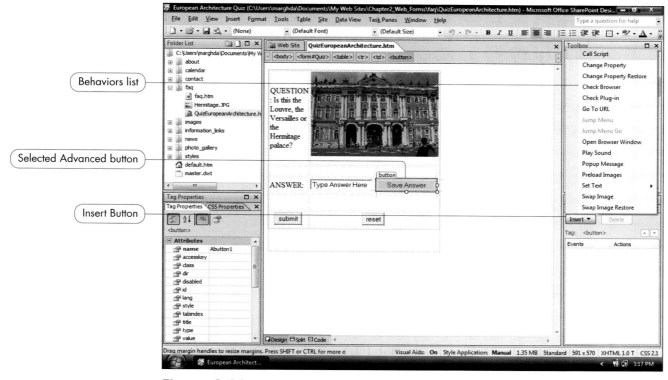

Figure 3.64 Selecting the Call Script Behavior

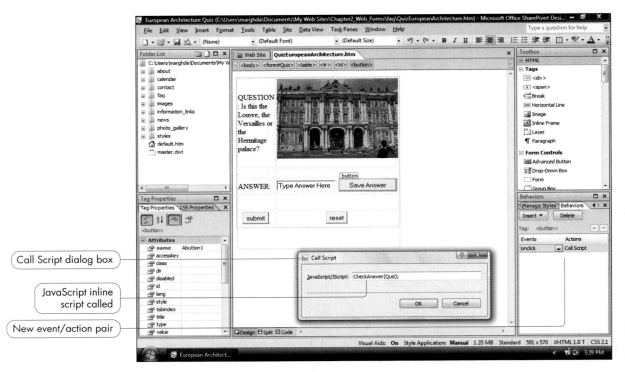

Figure 3.65 Working with the Advanced Button Form Field and Events

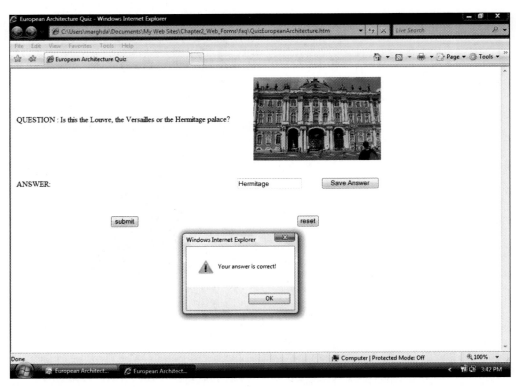

Figure 3.66 Action Generated by the Script Added to the Advanced Button

In the JavaScript/JScript text box, add the call to the script, as shown in Figure 3.65, which in this example is a JavaScript function that checks the correctness of a student's answer. Click OK to close the dialog box and see all the available event/action pairs added to the Behaviors task pane, as shown in Figure 3.65. The default event is onclick. If you want to change it, move the mouse over the onclick event, click the drop-down arrow at its right, and click another event. If you save the page, preview it in a browser, type the correct answer, and then click the advanced button (in this case, the Save Answer button), the action generated by the script will be launched. (In this case, a pop-up window is displayed, as shown in Figure 3.66.) The JavaScript function used in the example shown in Figures 3.65 and 3.66 can be found in the student data files. You can customize any push button using a JavaScript function and the Behaviors task pane.

TIP   Behaviors

The majority of behaviors are supported by Internet Explorer version 4.0 and higher, as well as Netscape Navigator version 4.0 and higher. However, some behaviors, such as Check Plug-in and Change Property, require Internet Explorer 5.0 and higher and Netscape Navigator 6.0 and higher.

You can also add a script function in the <head> section of a document by using the Microsoft Script Editor. To launch the Microsoft Script Editor, click the Tools menu, point to Macro, and then click Microsoft Script Editor, as shown in Figure 3.67.

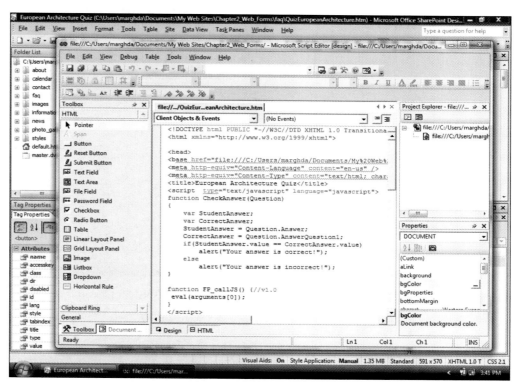

Figure 3.67 Microsoft Script Editor Window

TIP   Work with ASP.NET Controls and Data Sources

The Toolbox task pane includes a rich set of ASP.NET controls that enable you to connect to and view the content of different types of data sources. Using these tools, you can connect to an Access, Excel, or XML file. Figure 3.68 shows the Design view of an ASP.NET Web page that contains a FormView ASP.NET control connected to a SQLDataSource ASP.NET Control. The SQLDataSource ASP.NET control is connected to an Access 2007 .accdb file via an ASP.NET Connection. Figure 3.69 shows the same Web page displayed in Internet Explorer and Mozilla Firefox browsers. In Appendix A you will learn how to create a Data View of an XML Data Source.

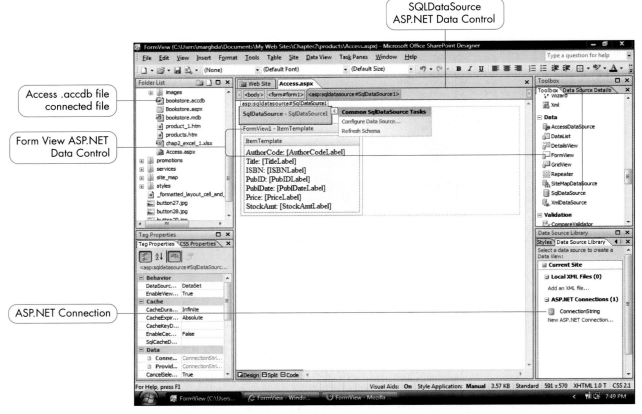

Figure 3.68   Working with ASP.NET Controls

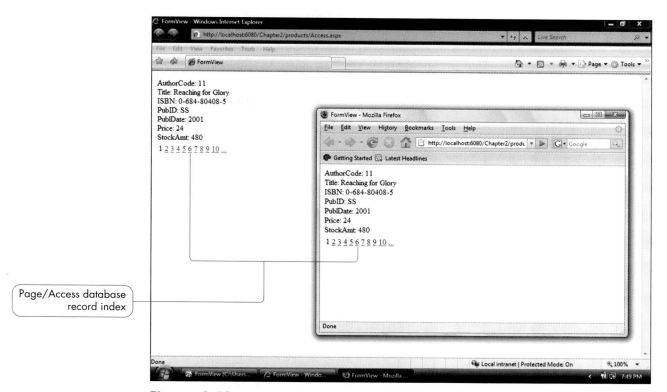

Figure 3.69 FormView ASP.NET Control Viewed in Internet Explorer and Mozilla Firefox Browsers

Hands-On Exercises

2 | Develop Web Forms with SharePoint Designer 2007

Skills covered: 1. Start SharePoint Designer, Open a Web Site, Create a New Blank Web Page, Insert a Layout Table, Insert an <h1> Line Text and an Image in the Cells of the Table, Insert Form Controls Within the Table Container Dotted Line, and Save the Web Page **2.** Modify the Properties of a Drop-Down Box and Modify the Properties of a Text Box **3.** Customize a Push Button Using JavaScript and the Behavior Task Pane, and View and Test a Form in Internet Explorer 7.0

<table>
<tr>
<td>

Step 1

Start SharePoint Designer, Open a Web Site, Create a New Blank Web Page, Insert a Layout Table, Insert an <h1> Line Text and an Image in the Cells of the Table, Insert Form Controls Within the Table Container Dotted Line, and Save the Web Page

</td>
<td>

Refer to Figure 3.70 as you complete Step 1.

a. Start SharePoint Designer, click **File** on the Menu bar, and click **Open Site**. Navigate to the chap3_ho2_solution_forms Web site folder, click, and then click the **Open button**. Create a backup **chap3_ho2_solution_forms_solution** Web site folder using the Remote Web Site view. Click the **Open your Remote Web site in SharePoint Designer hyperlink** in the *Status* section of the Remote Web Site view.

TROUBLESHOOTING: On the Windows taskbar, you should still see the SharePoint Designer tab opened in step a; right-click that tab and click Close on the shortcut menu to close it.

You should see the chap3_ho2_solution_forms _solution Web site in Folders view.

b. Click the **New button** on the Common toolbar to create a new blank Web page (**Untitled_1.htm**) within this Web site. Click the **Save button** on the Common toolbar to open the Save As dialog box. Navigate to the services folder and double-click. In the File name box, type **reservation_form.htm** and click the **Save button**.

The new reservation_form.htm Web page now shows in Design view.

c. Position the insertion point in the upper-left corner of the Web page, click **Table** on the Menu bar, and click **Insert Table** to open the Insert Table dialog box. In the *Size* section, select **1 row** and **2 columns**, and in the *Borders* section select **Size 0**. Click **OK**.

A table with 1 row and 2 columns is now added to the reservation_form.htm Web page.

d. Position the insertion point in the left cell of the table and type **Reservation Form**. Highlight the text, click the **down-arrow** to the right of the Style box on the Formatting toolbar, and click **Heading 1**.

e. Position the insertion point in the right cell of the table, click **Insert** on the Menu bar, point to **Picture**, and click **From File** to open the Picture dialog box. Navigate to the images folder, double-click to open it, and then double-click **condo_view.jpg**. Type **Condo View** in the Alternate Text box of the Accessibility Properties dialog box and click **OK** to insert the picture into the table.

The image now shows.

f. Right-click the **picture** and click **Picture Properties** on the shortcut menu to open the Picture Properties dialog box. Click the **Appearance tab**, and in the *Size* section, select **Width 133** and **Height 99** (in pixels). Click **OK** to close the Picture Properties dialog box.

</td>
</tr>
</table>

The image is now showing with the selected size.

g. Press ➡ and press **Tab**. Right-click **Form** in the *Form Control* section of the Toolbox task pane and click **Insert**.

h. Place the insertion point within the dotted line of the form container and press **Enter**. Click **Table** on the Menu bar and click **Insert Table** to open the Insert Table dialog box. In the *Size* section select **2 rows** and **2 columns**, and in the *Borders* section, select **Size 0**. Click **OK**.

The form container including a nested table is now shown.

i. Place the insertion point in row one, column one of the nested table and type **First Name:**. Press **Tab**, right-click **Input (Text)** in the *Form Control* section of the Toolbox task pane, and click **Insert**.

j. Place the insertion point in row two, column one and type **Last Name:**. Press **Tab**, right-click **Input (Text)** in the *Form Control* section of the Toolbox task pane, and click **Insert**.

k. Press ➡, and then press **Tab**. With the insertion point in row three, column one, type **Telephone:**. Press **Tab**, right-click **Input (Text)** in the *Form Control* section of the Toolbox task pane, and click **Insert**.

l. Press ➡, and then press **Tab**. With the insertion point in row four, column one, type **E-mail address:**. Press **Tab**, right-click **Input (Text)** in the *Form Control* section of the Toolbox task pane, and click **Insert**.

m. Press ➡, and then press **Tab**. Place the insertion point in row five, column one, and type **Type of Condominium:**. Press **Tab**, right-click **Drop-Down Box** in the *Form Control* section of the Toolbox task pane, and click **Insert**.

n. Press ➡, and then press **Tab**. Place the insertion point in row six, column one and type **For how many days?** Press **Tab**, right-click **Input (Text)** in the *Form Control* section of the Toolbox task pane, and click **Insert**.

o. Press ➡, and then press **Tab**. Place the insertion point in row seven, column one and type **Starting Date:**. Press **Tab**, right-click **Input (Text)** in the *Form Control* section of the Toolbox task pane, and click **Insert**.

p. Press ➡, and then press **Tab**. Place the insertion point in row eight, column one, right-click **Input (Submit)** in the *Form Control* section of the Toolbox task pane, and click **Insert**.

q. Press ➡, and then press **Tab**. Click **Table** on the Menu bar, point to **Modify**, and click **Split Cells**. In the Split Cells dialog box, click the **Split into columns option button** and select 2 in the Number of Columns drop-down list. Click **OK** to close the Split Cells dialog box.

r. Right-click **Input (Reset)** in the *Form Control* section of the Toolbox task pane and click **Insert**. Press ➡, and then press **Tab**.

s. Right-click **Advanced Button** in the *Form Control* section of the Toolbox task pane.

The advanced button is displayed and its button default label is highlighted.

t. Double-click the **advanced button** and type **Close Window** in the highlighted area of the advanced button to replace its default label with *Close Window*.

u. Click the **Save button** on the Common toolbar to save the Web page. Leave the Web site open to continue to the next step.

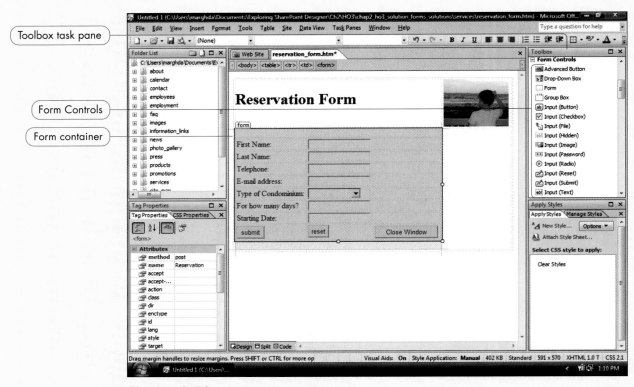

Figure 3.70 Creating a Web Form

Toolbox task pane

Form Controls

Form container

Step 2

Modify the Properties of a Drop-Down Box and Modify the Properties of a Text Box

Refer to Figure 3.71 as you complete Step 2.

a. Double-click the **drop-down box** to open the Drop-Down Box Properties dialog box. Click the **Add button** to open the Add Choice dialog box. In the Choice box, type **OneBedroom**, then select the **Specify Value check box** and the **Selected radio button**. Click **OK** to close the dialog box.

b. Click the **Add button** to open the Add Choice dialog box. In the Choice box, type **TwoBedrooms**, then select the **Specify Value check box** and the **Not Selected radio button**. Click **OK** twice to close the open dialog boxes.

You should see the *OneBedroom* choice in the drop-down box.

c. Double-click the **Starting Date text box** to open the Text Box Properties dialog box. In the Initial value box, type **mm/dd/yy**. Click **OK** to close the dialog box.

You should see the *mm/dd/yy* initial value in the Starting Date text box.

d. Right-click anywhere within the form container dotted line and click **Form Properties** to open the Form Properties dialog box. In the Form Name box, type **Reservation** and click **OK** to close the dialog box. Leave the Web site open to continue to the next step.

Figure 3.71 Modifying the Properties of a Web Form

Step 3

Customize a Push Button Using JavaScript and the Behavior Task Pane, and View and Test a Form in Internet Explorer 7.0

Refer to Figure 3.72 as you complete Step 3.

a. Double-click the **services folder** in the Folder List task pane and double-click **validationfunction.txt**. Click **Edit** on the Menu bar and click **Select All**. Right-click anywhere within the selected text and click **Copy** on the menu.

b. Click the **reservation_form.htm tab** to open the reservation_form.htm Web page. Click the **Code button** to see the Web page in Code view, place the insertion point underneath the <title> tag, right-click, and click **Paste** on the menu.

c. Click the **Design button,** click **Task Panes** on the Menu bar, and click **Behaviors** to display the Behaviors task pane. Click the **Submit button** to select it, click the **Insert button** on the Behaviors task pane, and click **Call Script** to open the Call Script dialog box.

d. In the JavaScript/Jscript box, type **Validate_OnSubmit (Reservation);** and click **OK** to close the dialog box.

e. Click the **Close Window button** to select it, click the **Insert button**, and click **Call Script** to open the Call Script dialog box.

f. In the JavaScript/Jscript box, type **window.close();**, as shown in Figure 3.72, and click **OK** to close the dialog box. Click the **Save button** to save the Web page.

g. Click **File** on the Menu bar, point to **Preview in Browser**, and click **Microsoft Internet Explorer 7.0**.

h. Fill in the form with simple information, but omit filling in one of the first text box form fields. Click the **Submit button**.

An alert box appears. Click the **OK button** in the alert box.

i. Fill in all the fields and click the **Submit button**.

No alert box should display now.

j. Click the **Close Window button** and then click **Yes** in the dialog box generated by the script to close the browser window.

The Internet Explorer window closes.

k. Close the Web site and exit SharePoint Designer.

Figure 3.72 Web Forms and Behaviors

Summary

1. **Work with Microsoft Word documents in SharePoint Designer.** As with all the Microsoft Office suite applications, Word enables integration with other applications. Its capability to create documents that can be cut and pasted into a Web page or even to create a document ready to be published on the World Wide Web (Single File Web Page, Web Page, and Web page, Filtered) has consistently improved in the past few years. Starting with Microsoft Word 2007, you can also save and export a Word document as a PDF (.pdf file format) or XPS Document (.xps file format). In SharePoint Designer, you can add Word content to your Web pages, import any Word document into a Web site, and edit Word content and files.

2. **Work with Microsoft PowerPoint and SharePoint Designer.** There are many ways to make content from PowerPoint or entire PowerPoint presentations available on a Web page, and SharePoint Designer can assist you in this process. From copying and pasting PowerPoint components to a Web page, to inserting an entire presentation into a Web page, saving a presentation for use on the Web, and publishing a PowerPoint presentation on a Web server, SharePoint Designer can assist Web developers in achieving their goals. Starting with Microsoft PowerPoint 2007, you can also save and export a PowerPoint presentation as a PDF (.pdf file format) or XPS Document (.xps file format). In SharePoint Designer, you can import any PowerPoint presentation into a Web site and edit PowerPoint content and files.

3. **Work with Microsoft Excel Spreadsheets in SharePoint Designer.** You can take advantage of the Microsoft Excel and SharePoint Designer content integration features and use content created in Excel in your Web pages. From copying and pasting Excel content to a Web page, to inserting an entire Excel spreadsheet into a Web page, saving an Excel spreadsheet or workbook for use on the Web, and publishing an Excel spreadsheet or workbook on a Web server, SharePoint Designer can assist Web developers in achieving their goals. Starting with Microsoft Excel 2007, you can also save and export an Excel spreadsheet or workbook as a PDF (.pdf file format) or XPS Document (.xps file format). In SharePoint Designer, you can import any Excel spreadsheet into a Web site and edit Excel content and files.

4. **Work with Microsoft Access Databases in SharePoint Designer.** Access enables integration of its objects with SharePoint Designer Web sites. Its capability to create databases that can be copied and pasted into a Web page or even to create a databases ready to be published on the World Wide Web has consistently improved in the past few years. Access 2007 empowers users with other options to export Access Objects in other formats, such as an Excel XML file format, Word RTF file, PDF (.pdf file format) or XPS Document (.xps file format), Access Database, Text File (.txt), XML file (.xml), ODBC Database, and HTML Document (.html). In SharePoint Designer, you can import any Access database into a Web site and edit Access content and files.

5. **Design a Web form.** Web forms are slowly but surely replacing many of the paper forms we all used to fill in, from the simple marketing survey to the mighty IRS 1040 form, from a sketchy request for information form to a complicated mortgage application form. A Web form is comprised of form fields such as text boxes, check boxes, option buttons, group boxes, drop-down boxes, text areas, push buttons, and advanced buttons. When designing a form, all the key factors of good Web page design, such as usability, navigation, compatibility, accessibility, consistency, validity, and attractiveness, need to be taken into consideration.

6. **Create a Web form with SharePoint Designer.** SharePoint Designer offers a complete set of tools for creating and editing Web forms, modifying their properties, and saving the Web form results. Using the SharePoint Designer HTML pane, you can insert and modify the properties of Form Controls, such as Input (Text), Input (Checkbox), Input (Radio), Group Box, Drop-Down Box, Text Area, Input (Button), and Advanced Button. You can also add one or more Input (Hidden) form controls that you might need to move information from one Web page to another page; to pull additional data, such as a login name, from your Web site visitors; or to indicate the e-mail address of the person who will receive the data entered by the Web site visitors as a form field value. You should always add explicit labels to each form field.

7. **Work with Web forms and scripts in SharePoint Designer.** In SharePoint Designer, you can add to a form field, using the Behaviors task pane, a custom script not included in FrontPage Server Extensions and SharePoint Services. These scripts can be embedded in a Web page or in an external file. You can use any combination of embedded script code and scripts placed in an external file. You can also use scripts to create your own customized functions. Functions can be embedded in a Web page or an external file as well. Scripts embedded in a

...continued on Next Page

Web page are placed between the <script> . . . </script> tags. An event causes a Web browser to trigger a script. When an event occurs, your script executes the code that responds to that particular event. An event handler, or action, is scripting code that executes in response to a specific event.

Key Terms

Multiple Choice

1. When you double-click a text box form field you cannot:

   (a) Attach a script to the form field.

   (b) Assign the form field an initial value.

   (c) Modify the tab order in which the form field can be selected by a visitor.

   (d) Decide the text or numeric format of the form field.

2. When adding a drop-down box form field to a form:

   (a) You prevent the visitor from selecting more than one choice.

   (b) You cannot display more than one choice.

   (c) You cannot assign an initial value.

   (d) You can disallow the first choice.

3. To build a usable and accessible form:

   (a) Use explicit labels.

   (b) Place form fields and explicit labels in the same cell of a table (if using a table layout).

   (c) Assign form fields an accesskey attribute.

   (d) All of the above.

4. Which of the following options is only included in the Text Box Properties dialog box?

   (a) Password field

   (b) Initial value

   (c) Validate

   (d) Tab order

5. You might want to use hidden form fields in which of the following situations?

   (a) You need to store information from one Web page on another page.

   (b) You need to pull additional data, such as a login name, from your Web site visitors.

   (c) You need to indicate the e-mail address of the person who will receive the data entered by the Web site visitors as a form field value.

   (d) All of the above.

6. Which of the following form fields cannot be used to enable visitors to select more options?

   (a) Drop-down box

   (b) Option button

   (c) Check box

   (d) Text area

7. In SharePoint Designer, you should modify a Word document with HTML content by doing which of the following?

   (a) Using the Open With command

   (b) Double-clicking its file name in the Folder List task pane

   (c) Editing the original Word source document in Microsoft Word

   (d) Both a and b

8. Which of the following statements about Excel and SharePoint Designer is not correct?

   (a) SharePoint Designer automatically converts the Excel content into HTML.

   (b) In SharePoint Designer, you should modify an Excel spreadsheet with HTML content by using the Open With command.

   (c) When you save an Excel spreadsheet as a PDF or an XPS Document you can publish the active sheet(s), the entire workbook, or just a selection (cell range) within a worksheet.

   (d) When you publish an Excel spreadsheet as a Web Page you may select the AutoRepublish option.

9. Which of the following statements about PowerPoint and SharePoint Designer is not correct?

   (a) When a visitor clicks a link to a PowerPoint presentation, the presentation, saved in the original PowerPoint format (.pptx) or the PowerPoint Slideshow format (.ppsx), opens in PowerPoint.

   (b) You can save a PowerPoint presentation directly as a Web page or as a Single File Web page.

   (c) If you import a .pptx, .ppsx, .mht, .pdf, or .xps PowerPoint presentation, the graphic files are not embedded in the file.

   (d) To add a link from a Web page to a PowerPoint presentation saved as a PDF (*.pdf) or an XPS document (*.xps) you will first need to import the files into the Web site.

10. Which of the following statements about Access and SharePoint Designer is not correct?

    (a) To copy and paste content from Access to SharePoint Designer you can use the Clipboard Task pane.

    (b) SharePoint Designer automatically converts Access content into HTML.

    (c) When you export an Access Object as a PDF or an XPS Document you can choose to publish all records, selected records, or selected pages.

    (d) Microsoft Access empowers users to export Access Objects in formats such as Excel XML file format, PDF (.pdf file format) or XPS Document (.xps file format), Access Database, and Single File Web page (.mht).

Practice Exercises

1 Integrate Microsoft Office 2007 and a SharePoint Designer E-Business Web Site for an Investment Management Company

Dan King, your e-business professor, is providing you with more information about new Web page elements for the home page. He is also providing you with a Microsoft Word document and a PowerPoint presentation that need to be published on your e-business Web site. You will publish the two documents using the Microsoft Word Web Page, Filtered (*.htm; *.html) format and Microsoft PowerPoint XPS Document (*.xps), and you will link them to the home page, as shown in Figure 3.73. Proceed as follows:

a. Start Microsoft Word. Locate and open *large_cap_growth.doc*. Click the **Office Button**, point to **Save As**, and click **Other Formats** to open the Save As dialog box. Locate and open the market_research folder in the Student Data Files folder, on the Save as type drop-down list, click **Web Page, Filtered (*.htm; *.html)**, and then click the **Save button**. Click **Yes** in the Microsoft Office Word Alert box and click **Continue** in the Microsoft Office Word Compatibility Checker dialog box if it displays.

b. Start Microsoft PowerPoint. Locate and open *tax_amt.ppx*. Click the **Office Button**, point to **Save As**, and click **Other Formats** to open the Save As dialog box. Locate and open the news folder and click **XPS Document (*.xps)** on the Save as type drop-down list. Click the **Options button**, make sure the **Document structure tags for accessibility check box** is selected, and then click **Save**.

c. Start SharePoint Designer. Locate and open the chap3_pe1_ebusiness Web site folder. Using the Remote Web Site view, create a **chap3_pe1_ebusiness_solution** Web site backup. Click the **Open your Remote Web site in SharePoint Designer link** to open the chap3_pe1_ebusiness_solution Web site folder. Open the market_research and news folders. Make sure the Microsoft Word document and PowerPoint presentation were properly published (as shown in Figure 3.73). Double-click *default.htm* in the Folder List task pane to open it in Design view.

d. Highlight the *Investing with Taxes in Mind* text line, right-click, and click **Hyperlinks** on the shortcut menu to open the Insert Hyperlink dialog box. Locate and double-click the **news folder**, and then click **tax_amt.xps**. Click the **ScreenTip button** to open the Set Hyperlink ScreenTip dialog box. Type **Long Cap Growth article** in the ScreenTip text area and click **OK** to close the Set Hyperlink ScreenTip dialog box.

e. Click the **Target Frame button** to open the Target Frame dialog box. Click **New Window** in the *Common targets* section and click **OK** two times to close all open dialog boxes.

f. Click the **Save button** on the Common toolbar to save all changes made to *default.htm*. The SharePoint Designer workspace should look as shown in Figure 3.73. Click **File** on the Menu bar, point to **Preview in Browser**, and click **Windows Internet Explorer 7.0** to preview *default.htm*.

g. Click the **Investing with Taxes in Mind hyperlink** to open the *tax_amt.xps* file in an XPS Viewer window, as shown in Figure 3.73. Close the XPS Viewer window. Click the **Learn More hyperlink** to open the *large_cap_growth.htm* Word document.

h. Close the Word, PowerPoint, and Internet Explorer application windows. Click **File** on the Menu bar and click **Close Site**. Click **File** again on the Menu bar and click **Exit** to close the SharePoint Designer window.

...continued on Next Page

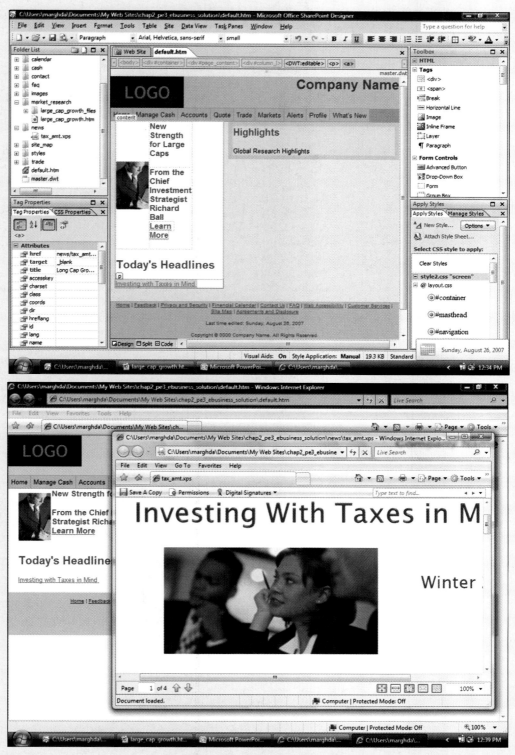

Figure 3.73 Integrating Microsoft Office 2007 and a SharePoint Designer E-Business Web Site for an Investment Management Company

...continued on Next Page

You have been asked by your faculty supervisor to develop a Web form that can be used by all instructors of a large course to add students entitled to a make up for a class midterm exam. Figure 3.74 shows how the SharePoint Designer workspace should look at the end of this exercise. Use this figure as a guide.

a. Start SharePoint Designer. Locate and open the chap3_pe2_IT_course Web site folder. Using the Remote Web Site view, create a **chap3_pe2_IT_course _solution** Web site backup. Click the **Open your Remote Web site in SharePoint Designer link** to open the chap3_pe2_IT_course_solution Web site folder.

b. Click the **New Document button** to create an Untitled_1.htm Web page. Click **Format** on the Menu bar, then point to **Dynamic Web Template** and click **Attach Dynamic Web Template** to open the Attach Dynamic Web Template dialog box. Locate and double-click **master.dwt**.

c. Highlight the *Heading 2* text line and type **Makeup Midterm Exams Web Form**. Double-click the **<p> tag** beneath the *Makeup Midterm Exams Web Form* headline, right-click **Form** in the *Form Controls* section of the Toolbox task pane, and click **Insert**.

d. Click **Table** and click **Insert Table** to open the Insert Table dialog box and insert within the dotted line of the form container a layout table with **8** rows and **2** columns.

e. Insert the form fields in column 2 and add the associated text prompt/questions in column 1 to approximate the Web page shown in Figure 3.74, using the Form Controls from the Toolbox task pane:

   • Insert an Input (Text) Form Control for the **Student's Last Name**, **Student's First Name**, and **Instructor's Name** form fields.

   • Insert a Drop-Down Box Form Control for the **Course Section** and **Midterm Exam** form fields.

   • Insert a Group Box Form Control for **Accommodation for Students with Special Needs** form field. Insert a nested table within the field with **3** rows and **2** columns for the three Input (Checkbox) Form Controls.

   • Insert a Text Area Form Control for the **Reason** form field.

   • Insert an Input (Submit) and an Input (Reset) Form Control for the **Submit** and **Reset** buttons.

f. Click the **Save button** on the Common toolbar to open the Save As dialog box, locate and double-click the **instructors folder**, type **makeup_list.htm** in the File name box, click **Change Tile**, and type **Makeup List** in the Page title text box. Click **OK**, and then **Save** to close all the open dialog boxes. The SharePoint Designer workspace should look very similar to the one shown in Figure 3.74. Click **File** on the Menu bar and click **Close Site**. Click **File** again on the Menu bar and click **Exit** to close the SharePoint Designer window.

...continued on Next Page

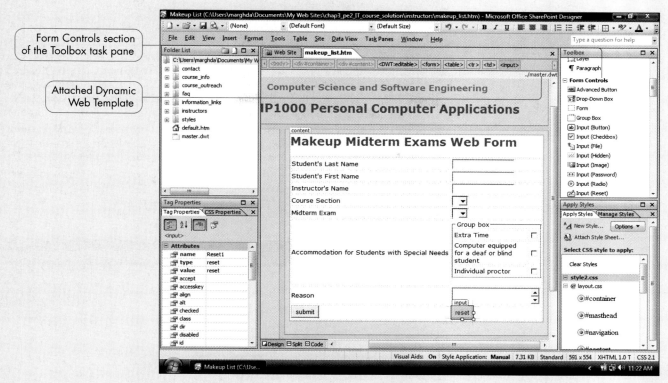

Form Controls section of the Toolbox task pane

Attached Dynamic Web Template

Figure 3.74 Creating a Web Form for a Multiple-Section Course Web Site

3 Customize the Midterm Exam Makeup Web Form of a Multiple-Section Course Web Site

Your faculty supervisor approved the design of the makeup Web form and gave you more information about how you need to further customize the Web form. Figure 3.75 shows how the SharePoint Designer workspace should look at the end of this exercise. Use this figure as a guide.

a. Start SharePoint Designer. Locate and open the chap3_pe3_IT_course Web site folder site. Using the Remote Web Site view, create a **chap3_pe3_IT_course_solution** Web site backup. Click the **Open your Remote Web site in SharePoint Designer link** to open the chap3_pe3_IT_course_solution Web site folder.

b. Open the instructors folder and open in Split view **makeup_list.htm.**

c. Position the insertion point, in Code view, before the <form> tag, type **<**, and, using the IntelliSense tool, type **Use the form below to add students to the Makeup List**. View the *Guidelines for Adding Students to the Makeup List* formatted with the Heading 6 style.

d. Point to **Import** on the File menu and click **File** to locate and import the *guidelines_makeup_list.pdf* file. The *guidelines_makeup_list.pdf* should be listed in the instructors folder. In Design view, highlight the *Guidelines for Adding Students to the Makeup List* text, right-click, and click **Hyperlink** on the shortcut menu to open the Insert Hyperlink dialog box and add a link to the *guidelines_makeup_list.pdf* file. Type the ScreenTip text of the hyperlink: **Guidelines for Adding Students to the Makeup List**.

e. Double-click the **drop-down box** in row 4 to open the Drop-Down Box Properties dialog box. Click the **Modify button** to open the Modify Choice dialog box. In the Choice box, type **1**, select the **Specify Value check box**, and click the **Selected option button**. Click **OK** to close the dialog box. Click the **Add button** to open the Add Choice dialog box. In the Choice box, type **2**, then select the **Specify Value check box**. Click **OK** to close the dialog box and click **OK** to close the Drop-Down Box Properties dialog box.

...continued on Next Page

f. Double-click the **drop-down box** in row 5 to open the Drop-Down Box Properties dialog box. Click the **Modify button** to open the Modify Choice dialog box. In the Choice box, type **Exam 1**, select the **Specify Value check box**, and click the **Selected option button**. Click **OK** to close the dialog box. Click the **Add button** to open the Add Choice dialog box. In the Choice box, type **Exam 2**, then select the **Specify Value check box**. Click **OK** to close the dialog box. Click the **Add button** to open the Add Choice dialog box. In the Choice box, type **Exam 3**, then select the **Specify Value check box**. Click **OK** to close the dialog box and click **OK** to close the Drop-Down Box Properties dialog box.

g. Click the **Save button** on the Common toolbar to save the modifications made to *makeup_list.htm*. Preview *makeup_list.htm* in Internet Explorer 7.0. The Internet Explorer 7.0 window should look very similar to the one shown in Figure 3.75.

h. Close the Internet Explorer 7.0 window, click **Close Site** on the File menu to close the chap3_pe3_IT_course_solution Web site, and click **Exit** on the File menu to exit SharePoint Designer.

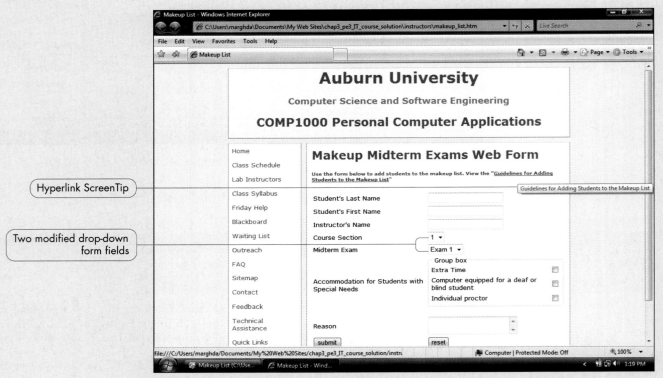

Figure 3.75 Customizing the Midterm Exams and Quizzes Makeup Web Form of a Multiple-Section Course Web Site

You have to develop a Feedback Form and Web page for the E-Business Web Site of an Investment Management Company using the Dynamic Web Template.

a. Start SharePoint Designer. Locate and open the chap3_mid1_ebusiness Web site folder site. Using the Remote Web Site view, create a **chap3_mid1_ebusiness_solution** Web site backup. Click the **Open your Remote Web site in SharePoint Designer link** to open the chap3_mid1_ebusiness_solution Web site folder.

b. Click the **New Document button** to create an Untitled_1.htm Web page. Click **Format** on the Menu bar, then point to **Dynamic Web Template** and click **Attach Dynamic Web Template** to open the Attach Dynamic Web Template dialog box. Locate and double-click **master.dwt**.

c. Highlight the *Headline 2* text line and type **Feedback**. Double-click the **<p> tag** beneath the *Feedback* headline, right-click **Form** in the *Form Controls* section of the Toolbox task pane, and click **Insert**.

d. Click **Table** and click **Insert Table** to open the Insert Table dialog box and insert within the dotted line of the form container a table with **5** rows and **2** columns.

e. Type **Your Name:** and press **Tab**. Right-click **Input (Text)** in the Toolbox task pane and click **Insert** to insert a text box field in the second column of the first row.

f. Position the insertion point in row 2, column 1, and type **You E-mail Address:**. Press **Tab**, right-click **Input (Text)** in the Toolbox task pane, and click **Insert** to insert a second text box field in the second column of the second row.

g. Position the insertion point in row 3, column 1, and type **You are a:**. Press **Tab**, right-click **Group Box** in the Toolbox task pane, and click **Insert** to insert a field set in the second column of the third row.

h. Click within the field set, click **Table**, and click **Insert Table** to open the Insert Table dialog box and insert a nested table with **3** rows and **2** columns within the field set.

   • Type **Personal Investor**, press **Tab**, right-click **Input (Radio)**, and click **Insert**.

   • Position the insertion point in row 2, column 1, type **Institutional Investor**, press **Tab**, right-click **Input (Radio)**, and click **Insert**.

   • Position the insertion point in row 3, column 1, type **Non-US Investor**, press **Tab**, right-click **Input (Radio)**, and click **Insert**.

i. Position the insertion point in row 4, column 1 of the external table and type **Your message:**. Press **Tab**, right-click **Text Area** in the Toolbox task pane, and click **Insert** to insert a text area tag in row 5, column 2.

j. Position the insertion point in row 5, column 1 of the external table right-click **Input (Submit)**, and click **Insert** to insert an input submit button.

k. Position the insertion point in row 6, column 2 of the external table, right-click **Input (Reset)**, and click **Insert** to insert an input reset button.

l. Click the **Save button** on the Common toolbar to open the Save As dialog box, locate and double-click the **contact folder**, type **feedback.htm** in the File name box, click **Change Tile**, and type **Feedback** in the Page title text box. Click **OK** and then **Save** to close all the open dialog boxes. The SharePoint Designer workspace should look very similar to the one shown in Figure 3.76.

m. Close *feedback.htm*, close the chap3_mid1_ebusiness_solution Web site, and exit SharePoint Designer.

...continued on Next Page

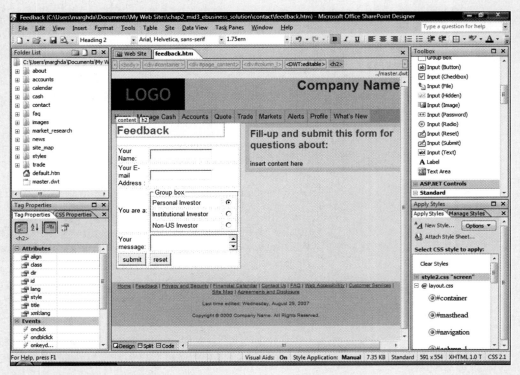

Figure 3.76 Feedback Form and Web Page for the E-Business Web Site of an Investment Management Company

2 Develop an Accessible Property Managers' Resources Subsite Using Microsoft Office Documents

You will create a new Property Managers' Resources subsite, and you will export, as an .html file, into this subsite an Access Table object. You will create a new home page for the subsite and add a link to the .html file. You will test for accessibility both documents and the hyperlink in your browser.

a. Start SharePoint Designer, open the chap3_mid2_management Web site folder, and create a **chap3_mid2_management_solution** back-up Web site. Start Microsoft Access and open the *chap3_mid2_reservations.accdb* file.

b. Export the *Reservations* table as **reservations.htm** in the managers folder of the chap3_mid2_management_solution Web site. Make sure you click the **Export data with formatting and layout check box** on the Export - HTML Document dialog box and the **Save export steps check box** in the Export - HTML Document Save Export Steps dialog box.

c. Click the **SharePoint Designer tab** on the Windows taskbar and convert the managers folder to a Web folder. Open the managers Web folder in a new SharePoint Designer window.

d. Open *reservations.html*, double-click the **Reservations table caption**, and type **Dolphin Beach Property Reservations**. Save **reservations.html**.

e. Create a new **managers.htm** Web page from the master.dwt Dynamic Web Template. Highlight the *Headline 2* text line and type **Property Managers' Resources**. Highlight the *Headline 3* text line and type **Property Reservations**. Highlight *the insert content here* text line beneath the *Property Reservations* text line and insert a **Dolphin Beach hyperlink** to *reservations.html*. The target of the hyperlink should be **New Window** and the ScreenTip text should be **Link to the Dolphin Beach Property Reservations**. Save **managers.html**.

f. Run the Accessibility Reports tool for *reservations.html* and *managers.html*. There should be no accessibility problems. The SharePoint Designer workspace should now look like the one shown in Figure 3.77.

...continued on Next Page

g. Preview *managers.html* in the Internet Explorer 7.0 browser and click the **Dolphin Beach hyperlink**. You should see *reservations.html*, as shown in Figure 3.77.

h. Close the chap3_mid2_management_solution Web site and exit SharePoint Designer, Internet Explorer 7.0, and Microsoft Office Access.

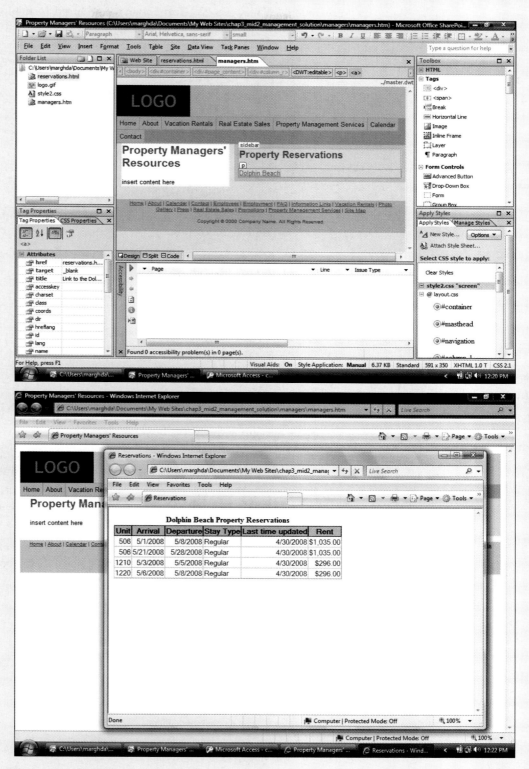

Figure 3.77 Developing an Accessible Property Managers' Resources Subsite Using Microsoft Office Documents

...continued on Next Page

You will validate the makeup Web form of an Information Technology course Web Site using the Form Field Properties tool. You will test the validation rules in a browser.

a. In SharePoint Designer, open the chap3_mid3_IT_course Web site folder and create a **chap3_mid3_IT_course_solution** backup Web site. Open the *instructors* folder, and then open *makeup_list.htm* in Design view.

b. Right-click the **form field** in row 1, column 2 of the layout table and click **Form Field Properties** to open the Text Box Properties dialog box.

Type **StudentLastName** in the Name box.

Click the **Validate button** and click the **Required check box** in the *Data length* section of the Text Box Validation dialog box.

Click **OK**, then click **OK** again to close the Text Box Properties dialog box and the Text Box Validation dialog box.

c. Right-click the **form field** in row 2, column 2 of the layout table and click **Form Field Properties** to open the Text Box Properties dialog box.

- Type **StudentFirstName** in the *Name* box.

- Click the **Validate button** and click the **Required check box** in the *Data length* section of the Text Box Validation dialog box.

- Click **OK**, then click **OK** again to close the Text Box Properties dialog box and the Text Box Validation dialog box.

d. Right-click the **form field** in row 4, column 2 of the layout table and click **Form Field Properties** to open the Drop-Down Box Properties dialog box.

Type **Section** in the Name box.

- Click the **Modify button**, type **Select Section** in the Choice box, select the **Specify Value check box**, click the **Selected option button**, and click **OK** to close the Modify Choice dialog box.

- Click the **Add button**, type **1** in the Choice box, select the **Specify Value check box**, and click **OK** to close the Add Choice dialog box.

- Click the **Add button**, type **2** in the Choice box, select the **Specify Value check box**, and click **OK** to close the Add Choice dialog box.

Click the **Validate button** and click the **Data Required check box** and the **Disallow first choice check box**.

Click **OK**, then click **OK** again to close the Drop-Down Box Properties dialog box and the Drop-Down Validation dialog box.

e. Right-click the **form field** in row 5, column 2 of the layout table and click **Form Field Properties** to open the Drop-Down Box Properties dialog box.

- Type **Exam** in the Name box.

- Click the **Modify button**, type **Select Exam** in the Choice box, select the **Specify Value check box**, click the **Selected option button**, and click **OK** to close the Modify Choice dialog box.

...continued on Next Page

- Click the **Add button**, type **Exam 1** in the Choice box, select the **Specify Value check box**, and click **OK** to close the Add Choice dialog box.

- Click the **Add button**, type **Exam 2** in the Choice box, select the **Specify Value check box**, and click **OK** to close the Add Choice dialog box.

- Click the **Add button**, type **Exam 3** in the Choice box, select the **Specify Value check box**, and click **OK** to close the Add Choice dialog box.

- Click the **Validate button**, then click the **Data Required check box** and the **Disallow first choice check box**.

- Click **OK**, then click **OK** again to close the Drop-Down Box Properties dialog box and the Drop-Down Validation dialog box.

f. Right-click the **Group Box form field** and click **Group Box Properties** to open the Group Box Properties dialog box, and then type, in the Label box, **Type of Accommodation**. Close the Group Box Properties dialog box.

g. Right-click the **form field** in row 7, column 2 of the layout table and click **Form Field Properties** to open the TextArea Box Properties dialog box.

Type **Reason** in the Name box.

- Click the **Validate button** and click the **Required check box** in the *Data length* section of the TextArea Box Validation dialog box.

- Click **OK**, then click **OK** again to close the TextArea Box Properties dialog box and the TextArea Box Validation dialog box.

h. Save the changes made to *makeup_list.htm*.

i. Preview *makeup_list.htm* in Internet Explorer 7.0. Every time you click the **Submit button** of the Web form without typing data in any of the form fields for which you checked the Required check box you should get an Internet Explorer 7.0 alert box, as shown in Figure 3.78.

j. Close the chap3_mid3_IT_course_solution Web site and exit SharePoint Designer and Internet Explorer 7.0.

...continued on Next Page

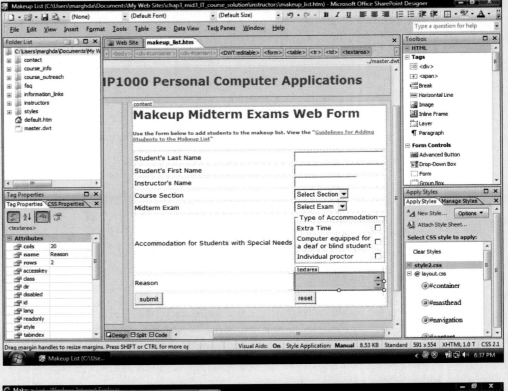

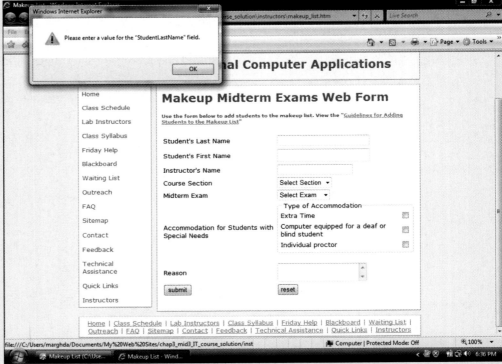

Figure 3.78   Validate and Customize a Web Form for an Information Technology Course Web Site

Capstone Exercise

The Personal Computer Applications course Web site was developed three years ago by a graduate student as part of his Master's Degree in Computer Software Engineering project, using FrontPage 2003 as the Web authoring tool. You did an excellent job building a new and enhanced version of the Web site using SharePoint Designer as a Web authoring tool. Your faculty supervisor wants you to continue working on the Personal Computer Applications course Web site by creating a subsite for Instructors' Resources and a course feedback form.

Opening and Creating a Backup Copy of the Personal Computer Applications Course Web Site

You will open in SharePoint Designer the Personal Computer Applications course Web site and use the Remote Web Site view to create a backup copy of it.

a. Start SharePoint Designer and open the chap3_cap_IT_course Web site folder.

b. Switch to Remote Web Site view and create a **chap3_cap_IT_course_solution** Web site.

c. Open the chap3_cap_IT_course_solution Remote Web site.

Develop an Instructors' Resources Subsite Using Microsoft Office Documents

You will create a new Instructors' Resources subsite, and you will export an Access Report object, as a .pdf file, into this subsite. You will add a link to the .pdf file and test the hyperlink in a browser.

a. Start Microsoft Access and open *chap3_cap_team_assignments.accdb*.

b. Export the Open Issues report as **open-issues.pdf** to the instructors folder of the chap3_cap_IT_course_solution Web site. Click the **Options button** on the Publish as PDF or XPS dialog box and make sure you click the **All option**, the **Document structure tags for accessibility check box**, and the **ISO 1905-1 compliant (PDF/A) check box** in the Options dialog box. Save Export Steps.

c. Click the **SharePoint Designer tab** on the taskbar and convert the instructors folder to a Web folder. Open the instructors Web folder in a new SharePoint Designer window.

d. Open *instructors.htm*. Type **Instructors' Resources** and format the text using the Heading 1 <h1> style. Beneath the <h1> heading, insert an **Open Issues** hyperlink to *open_issues.pdf*. The target of the hyperlink should be **New Window** and the ScreenTip text should be **Link to the team open issues report**.

e. Save **instructors.htm**. Preview *default.htm* in the Internet Explorer 7.0 browser, click the **Instructors hyperlink**, and click the **Open Issues hyperlink**. You should see *open-issues.pdf*.

Develop a Feedback Web Form for an Information Technology Course Web Site

You will create a feedback Web form using a SharePoint Designer general template.

a. Open the contact folder and then open *feedback.htm*. Attach the master.dwt Dynamic Web Template to *feedback.htm*. Highlight *Heading 2* and type **Feedback**. Press **Enter** and type **Use the form below to send feedback to the Course Faculty Coordinator**.

b. Insert a form including four input form fields that enable users to submit their name, e-mail address, subject, and message, as well as a Submit button and a Reset button. Use a table as the layout for the form fields. Each form field should have an initial value. Users are required to fill out all these form fields in order to submit their message.

c. Insert an explicit label for all form fields.

d. Use the Accessibility Reports to make sure *feedback.htm* has no accessibility problem(s).

e. Save **feedback.htm**, close the chap3_cap_IT_course_solution Web site, and exit SharePoint Designer.

Mini Cases

Use the rubric following the case as a guide to evaluate your work. However, keep in mind that your instructor may have additional grading criteria or may use a different standard to evaluate your work.

Creating a Stock Price Comparison Web Page for an E-Business Web Site

GENERAL CASE

You will develop a Stock Price Comparison Web page for the e-business Web site of an investment management company. Your e-business course professor provides you with a *chap3_mc1_stock_comparison* Excel workbook to use in creating the requested Web page. Because staff members who do not know how to handle an HTML document will need to update this Web page by modifying the Excel workbook, the Web page should be automatically republished every time the workbook is saved. Start Excel, open *chap3_mc1_stock_comparison*, and save it as **chap3_mc1_stock_comparison_solution**. Start SharePoint Designer, open the *chap3_mc1_ebusiness* Web site, and create a **chap3_mc1_ebusiness_solution** backup Web site using the Remote Web Site view. Open the *chap3_mc1_ebusiness_solution* Web site. Import the *chap3_mc1_stock_comparison_solution* workbook into the market_research folder. Double-click *chap3_mc1_stock_comparison_solution.xlsx* in the Folder List task pane to open in Excel the *chap3_mc1_stock_comparison_solution* workbook, and save it as **chap3_mc1_stock_comparison_solution.htm** (make sure you click the Autorepublish every time the workbook is saved check box in the Publish as Web Page dialog box) in the same market_research folder. Click the Excel tab corresponding to the *chap3_mc1_stock_comparison_solution* workbook in the market_research folder. Change the value of the Stock Price for 2006 from $30 to $32 and save the workbook. On the Microsoft Excel alert box (if it is showing) click the Enable the AutoRepublish option and click OK. Click the tab of the Internet Explorer window and click Refresh on the View menu. The Stock Price for 2006 should now be $32.

Performance Elements	Exceeds Expectations	Meets Expectations	Below Expectations
Import the Excel workbook	All requirements are correctly implemented.	All requirements are implemented.	No requirement was implemented.
Publish the Excel workbook as a Web page	All requirements are correctly implemented.	All requirements are implemented.	No requirement was implemented.
Modify the Excel workbook and republish it	All modifications and requirements are correctly implemented.	All modifications and requirements are implemented.	No modification or requirement was implemented.

Maximizing the Accessibility of the Stock Price Comparison Web Page for an E-Business Web Site

RESEARCH CASE

You have developed a Stock Price Comparison Web page for the e-business Web Site of an investment management company, starting from an Excel workbook. You want to make sure your Web page is in line with the Web Content Accessibility Guidelines (WCAG). Start SharePoint Designer, open the chap3_mc2_ebusiness Web site, and create a **chap3_mc2_ebusiness_solution** backup Web site using the Remote Web Site view. Open the chap3_mc2_ebusiness_solution Web site and open *chap3_mc2_stock_comparison.htm*. Run the Accessibility Checker. Go to the WebAIM Web site (http://www.webaim.org) and search the Web site for Creating Accessible Frames. Use Intellisense to eliminate all accessibility problems.

Performance Elements	Exceeds Expectations	Meets Expectations	Below Expectations
Identify the accessibility errors	Identifies all 4 accessibility errors.	Identifies 2 accessibility errors.	Identifies no accessibility errors.
Find useful information	Identifies and finds useful information for each error.	Information is too brief.	No information.
Accessibility Reports	Accessibility Reports runs with no errors.	Accessibility Reports runs with some errors.	Accessibility Reports runs with all errors.

Accessible Web Forms

DISASTER RECOVERY

Open the chap3_mc3_ebusiness Web site folder from the Exploring SharePoint Designer folder and create a **chap3_mc3_ebusiness _solution** backup Web site. Open the chap3_mc3_ebusiness_solution Web site, open the contact folder, and then open the *feedback.htm* Web page that contains several accessibility problems. Carefully study Appendices A and B. Use Intellisense and Accessibility Reports (make sure you select all three checkboxes in the Check for section— WCAG Priority 1, WCAG Priority 2, and Access Board Section 508—and the Errors and Warnings check boxes in the Show section) to help you identify the errors in *feedback.htm* related strictly to the form and form controls. Generate and save the accessibility HTML Report with the initial errors as **chap3_mc3_accessibility_report.htm**. Correct and explain all the errors related to the form and form controls.

Performance Elements	Exceeds Expectations	Meets Expectations	Below Expectations
Accessibility	Corrected all errors.	Corrected 1 error.	Corrected 0 errors.
Explain the error	Has a complete and correct explanation of each error.	Explanation is too brief to fully explain error.	No explanations.

Appendix A | **Microsoft Office SharePoint Designer 2007**

HTML, XHTML, XML, and CSS
Microsoft Office SharePoint Designer 2007
User-Friendly Tools for Working with HTML,
XHTML, XML, and CSS

Hypertext Markup Language (HTML) and Extensible Hypertext Markup Language (XHTML)

This book introduces you to the comprehensive set of tools that Microsoft Office SharePoint Designer 2007 offers to empower Web developers to create, edit, format, and optimize Hypertext Markup Language (HTML)/Extensible Hypertext Markup Language (XHTML) code without any actual HTML/XHTML knowledge. As stated earlier, in spite of the limitations and flaws of HTML, millions of Web pages have been, and continue to be, created with HTML. Consequently, a minimal level of HTML knowledge is a good addition to any Web developer's portfolio.

Let us start with a concise recap of what you have already learned about HTML/XHTML from this textbook's chapters, and let us also learn a little more about these two markup languages. The More Information section of this appendix provides a list of useful Web sites.

Getting Started with HTML

As discussed in Chapter 1, markup language is a language that describes the format of Web page content through the use of tags. Tags are specific codes that indicate how the text should be displayed when the document is opened in a Web browser. It is the job of the Web browsers to interpret these tags and render the text accordingly. Hypertext Markup Language (HTML), which was developed from the more complicated Standard Generalized Markup Language (SGML), is the markup language most commonly used to create Web pages. HTML is called the "language of the Web" because it defines the page layout and graphic elements of the page and provides links to other documents on the Web:

- HTML is the most common markup language.

TIP Physical and Logical Tags

Physical tags indicate the way information should be displayed and provide no indication about the type of information. Character tags are physical tags that format specific character selections. Character tags, such as <b> and <i>, are used for formatting. Although less common than physical tags, you can also use logical tags to format text in an HTML document. Logical tags, such as <strong> and <em>, concentrate on the type of information being displayed rather than how the information should be displayed. (The way logical tags are displayed is browser dependent, and future releases of HTML might not support certain logical tags.)

- Because HTML documents are created using unformatted text, you can create them in a simple text program (such as Windows Notepad), in a word processing program (such as Microsoft Word), or in a Web authoring program (such as SharePoint Designer 2007).
- HTML documents normally have the file extension .htm or .html.

TIP What is SHTML?

A Web file with the suffix of .shtml (rather than the usual .htm) indicates a file that includes some dynamic content that will be added by the server before it is sent to you. A typical use is to include a "Last modified" date at the bottom of the page.

- HTML documents need to follow a specific syntax, which is a set of standards or rules developed by the World Wide Web Consortium (W3C). The generic syntax of HTML tags that are used in pairs is <tag attributes> text </tag>. HTML tags are not case sensitive. Some HTML tags, such as the <br> tag that forces a break in the current line of text, are not used in pairs. W3C has created a set of standards indicating the correct format that should be applied to standard tags (http:// www.w3.org/MarkUp).
- In addition to the tags that define Web page elements, HTML provides attributes that further define the way elements are displayed in Web browsers. You can use these attributes to define the style, color, size, width, height, and source of the elements on your Web page. Web developers can assign a specific value to each attribute. The attribute of an HTML element is included within its start tag.
- You specify the style characteristics of the elements in your HTML using Cascading Style Sheets (CSS). W3C guidelines clearly indicate that standard HTML code should use styles in place of presentational attributes.
- HTML is not extensible, meaning it includes a finite set of tags and does not enable users to create their own custom tags (extensibility enables you to describe and define any new data by creating custom tags). Thus, it cannot be modified to meet the needs of specific developers. It does not enable users to structure, define, or process data. To add these features to a Web page, a Web developer needs to add code to the Web page. The code can be written in client-side scripting languages such as JavaScript, server-side scripting languages such as ASP.NET and JSP, or programming languages such as Java.

Getting Started with XHTML

XHTML is a newer markup language that was designed to overcome some of the problems generated by HTML. The main reason for considering XHTML as a transitional solution between HTML and XML is because XHTML is not extensible. Thus, until all browsers are upgraded to fully support Extensible Markup Language (XML), XHTML will continue to be used as a transitional solution.

Although there are many similarities between HTML and XHTML, there are also some important differences (see Figure A.1) such as the following:

- XHTML gives you the opportunity to write well-formed and valid documents that work in all browsers and that can be read by all XML-enabled applications. XHTML code has to be well-formed and valid.

- XHTML tags and attribute names must be lowercase.

- XHTML tags are case sensitive.

- In XHTML, the empty tags that were inherited from HTML, such as <img>, <br>, and <hr>, have the following syntax: <img/>, <br/>, and <hr/>.

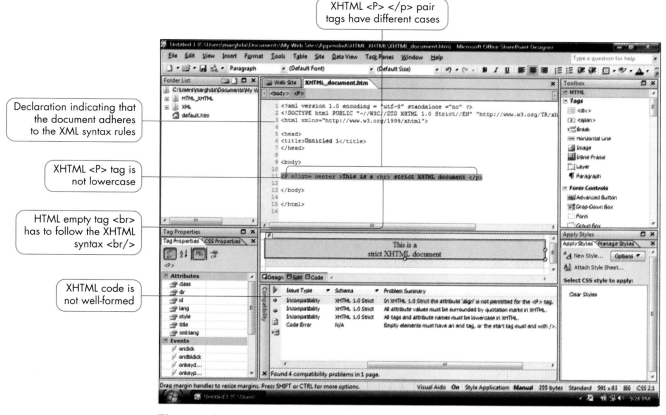

Figure A.1 Main Differences Between HTML and XHTML Documents

TIP   Creating an XHTML Document

Because all XHTML documents are also XML documents, the first line in any XHTML document should include a declaration indicating that the document adheres to the XML syntax rules, as shown in Figure A.1.

Developing Standard HTML/XHTML Documents

The way a Web page is displayed in different browsers can vary. Fonts, colors, tables, and hyperlinks are only a few of the many Web page elements that can appear differently, for example, in Mozilla® Firefox® than they do in Microsoft Internet Explorer.

The same Web page might also be displayed differently on computers using different operating systems. Fonts and colors are some of the Web page elements that might look different on an Apple® computer or a Sun® workstation than they do on a computer that uses Windows. Although organizations and corporations around the world are working on ways to eliminate these two issues, usually called cross-browser and cross-platform issues, they still pose a problem for Web developers.

To overcome the cross-browser and cross-platform issues, W3C declared many older HTML tags and tag attributes as deprecated, meaning that they might not be supported by all browsers. W3C has defined three variations of HTML 4.01 (http://www.w3.org/TR/REC-html40) and XHTML 1.0 (http://www.w3.org/TR/xhtml1): strict, transitional, and frameset. The strict version prohibits the use of any deprecated tag. The only difference between transitional and frameset is that the latter allows frames. When developing a Web page, you can indicate which version and variation you implement by using a DOCTYPE declaration like the one shown in Figure A.1.

DOCTYPE Declarations for HTML and XHTML | Reference

DTD	DOCTYPE
HTML 4.01 strict	<!DOCTYPE HTML PUBLIC "-//W3C//DTD HTML 4.01//EN" "http://www.w3.org/TR/html4/strict.dtd">
HTML 4.01 transitional	<!DOCTYPE HTML PUBLIC "-//W3C//DTD HTML 4.01 Transitional//EN" "http://www.w3.org/TR/1999/REC-html401-19991224/loose.dtd">
HTML 4.01 frameset	<!DOCTYPE HTML PUBLIC "-//W3C//DTD HTML 4.01 Frameset//EN" "http://www.w3.org/TR/1999/REC-html401-19991224/frameset.dtd">
XHTML 1.0 strict	<!DOCTYPE HTML PUBLIC "-//W3C//DTD XHTML 1.0 Strict//EN" "http://www.w3.org/TR/xhtml1/DTD/xhtml1-strict.dtd">
XHTML 1.0 transitional	<!DOCTYPE HTML PUBLIC "-//W3C//DTD XHTML 1.0 Transitional//EN" "http://www.w3.org/TR/xhtml1/DTD/xhtml1-transitional.dtd">
XHTML 1.0 frameset	<!DOCTYPE HTML PUBLIC "-//W3C//DTD XHTML 1.0 Frameset//EN" "http://www.w3.org/TR/xhtml1/DTD/xhtml1-frameset.dtd"

Once you finish a draft of your Web page, you can use a validator application to evaluate and see if it is in-line with the version and variation of the markup you used. W3C offers a freeware Markup Validation Service (http://validator.w3.org) that checks the markup validity of Web documents in HTML, XHTML, and so forth.

To help eliminate cross-browser and cross-platform issues, all browser manufacturers should comply with the W3C standards. Unfortunately, this is not always the case. Therefore, Web developers need to continue their efforts to develop standard Web sites that overcome cross-browser and cross-platform challenges.

Getting Started with Common HTML and XHTML Elements and Attributes

Table A.1 contains a listing of common HTML and XHTML elements and attributes, including the syntax of the tags and attributes and a short description. The Description column also indicates whether the HTML tag or any of its attributes are deprecated.

Table A.1 SharePoint Designer Status Bar Common HTML and XHTML Elements and Attributes

Type of Element	Element and Attribute	Description
Structure Tags	<html> . . . </html>	Encloses the entire HTML document.
	version="text"	Indicates the version of the HTML.
	<head> . . . </head>	Encloses the head of the HTML document.
	<body> . . . </body>	Encloses the body of the document.
	alink="color"	Indicates the color of active links; deprecated.
	background="url"	Indicates the file of the background image; deprecated.
	bgcolor="color"	Indicates the background color; deprecated.
	link="color"	Indicates the color of unvisited links.
	text="color"	Indicates the color of the page text; deprecated.
	vlink="color"	Indicates the color of visited links; deprecated.
	<!-- . . . -->	Indicates the beginning and the end of comments.
Title and Headings	<title> . . . </title>	Indicates the title of the document.
	<hi> . . . </hi>	Indicates the format of the included text as a heading, where the index i can vary between 1 for the smallest heading and 6 for the largest heading.
	align="left | center | right | justify"	Indicates the horizontal alignment of the heading text (left is the default value); deprecated.
Paragraphs	<p> . . . </p>	Indicates the formatting of the included text as a plain paragraph.
	align="left | center | right | justify"	Indicates the horizontal alignment of the heading text (left is the default value); deprecated.
	href="url"	Creates a link to another document or anchor.
	name="text"	Creates an anchor that can be a link target.

(continued)

	shape="rect | circle | polygon"	Indicates the shape hotspot used when creating an image map.
	title="text"	Indicates the ScreenTip text that will be displayed in a browser every time a user hovers the mouse over the link
	type="A | a | I | i | 1 | disc | square | circle"	Indicates the type of bullet or number/letter to be used to format the list; deprecated.
	value="integer"	Resets a list item number of an ordered/numbered list; deprecated.
	<menu> . . . </menu>	A menu list of items; deprecated.
	<dir> . . . </dir>	A directory listing; deprecated.
	<dl> . . . </dl>	A definition of glossary list.
	<dt> . . . </dt>	A definition term, part of a definition list.
	<dd> . . . </dd>	The definition that corresponds to a definition term.
	<ol> . . . </ol>	Indicates the beginning and ending of an ordered, numbered list.
	compact="compact"	Indicates the space between the list items; deprecated.
	start="integer"	Indicates the start value in the list.
	<ul> . . . </ul>	Indicates the beginning and end of an unordered, bulleted list.
	compact="compact"	Indicates the space between the list items; deprecated.
	type="disc | square | circle"	Indicates the type of bullet used to format the list; deprecated.
Tables	<table> . . . <table>	Indicates the beginning and the end of a table.
	align="left | center | right"	Indicates the horizontal alignment of the table; deprecated.
	background="url"	Indicates the URL of the image used as table background.
	bgcolor="color"	Indicates the color used as table background; deprecated.
	border="integer"	Indicates the size, in pixels, of the table border.
	bordercolor="color"	Indicates the color of the table border.
	cellpadding="integer"	Indicates the space, in pixels, between the table content and the cells' borders.
	cellspacing="integer"	Indicates the space, in pixels, between the table cells.
	cols="integer"	Indicates the number of columns in the table.

	height="integer"	Indicates the height, in pixels, of the table.
	width="integer"	Indicates the width, in pixels, of the table.
	\<tr> . . . \</tr>	Indicates the beginning and the end of a row in a table.
	align="left | center | right"	Indicates the horizontal alignment of the row; deprecated.
	background="url"	Indicates the URL of the image used as row background.
	bgcolor="color"	Indicates the color used as row background; deprecated.
	bordercolor="color"	Indicates the color of the row border.
	height="integer"	Indicates the height, in pixels, of the row.
	valign="baseline | bottom | middle | top"	Indicates the vertical alignment of the row content.
	\<td> . . . \</td>	Indicates the beginning and the end of a cell in a table.
	align="left | center | right"	Indicates the horizontal alignment of the cell; deprecated.
	background="url"	Indicates the URL of the image used as cell background.
	bgcolor="color"	Indicates the color used as cell background; deprecated.
	bordercolor="color"	Indicates the color of the cell border.
	colspan="integer"	Indicates the number of columns the cell spans.
	height="integer"	Indicates the height, in pixels, of the cell.
	nowrap="nowrap"	Disallows line wrapping within the table cell.
	rowspan="integer"	Indicates the number of rows the cell spans.
	valign="baseline | bottom | middle | top"	Indicates the vertical alignment of the cell content.
	width="integer"	Indicates the width, in pixels, of the cell.
	\<th> . . . \</th>	Indicates the beginning and the ending of a table header cell.
	align="left | center | right"	Indicates the horizontal alignment of the table header cell; deprecated.
	background="url"	Indicates the URL of the image used as table header cell background.

(continued)

		bgcolor="color"	Indicates the color used as table header cell background; deprecated.
		bordercolor="color"	Indicates the color of the table header cell border.
		colspan="integer"	Indicates the number of columns the table header cell spans.
		height="integer"	Indicates the height, in pixels, of the table header cell.
		nowrap="true | false"	Allows/disallows line wrapping within the table header cell.
		rowspan="integer"	Indicates the number of rows the table header cell spans.
		valign="baseline | bottom | middle | top"	Indicates the vertical alignment of the table header content.
		width="integer"	Indicates the width, in pixels, of the table header cell.
		<caption> . . . </caption>	Creates a table caption.
		align="bottom | left | center | right | top"	Indicates the alignment of the caption; deprecated.
		valign="top | bottom"	Indicates the vertical alignment of the caption; deprecated.
Frames		<frameset> . . . </frameset>	Creates a set of frames.
		cols="value list"	Indicates the layout of the frames in columns with the width specified in pixels, as percentage, or by an asterisk (the asterisk enables the browser to select the width).
		frameborder="1 | 0"	Indicates whether the frame border is visible.
		framespacing="integer"	Indicates, in pixels, the space in between frames.
		rows="value list"	Indicates the layout of the frames in rows with the height specified in pixels, as percentage, or by an asterisk (the asterisk enables the browser to select the width).
		border="integer"	Indicates, in pixels, the thickness of the frame border.
		bordercolor="color"	Indicates the color of the frame border.
		marginheight="integer"	Indicates, in pixels, the up and down space between the frame content and frame border.
		marginwidth="integer"	Indicates, in pixels, the left and right space between the frame content and frame border.
		name="text"	Indicates the frame name.

	noresize="noresize"	Does not allow users to resize a frame.
	scrolling="auto | yes | no"	Enables the browser to display or not display the scrollbar.
	src="url"	Indicates the URL of the Web page to be displayed in the frame.
	`<noframes>` . . . `</noframes>`	Alternate code for browsers that do not support frames
Character Formatting	`<b>` . . . `</b>`	Formats the enclosed text as bolded.
	`<em>` . . . `</em>`	Indicates emphasis text, usually italic.
	`<i>` . . . `</i>`	Formats the enclosed text as italic.
	`<strong>` . . . `</strong>`	Indicates stronger emphasis text, usually bold.
	`<sub>` . . . `</sub>`	Formats the enclosed text as subscripted.
	`<sup>` . . . `</sup>`	Formats the enclosed text as superscripted.
Forms	`<form>` . . . `</form>`	Marks the beginning and the ending of a Web page form.
	action="url"	Indicates the URL where the data collected by the form will be sent.
	method="get | post"	Indicates the method used to access the URL specified in the action attribute.
	name="text"	Indicates the form name.
	target="text"	Indicates the window (or frame) where the output of the form will be displayed.
Script	`<script>` . . . `</script>`	Places client-side scripts within an HTML document.
	event="text"	Indicates the event causing the script to be run.
	language="text"	Provides the language of the script; deprecated.
	src="url"	Indicates the URL of an external script.
	`<noscript>` . . . `</noscript>`	Encloses HTML tags for browsers that do not support client-side scripts.
Applet	`<applet>` . . . `</applet>`	Places a Java™ applet in an HTML document; deprecated.
	`<object>` . . . `</object>`	Places a Java applet and other embedded objects, such as an audio or video clip, in an HTML document.
	align="absbottom | absmiddle | baseline | bottom | left | middle | right | texttop | top | "	Indicates the alignment of an object within the body of a Web page.

(continued)

	border="integer"	Indicates, in pixels, the width of the border around the object; deprecated.
	classid="url"	Indicates the URL of the object.
	data="url"	Indicates the URL of the object's data file.
	datasrc="url"	Indicates the URL or ID of the data source bound to the object.
	height="integer"	Indicates, in pixels, the height of the object.
	name="text"	Indicates the name of the embedded object.
	width="integer"	Indicates, in pixels, the width of the object.
Images	`<img> . . . </img>`	Inserts an inline image into the document.
	src="URL"	Indicates the URL of the image to display.
	align="absbottom | absmiddle | baseline | bottom | left | middle | right | texttop | top | "	Indicates the alignment of an image within the body of a Web page; deprecated.
	alt="text"	Indicates the text displayed instead of the image if the browser does not display images.
	border="integer"	Indicates, in pixels, the width of the image border; deprecated.
	height="integer"	Indicates, in pixels, the height of the image.
	name="text"	Indicates the name of the image.
	width="integer"	Indicates, in pixels, the width of the image.
Other Elements	`<hr />`	Inserts a horizontal rule line.
	` `	Inserts a line break.
CSS Elements	`<style>` style declarations`</style>`	Defines a document's global style declaration—the declaration of a specific style applied to the document.
	type="mime_type"	Indicates the MIME type of the style sheet language (for CSS, it is "text/css").
	media="all | aural | Braille | handheld | print | projection | screen | tty | tv | "	Indicates the media used to display the style definition.
	title="text"	Indicates the title of the style definition.

Cascading Style Sheets

This book introduces you to the comprehensive set of tools that SharePoint Designer 2007 offers to empower Web developers to create, edit, modify, and optimize CSS styles without any actual CSS knowledge.

Let us start with a concise recap of what you already learned about CSS from this textbook's chapters, and let us also learn a little more about this style sheet language. The More Information section of this appendix includes a list of related Web sites.

Getting Started with CSS

Style sheets describe how documents are presented on screens, in print, or even how they are pronounced. Style sheet languages are computer languages for expressing style sheets. Although several style sheet languages have been developed, CSS is a robust formatting language that successfully separates a Web page's content from its appearance. CSS has become the standard style sheet language used on the Web. The Extensible Style Sheet (XSL) was developed by the W3C as an improved method for formatting XML documents, allowing developers to transform XML data files into a wide variety of popular file formats, such as HTML and portable document format (PDF). XSL is still supported by fewer browsers than CSS. Although the CSS was initially developed for HTML, it is currently used in HTML, XML, and XHTML.

You can use three different types of CSS style codes to format the HTML/XHTML code of your Web pages, inline styles, internal styles, and external styles. An inline style takes precedence over an internal style, which takes precedence over an external style sheet. If you have two styles with the same weight in a document, the style declared last has precedence.

CSS Types | Reference

CSS Type	Definition
Inline styles	Inline style codes are included in the start tag by using the tag's style attributes. Inline style codes override the styles defined in internal and external styles.
Internal styles	Internal style codes are usually included in the \<head> section of an HTML document and have the following syntax: \<style>style declarations\</style>. Internal style codes override the format defined in a linked external style sheet.
External styles	External style codes are included in separate files used to specify the formatting of any HTML document to which they are linked. These style codes are kept in a document with a .css file extension and are linked to the HTML document using the \<link> HTML tag.

TIP Linking External Style Sheets

An external style sheet also can be linked using the CSS @import directive added inside the HTML \<style> tag. The CSS @import directive is not supported by old browsers, such as Netscape® Navigator™ 4.0.

A single style defines the look of one Web page element by simply telling a Web browser how to format the content of a Web page, from turning a headline blue to drawing a table with an orange border. A style actually consists of two elements:

1. The Web page element that will be formatted by the browser, named the selector.

2. The formatting instructions, named the declaration block.

However, even a simple style like the one illustrated in Figure A.2 contains several elements, as illustrated in Figure A.3:

- **Selector:** Indicates to a Web browser which element(s) within a Web page to style. In Figures A.2 and A.3, the selector a refers to the tag \<a>; hence, the Web browser will format all \<a> tags using the formatting directions included in this style.

- **Declaration Block:** Starts with an opening brace { and ends with closing brace }. It includes all the formatting options to be applied to the selector.

- **Declaration:** The declaration block is comprised of one or more declarations, also known as formatting instructions. Each declaration includes a property and a value.

- **Property:** A property is a word or a group of hyphenated words indicating a style effect. In Figures A.2 and A.3, color and text-decoration are properties of the \<a> tag.

- **Value:** A value is required to be assigned to any property. In Figures A.2 and A.3, #04b is the value of the color property and underline is the value of the text-decoration property of the \<a> tag.

```
a {color: #04b; text-decoration: underline;}
```

Figure A.2 CSS Style

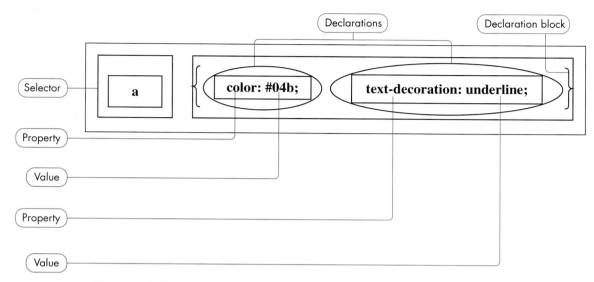

Figure A.3 Anatomy of a CSS Style

The CSS style selectors allow you to single out one specific Web page element or a collection of similar Web page elements:

- **Tag selectors:** Apply the style to all occurrences of the HTML tag. Tag selectors are easy to distinguish in a document because they have the same name as the HTML tag they style. For example, in the Web page shown in Figure A.4, a style was created for the p tag selector. Therefore, all the <p> tag occurrences implement this style.

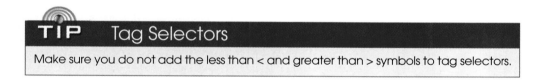

TIP Tag Selectors

Make sure you do not add the less than < and greater than > symbols to tag selectors.

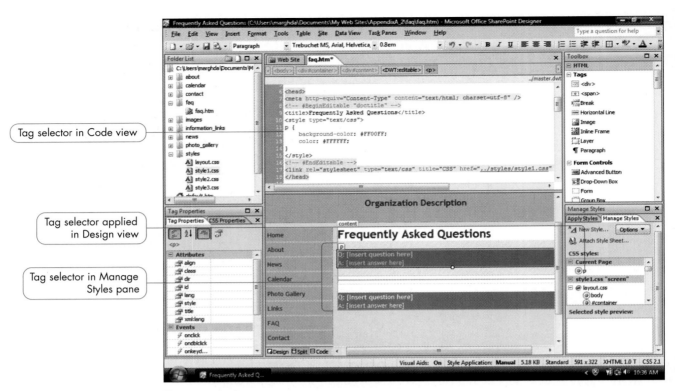

Figure A.4 Example of Tag Selector

- **Class selectors:** Apply to HTML sections of your Web page that can be, for example, identified by the <div> or <span> tags. Class selectors start with a period, and they are case sensitive. After the period, the name must start with a letter and can include only letters, numbers, hyphens, and underscores. They are usually defined in the head section of a Web page or in an external style sheet. For example, in the Web page shown in Figure A.5, a .style_bold class selector was created in the Web page's attached external style sheet and applied using the <span> tags.

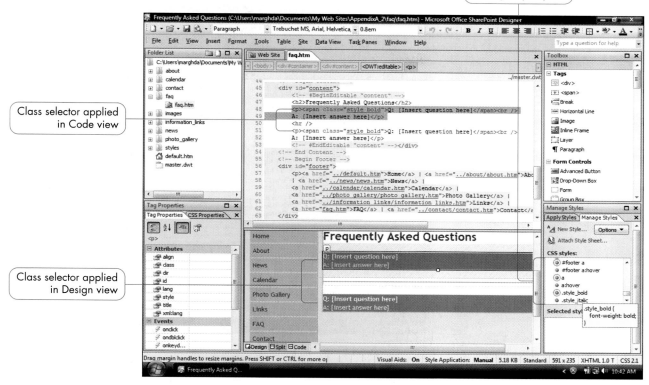

Figure A.5   Example of Class Selector

- **ID selectors:** Because they are connected to the id attribute of a Web page element and the id must be unique, ID selectors are used for identifying unique parts of your Web page, such as banners, navigation bars, or main content area. For example, in the Web page shown in Figure A.6, a #navigation id selector style was created in the Web page's attached external style sheet and applied to the section <div id = "navigation">.

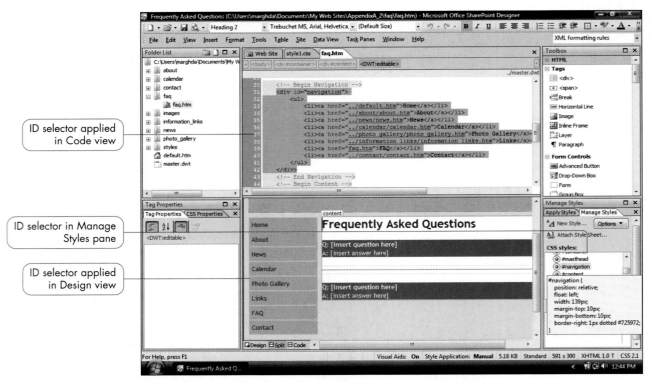

Figure A.6 Example of ID Selector

TIP Should I Use a Class or an ID?

When you need to use a style several times, you must use classes. When a browser encounters a class and ID for the same tag, it gives priority to the ID.

Developing Standard CSSs

One of the biggest advantages to using CSSs is that when the style sheet is changed, all the Web pages created with that style sheet are automatically updated. Although the CSS is useful and has experienced rapid growth on the WWW, it can still generate some problems. For example, some browsers still do not fully support it.

The specifications for CSS are maintained by W3C (http://www.w3.org/Style/CSS) and are made up of various levels, or versions, and profiles. Desktop browsers implement CSS level 1, 2, or 3, whereas other applications implement CSS profiles appropriate to their platform, such as PDA, cellular phone, television, printer, and speech synthesizer:

- CSS level 1 was developed between 1996 and 1999 and includes properties for fonts, margins, colors, and more.

- CSS level 2 was introduced in 1998 and includes all of CSS level 1, as well as new styles related to absolutely positioned elements, automatic numbering, page breaks, right to left text, and more.

- CSS level 3 is currently under development and includes all of CSS level 2, as well as new styles related to user interaction, accessibility, and speech.

- CSS Mobile Profile 1.0 (http://www.w3.org/TR/css-mobile) is for devices such as mobile phones and PDAs.

- CSS TV Profile 1.0 (http://www.w3.org/TR/css-tv) is for browsers that run on television sets.

- CSS Print Profile (http://www.w3.org/TR/css-print) is currently in the draft stage and is aimed at low-cost printers.

TIP   Always Think About the Users' Needs

You should be aware that a visitor can override any applied style to your Web pages. The best example is the Internet Explorer Accessibility dialog box, which is used mainly by people with disabilities to apply their own style sheet. Visitor style sheets take precedence over your style sheet and their browser's default styles. Thus, as discussed in Appendix B, your Web pages should be able to display properly with or without a style sheet.

Getting Started with Common CSS Styles and Attributes and Values

If you do not specify a style for an element of your Web page, the element inherits the style of its parent element. For example, all the styles specified for the <body> element will apply to any included <p> element that does not have a specified style. Some attributes use CSS units of measure to indicate properties, such as color, length, and spacing. For example, as discussed in Chapter 2, the text size can be expressed in HTML and CSS using a rather wide selection of units: keywords, ems, exs, pixels, percentages, picas, points, and even inches, centimeters, and millimeters. However, among these measurement units, only pixels, keywords, ems, and percentages are commonly used for sizing text for a computer monitor. When using these four measurement units, the text size is set either by adding to or subtracting from the text size already set on the viewer's browser screen. Hence, if you do not specify a size for text using CSS, Web browsers apply their base font size, which for most browsers is 16 pixels.

To learn about the CSS units of measure, visit the Webmonkey *Reference Stylesheets Guide* Web site (http://webmonkey.wired.com/webmonkey/reference/stylesheet_ guide/units.html).

Table A.2 includes the most common CSS styles, their common attributes, and standard values. The W3C working group is a dynamic one. To keep up with the most recent CSS developments, visit the W3C *Cascading Style Sheets* Web site (http://www.w3.org/Style/CSS).

Table A.2   CSS 2.1 Common Styles

	Style Syntax	Style Description	Style Values	Style Values Description
Background Style (http://www.w3.org/TR/CSS21/ colors.html#q2)	Background-color: color	Indicates the color of the background.	Keyword: inherit	Inherits the background color of the parent.
	See W3C CSS21 Specification (14.2.1) background-color for details.		Keyword: transparent	Shows the background image of the parent element.
			A CSS color name or value	Shows the background color indicated.

(continued)

	Background-image: url(url) See W3C CSS21 Specification (14.2.1) background-image for details.	Indicates the image file applied as background.	URL	The URL of the image file
	Background-position: x y See W3C CSS21 Specification (14.2.1) background-position for details.	Indicates the position of the background image.	The keywords left, center, or right, and top, center, or bottom Pixels or percentage of the parent element's width/ height	For the horizontal and vertical position of the background image The X and Y coordinates of background image in pixels or as percentage of the parent element's width/height
Box_model Style (http://www.w3.org/ TR/CSS21/box.html)	border: border-width border-style color See W3C CSS21 Specification (8.5) Border Properties for details.	Indicates the element border width, style, and color.	CSS units of measure Style A CSS color name or value	The width of the border The border design The border color
	margin: top, right, bottom, left See W3C CSS21 Specification (8.3) Margin Properties for details.	Indicates the size of the margins.	CSS units of measure CSS units of measure CSS units of measure CSS units of measure	The element margin size at the top The element margin size to the right The element margin size at the bottom The element margin size to the left
	Padding: top, right, bottom, left See W3C CSS21 Specification (8.4) Padding Properties for details.	Indicates the size of element padding.	CSS units of measure CSS units of measure CSS units of measure CSS units of measure	The element padding along the top margin The element padding along the right margin The element padding along the bottom margin The element padding along the left margin
Content Style (http:// www.w3.org/TR/ CSS21/generate. html#content)	Content: attr(X)	Provides the value of the element's X attribute.	String	The value of the element's attribute
	Content: text	Creates a text string and attaches it to the element's content.	Text string	The text string created and attached to the element's content

	Content: url (url)	Indicates the URL of an external file that will be attached to the element.	URL	The URL of the external file
Display Style				
Visual Effects (http://www.w3.org/TR/CSS21/visufx.html)	Clip: rect(top, right, bottom, left) See W3C CSS21 Specification (11.1.2) Clipping: the 'clip' property for details.	Indicates the portion of the content section that will be displayed.	CSS units of measure	Top, bottom, right, and left specify offsets of the top, bottom, right, and left edges from the upper-left corner of the element
			Keywords: auto and inherit	Enable browser to determine the clipping region
	Overflow: length See W3C CSS21 Specification (11.1.1) Overflow: the 'overflow' property for details.	Provides browser with the way it should handle content that overflows the element's dimensions.	Keyword: Hidden	Indicates that the content is clipped and that no scrolling user interface should be provided to view the content outside the clipping region
			Keyword: scroll	Indicates that the content is clipped and that if the Web page visitor uses a scrolling mechanism that is visible on the screen (such as a scrollbar) a mechanism should be displayed for a box whether or not any of its content is clipped
			Keyword: visible	Indicates that content is not clipped, and thus it may be rendered outside the block box
			Keyword: auto	Causes a scrolling mechanism to be provided for over-flowing boxes
			Keyword: inherit	Takes the same value as the property for the element's parent
	Visibility: length See W3C CSS21 (11.2) Specification Visibility: the 'visibility' property for details.	Indicates the element's visibility.	Keyword: hidden	Indicates that the element is invisible or fully transparent
			Keyword: collapse	When used for row, row group, column, and column group,

(continued)

				elements collapse; causes the entire row or column to be removed from the display and the space normally taken up by the row or column to be available for other content.
			Keyword: visible	Indicates that the element is visible.
			Keyword: inherit	Takes the same value as the property for the element's parent.
Visual Formatting (http://www.w3.org/ TR/CSS21/visuren. html#display-prop)	Display: type See W3C CSS21 (9.2.4) Specification the 'display' property.	Indicates the display type of the element.	Keywords: block, inline, inline-block, inherit, list-item, none, run-in, table, inline-table,table-caption, table-column, table-cell, table-column-group, table-header-group, table-footer-group, table-row, and table-row-group	Keyword block causes the element to generate a block box. Keyword inline causes the element to generate one or more inline boxes. Keyword list-item causes the element to generate a principal block box and a list-item inline box. Keyword none causes the element to generate no boxes in the formatting structure, which means that the element has no effect on layout.
Fonts and Text Style				
Colors (http://www.w3. org/TR/CSS21/ colors.html#propdef-color)	Color: color See W3C CSS21 Specification (14.1) Foreground color: the 'color' property.	Indicates the element foreground color.	Keyword: inherit CSS color name or a color value	
Fonts (http:// www.w3.org/ TR/CSS21/fonts. html)	Font-family: family See W3C CSS21 Specification (15.3) Font family: the 'font-family' property for details.	Indicates the font face used for displaying the text.	Keywords: sans serif, serif, fantasy, monospace, cursive, inherit, or the name of another installed font	
	Font-style: family See W3C CSS21 Specification (15.4)	Indicates the font style used for displaying the text.	Keywords: normal, italic oblique, and inherit	

	Font styling: the 'font-style' property for details.			
	Font-variant: type See W3C CSS21 Specification (15.5) Small-caps: the 'font-variant' property for details.	Indicates a variant of the font.	Keywords: inherit, normal, small-caps	
	Font-weight: value See W3C CSS21 Specification (15.6) Font boldness: the 'font-weight' property for details.	Indicates the weight of the font.	100, 200, 300, 400, 500, 600, 700, 800, 900 Keywords: normal, lighter, bolder or bold	
	Font-size: value See W3C CSS21 Specification (15.7) Font size: the 'font-size' property for details.	Indicates the size of the font.	Keyword: inherit CSS units of measure.	
Text Style (http://www.w3. org/TR/CSS21/ text.html)	Letter-spacing: value See W3C CSS21 Specification (16.4) Letter and word spacing: the 'letter-spacing' and 'word-spacing' properties for details.	Indicates the space between text's letters.	Keywords: normal, inherit CSS units of measure.	
	Text-align: type See W3C CSS21 Specification (16.2) Alignment: the 'text-align' property for details.	Indicates the horizontal alignment of the text.	Keywords: inherit, left, right, center, or justify	
	Text-decoration: type See W3C CSS21 Specification (16.3.1) Underlining, overlining, striking, and blinking: the 'text-decoration' property for details.	Indicates the type of decoration applied to the text.	Keywords: blink, line-through, none, overline, underline, inherit	
	Text-indent: length See W3C CSS21 Specification (16.1) Indentation: the 'text-indent' property for details.	Indicates the size of the first line of text's indentation.	CSS units of measure Percentage of the containing block width Keyword: inherit	

(continued)

	Text-transform: type See W3C CSS21 Specification (16.5) Capitalization: the 'text-transform' property for details.	Indicates a text case transformation.	Keywords: capitalize, lower case, none, upper case, or inherit	
	White-space: type See W3C CSS21 Specification (16.6) White space: the 'white-space' property for details.	Indicates the way white space (such as new lines, tabs, and blanks) should be handled.	Keywords: inherit, normal, pre (for handling text as preformatted text), or no wrap (for disabling the line-wrapping)	
	Word-spacing: length See W3C CSS21 Specification (16.4) Letter and word spacing: the 'letter-spacing' and 'word-spacing' properties for details.	Indicates the space between words included in text.	CSS units of measure Keyword: normal Keyword: inherit	When using normal space between words
Visual Formatting Style (http://www. w3.org/TR/CSS21/ visudet.html)	Vertical-align: type See W3C CSS21 Specification (10.8) vertical-align property for details.	Indicates the vertical alignment of the text with the surrounding content.	Keywords: baseline, middle, top, bottom, text-bottom, text-top, sub, super, inherit A percentage or CSS units of measure	
	Height: length See W3C CSS21 Specification (10.5) content height property for details.	Indicates the height of the element.	Keywords: auto or inherit CSS units of measure Percentage of the box's height	The element's height
	Width: length See W3C CSS21 Specification (10.5) content height property for details.	Indicates the width of the element.	Keywords: auto or inherit CSS units of measure Percentage of the box's width	The element's width
Layout (http://www.w3.org/ TR/CSS21/visuren. html)	Clear: type See W3C CSS21 Specification (9.5.2) Controlling flow next to floats: the 'clear' property for details.	Indicates the placement of the element after the selected margin is clear of any floating elements.	Keywords: inherit, none, left, right, both	
	Float: type See the W3C CSS21 Specification (9.5.1) Positioning the float: the 'float' property for details.	Indicates how the element, with content wrapped around it, will float on the selected box.	Keywords: inherit, none, left, or right	

Position: type	Indicates the element's positioning on the page.	Keyword: absolute	The element's position is specified with the 'top', 'right', 'bottom', and 'left' properties
See W3C CSS21 Specification (9.3) Choosing a positioning scheme: 'position' property for details.		Keyword: relative	The element's position is calculated according to the normal flow (or the position in normal flow)
		Keyword: fixed	The element's position is calculated according to the 'absolute' model, and the element is fixed with respect to some reference
		Keyword: static	The element's position is calculated according to the 'absolute' model, and the element is fixed with respect to some reference
		Keyword: inherit	The element's position is a normal box, laid out according to the normal flow. The 'top', 'right', 'bottom', and 'left' properties don't apply
Top: y See W3C CSS21 Specification (9.3.2) Box offsets: 'top', 'right', 'bottom', 'left' for details.	Indicates the vertical offset for the element's top edge.	CSS units of measure Percentage of the height of containing block Keywords: auto, inherit	
Right: x See W3C CSS21 Specification (9.3.2) Box offsets: 'top', 'right', 'bottom', 'left' for details.	Indicates the horizontal offset for the element's right edge.	CSS units of measure Percentage of the width of containing block Keywords: auto, inherit	
Bottom: y See W3C CSS21 Specification (9.3.2) Box offsets: 'top', 'right', 'bottom', 'left' for details.	Indicates the vertical offset for the element's bottom edge.	CSS units of measure Percentage of the height of containing block Keywords: auto, inherit	

(continued)

	Left: x See W3C CSS21 Specification (9.3.2) Box offsets: 'top', 'right', 'bottom', 'left' for details.	Indicates the horizontal offset for the element's left edge.	CSS units of measure Percentage of the width of the containing block Keywords: auto, inherit	
	Z-index: value See W3C CSS21 Specification (9.9.1) Specifying the stack level: the 'z-index' property for details.	Indicates the level of a box in a stack of overlapping elements.	An integer number. Keywords: auto, inherit	The stacking number
Lists Style (http://www.w3. org/TR/CSS21/ generate.html#q10)	List-style: list-style-type list-style-positionlist-style -image See W3C CSS21 Specification list-style (12.5.1) for details.	Specify the list style.	Keywords: disc, circle, square, decimal, decimal-leading-zero, lower-roman, upper-roman, lower-alpha, upper-alpha, and inherit Keywords: outside, inside URL Keywords: URL	Indicates the type of bullet or number used to create the list. Specifies the position of the marker Specifies the URL of the image file to be used as list marker.
	Marker-offset: length See the W3C CSS2 Markers: the 'marker-offset' property (12.6.1) for details.	Indicates the distance between the list marker and the box enclosing the list.	CSS units of measure Keywords: auto, inherit	
Tables Style (http://www.w3.org/ TR/CSS21/tables. html)	Border-collapse: type See W3C CSS21 Specification (17.6) Table Borders.	Selects a table border model.	Keyword: separate Keyword: collapse Keyword: inherit	Selects the sep-arated table border model Selects the collapsing table border model The style is inherited from the parent element
	Table-layout: type See W3C CSS21 Specification (17.5.2) Table width algorithms: the 'table-layout' property.	Indicates the algorithm in use for the table layout.	Keyword: auto Keyword: fixed Keyword: inherit	The layout is automatically established after all cells have been read The layout is established after the first row of the table is read The layout is inherited from the parent element.

SharePoint Designer 2007 Tools for Working with HTML, XHTML, and CSS

One of the greatest strengths of SharePoint Designer is that Web developers can use the SharePoint Designer graphical user interface to create a wide variety of Web pages and Web sites without extensive knowledge of HTML and XHTML. This interface shows you the page in WYSIWYG, which means What You See Is What You Get. In other words, the Web page looks nearly the same in SharePoint Designer as it does in a browser. SharePoint Designer 2007 excels in offering user-friendly tools that enable all categories of Web developers, from beginners to professionals, to work with HTML and XHTML code and CSS styles.

Let us review and learn more about the SharePoint Designer core tools for working with HTML, XHTML, and CSS. The More Information section of this appendix includes a list of related Web sites.

Working in SharePoint Designer 2007 with HTML and XHTML

SharePoint Designer 2007 includes a comprehensive set of tools that enable Web developers to create, edit, format, and optimize the HTML/XHTML code of their Web pages. Some of the most relevant tools are described here:

- **Code view and Split view**—These two views are extremely helpful for editing and formatting HTML/XHTML. Code view shows the HTML/XHTML code of the Web page. Split view, on the other hand, splits the screen into two horizontal sections: one displaying the Design view of the Web page and the second displaying the Code view of the Web page. When a designer selects an element or section of a Web page in the Design view side, that section is automatically highlighted in the Code view section, and vice versa.

- **IntelliSense tool**—The IntelliSense tool is a great built-in tutor for developers. It provides a content-specific list of HTML/XHTML code entries to select. If you type < while editing in Code view, or in the Code view section of Split view, SharePoint Designer2007 displays a list of appropriate HTML/XHTML tags for that specific HTML/XHTML section of the Web page. It provides the same type of assistance when typing an attribute of an HTML/XHTML tag.

- **XML formatting rules**—The Apply XML Formatting Rules tool is available in Code view and Split view (right-click the body of the Web page, and then click Apply XML Formatting Rules) and applies to the HTML/XHTML code XML formatting rules, such as end tags.

- **Accessibility and Compatibility tools**—The Accessibility Checker and Compatibility Checker are extremely powerful in assisting Web developers to create standard accessible and usable Web sites.

- **Find and Replace HTML tags**—This tool enables Web developers to perform more sophisticated searches using the HTML Rules feature, which enables you to create detailed search rules. With these detailed rules, you can refine the search to include HTML/XHTML tags, as well as their attributes and attribute values.

- **Optimize HTML**—This tool is available via the Optimize HTML tab of the Remote Web Site Properties dialog box, as well as in Code view and Split view (right-click the body of the Web page and then click Optimize HTML). Optimize HTML enables you to select the HTML elements that you want removed from the HTML code of your Web pages when they are published. Using the Optimize HTML tab, you can remove many HTML elements, including, but not limited to, selective HTML comments, all HTML comments, HTML leading spaces, or all HTML white spaces.

- **Reformat HTML**—This feature is available in Code view and Split view (right-click the body of the Web page and then click Reformat HTML). This command reformats the HTML code to follow predefined code formatting options as selected in the Code Formatting tab of the Page Options dialog box. To comply with the W3C requirements for standardizations, Tag names, which are lowercase, and Attribute names, which are lowercase checkboxes in the Page Formatting tab of the Options dialog box, need to be checked.

Working in SharePoint Designer 2007 with CSS

SharePoint Designer 2007 provides new and enhanced tools for working with CSS, which you can use to refine further your Web page layouts and formatting. CSS tools such as task panes assist you in managing, applying, and editing CSS rules and style sheets to design the look of your page. SharePoint Designer 2007 provides a CSS Style Application toolbar, CSS layout tools, and, for the first time, Microsoft IntelliSense for CSS.

Some of the most relevant tools are described here:

- **Applying and managing style sheet tools**—The new Apply Styles and Manage Styles task panes enable you to create, apply, and manage faster, easier, and more efficient CSS styles.

- **CSS Reports**—The new CSS Reports tool can help eliminate errors by providing a list of all unused styles, undefined classes, or mismatched cases (see Figure A.7 as an example). It also provides a comprehensive list of the CSS class, id, and element selectors (see Figure A.8 as an example).

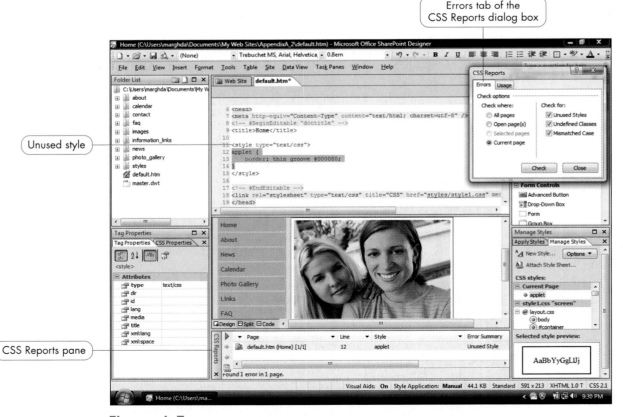

Figure A.7 Using the CSS Reports to Eliminate Errors

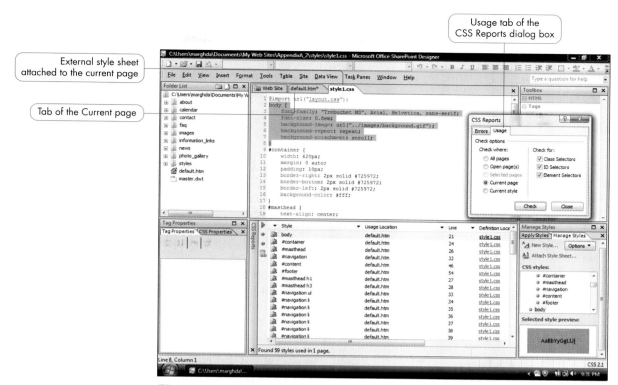

Figure A.8   Using the CSS Reports to Generate a Comprehensive List of the CSS Class, ID, and Element Selectors

- **IntelliSense tool**—The new IntelliSense tool for CSS is a great built-in tutor for developers. It provides a content-specific list of CSS code entries to select (see Figure A.9).

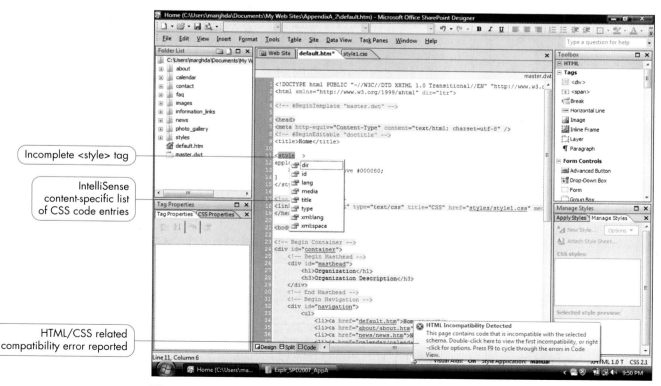

Figure A.9   Using the IntelliSense Tool for CSS

- **Compatibility Checker**—Using the Compatibility Checker you can identify any areas of your site that do not behave as anticipated and fix the problems before your site goes live. The Compatibility Checker enables you to verify that the pages in your site comply with the Web standards you are targeting. For example, you can check to see that your pages are compatible with XHTML 1.0 Strict and CSS 2.1 (or other combinations of CSS and HTML standards).

Extensible Markup Language

In Chapter 1, you were introduced to the fundamentals of the XML markup language and to the relationship between XML, HTML, XHTML, and CSS. Let us start with a concise recap of what you have already learned about XML from this textbook's chapters. (See the More Information section of this appendix for a list of related Web sites.)

Because XML is an extensible language, developers can create custom tags that describe the data or content in a document. Developers also like XML because they can prevent many code errors by employing an application called an XML parser. After an XML document is created, it has to be evaluated by an XML parser, which interprets the document code to make sure it meets the following criteria:

- **Well-formed.** The document contains no syntax errors and obeys all W3C specifications for XML code (http://www.w3.org/XML). Some common syntax errors can be caused by ignoring the case sensitivity of XML tags or by omitting one or more tags. As previously discussed, HTML never gives you any type of feedback regarding syntax errors.

- **Valid.** The document is well formed and satisfies the rules included in the attached document type definition or schema.

XML supports an optional document type definition and XML schema. These documents define all the components that an XML document is allowed to contain as well as the structural relationship among these components. A document type definition (DTD) can force an XML document to follow a uniform data structure, thus eliminating many code errors that can occur. The DTD can be internal, included in the XML document itself; external, stored in an external .dtd file; or a combination of internal and external components. The power of a DTD is increased when using external components because the same external DTD can be applied to more than one XML file. A schema is an XML document that includes the definition of one (or more) XML document's content and structure. Two of the most popular schemas are the XML schema (http://www.w3.org/XML/Schema.html), developed by W3C in 2001, and the Microsoft schema, XDR.

TIP   The Microsoft XML Parser

The Microsoft XML parser is called MSXML and is built into Internet Explorer versions 5.0 and above. However, it needs to be separately downloaded and installed. Netscape developed its own parser, called Mozilla, which is built into Navigator version 6.0 and higher. Although these are the most popular, many other XML editors and parsers are available, such as Altova® XMLSpy® *(http://www.altova.com/products/xmlspy/xml_editor.html)*, an award-winning XML editor for modeling, editing, transforming, and debugging XML technologies.

HTML can define the way data are formatted and displayed only on a Web page, whereas XML code describes the type of information contained in the document. The XML code does not indicate how data are to be formatted or displayed. Consequently, it must use CSSs or Extensible Stylesheet Languages (XSLs) to build style sheets that can be embedded into the XML document or linked to it. The CSS contains formatting instructions for each element. Using a CSS to format XML documents provides Web developers with the same formatting features found in HTML, but with greater flexibility:

- By attaching different style sheets to an XML document, you can change the way it appears in a browser.

- By changing a style sheet attached to multiple XML documents, you can change the way all these XML documents are displayed in a browser.

XSLT (Extensible Stylesheet Language Transformation) is a subset of XSL that enables you to display XML data on a Web page and "transform" it in HTML. XSLT pages can be used to create client-side or server-side XML transformations. If you perform a server-side XML transformation the server handles it, whereas when you perform a client-side transformation the browser will handle the transformation.

 TIP Extensible Stylesheet Language Transformation (XSLT)

The client-side XSLT transformations are still not supported by all browsers. However, the current versions of some of the most popular browsers (such as IE 6+, Firefox 1.02, Netscape 8) support client-side XSLT transformations.

SharePoint Designer 2007 Tools for Working with XML

In Chapter 2, you were introduced to the new XML–based Microsoft Office 2007 file formats called Microsoft Office Open XML Formats that apply to Microsoft Office Word 2007, Microsoft Office Excel 2007, and Microsoft Office PowerPoint 2007. You also learned that, by default, documents, worksheets, and presentations that you create in the 2007 Office release are saved in XML format with new file name extensions that add an "x" or an "m" to the file name extensions that you are already familiar with; the "x" signifies an XML file that has no macros and the "m" signifies an XML file that does contain macros. All Microsoft Office 2007 files can be exported as XML files.

SharePoint Designer includes a rich set of tools that enables you to connect, read, and modify the content of different type Data Sources (such as Access, Excel, or XML files). Taking into consideration all these user-friendly tools offered by the Microsoft Office 2007 suite applications, you can only benefit, as a SharePoint Designer Web site developer, by creating rather easily dynamic data-driven Web pages.

The majority of these tools require an ASP or ASP.NET server or a server running Windows SharePoint Services. This section briefly introduces you to some of the SharePoint Designer tools that apply to XML files and that may require the Microsoft ASP.NET Development Server.

Exporting Microsoft Office 2007 Access Data in SharePoint Designer 2007 as XML Files

The Microsoft Office Access 2007 user-friendly interface enables you to export as XML any data and generates the data (.xml file), schema (.xsd file), and presentation (.xsl file). An XML document enables people to exchange information between different applications and to distribute documents using many popular devices, such as computers, PDAs, and cell phones. If, when you export Access data as XML, you choose a client-side transformation, an .htm file will be generated, whereas if you choose a server-side transformation, an .asp file will be created. The .asp file will have to be published on an .ASP server to be properly displayed.

To export an Access table to XML, follow the step-by-step tutorial included in this section:

1. In the Navigation pane, click the table you want to export.

2. On the Ribbon, click the External Data tab, and then click the More drop-down box in the Export group. Then click XML file, as shown in Figure A.10, to display the Export - XML File dialog box.

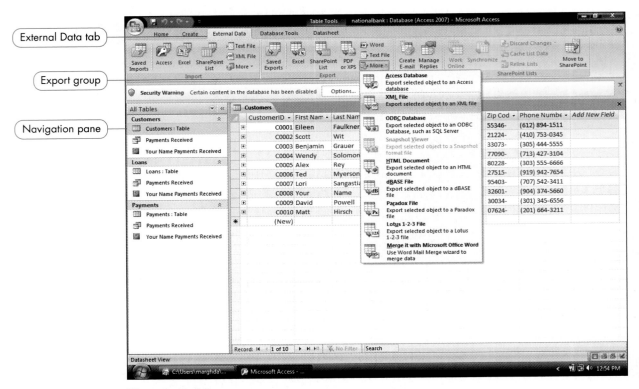

Figure A.10   Exporting Access Data as XML Files

3. Click Browse to navigate to the location and name for the .xml file and click OK. The Export XML dialog box appears. Click all three check boxes, as shown in Figure A.11, and click More Options.

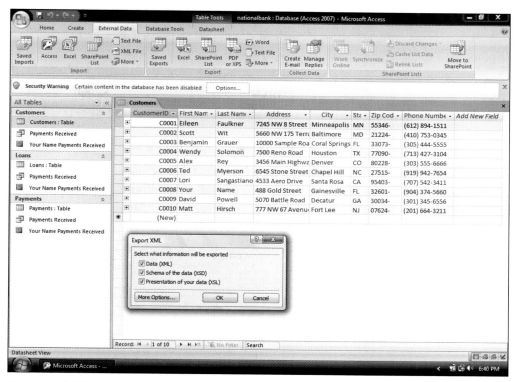

Figure A.11 Using the Export XML Dialog Box

4. Click the Presentation tab. To generate a client-side transformation, click the Client (HTML) option [to generate a server-side transformation, click the Server (ASP) option, and you will need to later publish the .asp file on an ASP server], as shown in Figure A.12.

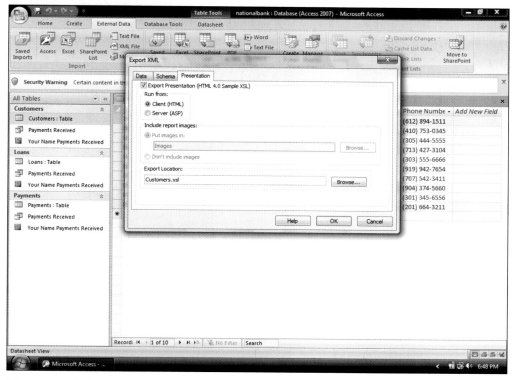

Figure A.12 Exporting an Access Data File as an XML File Using a Client-Side Transformation

5. Click the Save export steps check box, and then click Save Export.

6. The .htm client-side transformation, .xml, .xsd, and .xsl files are now showing on the destination Web site.

7. Open the .htm client-side transformation in Split view, as shown in Figure A.13. You can see the VBScript code generated by the Access wizard for exporting the data into an .xml file and creating a client-side transformation.

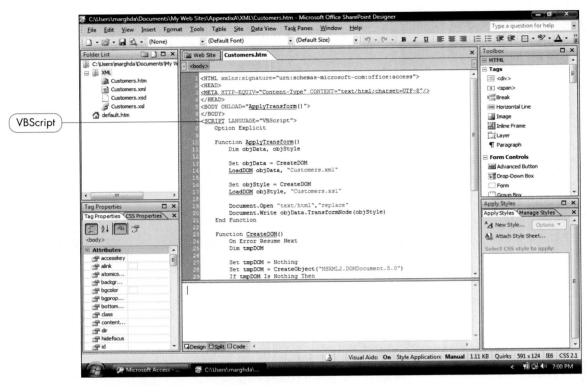

Figure A.13 VBScript Code

8. Preview in Internet Explorer 7.0 the .htm file. As you can see in Figure A.14, the table included in the .htm file is an accurate representation of the original Access data. Figure A.15 shows the sever-side transformation of an Access data table published on a FrontPage server.

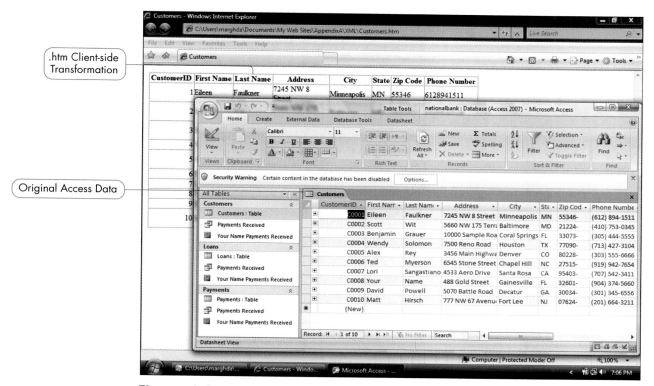

.htm Client-side Transformation

Original Access Data

Figure A.14 .htm Client-Side Transformation of Access Data

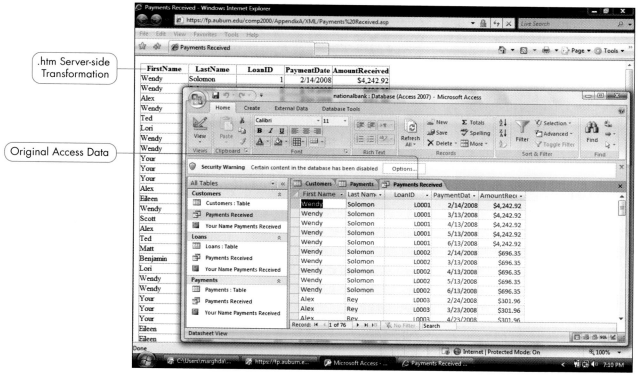

.htm Server-side Transformation

Original Access Data

Figure A.15 .htm Server-Side Transformation of Access Data

Using an XML Document as a SharePoint Designer 2007 Data Source

When you create or import an .xml file into SharePoint Designer, a connection is generated automatically and can be seen in the Data Source Library pane, as shown in Figure A.16.

The SharePoint Designer Data Views are built on ASP.NET form technology so that you can insert them either as read-only views of data or as forms in which users can write back to the data source by using the browser. A Data View can use as data sources only lists and libraries, database connections, and local XML files.

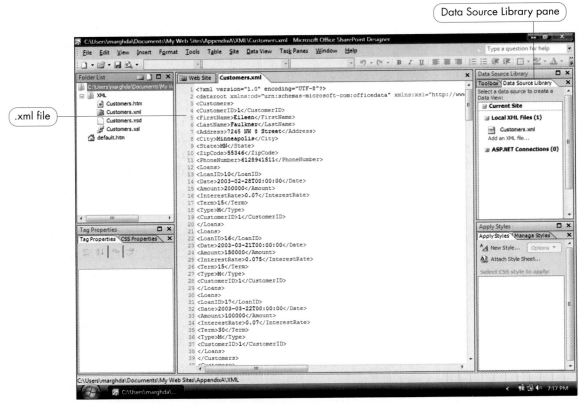

Figure A.16 Data Source Library Pane

To insert a Data View using an XML file as a data source, click .xml data source in the Data Source Library pane and click Show Data on the drop-down menu. You can insert all the content of the data source or select just the desired content. Then click Insert Selected Fields as and click Multiple Item View, shown in Figure A.17.

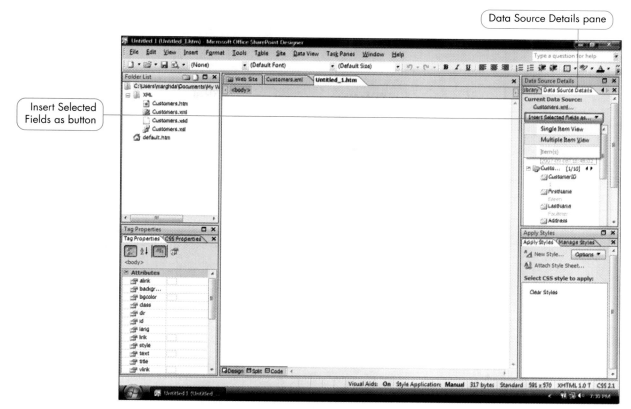

Data Source Details pane

Insert Selected Fields as button

Figure A.17 Data Source Details Pane

The Data View and its Common Data View Tasks menu are now showing, allowing you to further customize your Web page. If you click the Data View Properties, the Data View Properties dialog box is displayed, allowing you to modify the properties of the newly created Data View, as shown Figure A.18. If you save the Web

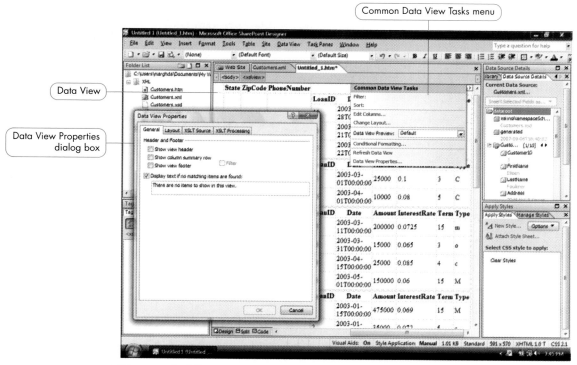

Common Data View Tasks menu

Data View

Data View Properties dialog box

Figure A.18 Data View

page including the Data View, the Save Embedded dialog box will appear. Preview the Web page in browsers, as shown in Figure A.19, and observe that its content is an accurate representation of the original Access data.

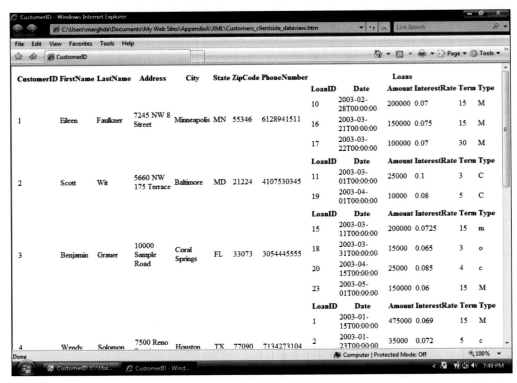

Figure A.19 Data View Rendered by the Internet Explorer Browser

TIP Working with XML Data Sources and SharePoint Server

If you have access to a SharePoint Server, you can build more sophisticated data-driven Web pages using an XML file as a data source, as shown in Figure A.20. For example, the form shown in Figure A.21 is a New Item Form that allows you to add new records to the XML data source. As you can see in Figure A.21, there are also more Common Data View Tasks that you can use to further customize your data-driven Web page.

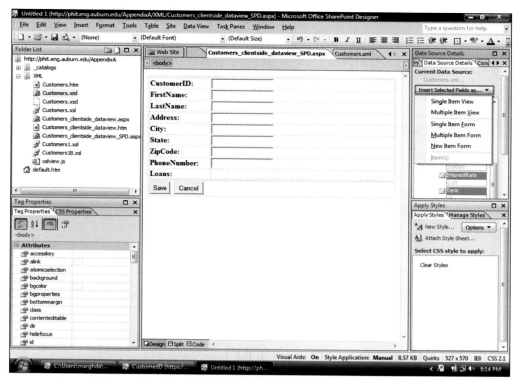

Figure A.20 Data-Driven Web Page Published on a SharePoint Server

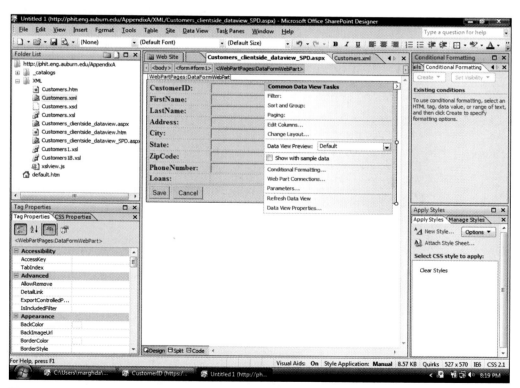

Figure A.21 More Common Data View Tasks

Keeping in Mind Good Web Design Rules

There are some excellent Web sites that synthesize all the dos and don'ts when it comes to Web design. The More Information section of this appendix provides you with a list of useful related Web sites.

This section includes the top ten Web design dos and don'ts of this book.

The Dos

- Do use color wisely. Colors should be used primarily for emphasizing text titles, sections, and keywords. Remember that color-blind people might not be able to see all colors. Do use color as background for your Web pages, but ensure that it doesn't diminish the readability of your Web page content.
- Do keep a balance between the need to use graphic, audio, and video files to enrich the content and the "look" of your Web page and the need to keep the size and amount of time required to display your Web pages at a reasonable level.

 TIP **More About Graphic, Audio, and Video Files**

Do make use of images for the background of your Web pages, so long as they do not diminish the readability of your Web page content. Do always add meaningful, alternative text and caption text to all graphic, audio, and video files employed in your Web pages so that visitors with visual and hearing impairments can fully understand what they represent.

- Do regularly update the content of your Web pages and remove any outdated content or content that is no longer relevant.
- Do implement a consistent style for all the Web pages included on a Web site by employing Web page and Web site templates and CSS external style sheets.
- Do build easy-to-navigate Web pages and Web sites.

The Don'ts

- Don't allow broken links and, whenever possible, don't publish Web pages under development.
- Don't use the underline style for the text of your Web pages because it might lead your users to believe that it is a hyperlink.
- Don't use sound without allowing visitors to control if and when they want to hear it, if you don't want to annoy your visitors.
- Don't use unethical wording, and try to avoid using professional jargon or slang.
- Don't use any kind of copyrighted material unless you have official permission to do so.

More Information

The following list presents some of the most useful Web sites that Web developers use to successfully develop standard Web sites. The list includes the Web sites of companies, organizations, and institutions developing Web-related software and hardware, guidelines and laws, and up-to-date articles, as well as online forums.

- W3C Index of Elements Web site: http://www.w3.org/TR/REC-html40/index/elements.html

- W3C Index of Attributes Web site: http://www.w3.org/TR/REC-html40/index/attributes.html

- W3C Index of HTML Special Characters Web site: http://www.w3.org/TR/REC-html40/sgml/entities.html

- W3C Recommended DTDs Web site: http://www.w3.org/QA/2002/04/valid-dtd-list.html

- David Siegal's "The Deadly Sins of Web Design" Web site: http://web.jccc.net/edtech/resources/technotes/webauthor/sins

- Stefan Mischook's Killersites.com Web site: http://www.killersites.com

- Jeff Johnson's "Web Bloopers Checklist" Web site: http://books.elsevier.com/companions/9781558608405/checklist.html

- Internet Engineering Task Force (IETF) Web site: http://ietf.org/home.html

- W3C CSS level 1 Web site: http://www.w3.org/TR/REC-CSS1

- W3C CSS level 2 Web site: http://www.w3.org/TR/CSS21

- W3C CSS level 3 Web site: http://www.w3.org/Style/CSS/current-work

- W3C CSS Mobile Profile 2.0 Web site: http://www.w3.org/TR/css-mobile

- W3C CSS TV Profile 1.0 Web site: http://www.w3.org/TR/css-tv

- W3C CSS Print Profile Web site: http://www.w3.org/TR/css-print

Microsoft Office SharePoint Designer 2007

Accessibility and Usability
Designing and Building Accessible and Usable Web Sites and Web Pages

Web Accessibility Guidelines

This book explained what it means to design for accessibility and usability. It also showed you how to use the Microsoft Office SharePoint Designer 2007 Accessibility Reports tool and Compatibility Reports tool to maximize the accessibility and usability of your Web pages. The chapters alerted you about accessibility and compatibility requirements to keep in mind when using Web page elements such as images, tables, multimedia, and forms. In this appendix, you learn more about the Web design guidelines that are included in the World Wide Web Consortium's (W3C) Web Accessibility Initiative (WAI) and in subsection 1194.22 of Section 508 concerning Web-based intranet and Internet information and applications. This appendix also introduces you to some of the most popular assistive and adaptive technologies. At the time this manuscript is being finalized, the Telecommunications and Electronic and Information Technology Advisory Committee (TEITAC) is working on the fourth draft of the revised Section 508 (http://teitac.org/wiki/TEITAC_Wiki). Upon the official publication of the revised Section 508, this appendix and any related information published in this textbook will be updated as soon as possible.

The 2000 United States Census estimated that 19.4% of noninstitutional civilians in the United States have a disability. Almost half of these people have a severe disability. (To learn more about these figures go to http://factfinder.census.gov, point to People on the vertical navigation bar, and click Disability on the short menu.) As Article 27.1 of the Universal Declaration of Human Rights (http://www.un.org/Overview/rights.html) states it best, "Everyone has the right freely to participate in the cultural life of community, to enjoy the arts and to share in scientific advancement and its benefits." When, as a Web developer, you create accessible content, you help to realize this promise for your users.

This section introduces the W3C WAI accessibility guidelines and Section 508 law. The More Information section of this appendix provides you with a helpful list of related Web sites.

TIP International Accessibility and Disability Initiatives

Efforts are made around the world toward raising awareness of accessibility and disability and maximizing World Wide Web (WWW) accessibility. W3C's WAI works with organizations and governments toward maximizing the accessibility of the WWW through five primary areas: technology, guidelines, evaluation and repair tools, education and outreach, and research and development. Governments around the world (such as those of the United Kingdom, Japan, Canada, Australia, Greece, France, Italy, and Sweden) have adopted or are in the process of implementing the W3C Web Content Accessibility Guidelines 1.0.

W3C Web Accessibility Initiative (WAI)

In April 1997, the W3C announced the launch of the WAI (http://www.w3.org/WAI) to promote and achieve Web functionality for persons with disabilities. W3C WAI works with organizations and governments around the world toward maximizing the accessibility of the Web through five primary areas: technology, guidelines, evaluation and repair tools, education and outreach, and research and development.

As stated on the W3C Web site, the Web Content Working Group (WCAG WG) is part of the WAI and was first chartered in August 1997 to produce the Web Content Accessibility Guidelines 1.0 (WCAG 1.0), which became a W3C Recommendation in May 1999. WCAG 1.0 provides Web designers with a set of 14 guidelines. These 14 guidelines are general principles of accessible design, and each guideline includes a set of checkpoints specifying how Web developers should apply the guideline. Each checkpoint has a priority level assigned to it by WCAG based on its impact on the Web page's accessibility. The three priority levels of WCAG 1.0 are described in Table B.1.

Table B.1 W3C WCAG Priority Levels

Priority Levels	Description
I	A Web content developer must satisfy this checkpoint. Otherwise, one or more groups will find it impossible to access information in the document. Satisfying this checkpoint is a basic requirement for some groups to be able to use Web documents.
II	A Web content developer should satisfy this checkpoint. Otherwise, one or more groups will find it difficult to access information in the document. Satisfying this checkpoint will remove significant barriers to accessing Web documents.
III	A Web content developer might address this checkpoint. Otherwise, one or more groups will find it somewhat difficult to access information in the document. Satisfying this checkpoint will improve access to Web documents.

TIP Web Content Accessibility Guidelines (WCAG) 2.0

The WCAG Working Group (WG) was rechartered in November 2000 to continue the W3C's work on guidelines for creating accessible Web content. The mission of the WCAG WG is to develop guidelines to ensure that Web content is accessible to people with disabilities. The WCAG WG is currently working on developing WCAG 2.0 as a W3C Recommendation. Until WCAG 2.0 advances to W3C Recommendation, the current and referenceable document is WCAG 1.0.

Section 508 Law

In 1998, the Section 508 Law (http://www.section508.gov) was enacted by Congress as an amendment to the Rehabilitation Act of 1973, "to require Federal agencies to make their electronic and information technology accessible to people with disabilities. Inaccessible technology interferes with an individual's ability to obtain and use information quickly and easily." The purpose of this amendment is to ensure that all Americans have access to information technology. The law applies to all Federal agencies when they develop, procure, maintain, or use electronic and information technology. Under Section 508 (29 U.S.C. 794d), agencies must give disabled employees and members of the public access to information that is comparable to the access available to others.

The United States Access Board (http://www.access-board.gov) is the federal agency that "develops and maintains design criteria for the built environment, transit vehicles, telecommunications equipment, and for electronic and information technology. It also provides technical assistance and training on these requirements and on accessible design and continues to enforce accessibility standards that cover federally funded facilities." *Built environment* refers to buildings and facilities. Subsection 1194.22 of the Section 508 guidelines provides information covering all aspects of maximizing accessibility in Web site design. The majority of the subsection 1194.22 guidelines are based on Priority Level I of the WCAG, with a few additional rules unique to the law. Part 1194—electronic and information technology accessibility standards (go to http://www.access-board.gov and click on Section 508 in the left-side vertical navigation bar)—includes subsection 1194.22, which concerns Web-based intranet and Internet information and applications.

At the time this manuscript is being developed, the Access Board is conducting a review and update of its access standards for electronic and information technology covered by Section 508 of the Rehabilitation Act. These standards, which were initially published in 2000, cover products and technologies procured by the Federal government, including computer hardware and software, Web sites, phone systems, fax machines, and copiers, among others. This effort will also cover Access Board guidelines for telecommunications products and equipment covered by section 255 of the Telecommunications Act (go to http://www.access-board.gov and click on "Telecommunications" in the left-side vertical navigation bar). To achieve these goals, the Access Board has organized an advisory committee, the elecommunications and Electronic and Information Technology Advisory Committee (TEITAC; http://teitac.org), to review its standards and guidelines and to recommend changes. The committee's membership includes representatives from industry, disability groups, standard-setting bodies in the United States and abroad, and government agencies, among others. The revised Section 508 is expected to be released in early 2008.

Using SharePoint Designer 2007 to Develop Web Pages in Compliance with Section 508

Microsoft has a strong commitment "to enable people and businesses throughout the world to realize their full potential." To better understand and address the computing-related needs of people with disabilities, Microsoft commissioned a study in 2003, which was conducted by Forrester Research, Inc. (go to http://www.microsoft.com/enable and click on Research studies about accessible technology in the More Information section). This study showed that among the adult computer users in the United States one in four has a vision difficulty, one in five has a hearing difficulty, and one in four has a dexterity difficulty (dexterity difficulties consist of pain, discomfort, or complete loss of feeling in fingers, hands, wrists, or arms).

TIP Microsoft "Accessible Technology: A Guide for Educators"

Microsoft's "Accessible Technology: A Guide for Educators" (go to http://www.microsoft.com/enable and click on Educators in the Information for section of the side bar) is an excellent source of information for accessibility features and assistive-technology products that help individuals with specific disabilities.

The Microsoft and Section 508 Web site provides in-depth documentation about the way each Microsoft application's design, including SharePoint Designer 2007, complies with the Section 508 law (go to http://www.microsoft.com/enable and click on Government in the Information for: section of the side bar). SharePoint Designer provides two good tools for maximizing the accessibility and usability of its Web sites, the Accessibility Reports and the Compatibility Reports. The SharePoint Designer 2007 Accessibility Reports tool enables you to maximize the accessibility of your Web pages by identifying the design elements that do not comply with WCAG Priority 1, WCAG Priority 2, and Section 508.

Let us take a closer look at the 15 paragraphs of subsection 1194.22 and how they can be addressed using SharePoint Designer.

TIP Web Accessibility in Mind (WebAIM) Article on How to Make Accessible Web Content Using SharePoint Designer

The Web Accessibility in Mind (WebAIM) organization published a very useful article on how to make accessible Web Content using Microsoft Expression© Web. Because the Microsoft Expression Web user interface is almost identical to the Microsoft SharePoint Designer user interface, and all Microsoft Expression Web accessibility-related features are also offered by Microsoft SharePoint Designer, you should definitely review the WebAIM article, "How to Make Accessible Web Content Using Microsoft Expression Web" (go to http://www.webaim.org and search for How to Make Accessible Web Content Using Microsoft Expression Web).

Graphics and Images

(a) A text equivalent for every non-text element shall be provided (e.g., via "alt," "longdesc," or in element content).

The first paragraph requires that all graphic images have alternative text attached. If no alternative text is present, the screen reader application attempts to read the graphic image file, which will not help a visually impaired user. You can use the alt attribute, used for short descriptions, or the longdesc attribute, if a longer description is required. If you provide a longer description, it is stored in a separate file from the one in which the graphic element is included.

Screen readers and nonvisual (talking) browsers implement a technique called *linearizing*, which converts Web page content into a sequence of words and lines. Checking the linearization of a Web page is extremely important to ensure accessibility for blind users who use screen readers because a screen reader must be able to convert a two-dimensional graphical Web page into a one-dimensional stream of characters, which is usually fed into a speech synthesizer. You can use Lynx to test the linearization of an entire Web page and of individual tables. Lynx is a text-based Web browser available on UNIX©, DOS, and Windows© operating systems. It was developed by Academic Computing Services at the University of Kansas.

TIP The Web Page Linearizing Process

In the first step of the Web page linearizing process, an assistive technology application converts images to alternative text. In the second step, it linearizes tables. The table linearizing process consists of laying out the text a line at a time, starting with the first cell of the first row, then moving across the columns of the first row, then proceeding to the second row, and so on. If a table's cell includes a nested table, the nested table is linearized before the application moves to the next cell. Lynx does not support graphics, plug-ins, JavaScript, Java, or Cascading Style Sheets (CSS). Thus, it is an excellent test vehicle to evaluate whether your page is usable and readable with these technologies turned off. DJ Delorie has developed a free Lynx viewer (go to http://www.delorie.com and click Lynx Viewer). The viewer enables you to submit a URL and see what the Web page looks like when viewed in Lynx.

SharePoint Designer automatically opens the Accessibility Properties dialog box when you insert a picture in a Web page, enabling you to add the alt or longdesc attribute, as shown in Figure B.1.

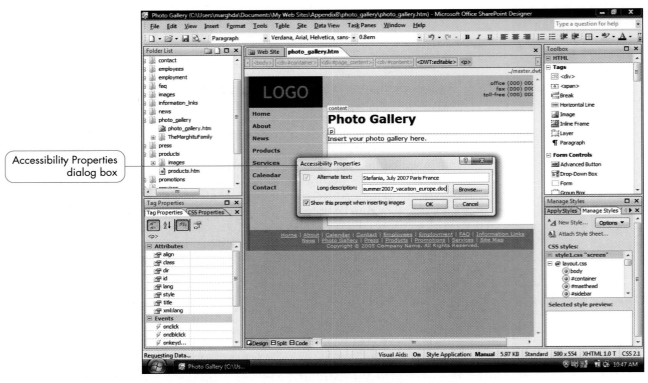

Accessibility Properties
dialog box

Figure B.1 SharePoint Designer Accessibility Properties Dialog Box

In SharePoint Designer, you can also add the alt or longdesc attribute to any inline image by right-clicking the image, clicking Picture Properties on the shortcut menu, and then clicking the General tab, as shown in Figure B.2. In browsers that support the longdesc attribute, the value assigned to the attribute is displayed as a link.

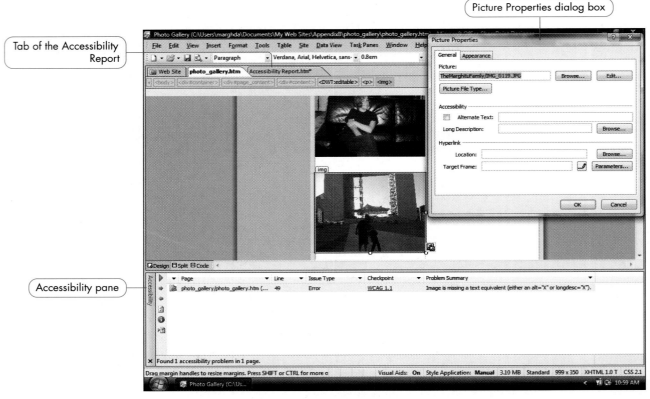

Picture Properties dialog box

Tab of the Accessibility
Report

Accessibility pane

Figure B.2 Working with the SharePoint Designer Accessibility Checker and Inline Images

However, not all browsers and assistive technologies support the longdesc attribute. To make your content accessible to browsers and assistive technologies that do not support the longdesc attribute, you can add a D-Link. A D-Link is a link to the same descriptive file contained in the longdesc attribute that is inserted near the image, as shown in Figure B.3.

In SharePoint Designer, to insert a D-Link, make sure you are in Design view, position the insertion point to the right of the image, click Insert on the Menu bar, and click Hyperlink to open the Insert Hyperlink dialog box. Type D in the Text to display box; in the Address box, type or browse for the descriptive file to add, and click OK to insert the hyperlink and close the dialog box. The HTML code example shown in Figure B.3 includes the three ways you can add a description to an inline image. The second <img> tag includes the longdesc attribute as well as a D-Link to the file including the long description for browsers and assistive technologies that do not support the longdesc attribute.

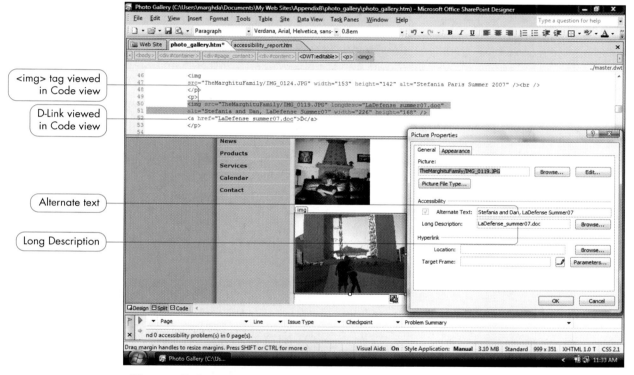

Figure B.3   Adding the Longdesc Attribute and a D-Link to an Inline Image

You can use the SharePoint Designer Accessibility Checker to generate a report that lists all the images that are missing alternative text or long description, as shown in Figure B.2. For decorative images, such a list bullets, you do not need to include an equivalent text. You can simply add the alt attribute and assign it an empty text string (alt=" ").

TIP   Animated Images and Thumbnails

You should avoid using animations, which can be debilitating for some of your users. You should provide access to large images via thumbnails or text links (large images still take a long time to download). In SharePoint Designer, you can very easily generate a thumbnail image if you right-click on the original image and click AutoThumbnail on the shortcut menu.

Multimedia

(b) Equivalent alternatives for any multimedia presentation shall be synchronized with the presentation.

To maximize the hearing impaired users' access to audio you should supply a text transcript for audio content; when audio is part of a video, you should synchronize the transcript as captions. To maximize the visually impaired users' access to video you should use synchronized descriptions about the video and provide separate text descriptions as well as the audio transcript. Specialized multimedia applications are required to generate audio content transcripts and captions for video content. To learn more about audio content transcripts and captions for video content, check out the following Web sites:

- **Captions and audio descriptions for PC multimedia**—go to http://msdn2.microsoft.com and search for "captions and audio descriptions for PC multimedia"
- **The National Captioning Institute**—http://www.ncicap.org
- **Relay Conference Captioning**—http://www.fedrcc.us/FedRcc
- **Media Access Group**—http://access.wgbh.org
- **Microsoft SAMI 1.0**—go to http://msdn2.microsoft.com and search for understanding SAMI 1.0
- **The W3C Synchronized Multimedia**—http://www.w3.org/AudioVideo
- **The Media Access Generator (MAGpie)**—go to http://ncam.wgbh.org/index.html and click MAGPIE
- **HiSoftware© Hi-Caption™**—go to http://www.hisoftware.com, point to Products&Solutions, and click Hi-Caption
- **Adobe© Captivate©**—go to http://www.adobe.com and search for Adobe Captivate 3 accessibility
- **CPC Computer Prompting and Captioning Co**—http://www.cpcweb.com

TIP   CSS Level 3 Speech Module

The CSS level 3 speech module (go to http://www.w3.org and search for CSS level 3 speech module) allows you to give guidance to screen readers as to how content can be best presented in audio to the user. CSS level 3 is under development. It includes all of CSS level 2 and extends it with new selectors, fancy borders and backgrounds, vertical text, user interaction, speech, and much more.

Color

(c) Web pages shall be designed so that all information conveyed with color is also available without color, for example from context or markup.

As documented in Chapter 2 and Appendix C (available on the Companion Web site), color is an important Web design element that, when properly used, can improve the look of your Web page and help to convey the purpose of the information. However, color can create serious problems for Web site users who are blind or color blind. Consequently, you should always consider the following options:

- Set colors of your Web pages in style sheets so users can easily override color settings. When colors are defined in HTML, your users cannot override color settings.
- Provide a black and white or grayscale alternative version of your Web page for users who are color blind. You can create a Web page template using black and white or grayscale colors and images using an image editing program. You can find out more about using image editing programs at the Web developers notes

Web site (go to http://www.webdevelopersnotes.com and search the Web site for image editing programs using the Google search box placed at the bottom of the home page).

- Use brighter colors when possible, because they are easier for color-blind users to differentiate.

- Make sure you offer text equivalent clues if you use important color clues in your Web page. For example, if you use a statement, such as click the red button to log out, in your Web page, the red button needs to be identified with a text label that makes it recognizable to people who are color blind.

- Provide sufficient contrast between text colors and backgrounds.

- Avoid using red and green, which are challenging for the majority of color-blind people.

Two simple methods can help you verify that your Web page is in compliance with guideline (c). Try viewing the Web page on a black and white monitor, or print the Web page on a black and white printer. If the usability of the Web page is not affected by the removal of color, your Web page should be easy to use by color-blind people.

Several Web sites enable you to test the accessibility of your Web site for color-blind users. aDesigner is one of the best disability simulators to use for testing Web pages for accessibility and usability problems related to visual and color deficiencies. aDesigner checks for compliance with the Section 508 guidelines, the W3C WCAG 1.0 guidelines, the Japanese Industrial Standard (JIS), and IBM's Web Accessibility Checklist. There are two modes or settings available in aDesigner:

- **Blind**—The blind mode runs three types of tests on Web pages: blind usability visualization, accessibility and usability checking, and compliance checking. This setting helps you understand how blind users who depend on voice browsers and screen readers experience their Web pages. By using this setting, you can correct the most crucial factor in improving usability for the blind: navigability.

- **Low Vision**—The low-vision mode simulates how users with weak eyesight, color vision deficiencies, cataracts, and combinations of impairments perceive Web pages. This mode enables you to detect accessibility problems from simulated Web pages or images.

The Vischeck (http://www.vischeck.com/downloads) Web site provides you with free downloadable software tools, which let you see how your Web pages appear to people with different types of color blindness.

Style Sheets

(d) Documents shall be organized so they are readable without requiring an associated style sheet.

By using style sheets to separate content from presentation, Web pages load faster and are more usable and accessible in most Web browsers. However, you need to ensure that pages display properly even if your visitor is using a browser that does not support style sheets, has style-sheet support turned off, or has to use another custom style sheet. When using CSSs in developing your Web pages, you should always consider the following recommendations:

- Do not rely on specific fonts or colors to convey relevant information because the specified fonts and colors might not exist on all computers. If they do not exist, the browser uses its default colors and fonts.

- Do not fix the size of your text in points or pixels. If someone with low vision needs to increase the size of the text on your page, they will not be able to change the size of fixed text. Instead use the em unit to set font sizes as required by CSS Techniques for Web Content Accessibility Guidelines 1.0 (go to http://www.w3.org and search for CSS Techniques for Web Content Accessibility Guidelines 1.0).

- The heading tags (<h1>–<h6>) should be used to emphasize the organization of your Web page, not to modify the text font size.
- Use an adjustable layout (relative length units and percentages of the browser window size) that shrinks or expands as necessary so that visitors with different browser window sizes and screen resolutions can properly see your Web pages. See the Units of Measure section of the CSS Techniques for Web Content Accessibility Guidelines 1.0 for more information (see bullet regarding text size, above).
- Use linked style sheets rather than imported style sheets or internal styles on each Web page.

Linked style sheets offer the best solutions for maximizing the universal usability of your Web pages. Here are some reasons for choosing linked style sheets over internal styles or imported style sheets:

- Linked style sheets enable alternative views for different types of devices (such as printers, PDAs, and cellular phones), different options for viewing your Web pages (such as larger-size fonts or higher color contrast), or custom-made views for different browsers.
- Linked style sheets are virtually supported by all CSS-capable browsers, in contrast to the imported style sheets (using the @import method) that work only in Internet Explorer 5.0 or later browsers.
- Linked style sheets minimize the time needed to download your Web pages because they are downloaded only one time and applied to each Web page of your Web site that is linked.
- Linked style sheets help maximize the consistency of your Web site. Your users will need to get acquainted with only one design.

However, even when using CSS linked style sheets, you might have to deal with browser incompatibilities that will force you to create alternate versions of your Web page for different browsers. SharePoint Designer can help you identify these incompatibilities and create alternate versions of your Web pages. Figure B.4 shows a Web page viewed in Internet Explorer and Mozilla Firefox© browsers using the SharePoint Designer Preview in Multiple Browser command. There is obviously a problem with the bulleted list viewed in Mozilla Firefox. Therefore, an alternate Web page was created simply by adequately modifying the external style sheet. To ensure that your Web page will display correctly in Mozilla Firefox you can use the SharePoint Designer Check Browser behavior. After you create the alternate version of the Web page, click Behaviors on the Task Panes menu. Select the <body> tag on the Quick Tag Selector and click Insert on the Behaviors task pane to open the Check Browser dialog box. From the current browser type select the browsers for which the Web page does not display correctly. Then, from the Version list, check a specific version, if required. Click the first Go to URL check box, click Browse to navigate to the location of the alternate page (see Figure B.5), and click OK to apply the behavior.

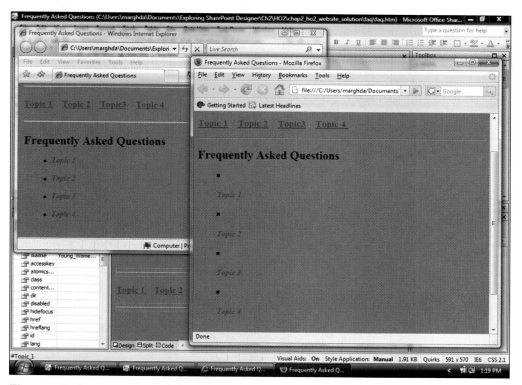

Figure B.4 SharePoint Designer Preview in Multiple Browsers

Check Browser dialog box

Quick Tag Selector bar

Behaviors task pane

Tag Properties pane

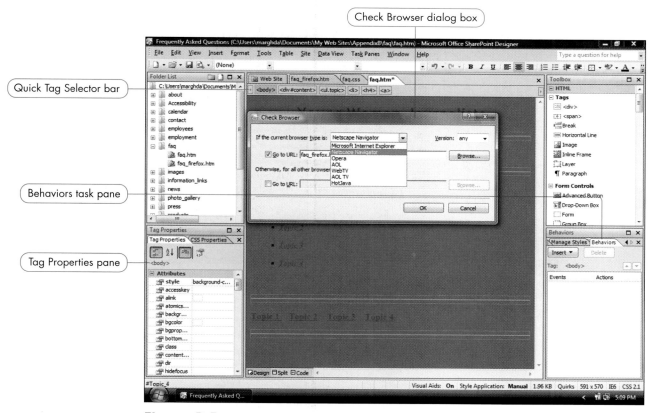

Figure B.5 Working with the SharePoint Designer Check Browser Behavior

Image Maps

(e) Redundant text links shall be provided for each active region of a server-side image map.

(f) Client-side image maps shall be provided instead of server-side image maps except where the regions cannot be defined with an available geometric shape.

Client-side image maps are starting to replace server-side image maps, especially because client-side image maps enable polygon hotspots, and therefore all shapes can be defined on a client-side map. To make a Web page containing a client-side image map accessible, you need to add alternate text to the original map image and each hotspot within the map.

Figure B.6 shows how you can add a hotspot to an image in SharePoint Designer using the Pictures toolbar. Figure B.7 shows the client-side image map in Split view as well as the Accessibility pane with no error.

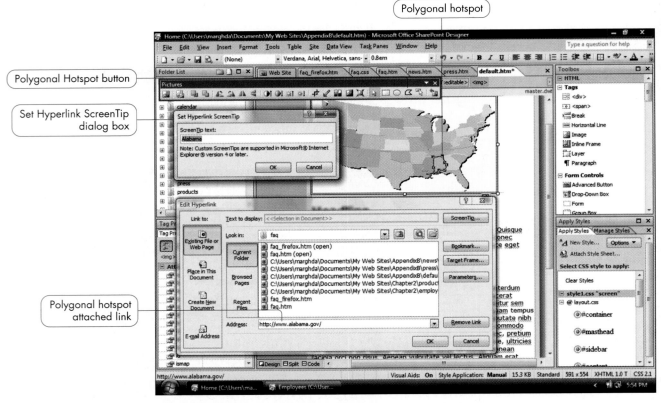

Figure B.6 Creating a Hotspot in SharePoint Designer

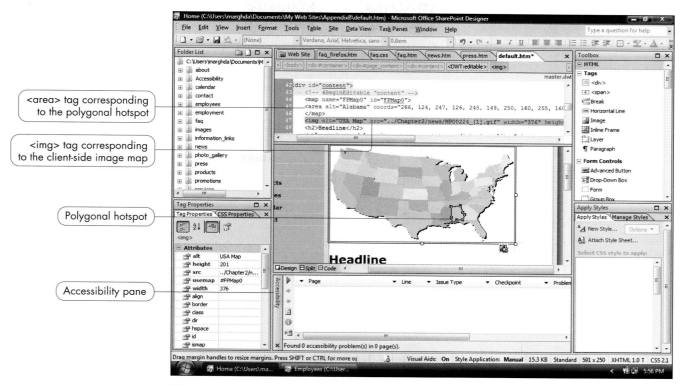

Figure B.7 Accessible Client-Side Image Map Created in SharePoint Designer

The following labels appear in the figure:

- <area> tag corresponding to the polygonal hotspot
- <img> tag corresponding to the client-side image map
- Polygonal hotspot
- Accessibility pane

Tables

(g) Row and column headers shall be identified for data tables.

Chapter 2 covers the use of tables to organize data, the use of tables as layout tools, and the use of tables that have two or more levels of row or column headers, which means that tables include one or more levels of nested tables. To comply with guideline (g), when using data tables, you need to use the <th> tag for any cell that contains a row or a column header.

By default, SharePoint Designer uses the <td> tag and enables you to handle this issue using the Cell Properties dialog box, in which you need to check the Header cell option, as shown in Figure B.8. Adding a table caption can also help visually impaired users by providing them with more information about the table's content, as shown in Figure B.8. Providing a table summary using the summary attribute is useful for nonvisual readers as well (summary is not displayed and it is used only by screen reader users).

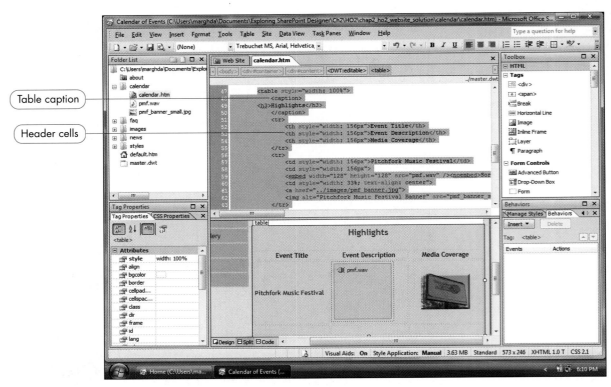

Table caption

Header cells

Figure B.8 Working with Tables

(h) Markup shall be used to associate data cells and header cells for data tables that have two or more logical levels of row or column headers.

To comply with guideline (h) use the <th> tag for any cell that contains a row or a column header in any nested table. This can be quite tedious and might convince you that nested tables should be used only when absolutely necessary. As previously discussed, an excellent way to test that your Web page is accessible is by viewing it in the Lynx browser.

If a table is used as a layout tool, do not use any structural HTML tags for the purpose of visual formatting (for example, the <th> tag that displays its content visually as centered and bold). For a browser to render a table's side-by-side text correctly, you will need to linearize the table. To learn more about how to linearize a table, see the Creating Accessible Tables section of the WebAIM Web site (go to http://www.webaim.org and search the Web site for creating accessible tables). One of the best tools for creating accessible tables is the WebAIM free online WAVE 3.0 Accessibility Tool (go to http://www.webaim.org and search the Web site for WAVE Accessibility Evaluation Tool).

Frames

(i) Frames shall be titled with text that facilitates frame identification and navigation.

A frame can be defined as a layout tool for creating framed Web pages based on the structure of a frameset. A frameset is the actual layout that lets the browser know how to display the framed pages. Sometimes, Web designers want to include the contents of one Web page in another Web page (using all the display features of a frame) without having to build a frameset layout. The inline frame, also known as a floating frame, is basically a frame that does not need to be framed in a frameset, and it embeds a document or another Web page into an HTML document so that embedded data is displayed inside a subwindow of the browser's window. The two documents are absolutely independent, and both are treated as complete documents.

When opening a frames page, assistive technology applications for visually impaired people enable users to open only one frame at a time. Thus, it is extremely important to provide information about the contents of each frame and inline frame included in your Web page. You can do this by adding the title or name attribute to each frame. Because some browsers and assistive technology applications support the *title* attribute and others support the *name* attribute it is wise to add both of them. Users without access to frames should still have access to the Web page content if appropriate navigation links are provided in the <nonframes> tag (see Figure B.9).

SharePoint Designer provides you with ten Frames Pages Web page templates via the Page tab of the New dialog box. All frames included in these Frames Pages Web page templates have already been assigned the name attribute. SharePoint Designer enables you to add the name and title attributes to each frame or inline frame. You right-click within each frame and inline frame to open the Frame Properties dialog box or the Inline Frame Properties dialog box. Type the descriptive name and title, and then click OK to close the dialog box. You can also add attributes and assign attribute values to each frame using the Tag properties pane (see Figure B.9).

Using the Insert/Inline Frame command, you can easily insert in your Web pages an Inline Frame that you can easily format later using the Inline Frame Properties dialog box or the Tag Properties pane, as shown in Figure B.10.

The SharePoint Designer Accessibility Checker reports each frame and inline frame that does not comply with guideline (i). Even if, in general, the accessibility issues related with frames can be addressed, it is highly recommended not to use frames if you wish to build standard, accessible Web pages.

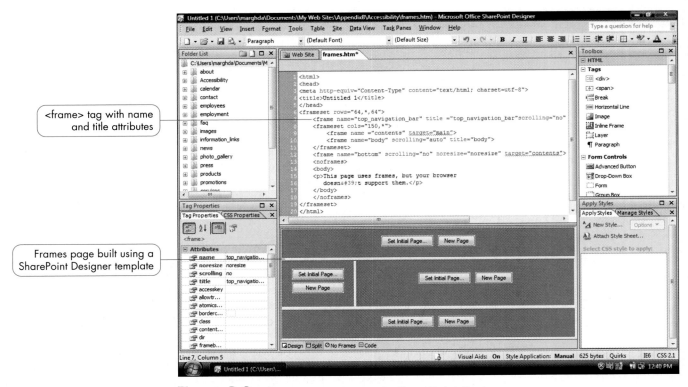

Figure B.9 Working with Frames in SharePoint Designer

Callout labels for Figure B.9:
- <frame> tag with name and title attributes
- Frames page built using a SharePoint Designer template

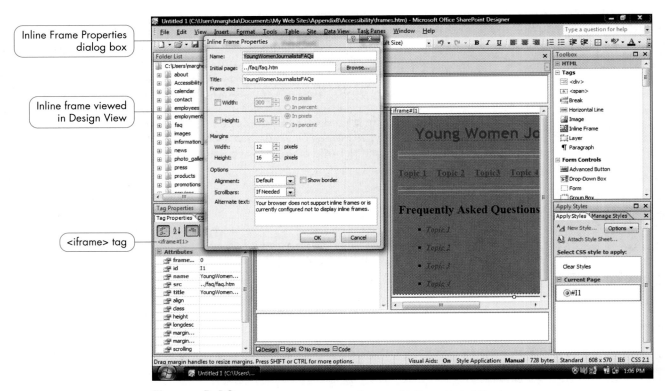

Figure B.10 Working with Inline Frames in SharePoint Designer

Callout labels for Figure B.10:
- Inline Frame Properties dialog box
- Inline frame viewed in Design View
- <iframe> tag

TIP   Frames or No Frames

The only way a user can view any of the contents included in a Web page using frames and when using a browser that does not support frames is if you create an alternative version of the Web page. Therefore, you should always provide users access to an alternate Web page using the <noframes></noframes> tags.

Animation and Scrolling Text

(j) Pages shall be designed to avoid causing the screen to flicker with a frequency greater than 2 Hz and lower than 55 Hz.

Using flashing or flickering elements, such as GIF images, blinking text, and scrolling text, can affect the accessibility of your Web pages. People with photosensitive epilepsy can have seizures caused by elements that flicker, flash, or blink with an intensity and frequency outside the range indicated by guideline (j). The majority of screen reader applications cannot read moving text. People with cognitive disabilities might also find it challenging to read moving text.

Text-Only Version

(k) A text-only page, with equivalent information or functionality, shall be provided to make a Web site comply with the provisions of this part, when compliance cannot be accomplished in any other way. The content of the text-only page shall be updated whenever the primary page changes.

A text-only Web page must contain all the information included in the original page and must have the same functionality the original page has. Anytime you update a Web page, you need to update its text-only version. A link to the text-only version must be included in the original Web page. The home page of the DisabilityInfo.gov Web site is an excellent example of how to implement this guideline, as shown in Figure B.11. The DisabilityInfo.gov Web site is also a rich source of information for any disability issue related to the federal government.

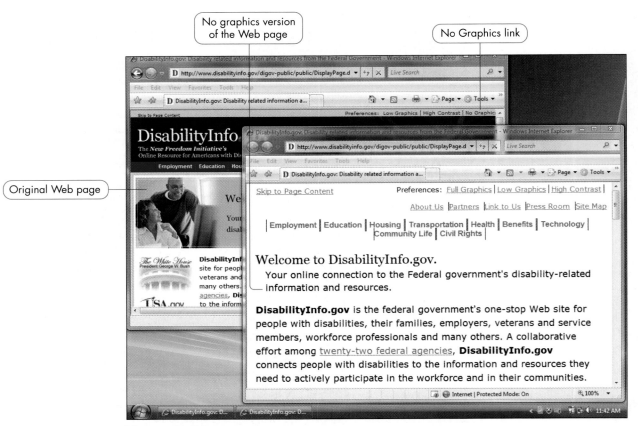

Figure B.11 Working with Text-Only Web Pages

Scripts, Applets, and Plug-Ins

(l) When pages utilize scripting languages to display content, or to create interface elements, the information provided by the script shall be identified with functional text that can be read by assistive technology.

(m) When a web page requires that an applet, plug-in, or other application be present on the client system to interpret page content, the page must provide a link to a plug-in or applet that complies with [s]1194.21(a) through (l) [go to http://www.access-board.gov/508.htm, click on "Guide to the Standards," and then click "Web-based Intranet and Internet Information and Applications (1194.22)"].

This book's chapters briefly introduced scripting languages and how they are used to develop Web pages:

- They automatically change a formatted date on a Web page.
- They cause a linked-to-page to appear in a pop-up window.
- They cause text or a graphic image to change during a mouse rollover.
- They obtain information about the current Web browser.
- They enable navigation to Web pages that have been opened during a Web browser session.
- They process data submitted via an HTML form.
- They retrieve data from a database via an HTML form.

Many of these scripting language applications require the use of the mouse. Some people with motor disabilities might not be able to use a mouse. Furthermore, some assistive technology applications have browsers with scripting turned off; thus, you should provide alternative methods for users with disabilities. Your Web pages should include access keys (keyboard shortcuts) that enable users to achieve the same functionality.

SharePoint Designer's IntelliSense© tool enables you to assign keyboard shortcuts (accesskey attributes) to the links and form fields on each Web page, so keyboard users can navigate the page by using a combination of Alt plus a letter key. For consistency and usability, you should use the same keyboard shortcuts for the same links on all Web pages included in a Web site. You can add an accesskey attribute to a hyperlink in Code view or Split view by typing <a> tag accesskey="", and with a letter between the quotation marks, as shown in Figure B.12. To add an accesskey attribute to a form field, type accesskey="", with a letter between the quotation marks in the form field tag, as shown in Figure B.13.

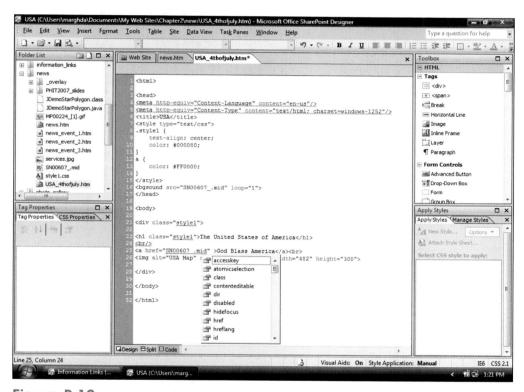

Figure B.12 Assigning a Keyboard Shortcut to a Hyperlink

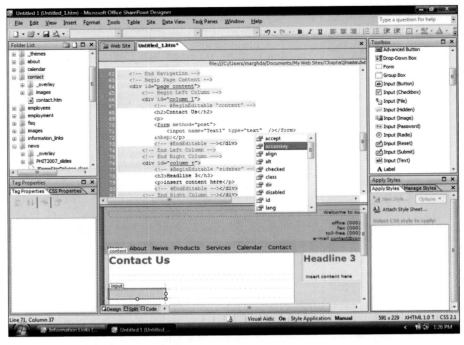

Figure B.13 Assigning a Keyboard Shortcut to a Form Field

Chapter 2 and Chapter 3 cover the SharePoint Designer tools that enable you to add an applet to a Web page and multimedia elements that might require a plug-in or another application to be properly displayed in a browser and empower the user with the decision of when to access media. When using any of these elements in a Web page, a link to the source of a required plug-in or application, such as Flash, Java, or Shockwave, should be added to the Web page. Applets and plug-ins can be detected in the HTML code of a Web page by searching for the <object> tag or <embed> tag. Applets might also be implemented using the deprecated <applet> tag. SharePoint Designer 2007 is actually using the <applet> tag when inserting a Java© Applet Advanced Control and the <embed> tag when inserting a Plug-in Advanced Control. See Figure B.14.

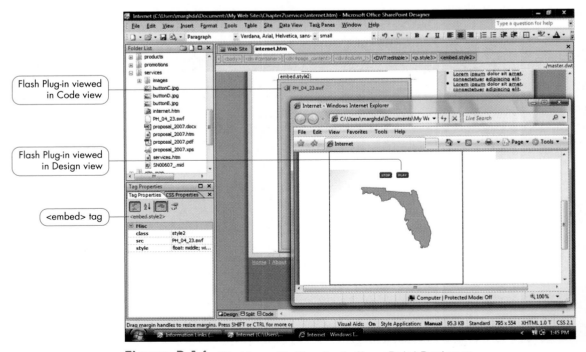

Figure B.14 Working with Plug-Ins in SharePoint Designer

Web Forms

(n) When electronic forms are designed to be completed online, the forms shall allow people using assistive technology to access the information, field elements, and functionality required for completion and submission of the form, including all directions and cues.

Chapter 3 covers the techniques for developing interactive Web forms. Web forms tend to cause problems for people with disabilities if the form elements are improperly labeled and titled or if they have not been coded in compliance with guideline (n). As documented in Chapter 3, Web forms consist of text boxes, text areas, check boxes, option buttons, and drop-down menus. Because form layouts are usually structured using a table, you must be careful to make sure the table is linearized. To improve a screen reader's ability to process an HTML form, each form element should have an initial default value to give the user guidance in completing the form.

All form elements must have explicit labels (placed in the same table cell). The W3C HTML 4.0 specifications (go to http://www.w3.org/html and click HTML 4.01 in the Work section) require you to include a <label> tag associated with a form element. You can use the <label> tag in two distinctive ways:

1. **Explicit labels**—These labels can be implemented using the <label> tag with the "for" attribute. The id attribute of the form element is assigned as the value of the for attribute. The majority of assistive technology applications work extremely well with explicit labels.

2. **Implicit labels**—These labels can be implemented by including the form element and its associated label within the <label> tag. The majority of assistive technology applications, especially screen readers, do not properly support implicit labels.

SharePoint Designer cannot create explicit labels and does not add the id attribute to form elements. You need to add explicit labels and the id attribute to the associated form elements manually in Code view or Split view, as shown in Figure B.15.

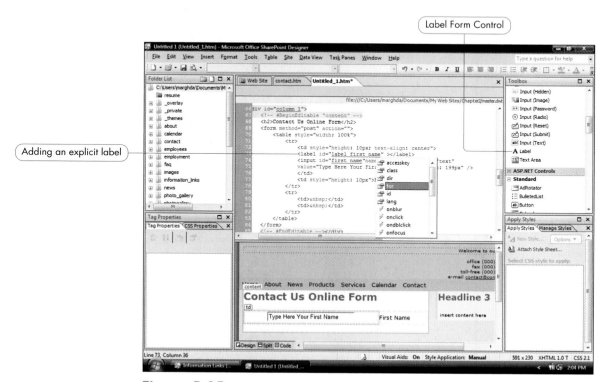

Figure B.15 Working with Forms in SharePoint Designer

TIP   Alternative Contact Methods

It is not easy to design and develop accessible forms for your users with different types of special needs. That is why you should always include an alternative contact method such as telephone or e-mail in your Web pages with forms.

Links

(o) A method shall be provided that permits users to skip repetitive navigation links.

Chapter 2 introduced bookmarks as hyperlinks that link to a specific location within a Web page. The most commonly used bookmark for accessibility is Skip Navigation Links. The Skip Navigation Links link enables a user to skip the Web page title and navigation links by directing the focus to the main contents of the Web page being viewed. This link is especially important for visually impaired people who use a screen reader. In the example shown in Figure B.16, the Skip to Page Content link enables visually impaired users to skip directly to the main content of a Web page so that they are not forced to listen to the Web page title and navigation links each time they access the Web page.

Figure B.16 Working with Links

Timed Response

(p) When a timed response is required, the user shall be alerted and given sufficient time to indicate more time is required.

For security reasons and to accommodate visitor traffic on busy servers, Web developers use scripts that disable the functionality of Web pages when a response is not received within a certain time limit. People with cognitive disabilities or different levels of visual impairment might need more time to provide a response. Consequently, you should always alert users if there is a time limit for providing a response. You should also consider establishing a response time that accommodates all users or enables them to change the time. The W3C How People with Disabilities Use the Web Web page (go to http://www.w3.org and search the W3C Web site for how people with disabilities use the Web) is an excellent resource for this topic.

Assistive Technology and Accessibility and Evaluation Tools

Web pages designed in compliance with Section 508 and the WCAG guidelines can be made accessible to the majority of people with disabilities using software applications and devices that are grouped under the umbrella of assistive technologies:

- Screen readers use text-to-speech (TTS) technology to verbalize screen text and textual representations of graphical elements if available.
- Speech-to-text converters automatically transform dialogue into text.

Accessibility and Evaluation Tools refer to the tools used to make the WWW accessible. W3C provides two free online validation services: the Quality Assurance Markup Validation Service (http://validator.w3.org) and CSS Validation Service (http://jigsaw. w3.org/css-validator). The Markup Validation Service checks documents like HTML and XHTML for conformance to W3C Recommendations and other standards. The CSS Validation Service checks CSS in HTML and XHTML documents or stand-alone CSS documents for conformance to W3C recommendations.

Assistive Technologies and Accessibility and Evaluation Tools | Reference

Category	Application	WWW address
Accessibility and evaluation tools	Bobby™ designed by Watchfire®	http://webxact.watchfire.com/ScanForm.aspx
	aDesigner designed by IBM®	http://www.alphaworks.ibm.com/tech/adesigner
Screen readers	JAWS® for Windows developed by Freedom Scientific®	http://www.freedomscientific.com
	Dolphin Pen by Dolphin Computer Access	http://www.yourdolphin.com
	Window-Eyes Professional developed by GW Micro	http://www.gwmicro.com
Speech-to-text converters	Dragon Naturally Speaking developed by Advanced Speech	http://www.advancedspeech.com
	MacSpeech®	http://www.macspeech.com
	IBM ViaVoice®	http://www.nuance.com/viavoice

More Information

The task of building accessible Web pages is not an easy one. Web developers are required to accumulate a lot of knowledge to successfully accomplish this task. The good news is that more and more companies and organizations are developing competitive assistive and accessibility technology applications that can help you in your quest to assist people with disabilities and special needs. As of now, Section 508 law applies only to Federal agencies; however, many companies and organizations are now complying with Section 508 and the W3C Guidelines.

The following list presents some of the most resourceful Web sites that Web developers use to develop accessible Web sites. The list includes Web sites of software companies that are providing successful assistive and accessibility technologies, Web sites of organizations and institutions developing accessibility guidelines and laws, up-to-date articles, and Web accessibility online forums.

- **Microsoft Accessibility Technology for Everyone**—go to http://www.microsoft.com/enable and click on Microsoft's longstanding commitment to accessibility in the More Information section
- **IBM Human Ability and Accessibility Center**—http://www-306.ibm.com/able/index.html
- **W3C Web Accessibility Initiative (WAI) Guidelines and Techniques**—go to http://www.w3.org/WAI click on Guidelines&Techniques in the vertical navigation bar
- **Web Accessibility in Mind** (WebAIM)—http://www.webaim.org
- **Web Content Accessibility Guidelines 1.0**—go to http://www.w3.org/WAI/, click on Guidelines&Techniques in the vertical navigation bar, click on Web Content (WCAG) in the vertical navigation bar, and then click on How the Guidelines are Organized in the What is in WCAG 1.0 section

- **Freedom Scientific: JAWS for Windows**—go to http://www.freedomscientific.com, then click on JAWS Headquarters
- **IBM Alpha Works: aDesigner**— http://www.alphaworks.ibm.com/tech/adesigner
- **AskAlice: Accessibility Evaluation Tool**—http://askalice.ssbtechnologies.com
- **InFocus**—http://www.ssbtechnologies.com/products/infocus/index.html
- **LIFT: Accessibility Evaluation Tool**—http://www.usablenet.com
- **Illinois Accessible Web Publishing Wizard**— http://www.accessiblewizards.uiuc.edu
- **Windows-Eyes**—http://www.gwmicro.com
- **Lynx—Internet Software Consortium**—http://lynx.isc.org
- **Lynx Viewer**—http://www.delorie.com/web/lynxview.html
- **ScanSoft: Dragon Naturally Speaking 7**—http://www.nuance.com
- **Section 508**—http://www.section508.gov
- **University Web Accessibility Policies: A Bridge Not Quite Far Enough**— http://www.webaim.org/coordination/articles/policies-pilot
- **WAVE 3.0 Accessibility Tool**—http://wave.webaim.org/index.jsp
- **HiSoftware CynthiaSays™ portal**—http://www.cynthiasays.com/Default.asp
- **A-Prompt Web Accessibility Verifier**— http://aprompt.snow.utoronto.ca/download.html
- **Vision Australia Web Accessibility Toolbar**— http://www.visionaustralia.org.au/ais/toolbar
- **Rehabilitation Engineering and Assistive Technology Society of North America**—http://www.resna.org
- **The Alliance for Technology Access (ATA)**—http://www.ataccess.org
- **Disabilities, Opportunities, Internetworking, and Technology** (DO-IT)— http://www.washington.edu/doit/Resources/udesign.html
- **Association for Computing Machinery's (ACM) Special Interest Group on Computer-Human Interaction (SIGCHI)**—http://www.sigchi.org
- **ACM's Special Interest Group on Accessible Computing, SIGACCESS**— http://www.acm.org/sigaccess

Glossary

All key terms appearing in this book (in bold italic) are listed alphabetically in this Glossary for easy reference. If you want to learn more about a feature or concept, use the Index to find the term's other significant occurrences.

Absolute URL Provides the full path to a Web page or file.

Accessibility Means that a page can be accessed—read and used—by any person regardless of special needs or disabilities.

Accessibility Checker Assists in creating universally accessible Web sites that are in compliance with the W3C Web Content Accessibility Guidelines (WCAG) and Section 508 of the Rehabilitation Act: Electronic and Information Technology Accessibility Standards.

Accesskey A form field attribute that enables visitors to use a keyboard instead of the mouse to navigate between form fields.

Action (or event) handler Scripting code that executes in response to a specific event.

Active page The Web page that is being edited.

Adobe Flash A popular application used to create Flash animated graphics.

Advanced button Enables visitors to use all the functionalities provided by a push button; provides Web developers with more control over form functionality and button display.

Advanced controls Enable Web designers to add more advanced components to their Web pages, such as Java applets, audio and video files, Plug-In, and Active-X.

Alink attribute Determines the color of an active hyperlink (a link as it is clicked by the user) and corresponds to the a:active {color: #value;} CSS style and Active Hyperlink color setting in the Page Properties dialog box.

Animated GIFs Combine several images and display them one after the other in rapid succession.

ASCII Created by the American National Standards Institute and is the common numeric code used by computers. The standard ASCII character set consists of 128 decimal numbers ranging from zero through 127 assigned to letters, numbers, punctuation marks, and the most common special characters. The extended ASCII character set consists of 128 decimal numbers and ranges from 128 through 255, representing additional special, mathematical, graphic, and foreign characters.

Auto Thumbnail Creates a thumbnail of the image to appear on your page.

Background sound An audio file that plays for as long as a Web page is open in a browser or for a limited number of loops, or cycles, depending on the designer's preference.

Bar based on navigation structure An option that is built upon the navigational structure of your Web site.

Bar with back and next links An option includes only Back and Next buttons.

Bar with custom links An option that includes links and text.

Bookmark link A link to a specific position within the same document or another document.

Broken hyperlinks Target unavailable files.

Caption A word or a phrase that, in general, identifies the content of the table or figure. By default, the caption is positioned at the top of the table and centered. However, you can position it at the top or bottom of the table and set the alignment to left, center, right, or justified.

Cascading Style Sheet (CSS) Has become the standard style sheet language used on the Web.

Cell The intersection of a column and a row.

Check box Enables visitors to check or clear one or more boxes from a group of boxes representing a set of options.

Client A user machine that connects to the server and receives information from it.

Clip Art task pane Provides you with a wide variety of media files, generically called clips, stored in a comprehensive group of collections.

Code view A type of Page subview in which you view, add, and edit HTML tags.

Comment Text that can be seen only in Design, Split, and Code views, but that is not visible in Preview in Browser view.

Communications The process of moving data within or between computers.

Communications devices Provide the hardware and software support for connecting computers to a network.

Compatibility Checker Assists in creating Web pages based on Web standards such as HTML, XHTML, and CSS.

Current page The Web page that is being edited.

Database Consists of fields, records, and tables.

Database table A collection of records.

Date and Time An option that opens the Date and Time dialog box and includes a few options about when to update the date and time and how to format each.

Deprecated HTML tags and tag attributes are tags that might or might not be supported by all browsers, and thus, they are not recommended for use.

Design view A type of Page subview in which you design and edit Web pages.

Disk-based Web sites Web sites located on a floppy disk, zip disk, CD, USB flash drive, or hard disk on your local machine or any other machine on a network that you can access.

Document type definition (DTD) Can force an XML document to follow a uniform data structure, thus eliminating many code errors that can occur.

Document window Displays the content of the latest open Web page. If no Web page is open, it displays a view of all Web site files.

Domain name Comprises the first part that identifies the Web page's host, which can be a Web server or computer on the Internet, and a second part called the top-level domain.

Drop-down box (or Menu) Enables visitors to select one or more options from a list of options.

Dynamic HTML (DHTML) An extension of HTML that adds multimedia, database access, and an object model that programs use to change the styles and attributes of page elements and to replace existing elements with new ones.

Dynamic Web page Content that changes as users interact with it.

Dynamic Web template Enables you to automatically update common features of many attached Web pages.

Editable regions Sections of the Web template that can be modified within any Web page built upon the Dynamic Web template.

Empty Web site Creates just the Web site folder with no files included.

Event Causes a Web browser to trigger a script. When an event occurs, your script executes the code that responds to that particular event.

Event handler (or action) Scripting code that executes in response to a specific event.

Extensible Hypertext Markup Language (XHTML) A newer markup language that was designed to overcome some of the problems generated by HTML. XHTML is considered a transitional solution between HTML and XML because it is not extensible.

eXtensible Markup Language (XML) Based on the SGML standard. Enables data to be shared and processed via the Internet and across software applications, operating systems, and hardware computer platforms.

External styles Codes that are included in separate files used to specify the formatting of any HTML document to which they are linked. These style codes are kept in a document with a .css file extension and are linked to the HTML document using the <link> HTML tag.

Extranet Falls somewhere between the Internet and an organization's intranet. Only selected users, such as customers, suppliers, or other trading partners, are allowed access.

Field A single piece of information represented as a column.

File Transfer Protocol (FTP) The second most popular protocol on the Internet. It is used to transfer files between computers.

Find and Replace A feature that enables designers to find and replace text using expressions or HTML code.

Folders view The default web site view when you create a new Web site, which can be used to open, close, create, delete, copy, rename, and move folders and files; to preview files in the browser; to select files you do not need to publish; and to publish files. Folders view can also provide useful information about files.

Form A set of form fields used to collect information from visitors for additional processing.

Form field The basic form element that enables visitors to supply information.

Form handler A program residing on a Web server that processes the information the visitor submitted.

Graphics Interchange Format (GIF) Supports transparent colors, is most often used to create animated images, can display only 256 colors, and has large file sizes compared, for example, with the Joint Photographic Experts Group (JPEG) format.

Group box A titled border placed around a group of related fields.

Handles (sizing) Look like little squares evenly distributed around the picture; they enable you to resize the picture.

Hidden form field A form field that does not appear on the visitors' view of the Web page; thus, they cannot make changes to it.

Hit counter A SharePoint Designer Web component that keeps track of the number of people visiting your Web site. It is a generic name for any number of hit counters created any number of ways (that do not require FrontPage Server Extensions or SharePoint Services).

Hyperlink target The file that opens when a hyperlink is clicked.

Hyperlinks view Provides a graphical layout of all the hyperlinks included in a Web site.

Hypertext documents Electronic files that can be easily accessed by a mouse click.

Hypertext links (or links) Text or objects that connect Web pages. Hypertext links on a Web site can link to their own documents or to other locations on the Web.

Hypertext Markup Language (HTML) The markup language most commonly used to create Web pages and was developed from the more complicated Standard Generalized Markup Language (SGML).

Hypertext Transfer Protocol (HTTP) The most popular communication protocol used to transfer Web pages.

Image map A more elaborate inline image; its area is divid

Import Web Site Wizard Allows you to create a new Web site by importing files either from an existing Web site or from a folder on your computer or a network.

Included Content Represents an extremely helpful and popular set of Web components that enable you to include different types of components, such as Web page configuration variables, another Web page, and a picture or Web page, based on a predefined time schedule.

Inline images Display graphic images that are stored in a separate file that can be located within the same Web site or outside the Web site.

Inline style Codes that are included in the start tag by using the tag's style attributes.

Insert Table grid A graphical table that enables you to select the number of rows and columns for your table.

Interactive buttons Buttons that change in appearance when users click them or hover over them with the mouse. You can also attach a hyperlink to an interactive button. You can use interactive buttons to build navigation bars and tables of contents. You can also use them in forms.

Interlacing A technology used for displaying images in stages.

Internal styles Codes that are usually included in the <head> section of an HTML and have the following syntax: <style>style declarations</style>. Internal style codes override the format defined in a linked external style sheet.

Internet A huge collection of computers and networks located all over the world. It is used in a great variety of ways, such as to gather information, share resources, read and send e-mail, shop online, trade stocks, participate in discussions and chat groups, and download software.

Internet law The application of many different types of traditional law to the virtual world of the Internet. Internet law comprises a number of distinct subcategories including the Internet Copyright.

Internet Service Provider (ISP) Asynchronous tool for communications that is part of the standard default workspace. It accepts topic and response postings that can be reviewed and added to at a later time.

Intranet Consists of Web pages and other resources that are only available inside the company. Intranets have a low cost of ownership because they use the standard technologies of the Internet.

Joint Photographic Experts Group (JPEG) Does not support animation and transparent colors, displays all 17.6 million colors that are available in the color palette, and uses an image compression algorithm.

Keep aspect ratio A check box that enables you to maintain the aspect ratio of the picture as you resize it.

Language bar A toolbar that automatically appears on your desktop, in the Windows Vista operating system, when you add text services such as input languages, speech recognition, handwriting recognition, or Input Method Editors (IME).

Layout cells The building bricks for Layout tables.

Layout tables Web page layout frameworks that consist of a regular one-cell table to which SharePoint Designer attaches an identification tag.

Link attribute Defines the color of hypertext links and corresponds to the a:link {color: #value;} CSS style and Hyperlink color setting in the Page Properties dialog box.

Link bars Extremely helpful navigational components of a Web site; they can contain custom links or links based on the Web site's navigational structure.

List A common format seen on many Web pages that helps you organize and present your content in a consistent and concise fashion.

Local Web site The initial source Web site that is opened by developers in SharePoint Designer.

Mailto link A common type of hyperlink that connects the user to an e-mail address.

Markup language A language that describes the format of Web page content through the use of tags.

Marquee An attractive Web component that looks much like the tickers that you see at the bottom of your TV set when you watch news channels. It is an easy way to add a dynamic effect to your Web page. It is often used to display news or updated information related to the Web page's topic.

Menu bar Located directly beneath the title bar and displays the names of each of the SharePoint Designer menus. When you click a menu name, the menu appears.

Meta tags Represent one of the tools that you can use to ensure that the content of your Web site has the proper topic identification and ranking by search engines.

Microsoft ASP.NET Development Server Available in Microsoft Office SharePoint Designer as well as Microsoft Expression Web.

Microsoft Clip Organizer Simplifies your searches by cataloging all the clips available to you.

Microsoft IntelliSense technologies (IntelliSense) Help you minimize errors when working directly in the Code view with the markup language and tags that comprise the site, including HTML, XHTML, ASP.NET, and CSS.

Microsoft Office open XML formats New Microsoft Office 2007 file formats that are based on XML and that apply to Microsoft Office Word 2007, Microsoft Office Excel 2007, and Microsoft Office PowerPoint 2007.

My Collections Includes your personal collection of media files.

My Templates An induced category of templates that appears on the Web site tab of the New dialog box only if you have previously saved a Web package in the user Web template folder on your computer.

Navigation view A Web site view which provides a tree-like diagram of your Web pages and helps you add a new/already existing Web page or remove a Web page from a Web site and/or to the Web site navigational structure.

Nested lists Popular features used by Web designers to emphasize text categories and subcategories.

Nested table A table inserted within a cell of another table.

Network Consists of a group of computers connected to share resources such as output devices (for example, printers), servers, and information.

Noneditable regions (static regions) Sections of the Dynamic Web template that can be edited only through the Dynamic Web template.

Office Collections Includes media files stored in the Office Collections folder when SharePoint Designer was installed.

Older files Files that have not been updated within 72 days.

One Page Web site Creates a Web site incorporating only one blank page.

Optimize HTML Tab of the Remote Web Site Properties dialog box that enables you to select the HTML elements that you want to remove from the HTML code of your Web pages while they are being published.

Option button Enables visitors to check only one option button from a group of option buttons.

Padding Increases the space between any element content and its borders, whereas margins represent the space outside the element's borders.

Page A component that inserts an entire page into a Web page so that any changes made and saved in the inserted page's original file appear in all pages where this page was inserted as a page component.

Page Banner A component that displays the page titles as they appear in Navigation view and will not be displayed on the Web page unless the page is included in the navigation structure.

Page Based on Schedule A component that enables you to add an entire separate page to your Web page at regularly scheduled intervals.

Page template A template that includes all the appropriate Web page elements, including page settings and formatting.

Page view Displays the Web page that is being edited. The Web page that is being edited is referred to as the current page or the active page.

Path name In conjunction with the file name of the URL, it specifies the location of the Web page on the host computer.

Photo Gallery A component that arranges your photos in one of four predesigned layouts.

Picture Based on Schedule A component enables you to insert a picture in a Web page at regularly scheduled intervals.

Plug-in A software application that can be an integral part of a browser or can give the browser additional multimedia capabilities.

Portable Document Format (PDF) A fixed-layout electronic file format that preserves document formatting, enables file sharing and is also useful for documents that will be reproduced by using commercial printing methods.

Portable Network Graphics (PNG) A format that supports transparent colors, can be used for animated graphics, can display all 17.6 million colors available in the color palette, but is not yet fully supported by all browsers.

Portal A special kind of Web application. Its role is to act as a gateway into a number of other applications. Portal architecture is typically used to present a number of portlets, which are window-based links into other applications. Portals also commonly provide features for personalization, so that users can customize the portlets that are represented and also change the layout, look, and feel of the portal.

Preview in Browser view A type of Page subview in which you can see what a Web page will look like in a Web browser without having to first save or publish your page.

Print Preview Allows you to see how a Web page will appear when printed; this feature paginates and assigns page numbers, whereas Web browsers do not.

Protocol Represents a set of rules used to transmit data on the Internet. The most well-known and commonly used part of the Internet is the World Wide Web (WWW).

Publishing (a Web site) Consists of transferring all the Web site's files and folders to a Web server.

Push button Enables visitors to submit the information entered in a form (the Submit button), to clear form fields by resetting the form (the Reset button), or to run a custom script attached to the button.

Record One complete set of fields represented as a row.

Relative URL Provides the path to a Web page or a file relative to another file.

Remote Web site The destination site to which you publish your Web site.

Remote Web site view A Web site view that can be used publish an entire Web site or individual Web pages to a local or remote site and to save a backup copy of your Web site.

Reports view A Web site view that provides access to a set of site reports, organized in five categories.

Resample To modify physical size (of a picture).

Reset button Enables visitors to return the contents of the form fields to their default status.

Resize To modify display size (of a picture).

Root Web site A Web site that includes nested subsites.

Schema An XML document that includes the definition of one or more XML document's content and structure.

ScreenTip Text that displays in the body of the Web page whenever a mouse is moved over the hyperlink.

Search engines Usually refer to Web search engines, which are specialized software applications that help you to find information on the WWW and Internet.

Server A computer that provides clients with access to files and printers as shared resources on a computer network.

Server-based Web sites Web sites published on a Server.

Set Transparent Color A button that enables you to change the background color of the picture (or any specific color within the picture) to be transparent.

SharePoint Services 3.0 The latest release of SharePoint Services; provides support for authoring, publishing, organizing, and finding information on the Web and a foundation for Web-based applications.

Shortcut menus Short menus that display a list of commands related to the item you right-clicked within the SharePoint Designer window.

Single File Web page An option that saves the entire document as a single .mht-format file, which is supported only by Internet Explorer version 4.0 and higher.

Site map A hierarchical outline of a Web site's sections, which provides a Web site overview to help users locate the Web page they are looking for in the Web site architecture.

Site Summary Category of reports that contains comprehensive overview information about all the Web site's statistics.

Slow pages Pages that might need more than 30 seconds to be downloaded at a speed of 56 Kbps.

Spacer image A transparent GIF image that you can use to control spacing in autostretch tables; it consists of a single-pixel transparent image, outstretched to represent a specified number of pixels in width.

Split view A type of Page subview in which you can simultaneously display the Code view and Design view of the Web page content in a split screen format.

Spreadsheet The computerized version of a ledger; it consists of rows and columns of data.

Static Web page Content that displays the same information every time it is viewed unless the Web developer makes and saves specific changes in the HTML code.

Status bar Formed by five sections providing information about the open files and enables you to customize the SharePoint Designer interface and some of its functionalities.

Style A feature that enables Web designers to format text using built-in HTML styles.

Style sheet languages Computer languages for expressing style sheets.

Style sheets Describe how documents are presented on screens or in print, or even how they are pronounced.

Submit button Enables visitors to submit the information to a Web server for further processing.

Subsite A Web site nested in another Web site.

Substitution A component that inserts a page configuration variable, such as author, description, modified by, and page URL, into your Web site.

Synchronize Transferring files between two Web sites (the local and remote versions) so that their contents are identical.

Table A collection of rows having one or more columns.

Tags Specific codes that indicate how the text should be displayed when the document is opened in a Web browser.

Task panes Contain the most common options for the particular view that you are using. This feature can improve your productivity by eliminating the need to hunt through menus to find the options you need (for example, the Toolbox task pane assists you in inserting HTML tags).

Telnet A popular Internet resource that allows users to log in to and use a remote computer.

Text area Enables visitors to enter up to 999 columns and 999 rows of text in a scrolling text box.

Text box Enables visitors to enter up to 500 alphanumeric characters. If no character is entered, only the text box name is sent to the server.

Title bar Provides information about the file that you have open and always shows the name of the application as well as the location and name of the Web site that you are creating or editing.

Toolbars Combinations of related buttons that you can choose to perform tasks without using the menus. Each button displays a graphic icon suggesting its functionality. A common toolbar, the default SharePoint Designer toolbar, which includes the most frequently used functionalities from the Standard toolbar and the Formatting toolbar.

Top-level domain Can be either a generic three-letter suffix indicating the type of organization to which the Web page host belongs (such as .edu and .org) or a two-letter suffix designated for each country.

Transmission Control Protocol (TCP)/Internet Protocol (IP) Represents the main set of protocols used for transmitting data on the Internet. TCP/IP includes a variety of interrelated protocols, among which TCP, IP, FTP, Telnet, and Hypertext Transfer Protocol (HTTP) are some of the most important.

Uniform Resource Identifier (URI) A compact string of characters used to identify or name a resource. The main purpose of this identification is to enable interaction with representations of the resource over a network, typically the WWW, using specific protocols.

Uniform Resource Locator (URL) A specific kind of URI that assigns each Web page a unique WWW address.

Unlinked files Files that cannot be reached by starting from the Web site's homepage.

Usability (of a Web site) A measure of the quality of your Web site visitors' experience.

Valid An XML document that is a well-formed and also satisfies the rules included in the attached document type definition or schema.

Views bar Enables you to change the view of an open file or of all Web pages included in the Web site. When a Web page is open, you can select Design View, Code View, or Split View. When a Web site is open and no Web pages are open, the Views bar shows the six Web site views. You learn about Web page and Web site views later in this chapter.

Vlink attribute Defines the color of links that have been visited by the user and corresponds to the a:visited {color:

#value;} CSS style and Visited Hyperlink color setting in the Page Properties dialog box.

Web application (webapp) A software application that is accessed with a Web browser over a network such as the Internet, an intranet, or an extranet. The main reason for the increased popularity of Web applications is that Web applications can be updated and maintained without distributing and installing software on potentially thousands of client computers.

Web browsers Software applications, installed on your computer, designed to assist you with navigating the Web, retrieving a Web page from its host server, interpreting its content, and displaying it on your computer.

Web Collections Includes media files downloaded from the Web and stored in the Web Collections folder.

Web components Represent another great collection of SharePoint Designer features that you can use to enhance content and improve navigation on your Web site.

Web Package (.fwp) Enables you to share or reuse Web pages or an entire Web site.

Web page A document on the WWW that has been coded to provide static or dynamic content for users to view and access; an option that saves the document as an .htm file with a set of files grouped in a folder that enables you to rebuild the original Word document.

Web page, Filtered An option that saves the document in an .htm file format with an additional set of files grouped in a folder, but it filters and removes all the Word-specific metadata.

Web page label The name displayed in SharePoint Designer Web component page banners and navigation bars.

Web server A special kind of server that is connected to the Internet and that runs specialized software applications, enabling it to handle requests from clients to access information from Web sites.

Web site A collection of Web pages, files, and folders gathered together and published on the Internet.

Web site template A template formed by a group of page templates and contains navigation elements that connect the pages.

WebDAV An application protocol for creating, editing, and publishing files on a Web server. It enables multiple authors of a Web site to change files and file properties simultaneously without overwriting each other's work.

Well-formed An XML document that contains no syntax errors and obeys all W3C specifications for XML code.

Wizard Consists of a series of steps that guide you through the process of designing Web pages and Web sites or importing already created Web sites.

Workbook A set of related worksheets contained within a file.

Worksheet A single spreadsheet consisting of a grid of columns and rows that can contain descriptive labels, numeric values, formulas, functions, and graphics.

World Wide Web (Web or WWW) Graphical, user-friendly side of the Internet, which enables users to view and share graphics and multimedia documents electronically and remotely over the Internet. The WWW has no centralized control or any type of central administration. Theoretically, anybody can retrieve information from the WWW and publish information on it. The WWW is basically a huge collection of Web sites created by individuals and governmental, professional, and academic organizations.

World Wide Web Consortium (W3C) An open forum of companies and organizations with the mission to lead the Web to its full potential.

XML Paper Specification (XPS) A fixed-layout electronic file format that preserves document formatting and enables file sharing.

XML parser An application that evaluates XML documents. It interprets the document code to make sure that the document meets certain criteria.

Multiple Choice Answer Keys

Chapter 1

1. c
2. c
3. d
4. b
5. c
6. d
7. d
8. d
9. c
10. c
11. c
12. d
13. d
14. c
15. a
16. b

Chapter 2

1. b
2. a
3. a
4. d
5. c
6. d
7. b
8. d
9. a
10. b
11. d
12. a
13. d
14. c
15. b
16. d
17. c
18. c
19. b
20. b
21. a

Chapter 3

1. a
2. d
3. d
4. a
5. d
6. d
7. c
8. b
9. c
10. d

Index

SharePoint Designer 2007 (*continued*)
  Office 2007 integration with, 259–286, 288–296
  online tips/features, 26
  opening, 27
  opening PDF file in, 264, 281
  opening XPS file in, 264, 281
  PowerPoint and, 265–274, 290–292, 327
  software/hardware requirements, 26
  tools for XML, 373–381
  Word and, 260–265, 288–290, 327
SharePoint Designer interface
  components, 26–35, 45–47
  customization, 35–42, 99–100
SharePoint Designer Permissions
    Administration Page, 137–138
SharePoint Designer wizard, 50
SharePoint Products and Technologies
    Community, 26
SharePoint Server, 380
SharePoint Server 2007 Site Settings Web
    site, 137
SharePoint Services, Microsoft Windows
    2.0, 51
  3.0, 51, 52, 137, 316
  Overview Web site, 51
Shortcut menus, 28
Show/Hide Outline button, 272
SHTML, 346. *See also* HTML
.shtml, 346
Single File Web page option, 262, 278
Site map(s), 224, 225, 226
  accessibility and, 226
Site Map option, 67
Site Summary reports, 130
Sixteen original colors, 74
Size, font, 156
Sizing handles, 196, 310
Slides. *See* PowerPoint slides
Slow pages, 130
Slow Pages report, 131
Software/hardware requirements,
    SharePoint Designer, 26
Sounds. *See* Audio files
Spacer images, 187
Spaces, in HTML, 151
Specify value option, 309
Speech recognition features, 37
Spelling
  dialog box, 158
  text, 158–159
Spiders, 23
Split Cells dialog box, 182
Split view, 61, 369
Splitting/merging cells, 182–183
Spreadsheets. *See* Excel spreadsheets
SQLDataSource ASP.NET Data Control, 320
Stacking task panes, 39
Standard Generalized Markup Language
    (SGML), 8, 9. *See also* HTML;
    XHTML; XML
Standard toolbar, 30
  components, 30
Standard Web Pages exercise, 110
Starbright Children's Foundation Web site
    exercise, 91–94
  enhancing, 251–252
  subsite for, 250–251
Static Web pages, 19
Status bar, 28, 31–33

areas/features, 32
  customization, 32
Stock Price Comparison Web page, 342
Streaming video, 208
String of data, from form, 299
Structure tags, HTML/XHTML
    elements/attributes, 349
Style Application Setting indicator, 32, 33,
    150, 151
Style feature, 157
Style sheets, 15, 355, 393–395. *See also* CSS;
    External style sheets
  group, 67
  inline, 16, 356
  internal, 16, 17, 356
  languages, 15
  Section 508 guidelines, 393–395
Submit button (form field), 298, 314
Subsites (subwebs), 122–124. *See also* Web
    site(s)
  Navigation view, 124
  permissions, 137
  publishing, 18, 124–129, 144
  for Starbright Children's Foundation Web
      site, 250–251
Substitution component, 221, 222
Subwebs. *See* Subsites
Summaries
  chapter 1, 95–96
  chapter 2, 239–240
  chapter 3, 327–328
Sun Java Server Pages. *See* JSP
Symbols, 152
  cross-platform issues, 153
  inserting, 152
Synchronize button, 128
Synchronizing files, 128–129
  with Remote Web Site view, 56
Syntax, 10

T

Tab order option, 303, 304, 305, 308
Table Layout Template, 189
Table Properties dialog box, 179–180
  options/functionality, 180
Tables, 63, 172–186, 282. *See also* Cells;
    Layout tables
  accessible, 185
  captions added to, 178–179
  CSS Style, 368
  data entered in, 176–177
  defined, 172
  dimensions setting, 173
  dragging, 184
  HTML, 173
  HTML/XHTML elements/attributes,
      350–352
  images added to, 177–178
  Insert Table grid, 173
  nested, 172, 183–184
  properties, editing, 179–180
  rows/columns added to, 174
  rows/columns deleted from, 174–176
  Section 508 guidelines, 397–398
Tables toolbar, 31, 185–186
  buttons, 186
  reference, 186
Tabs. *See specific tabs*

Tag(s), 8, 10
  <div>, 203, 205
  empty, 10
  HTML, 10, 93
  logical, 346
  meta, 18
  physical, 346
  selectors, 357
Tag Inspector, 30
Tag Properties/CSS properties task pane,
    34, 89, 315
Target, hyperlink, 160
Task panes, 28. *See also specific task panes*
  closing, 39
  docking, 39
  floating, 35, 39
  layout arrangement options, 39
  menu, 34, 35
  merging, 35, 39
  open, 39
  resizing, 39
  stacking, 39
  types, 34
TCP/IP. *See* Transmission Control Protocol
    /Internet Protocol
Teaching and Research Lab Web site,
    101–102, 105–106
Telnet, 5
Templates. *See also* Dynamic Web
    templates; Web site templates
  My, 52, 53
  page, 49
  Table Layout, 189
  VPAT, 87
Terms/terminology. *See* Key terms
Testing/validating Web sites, 129–135, 145
  on multiple computer platforms, 85
Text, 152–159
  accessible, 156
  adding, 152–154
  copy-and-paste method, 153–154
  editing/formatting, 154–157
  effects, 156
  graphic, 156
  spelling, 158–159
  underlined, 157
Text area(s) (form field), 297, 298, 309–310
  inserting/modifying, 309–310
Text area Form Control, 297
Text box(es) (form field), 297, 298, 302–303
  inserting, 302–303
  modifying, 302–303, 324–325
Text Box Properties dialog box, 302–303
Text Box Validation dialog box, 303
Text CSS Style, 365–366
Text Editor, HTML document in, 9
Text File option, 66
Text hyperlinks, 6. *See also* Hyperlinks
Text prompt/question, 305
TextArea Box Properties dialog box, 309–310
Text-only Web pages, Section 508
    guidelines, 401–402
Tiles button, 264, 273, 281
Timed response, Section 508
    guidelines, 407
Title(s), Web page, 28, 149
  Web page labels v., 149
Title and headings, HTML/XHTML
    elements/attributes, 349
Title bar, 28, 149